8TH EDITION THE ULTIMATE KAUAI GUIDEBOOK
KAUAI REVEALED

ANDREW DOUGHTY

PHOTOGRAPHS BY ANDREW DOUGHTY & LEONA BOYD

WIZARD PUBLICATIONS INC

The Ultimate Kauai Guidebook
Kauai Revealed; 8th Edition

Published by Wizard Publications, Inc.
Post Office Box 991
Lihu'e, Hawai'i 96766–0991

© Copyright 2012 Andrew Doughty. All rights reserved.

ISBN: 978–0–9814610–8–3   1061
Library of Congress Control Number 2011930940
Printed in China

Cataloging-in-Publication Data

Doughty, Andrew
    The Ultimate Kauai guidebook : Kauai revealed / Andrew Doughty -- 8th ed.
Lihue, HI : Wizard Publications, Inc., 2012
    p. 268: col. illus., col. photos, col. maps ; 21 cm.
    Includes index.
    Summary: A complete traveler's reference to the Hawaiian island of Kauai, with
full color illustrations, maps, directions and candid advice by an author who resides in
Hawaii.
    ISBN-13: 978-0-9814610-8-3
    LCCN: 2011930940
    1. Kaua'i (Hawaii) - Guidebooks. 2. Kaua'i (Hawaii) – Description and travel.
    I. Title.

DU628.K3   919.69'41_dc22

All photographs (except the cover) taken by Andrew Doughty and Leona Boyd.
Cover space imagery courtesy of Earthstar Geographics (www.earth-imagery.com).
Cartography by Andrew Doughty.
All artwork and illustrations by Andrew Doughty.

Pages 2–3: Wai'ale'ale Crater, with its 3,000-foot waterfall-etched walls, was the
spiritual center of the ancient Hawaiian universe.

We welcome any comments, questions, criticisms or contributions you may have,
and have incorporated some of your suggestions into this edition. Please send to the
address above or e-mail us at **aloha@wizardpub.com**

Check out our website at **www.wizardpub.com** for up-to-the-minute changes.

Dedicated to Sammie Dollar, who soars on the wind with the white-tailed tropic birds.

CONTENTS

CONTENTS

ACTIVITIES
120

ADVENTURES
188

ISLAND DINING
204

WHERE TO STAY
240

INDEX
262

In a sense, this is not a guidebook, it's more of a love story. Having first seen the island as a tourist, I was immediately smitten. I had no idea that a place like this could exist anywhere in the world. Now as a resident, I marvel at its beauty every day.

Longtime locals have been stunned at some of the items in our book. We've found many special places that people born and raised here never knew about. Visitors will find this book as valuable as having a friend living on the island.

Kaua'i is a unique place. People who visit here recognize this immediately. There are plenty of places in the world featuring sun and sea, but no other place offers the incomparable beauty, lushness and serenity of Kaua'i. Living here, we get to see first-time visitors driving around with their jaws open, shaking their heads in disbelief at what they see. Without a doubt, you will never see more smiles than during your visit to Kaua'i.

Our objective at Wizard Publications is to assist you in finding the bliss that can accompany a Kaua'i visit. We recognize the effort people go through to visit here, and our goal is to expose you to every option imaginable so you can decide what you want to see and do.

We took great pains to structure this book in such a way that it would be fun, easy reading and loaded with useful information. This book is not a bland regurgitation of facts arranged in textbook fashion. We feel strongly that guidebooks should present information so you don't have to read through every page every time you want to find something. If you're here on vacation, your time is extremely precious. You worked all year to get here, and you don't want to spend all your time flipping through a book looking for something. You

want to be able to locate what you want when you want it. You want to be able to access a comprehensive index, a thorough table of contents and refer to high-quality maps that were designed with *you* in mind. You want to know which helicopter, SCUBA, boat tour or lu'au is the best on the island. You want to be shown those things that will make this vacation the best of your life.

A quick look at this book will reveal features never before used in a guidebook. Let's start with the maps. They are more detailed than any other maps you will find, yet they omit extraneous information that can sometimes make a chore of reading a map. We know that people often have a hard time determining where they are on a map, especially here, so we have included landmarks. Most notable among these are mile markers. At every mile on main roads, the government has erected numbered markers to tell you where you are. We were the first to put these markers on a map so you can use them as reference points. We also made every effort to place north at the top of the page. It can be confusing when you see a map with south pointing up or to the right. Only a couple of trail maps deviate from this rule. Additionally, we repeatedly drove and GPSed every inch of every road and trail on the maps. This is important because *many* of the roads and trails represented on existing maps have been shifted, moved or eliminated. You could become very frustrated trying to find certain beaches or other scenic spots using other maps. We physically check every place and often use aerial photography and a GPS to determine the best methods for getting to certain places.

Early on, I spent three days trying to find a certain secluded beach using existing maps. When I checked aerial shots, I discovered that *every single map was wrong*. Getting to the beach was a snap—if you knew where to go. Where needed, we've drawn legal public beach access in yellow, so you'll know when you are legally entitled to cross someone's land. Lastly, all the maps are 3-D. We've found that *accurate* shaded relief maps easily convey much more information to the map reader.

One of the things unique to this book is the acceptance of change. We produce brand new editions of our books every two years or so, but in the intervening time we are constantly incorporating changes into the text nearly every time we do a new printing. We also post these changes on our website. This allows us to make some modifications throughout the life of each edition. We don't have the luxury of making every change that happens on a weekly basis, but it does give us more flexibility than if we only acknowledged changes every two years.

Slick (and not so slick) free magazines and publications are strewn throughout the island. Most claim to point you to assorted wonders. There's nothing wrong with that. But the adage, "You get what you pay for," applies. Let's put it this way: If all the companies in this book were companies that we had to solicit for advertising, how much candor do you think we could provide? That's why *you* pay for the book, not the companies we describe. We're free to be as brutally honest as we want to be. Since we accept no advertisements, our allegiance is to our readers, not advertisers. Nonetheless, these free publications can be useful for the coupons that advertisers put inside.

As you read this book, you will notice that we are very candid in assessing businesses. Unlike some other guidebooks

that send out questionnaires asking a business if they are any good (gee, they *all* say they're good), we've had *personal* contact with the businesses listed in this book. We accept no payment for our reviews, we make no deals with businesses for saying nice things, and again, there are *no advertisements* in our book. If we gush over a certain company, it comes from personal experience with the company. If we rail against a business, it is for the same reason. All businesses mentioned in this book are here by *our* choice. None have had any input into what we say, and we have not received a single cent from any of them for their inclusion. (In fact, some would probably pay to be left out of this book, given our comments.) We always approach businesses as *anonymous travelers* and later by phone as guidebook writers only if we need more information. This ensures that we are treated the same as you. (I was once *anonymously* reviewing a restaurant when a writer from another guidebook walked in, told the manager their identity and asked for food. Not surprisingly, the food was "great." But mine was lousy!) What you get here is our unbiased opinion on how companies operate—nothing more, nothing less.

This book is intended to bring you independence in exploring Kaua'i. We don't want to waste your precious time by giving you bad advice or bad directions. We want you to experience the best that the island has to offer. In the end, it's probably fair to say that our ultimate objective is to have you leave Kaua'i shaking your head saying, "I never knew a place like this existed."

We hope we succeed.

Andrew Doughty
Kapa'a, Hawai'i

The walls of Wai'ale'ale Crater, from which the island of Kaua'i burst forth in a fiery cataclysm, are now home to innumerable waterfalls. This part of the crater is called the Weeping Wall.

As with people, volcanic islands have a life cycle. They emerge from their sea floor womb to be greeted by the warmth of the sun. They grow and mature and eventually die before sinking forever beneath the sea.

HOW IT BEGAN

The Hawaiian Islands were born of fire thousands of feet below the surface in the icy cold waters on the Pacific Ocean floor. A rupture in the earth's crust caused a vent to spew hot magma that built upon itself as it reached upward. When it began, no one knows exactly, but the first of the still existing islands to boil to the surface was Kure. Nothing remains of that island today but its fringing coral reef, called an atoll.

As the Pacific plate shifted over the opening of the vent like steel over a cutting torch, more islands were created. Midway, French Frigate Shoal, Necker, Nihoa—all of these once-great islands were born and then mostly consumed by the angry ocean. What we call Hawai'i is just the last in a series of islands created by this vent. Someday these, too, will be nothing more than atolls, footnotes in the geologic history of the earth. But this vent isn't finished yet. The Big Island of Hawai'i is still expanding as lava from its active volcano continues even now to create additional real estate on that island. As we sit here, the future island of Lo'ihi is being created 20 miles southeast of the Big Island. Although still 3,200 feet below the surface of the ocean, in but a geologic moment, the Hawaiian volcano goddess Pele will add yet another piece of paradise to her impressive domain.

These virgin islands were barren at birth. The first life forms to appreciate these new islands of volcanic rock were marine creatures. Fish, mammals and microscopic animals discovered this new underwater haven and made homes for themselves. Coral polyps attached themselves to the lava rock, and succeeding generations built upon these, creating what would become a coral reef.

Meanwhile, on land, seeds carried by the winds were struggling to colonize the rocky land, eking out a living and breaking down the lava rock. Storms brought the occasional bird, hopelessly blown off course. The lucky ones found the islands. The even luckier ones arrived with mates or had fertilized eggs when they got here. Other animals, stranded on a piece of floating debris, washed ashore against all odds and went on to colonize the islands. These introductions of new species were rare events. It took an extraordinary set of circumstances for a new species to actually make it to the islands. Single specimens were destined to live out their lives in lonely solitude. On average, a new species was successfully deposited here only once every 20,000 years.

As the plants and animals lived out their lives, they broke up the rock, forming soil and organic debris. The ocean, meanwhile, was busily working to reclaim the horizon from these interruptions of land. Waves battered unmercifully against the fragile lava rock. In this battle between titans, there can be but one winner. While the creation of land eventually ceases on an individual island, the ocean never gives up. Wave after wave eventually takes its toll.

In addition to the ocean, rain carves up the islands. As the islands thrust them-

Each successive wave is like a sculptor's chisel, slowly shaping the island. Large storms can generate powerful waves, such as this one, which, over the eons, patiently return the island to the sea.

On rare occasions this ancient Hawaiian petroglyph is exposed in the mouth of the Wailua River.

selves upward into the moisture-laden trade winds, their challenge to the rain clouds is accepted. As the air encounters the slopes of these tall islands, it rises and cools, causing the air to release its humidity in the form of rain. This rain forms channels that easily carve valleys in the soft lava rock.

So what is the result of all this destruction? Paradise. Absolute paradise. There are few things more beautiful than Mother Nature reclaiming that which she gave birth to. The older the island, the more beautiful the landscape. A Hawaiian island is never more lovely than in its middle age, when the scars of constant environmental battles are carved into its face. Lush landscaped valleys, razorback ridges, long, sandy beaches—those things we cherish so much are the result of this destructive battle.

Kaua'i consists of 553 square miles of beach, rainforest, desert, mountains and plains. The island's landscape is as varied as its people. At Wai'ale'ale in the island's center, it rains nearly every day, making it the wettest place on earth. Just a few miles to the west, rain is rare, creating dry, almost arid conditions. The north shore is as lush as any place on the plan-

et. The south shore is a sunny playground. The island's first inhabitants surely must have felt blessed at the discovery of this diversity.

THE FIRST SETTLERS

Sometime around the fourth or fifth century AD, a large, double-hulled voyaging canoe, held together with flexible sennit lashings and propelled by sails made of woven pandanus, slid onto the sand on the Big Island of Hawai'i. These first intrepid adventurers encountered an island chain of unimaginable beauty.

They had left their home in the Marquesas Islands 2,500 miles away for reasons we will never know. Some say it was because of war, overpopulation, drought or just a sense of adventure. Whatever their reasons, these initial settlers took a big chance and surely must have been highly motivated. They left their homes and searched for a new world to colonize. Doubtless, most of the first groups perished at sea. There was no way for them to know that there were islands in these waters. The Hawaiian Islands are the most isolated island chain in the world. Those who did arrive brought with them food staples from home: taro, breadfruit, pigs, dogs and several types of fowl. This was a pivotal decision. These first settlers found a land that contained almost no edible plants. With no land mammals other than the Hawaiian bat, the first settlers subsisted on fish until their crops could mature. From then on, they lived largely on fish and taro. Although we associate throw-net fishing with Hawai'i, this practice was introduced by Japanese immigrants much later. The ancient Hawaiians used fishhooks and spears for the most part or drove fish into a net already placed into the water. They also had domesticated animals that were used as ritual foods or reserved for chiefs.

As the culture evolved and flourished, it developed into a hierarchical system of order. The society was governed by chiefs, called *ali'i*, who established a long list of taboos called kapu. These kapu were designed to keep order, and the penalty for breaking one was usually death by strangulation, club or fire. If the violation was serious enough, the guilty party's family might also be killed. It was kapu, for instance, for your shadow to fall across the shadow of the ali'i. It was kapu to interrupt the chief if he was speaking. It was kapu to prepare men's food in the same container used for women's food. It was kapu for women to eat pork or bananas. It was kapu for men and women to eat together. It was kapu not to observe the days designated to the gods. Certain areas were kapu for fishing if they became depleted. This allowed the area to replenish itself.

While harsh by our standards today, this system kept order. Most ali'i were sensitive to the disturbance their presence caused and often ventured outside only at night, or a scout was sent ahead to warn people that an ali'i was on his way. All commoners were required to

Who Were the Menehune?

Although the legend of Menehune exists throughout the Hawaiian Islands, the folklore is strongest on Kaua'i. Hawaiian legend speaks of a mythical race of people living in the islands before the Polynesians. Called the Menehune, these people were always thought of as being small in stature. The legend initially referred to their social stature, but evolved to mean that they were physically short and lived in the jungle away from the Hawaiians. (The ancient Hawaiians avoided living in the jungle, fearing that it held evil spirits, and instead settled on the coastal plains.) The Menehune were purported to build fabulous structures, always in one night. Their numbers were said to be vast, as many as 500,000. Today, archeologists speculate that a second wave of colonists, probably from Tahiti, may have subdued these initial inhabitants, forcing them to live in the woods. It is interesting to note that in a census taken of Kaua'i around 1800, 65 people from the upper region of the Wainiha Valley identified themselves as Menehune.

Today, Menehune are jokingly blamed for anything that goes wrong. If you lost your wallet, Menehune took it. If your car won't start, Menehune have been tinkering with it. Kaua'i residents greatly cherish their legends of the Menehune.

pay taxes to the ali'i in the form of food, labor and in other ways.

In January 1778 an event occurred that would forever change Hawai'i. Captain James Cook, who usually had a genius for predicting where to find islands, stumbled upon Hawai'i. He had not expected islands to be there. He was on his way to Alaska to search for the Northwest Passage linking the Atlantic and Pacific oceans. As Cook approached the shores of Waimea, Kaua'i, on January 19, 1778, the island's inhabitants thought they were being visited by gods. Rushing aboard to greet their visitors, the Kauaians were fascinated by what they saw: pointy-headed beings (the British wore tricornered hats) breathing fire (smoking pipes) and possessing a death-dealing instrument identified as a water squirter (guns). The amount of iron on the ship was incredible. (Hawaiians had only seen iron in the form of nails on driftwood but never knew the source.) Cook left Kaua'i and briefly explored Ni'ihau before heading north for his mission on February 2, 1778. When Cook returned to the Big Island of Hawai'i after failing to find the Northwest Passage, he was killed in a petty skirmish over a stolen rowboat. The Hawaiians were horrified that they had killed a man they had earlier presumed to be a god.

Just after this, Kamehameha the Great of the Big Island began consolidating his power by conquering the other islands in the chain. Kaua'i, however, presented a unique problem. Cut off from the rest of the chain by the treacherous Kaua'i Channel, Kaua'i's King Kaumuali'i had no intention of submitting himself to Kamehameha. In the spring of 1796 Kamehameha tried to invade Kaua'i. He and his fleet of 1,200 canoes carrying 10,000 soldiers left O'ahu at midnight hoping to reach Wailua, Kaua'i, by daybreak. They were in the middle of the Kaua'i Channel when the wind and seas picked up. Many of the canoes were swamped. Reluctantly, he ordered a retreat, but too late to stop some of his advance troops who were slaughtered after they arrived at the south shore beach of Maha'ulepu.

Ancient Hawaiians lived off the sea. With reefs teeming with life, Hawaiian waters have always been generous to the people of Hawai'i.

The earliest Hawaiians built elaborate terraces to grow taro, used to make poi. This one, in the Limahuli Garden, is estimated to be 700 years old.

In 1804 Kamehameha tried again. He gathered 7,000 men, all heavily armed, and prepared to set sail for Kauaʻi. Just before they were to leave, typhoid struck, decimating his troops and advisers. Kamehameha himself contracted the disease but managed to pull through. Kauaʻi's king must have seen the writing on the wall and agreed to give his kingdom of Kauaʻi over to Kamehameha. When Kamehameha died, his son, in order to solidify his power on Kauaʻi, arranged to kidnap Kauaʻi's King Kaumualiʻi and forced him to marry his stepmother, the powerful widow of Kamehameha. Kauaʻi's last king would never return and was eventually buried on Maui.

During the 19th century, Hawaiʻi's character changed dramatically. Businessmen from all over the world came here to exploit Hawaiʻi's sandalwood, whales, land and people. Hawaiʻi's leaders, for their part, actively participated in these ventures and took a piece of the action for themselves. Workers were brought in from many parts of the world, changing the racial makeup of the islands. Government corruption became the order of the day, and everyone seemed to be profiting except he Hawaiian commoner. By the time Queen Liliʻuokalani lost her throne to a group of American businessmen in 1893, Hawaiʻi had become directionless. It barely resembled the Hawaiʻi Captain Cook had encountered in the previous century. The kapu system had been abolished by the Hawaiians shortly after the death of Kamehameha the Great. The *Great Mahele*, begun in 1848, had changed the relationship Hawaiians had with the land. Large tracts of land were sold by the Hawaiian government to royalty, government officials, commoners and foreigners, effectively stripping many Hawaiians of land they had lived on for generations.

The United States recognized the Republic of Hawaiʻi in 1894 with Sanford Dole as its president. It was later annexed and then became a territory in 1900. During the 19th and 20th centuries,

INTRODUCTION

What's it Like in the Wettest Spot on Earth?

The center of the island is called Mount Wai'ale'ale, meaning "rippling waters." It is here that you will find the rainiest spot on the planet with an average of 432 inches. Rain around the rest of the island is a fraction of this (see chart on page 27). The ancient Hawaiians recognized the importance of this spot and built a temple on the summit, its remains visible to this day. The only way you will get to see Wai'ale'ale up close and personal is by air.

The top of Mount Wai'ale'ale is somewhat barren. While this might sound strange given its moniker as the wettest spot on Earth, remember that few plants in this world are genetically programmed to deal with that much rain at that altitude. Plus the ever-present rain clouds prevent sunshine from enriching the plants. The bogs on top of the mountain make for a less-than-well-defined soil base, and fungi and lichen flourish in the constant moisture. The result is few trees. Those trees that do survive are stunted by nature's over-generous gift of water.

Just below the summit—3,000 feet straight down, to be precise—exists the unimaginable lushness one would expect from abundant rain. As the clouds are forced up the walls of Wai'ale'ale Crater, they shed a portion of their moisture. With the majority of the rain

falling on the summit, the crater floor is left with just the perfect amount. With volcanically rich soil left over from the fiery eruptions, the crater floor has become a haven for

The summit of Wai'ale'ale feeds the Wailua River 3,000 feet below the sheer cliffs.

anything green. Ferns rule the crater. The ground shakes beneath your feet as your footsteps echo through generations of water-saturated fallen ferns, which have created a soft underbelly on what was once a savage, lava-spewing giant.

There is a surprising lack of insect presence. And most that do live there are endemic, appearing nowhere else on earth. Aside from mosquitoes in the stream beds, we encountered almost no insects in the dense fern growth of the crater. The only exception was a single flightless grasshopper. We found some 'o'opu fish inhabiting streams between towering waterfalls. They live in these isolated pools and use their pelvic fins to actually climb the falls.

Everywhere one looks, plants have taken root. Every rock has moss, every fallen tree has other plants growing on it, every crevice has growth. Surely no other place on earth is as lush as Wai'ale'ale Crater.

sugar established itself as king. Pineapple was also heavily grown in the islands, and the entire island of Lana'i was purchased for the purpose of growing pineapple. As the 20th century rolled on, Hawaiian sugar and pineapple workers found themselves in a lofty position—they became the highest paid workers for these crops in the world. As land prices rose and competition from other parts of the world increased, sugar and pineapple became less and less profitable. Today, these crops no longer hold the position they once had. In the 1990s the "Pineapple Island" of Lana'i completely shifted away from pineapple and started luring tourists. And where dozens of sugar companies once dotted the islands, today only one remains, and it's on Maui. Former sugar workers have moved into other vocations, usually tourist-related or farming.

The story of Hawai'i is not a story of good versus evil. Nearly everyone shares in the blame for what happened to the Hawaiian people and their culture. Nevertheless, today Hawai'i is struggling to redefine its identity. The Islands are looking back to the past for guidance. During your stay you will be exposed to a place that is attempting to recapture its cultural roots. There is more interest in Hawaiian culture and language than ever before. Sometimes the process is clumsy, sometimes awkward. There is no common agreement regarding how to do it, but in the end, a reinvigoration of the Hawaiian spirit will no doubt be enjoyed by all.

NI'IHAU

No man is an island, or so they say. But in Hawai'i, one family can own one. The island of Ni'ihau is a dry, somewhat barren island of 46,000 acres located 17

On Kaua'i, the first settlers found an Eden more beautiful than any place they'd ever known.

miles to the west of Kaua'i. When Scottish-born Eliza Sinclair was sailing in the islands with her family in 1863, they were looking for land on which to settle. Having turned down offers of several tracts on O'ahu (including Waikiki, which they dismissed as showing no promise), they were about to leave for California when King Kamehameha V offered to sell them Ni'ihau. When Eliza's sons went to look at it, they found a green, wet island with abundant grass—perfect for raising cattle. What they were unaware of at the time was that Ni'ihau had experienced a *rare* rainy period and was flourishing as a result. They offered $6,000, the king countered with $10,000, and they took it.

This was 1864 and, unfortunately for the Sinclairs, the residents of Ni'ihau did not respect their ownership and resisted them. They had a further setback when an old Hawaiian showed them a deed indicating ownership to a crucial 50-acre sliver of Ni'ihau deeded to the old man by King Kamehameha III. The Sinclairs were in a bind and elicited the aid of Valdemar Knudsen to negotiate the purchase of the remaining 50 acres. He spoke fluent Hawaiian and was well known and respected by the islanders.

Knudsen went to Ni'ihau and offered $1,000 to the old man by slowly stacking the silver coins on a table while he explained how much better off the old man would be if he sold his land and lived in comfort on Kaua'i. After repeated refusals from the man, Knudsen went to take the money away when the old Hawaiian's wife grabbed the money, and the deal was consummated on the spot.

When the Sinclairs discovered that the land was actually dry and barren, unsuitable for a cattle ranch at that time, they arranged to buy 21,000 acres of West Kaua'i. (They would continue to buy land on Kaua'i, eventually acquiring 51,000 acres of the island, which they own to this day.) If you take a helicopter ride, you may see their fabulous estate nestled high in the mountains near Olokele.

Today, about 170 Hawaiians live on Ni'ihau. There is one unpaved road going halfway around the island, no telephones, except for a wireless two-way to Kaua'i, and no cable TV. (Some residents tell us they've unsuccessfully tried to talk the Robinsons—the descendants of Eliza Sinclair—into getting a satellite dish so they can get CNN.) In-

So close and yet so far. This is as close as most will ever come to the "forbidden" island of Ni'ihau.

termittent power is supplied by generator and solar.

Ni'ihau's one school hosts around 40 students. The sense of family on the island is strong, and only Hawaiian is spoken in most homes. (Classes, however, are taught in English.) Ni'ihau residents are a deeply religious people, and crime against one another is almost unknown. They are intensely proud of their community and feel strongly that their people, their heritage and their way of life are special and are protected by God.

They live in one village called Pu'uwai (located in the only part of Ni'ihau where you can't see Kaua'i) and receive their mail once a week –the Post Office only delivers as far as Makaweli on Kaua'i. They shop for clothes and other durable items on Kaua'i, where most have family.

Time is fluid there. If someone says they'll see you on Wednesday, it could be any time of the day. There's no such thing as being late on Ni'ihau.

With a warehouse for staples and gardens for their fruits and vegetables, Ni'ihau islanders are reasonably self-sufficient. Travel to and from the island is via old military transport boats (like the kind in *Saving Private Ryan*), and the rough, bumpy ride takes around 3 hours each way (during which many get seasick).

Life on Ni'ihau is certainly not without problems. No drugs or alcohol are allowed on the island, and families have been banished forever from the island for growing pakalolo (marijuana). Their mortality rate is high. Virtually everyone receives welfare and/or food stamps. With no permanent streams on the island, water is sometimes scarce. Although the largest lake in the state is on Ni'ihau, it is usually only a few feet deep, muddy and generally unpleasant.

The Robinson's land is valued at well over a *billion* dollars, but crushing tax burdens and losses (from Kaua'i operations) leave them relatively cash poor. Though the land has been in the family for almost a century and a half, every time a land-owning relative dies, the government takes a huge bite out of the family in massive inheritance taxes. They claim that they can only afford to go out to dinner a few times a year. (You can dry your eyes now after that one.) They warmed to the idea of using some of their Kaua'i land for tourism for a few years, then backed away. They almost allowed the federal government to install (for a fee) rocket launchers on Ni'ihau as part of an expansion of the Pacific Missile Range Facility on Kaua'i's west side. The deal fell through when the government insisted on an ethnographic survey, which the secretive Robinsons feared would be used to create precedents that would allow native Hawaiians *from Kaua'i* to visit the island (for constitutionally allowed ritual or gathering purposes). Instead, they now lease much of their Kaua'i land to large, mainland seed growers cultivating genetically modified plants and have been in talks with outsiders *for years* about using some of their former sugar lands to make ethanol. Lots of talk, lots of plans. But nothing has come of any of it.

The Robinsons claim that their unique deed to the island gives them ownership of Ni'ihau's beaches—directly in conflict with state law that proclaims that *all* beaches in Hawai'i are public beaches. To date nobody has challenged them in court. If you land on a beach on Ni'ihau, you will be asked to leave. If you refuse, a truly *gargantuan* Hawaiian gentleman will be summoned, and he will ask you a bit more firmly. This request is usually sufficient to persuade all but the most determined individuals to leave.

The bird-of-paradise is a striking flower found all over the island.

In order to get to Kaua'i, you've got to fly here. (You might be able to find a cruise to Hawai'i, but it's a pretty big and featureless piece of water to cross in a boat.)

GETTING HERE

When planning your trip, a travel agent can be help-ful, though that method is becoming less and less common. The Internet has sites such as Orbitz, Expedia, Cheap-tickets, Cheapair, Pandaonline, Price-line, Travelocity, Kayak, etc. If you don't want to or can't go through these sources, there are large wholesalers that can get you airfare, hotel and a rental car, often cheaper than you can get airfare on your own. **Pleasant Holidays** (800–742–9244) provides complete package tours.

The prices listed in the WHERE TO STAY section reflect the RACK rates, meaning the published rates before any discounts. Rates can be significantly lower if you go through a travel company or book online.

When you pick your travel source, shop around—the differences can be dramatic. A diligent effort can make the difference between affording a *one-week* vacation and a *two-week* vacation.

Though most visitors fly into Honolulu before arriving, there are some direct flights to Kaua'i. Not having to cool your heels while changing planes on O'ahu is a *big* plus since interisland flights aren't quite as convenient—or cheap—as they used to be. If you fly to Kaua'i from Honolulu, the best views are usually on the left side (seats with an "A"). When flying to Honolulu from the mainland, sit on the left side coming in, the right going home. Interisland flights are done by **Hawaiian** (800–367–5320), **Go!** (888–435–9462) and **Island Air** (800–652–6541). Flight attendants zip up and down the aisle hurling juice at you for the short, interisland flights.

WHAT TO BRING

This list will be helpful in planning what to bring. Obviously, you won't bring everything on the list, but it might help you think of things you may otherwise overlook:

- Waterproof sunblock (SPF 15 or higher)
- Two bathing suits
- Shoes—flip-flops, trashable sneakers, water shoes, hiking or trail shoes
- Mask, snorkel and fins
- Digital camera
- Hiking sticks (carbide-tipped ones are good for boulder-hopping hikes)
- Mosquito repellent for some hikes (*Lotions,* not liquids, containing DEET seem to work longest.)
- Shorts and other cool cotton clothing
- Hat or cap for sun protection
- Light windbreaker jacket (for trip to Kalalau Lookout or helicopter trip)
- Cheap, simple backpack—you don't need to go backpacking to use one; a 10-minute trek down to a secluded beach is much easier if you bring a simple pack.
- Long, lightweight pants for hiking if you are going through jungle country.

GETTING AROUND
Rental Cars

The rental car prices in Hawai'i *can be* (but aren't always) cheaper than almost anywhere else in the country, and the competition is ferocious. Nearly every visitor to Kaua'i gets around in a rental car, and for good reason. The island's towns are separated by distances sufficient to discourage walking. Many of Kaua'i's best sights can only be reached if you have independent transportation.

At Lihu'e Airport, rental cars can easily be obtained from the booths across the street from the main terminal. It's usually a good idea to reserve your car in advance since companies can run out of cars during peak times.

Below are the companies currently operating on Kaua'i:

The Big Guys

Alamo	(877) 222–9075
	(808) 246–0645
Avis	**(800) 321–3712**
	(808) 245–3512
Budget	**(800) 527–0700**
	(808) 245–9031
Dollar	**(800) 800–4000**
	(808) 245–3652
Hertz	**(800) 654–3131**
	(808) 245–3356
National	**(877) 222–9058**
	(808) 245–5636
Thrifty	**(800) 367–5238**
	(877) 283–0898

The Little Guys

Island Cars	**(800) 246–6009**
	(808) 246–6000
Kaua'i Rent A Car	**(808) 246–1881**
Timeshare Auto & U-Haul	**(808) 632–0741**

If you're 21–24 years old, most of the companies will rent to you, but you'll pay about $25 extra *per day* for the crime of being young and reckless. If you're under 21—rent a bike or moped or take the bus. Below are a few tips to keep in mind when you rent your car on Kaua'i.

Many **Collision Damage Waivers** will not cover vehicles on unpaved roads or beaches. Consider this when driving on dirt roads or at Polihale.

Car break-ins can be a problem anywhere. They seem to be more frequent in the summer due to school vacations. The places usually hit are those that require you to leave your car in a secluded place for an extended period of time. Contrary to popular belief, locals are targeted nearly as often as tourists. To protect yourself, don't leave anything valuable in the car. (Well...maybe the seats can stay.) At secluded spots that have recently been robbed, savvy locals will often leave their doors unlocked and the windows partially open to prevent having their windows smashed, but doing so *might* negate your rental car insurance. If you park in a secluded spot and notice several piles of glass on the ground, it's evidence that some juvenile has a new hobby. Don't kid yourself into believing that trunks are safe—they are often easier to open than doors. One place thieves rarely look is under the hood. But don't put something there after you arrive at your destination since someone might be watching. We once drove up to the parking area at Secret Beach, and there was a suspicious looking guy there. Mr. Slick acted busy by spending considerable time checking the oil in his car—*but the rusted hulk had no wheels all the way around.* Be alert and you should be OK.

All of this is not meant to convey the impression that car break-ins are rampant. In fact, the opposite is true. You could probably spend your entire life here and never experience one. (We haven't.) But if you lose your brand new $1,000 auto-everything digital SLR camera to some juvenile dipstick because you were one of the few...well, won't *you* feel sick?

4-Wheel Drive

With its many rugged roads, one of the best ways to see Kaua'i is by four-wheel drive. These can be difficult to come by at times. Ask the rental car company if they have disabled the 4WD mechanism. If you use a gold credit card for the automatic insurance, check with the card carrier to see if you are covered when you're on unpaved roads. Another tip is to avoid deep, soft sand. Even 4WD vehicles can get stuck in sand if they have the wrong tires. If you must drive on sand, let much of the air out of the tires to get more sand traction. (We'll leave it up to you how to get the air back in.) If you already *are* stuck in sand, try pulling the carpet from the trunk and driving on it to get out. (Oh, the car companies will love us for *that* one.) Rental car companies are always changing the vehicles to keep them new. At press time, all the *big* companies we list had SUVs or other 4WD vehicles. Expect to pay up to $60–$90 per day for the privilege of cheating the road builders.

Buses

Kaua'i has a bus system called the Kaua'i Bus (clever, eh?). It goes from Kekaha to Hanalei, and fares are $2. A monthly pass is $25, and most have bike racks. There are stops all along the main highway, but they aren't always marked as well as they should be. For a bus schedule or more information, call 241–6410.

Less Than 4 Wheels

If you really want to ham it up, try renting a HOG. (*Note:* The Supreme Court recently ruled that publishers cannot be held liable for bad puns.) Kaua'i Harley-Davidson on the highway in Puhi (241–7020) rents HOGs and other bikes. Good selection. Rates are $139 for 8 hours and $179 for overnight for HOGs. Expensive? You bet! But nothing else feels like a genuine Harley.

Scooters/mopeds are also available. We've seen some pretty close calls and consider them too unstable to rec-

Hey, I Recognize That Place…

When Hollywood wants to convey the impression of beauty, lushness and the exotic, it's no contest what location they choose. Kaua'i has long been the location of choice for movie directors looking for something special. As you drive around the island, keep an eye out for the locations of scenes from some of these movies: Pirates of the Caribbean 4, The Descendents, Just Go With It, Soul Surfer, all three Jurassic Park movies, Tropic Thunder, Dragonfly, To End All Wars, Six Days/Seven Nights, Mighty Joe Young, George of the Jungle, Outbreak,

North, Honeymoon in Vegas, Hook, Lord of the Flies, Flight of the Intruder, Throw Momma From the Train, The Thorn Birds, Uncommon Valor, Body Heat, Raiders of the Lost Ark, Fantasy Island, King Kong, Acapulco Gold, Islands in the Stream, The Hawaiians, Lost Flight, Hawai'i, Paradise Hawaiian Style, Girls! Girls! Girls!, Donovan's Reef, Blue Hawai'i, South Pacific, Miss Sadie Thompson and many more. Hollywood discovered Kaua'i years ago.

Harrison Ford rehearsing at Maha'ulepu for the movie, Six days/Seven Nights.

It's cool when you literally stumble across movie props, as we did with this shipwreck from Tropic Thunder, local resident Ben Stiller's film.

Even a beach with no sand can have something to offer.
Queen's Bath on the north shore is an example.

ommend. Be *real* careful on hills, and stay off the highway between Lihu'e and Kapa'a. **Kaua'i Car and Scooter Rentals** (245–7177) rents them for a confiscatory *$75* a day.

Taxis

If you want to tour the island by taxi...you have entirely too much money to burn. For those who need an occasional taxi service, you will find these available: **Sue's North Side Taxi** (635–0882), **Akiko's** (822–7588) on the east shore, or **City Cab** (245–3227) on the south shore.

Wheelchair Accessible Vans

These are available from **Wheelchair Getaways** (800–638–1912). Rates are $95 per day if you rent for a week, plus $200 for pickup at airport. Don't forget to bring your placard. Also, if you're looking to rent a wheelchair, **Gammie HomeCare** (632–2333) in Lihu'e has beach wheelchairs, but reserve them well in advance.

GETTING MARRIED ON KAUA'I

The beauty of Kaua'i has provided the backdrop for many engagements, weddings and vow renewals. And why not? It's in the air here. People are genuinely happy on Kaua'i, and the aroma of joy can make your life together even sweeter. Whether you choose a natural or man-made waterfall, a sunset on a beach, an elegant chapel, beautiful garden or an ancient Hawaiian temple, Kaua'i can create nuptial memories that will last a lifetime.

Thanks to e-mail and the Internet, you can arrange your own wedding, no matter how far away you are. All of the legal requirements, as well as possible wedding locations, are just a click away. Everything—from helicopter flights landing at private waterfalls to just the two of you on a beach at sunset with a minister—is available.

Some of the more popular wedding locations are at the St. Regis Princeville, Hanalei Colony Resort, Marriott, Hyatt, Sheraton and the Waimea Plantation Cottages. Many resorts have wedding coordinators and private wedding sites on property. You might also want to consider renting a private home for you and your guests. Don't let the RACK rates and wedding package prices scare you off. Nothing's carved in stone.

The number of details in planning a wedding is dizzying, and many couples prefer the assistance of an independent wedding coordinator. They can be tremendously helpful in navigating the complicated waters of your marriage. (Well, the ceremony, at least. After that, you're on your own.) Don't let yourself get herded into activities (for which they get a commission), and be on the lookout for add-ons that can ratchet up the price. Be especially selective of your photographer and videographer. This is a one-time event that can't be duplicated.

Some of the more reputable companies are listed below. Unlike most activities, we can't review each in depth. It's not possible to get married a dozen times and critique the way each coordinator did their job. We have, however, anonymously contacted virtually all of the coordinators on the island (in the guise of planning a wedding) and these stood out.

Coconut Coast Weddings
(800) 585–5595 or (808) 822–2020
Weddings on the Beach
(808) 742–7099
Island Weddings & Blessings
(800) 998–1548 or (808) 828–1548

WEATHER

Kaua'i doesn't have the best weather in the state, but the best weather in the state is on Kaua'i. What do we mean by that? Well, when it's good here, it's as good as weather can get—brilliant sunshine, crystal clear air, and gentle but constant breezes. That's when it's good.

Yeah, but I've heard it always rains on Kaua'i. We heard this many times before we came here for the first time. The reality of Kaua'i is that it gets more rain than the other Hawaiian islands. In fact, the rainiest spot on earth is smack dab in the middle of the island. Mount Wai'ale'ale is the undisputed *year-round* rain magnet, receiving an average of 432 inches per year over the past 70 years, which is a staggering 36 *feet* annually. (Though they've measured rainfall there for over a century, stating an average is more of an art than a science since there were times in the past they went up to read that gauge, perhaps after a year, only to find it overflowing—so they guessed.)

The mountain is shaped like a funnel pointing directly into the moisture-laden trade winds, which are forced to drop their precious cargo during their march up the slopes. The summit of Wai'ale'ale is other-worldly, with plants stunted and dwarfed by the constant inundation of rain. Moss, fungi and lichen flourish in the swamp just west of the actual peak. Alaka'i Swamp contains flora and fauna found nowhere else in the world. On the opposite side of the mountain, the spent clouds can do no more than drift by, making the west side of the island rather arid. What rain it does get comes from the sporadic Kona winds. (Throughout the islands, Kona winds refer to winds that come from the southwest and are often associated with inclement weather.)

All that said, the odds are overwhelming that rain will *not* ruin your Kaua'i vacation. The coast gets *far* less rain than the waterlogged central interior, and throughout Kaua'i the lion's share of rain falls at night. When it does rain during the day, it is usually quite short-lived, often lasting a matter of a few minutes.

One of the things that takes a little getting used to is the fleeting nature of the weather here. In many parts of the country, rain or sunshine are words used *by themselves* to describe the day's weather. On Kaua'i, a warm, passing shower is to be expected and rarely signifies that a long period of rain is to follow. If you call the local telephone number for the National Weather Service (see page 28), you will probably hear something like this. "Today—mostly sunny, with a few passing windward and *mauka* (mountain) showers. Tonight—mostly fair with a few passing windward and *mauka* showers. Tomorrow—mostly sunny, with a few passing windward and *mauka* showers." So don't get bummed if it suddenly looks ominous in the sky. It'll probably pass within a few minutes, leaving happy plants in its wake.

If you want to know whether to take the top down on the convertible, look into the wind, and you'll be able to see the weather coming. Dark clouds drop rain—the darker the cloud, the harder the rain. It's as simple as that, and you will often see locals looking windward if they feel a drop on their heads. If you're inland, you will often be able to *hear* the rain approaching. When you hear the sound of a rushing river but there isn't one around, take cover until it passes. (Mango trees are ideal for this purpose and have ancillary benefits, as well.)

In planning your daily activities, a good rule of thumb is that if it is going to be a rainy day, the south shore will probably be sunny, and the west shore will almost certainly be sunny. The exception is during Kona winds when weather is the opposite of normal.

Storm systems do discover the state from time to time. Sometimes they're here for days. If one happens to hang around during your trip, don't despair. I first met Kaua'i during one of the wettest times in decades. There was even lightning, which is rare. And it was during that stay that I fell in love with the island and vowed to make it my home. Kaua'i in the rain is still Kaua'i.

As far as hurricanes are concerned, don't waste your time worrying about them. It's true, we had a real 'okole kicker back in 1992. Hurricane 'Iniki was a category 4 storm that stripped the island bare, ironically striking on Sept. 11 of that year. But after this pruning, the island recovered and became greener than ever. Hurricanes are few and far between here. The only previous hurricanes to hit the state this century were 'Iwa in 1982 and Dot in 1959. When Isabella Bird traveled here in 1873, where she penned her excellent book, *Six Months in the Sandwich Isles,* she reported that "hurricanes are unknown in the islands," which means that there hadn't been one in living memory. (Of course, if one *does*

strike during your stay, kindly disregard this last statement.)

As far as **temperatures** are concerned, Kaua'i is incredibly temperate. The average *high* during January is 78°, whereas our hottest time, late August/ early September, has an average *high* of 85°. With humidity percentages usually in the 60s and low 70s, Kaua'i is almost always pleasant. The exception is the extreme west side, which is about 3 degrees hotter. (That might not sound like much, but you sure do notice it.)

Kaua'i's surface **water temperatures** range from a low of 73.4° in February to a high of 80° in October. Most people find this to be an ideal water temperature range. (Ocean water near a river mouth, such as Lydgate Beach Park, can get colder—we've seen the ocean get as low as 70° there during unusually cold Februarys.)

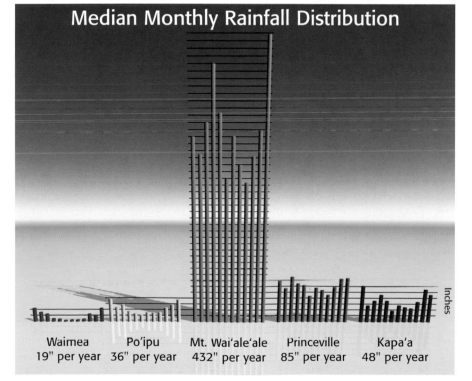

Median Monthly Rainfall Distribution

Waimea	Po'ipu	Mt. Wai'ale'ale	Princeville	Kapa'a
19" per year	36" per year	432" per year	85" per year	48" per year

Inches

To get current weather or ocean information, call the **National Weather Service: Weather Forecast** (245–6001) and **Hawaiian Waters Forecast** (245–3564).

Where Should I Stay?

If your decision about when to visit and where to stay takes rainfall amounts into account, the graph on the previous page should be of interest. Winter is our rainiest season. (But that's also when you will see the waterfalls at their best.) The north shore is a more popular place to stay in the summer, and the south shore is more popular in the winter due to rainfall distribution and surf.

GEOGRAPHY

Kaua'i is located in the tropics at 22° latitude, meaning that it receives direct overhead sunlight twice each year three weeks before and after the summer solstice. (No part of the mainland United States *ever* receives direct overhead sunshine due to its more northern location.) The island is 553 square miles, with 50 of its 113 miles of shoreline composed of sand beaches. Compared to the other Hawaiian Islands, Kaua'i and O'ahu have by far the highest proportion of sand beach shorelines. You might read in brochures about "white sand beaches." Actually, they are *golden* sand beaches, unlike the truly white sand beaches found in other parts of the world. Kaua'i is too old to have any volcanic black sand beaches since the creation of *volcanic* black sand ends when the lava flow stops. (Waimea's black sand beach is from lava flecks chipped from riverbeds and from dirt.)

Kaua'i's interior is mountainous, with deeply eroded valleys and large plains around most of the coastal areas. Its rainfall is more varied than any place in the world. The northern and eastern parts of the island (called the windward side) receive the majority of the rain, with the southern and western sections (leeward side) considerably drier. (See rain graph on previous page.)

Looking at the map on the fold-out back cover, you will notice that a highway stretches *almost* all the way around the island. This means that Ke'e is as far as you can go by car on the north shore, and Polihale or the top of Waimea Canyon Drive is as far as you can go on the west

Thunderstorms are relatively uncommon on Kaua'i.
But when we get 'em, they can be dramatic.

side. An attempt to link the two a few years back ended with almost comic results. (See page 92 for more on that.)

The maps in this book are unique in that they show the roadside mile markers. These correspond to the little green signs you will see along the main roads of Kaua'i. This will give you a perspective regarding distances beyond the map scales. Another feature of our maps is that north *usually* points up. We have found that many people get confused when they try to use a map where south is pointing to where east should be, etc. The only exceptions we made were a couple trail maps that benefited from using a specific elevated perspective.

In getting around, distances are usually measured in time, rather than miles. See the back fold-out map for a chart of **driving times between towns.**

HAZARDS
The Sun

Excluding our food prices, the hazard that affects by far the most people is the sun. Kaua'i's latitude means we receive sunlight that's more direct overhead than anywhere on the mainland. (The more overhead the sunlight is, the less atmosphere it is filtered through, and it's also more concentrated than it is farther north.) If you want to enjoy your *entire* vacation, make sure that you wear a strong sunblock. We recommend a waterproof sunblock with *at least* an SPF of 15. **Gels** work best in the ocean, **lotions** are best if you're staying dry, and lotions meant for infants and kids works best on your head. (Less painful if it gets in your eyes.) Try to avoid the sun between 11 a.m. and 2 p.m. since the sun's rays are particularly strong during this time. If you are fair-skinned or unaccustomed to the sun and want to lay out, 15–20 minutes per side is all you should consider the first day. You can increase it a bit each day. *Beware of the fact that Kaua'i's ever-constant trade winds will hide the symptoms of a burn until it's too late.* You may find that trying to get your tan as golden as possible isn't worth it; tropical suntans are notoriously short-lived, whereas you are sure to remember a bad burn far longer.

Water Hazards

The most serious water hazard is the surf. During the winter, many beaches are not swimmable. Eastern and northern beaches are especially dangerous, and the sad fact is that more people drown in Hawai'i each year than anywhere else in the country. This isn't said to keep you from enjoying the ocean, but rather to instill in you a healthy respect for Hawaiian waters. See BEACHES chapter for more information on this.

Ocean Critters

Hawaiian marine life, for the most part, is quite friendly. There are, however, a few notable exceptions. Below is a list of those that you should be aware of. This is not mentioned to frighten you out of the water. The odds are overwhelming that you won't have any trouble with any of the beasties listed below. But should you encounter one, this information should be of some help.

Sharks—Kaua'i does have sharks. They are mostly white-tipped reef sharks with an occasional hammerhead or tiger shark. Contrary to what most people think, sharks are in every ocean and don't pose the level of danger people attribute to them. In the past 25 years, there have been so few documented shark attacks off Kaua'i—less than one per year—that they haven't been able to create a statistical average. When one *does* occur it's mostly tigers attacking surfers. Considering the number of people who swam in our waters during that time, you are more likely to choke to death on a bone at a lu'au than be attacked by a shark. If you do happen to come upon a shark, however, swim away slowly. This kind of movement doesn't interest them. *Don't* splash about rapidly. By doing this you are imitating a fish in distress, and you don't want to do that. The one kind of ocean water you want to avoid is murky water, typically found near river mouths. These are not interesting to swim in anyway. Most shark attacks occur in murky water at dawn or dusk since sharks are basically cowards who like to sneak up on their prey. In general, don't go around worrying about sharks. *Any* animal can be threatening, not just Jaws.

Sea Urchins—These are like living pin cushions. If you step on one or accidentally grab one, remove as much of the spine as possible with tweezers. See a physician if necessary.

Cone Shells—People tend to forget that shells are created by organisms to serve as housing. Most of these creatures are capable of protecting themselves by the use of a long stinger called a proboscis, which injects venom. You might hear that it's safer to pick up a shell by the large end. You should be aware that many shells have stingers that can reach any part of the shell and can penetrate gloves. Therefore, it is recommended that you do not pick up live shells. If you do find yourself stung, immediately apply hot water, as it breaks down the protein venom.

Portuguese Man-of-War—These are related to jellyfish but are unable to swim.

They are instead propelled by a small sail and are at the mercy of the wind. Though small, they are capable of inflicting a painful sting. This occurs when the long, trailing tentacles are touched, triggering hundreds of thousands of spring-loaded stingers, called nematocysts, which inject venom. The resulting burning sensation is usually very unpleasant but not fatal. Fortunately, the Portuguese Man-of-War is not a common visitor to Kaua'i. When they *do* come ashore, usually during the summer and fall on the east shore, they might do so in great numbers, jostled by a strong storm offshore. If you see them on the beach, don't go in the water. If you do get stung, immediately remove the tentacles with a gloved hand, stick or whatever is handy. Rinse thoroughly with salt or fresh water to remove any adhering nematocysts. Then apply ice for pain control. If the condition worsens, see a doctor. The folk cure is urine, and for some of us it comes in a handy applicator, but you might look pretty silly applying it.

Coral—Coral skeletons are very sharp and, since the skeleton is overlaid by millions of living coral polyps, a scrape can leave proteinaceous matter in the wound, causing infection. This is why coral cuts are frustratingly slow to heal. Immediate cleansing and disinfecting of coral cuts should speed up healing time. We don't have fire coral around Kaua'i.

Sea Anemones—Related to the jellyfish, these also have stingers and are usually found attached to rocks or coral. It's best not to touch them with your bare hands. Treatment for a sting is similar to that of a Portuguese Man-of-War.

Bugs

Though devoid of the myriad of hideous buggies found in other parts of the world, there are a few evil critters brought here from elsewhere that you should know about. The worst are **centipedes**. They can get to be six or more inches long and are aggressive predators. If you do happen to get stung, you won't die (but you might wish you had). You'll probably never see one, but if you get stung, even by a baby, the pain can range from a bad bee sting to a mild gunshot blast. Some local doctors say the only cure is to stay drunk for three days. Others say to use meat tenderizer.

Cane spiders are big, dark and look horrifying, but they're not poisonous. (But they seem

Hey...what are you looking at?

to *think* they are. I've had *them* chase *me* across the room when *I* had the broom in my hand.) We *don't* have no-see-ums, those irritating sand fleas common in the South Pacific and Caribbean.

Mosquitoes were unknown in the islands until the first stowaways arrived on Maui on the *Wellington* in 1826. Since then they have thrived. A good mosquito repellent containing DEET will come in handy, especially if you plan to go hiking. *Lotions* (not thin liquids) with DEET seem to work and stick best. Forget the guidebooks that tell you to take vitamin B$_{12}$ to keep mosquitoes away; it just gives the little critters a healthier diet. If you find one dive bombing you at night in your room, turn on your overhead fan to help keep them away.

Bees are more common on the drier west side of the island. Usually, the only way you'll get stung is if you run into one. If you rent a scooter, beware: I received my first bee sting while singing *Come Sail Away* on a motorcycle. A bee sting in the mouth can definitely ruin one of your precious vacation days. Watch for them rolling around and disoriented at the beach.

Regarding **cockroaches**, there's good news and bad news. The bad news is that here, some are bigger than your thumb and can fly. The good news is that you probably won't see one. One of their predators is the **gecko**. This small, lizard-like creature makes a surprisingly loud chirp at night. They are cute and considered good luck in the islands (probably because they eat mosquitoes and roaches).

One thing nearly all visitors have heard is there are no **snakes** in Hawai'i (aside from a rare, tiny, worm-like blind burrowing snake said to be found here on occasion). There is concern that the brown tree snake *might* make its way onto the islands from Guam. Although mostly harmless to humans, these snakes can spell extinction to native birds. Guam has lost nearly all of its birds due to this egg-eating curse. Once they are fertilized, the snakes can reproduce for life from a single specimen. If there are any on Kaua'i (none are known to be on the island at this time), it would be a major disaster. Government officials aren't allowed to tell you this, but we will: If you ever see one anywhere in Hawai'i, please *kill it* and contact the **Department of Forestry and Wildlife** (274–3433). At the very least, call them immediately. The entire bird population of Hawai'i will be grateful.

Watch where you choose to take a nap.

Road Hazards

There are a couple things you should know about driving around Kaua'i. The speed limits here are probably slower than what you are used to, and Kaua'i police do have a few places where they regularly catch people. (That's code for speed traps.) We mention some in the tours. Also be aware that we have something on Kaua'i called **contra flow**. During commute hours, orange cones are placed on the lane divisions forcing you to drive on the wrong side of the road. The area between Lihu'e and Wailua is an example of contra flow, and it can be a bit unnerving for the uninitiated. **Seat belt** and **child restraint** use are required by law, and the police will pull you over for this alone. It's also illegal for drivers to use a **cell phone** without a headset. You should know that the Kaua'i Police Department regularly receives funds to enhance their seat belt violation enforcement, speeding enforcement and their sobriety checkpoints. So don't even think about violating these laws, or you'll likely get stung.

Lastly, even in paradise we have our **traffic**. Don't overlook the Kapa'a Bypass on the east shore, the Koloa Bypass on the south shore and the Puhi Bypass near Lihu'e. In fact, driving *south* through Kapa'a can be a pain almost *any time* of day. If you don't take the bypass, consider taking the scenic route up 581 (at the ABC Store) to 580. Might not save any time, but it's prettier than someone else's bumper.

Dirt

Dirt? Yes dirt. Kaua'i's infamous red dirt has ruined many new pairs of Nikes in its time. If you are driving on a cane road on the west side and have your window rolled down, you will eat a lot of it. It's always best to bring some trashable sneakers if you plan to do any hiking. And leave your silk argyle socks at home. If you want to know how staining it can be, just ask the makers of *Red Dirt Shirts.* They use one bucket of Kaua'i mud to dye *five hundred* shirts.

Dehydration

Bring and drink lots of water when you are out and about, especially when you are hiking. Dehydration sneaks up on people. By the time you are thirsty, you're already dehydrated. It's a good idea to take an insulated water jug with you in the car or one of those 1½ liter bottles of water. Our weather is almost certainly different than what you left behind, and you will probably find yourself thirstier than usual. Just fill it before you leave in the morning and *suck 'em up* (as we say here) all day.

Swimming in Streams

Kaua'i offers lots of opportunities to swim in streams and sometimes under waterfalls. It's a fulfillment of a fantasy for many people. But there are several hazards you need to know about.

Leptospirosis is a bacteria that is found in some of Hawai'i's fresh water. It is transmitted from animal (usually pig and cattle) urine and can enter the body from open cuts, eyes and by drinking. Around 100 people a year in Hawai'i are diagnosed with the bacteria, which is treated with antibiotics if caught relatively early. You should avoid swimming in streams if you have open cuts, and treat all water found in nature with treatment pills before drinking. (Most filters are ineffective for lepto.)

Also, while swimming in freshwater streams, try to use your arms as much as possible. Kicking an unseen rock is easier than you think. Consider wearing water shoes or, better yet, tabis, while in streams. (Tabis are sort of a fuzzy mitten for your feet that grab slippery rocks quite effectively.) You can get them at Kmart or Walmart in Lihu'e, or the Waipouli Variety Store in Waipouli Plaza in Kapa'a.

Though rare, **flash floods** can occur in any freshwater stream anywhere in the world, even paradise. Be alert for them.

Lastly, remember while lingering under waterfalls that not everything that comes over the top will be as soft as water. Rocks coming down from above could definitely ruin the moment.

Grocery Stores

Definitely a hazard. Restaurants may be expensive, but don't think you'll get off cheap in grocery stores. Though you'll certainly save money cooking your own food, a trip to the store here can be startling. Phrases like *they charge how much for milk?* echo throughout the stores. One tip: **Foodland** and **Safeway** both offer discount cards (called Maika'i Cards and Safeway Club Cards, respectively) that can bring pretty big savings off their otherwise confiscatory rates. Kapa'a's stores are easily seen along the highway; north shore has Foodland at Princeville Shopping Center and **Big Save** in Hanalei. The south shore has Big Save in Koloa on Koloa Road. If you're a **Costco** member, we have one near Kukui Grove in Lihu'e. If you're not a member and will be here awhile, consider joining as they have the best prices. If you just don't want to shop, **Island Grocery Service** (922–4670) and **Grocery Guys** (635–4140) will shop and deliver for around $25 plus cost of food.

Roosters

OK, so you don't normally think of roosters as hazards. And normally they're not. These guys are wild in many parts of the island and can be charming. But our roosters have proliferated since Hurricane 'Iniki freed so many back in 1992, and they are particularly stupid here. They don't seem to know when they're supposed to crow, so they do it *all day long* just to cover themselves. (Probably for liability purposes.) If any of these two-legged alarm clocks are near where you're staying, you may find yourself waking up *real* early.

TRAVELING WITH CHILDREN (KEIKI)

Perhaps we should have put this section under HAZARDS. If you are looking for baby-sitters, nearly every lodging on the island has lists of professional services, as well as employees who baby-sit. **Babysitters of Kaua'i** (632–2252) and **Kaua'i Babysitting** (652–5373) charge around $18 per hour. Some hotels, such as the **Hyatt** and the **Marriott**, offer rather elaborate services that can be a rug-rat's dream. If you are staying at a place that has no front desk, contact your rental agent for an up-to-date list of sitters.

If you need a crib, stroller, car seat and the like, **Ready Rentals** (823–8008 or 800–599–8008) from the mainland can help.

As far as swimming in the ocean with your little one, **Lydgate Beach Park** in Wailua has a boulder-enclosed keiki (kid) pond that is wildly popular. (See the aerial photo on the inside back cover.) It also has two playgrounds (Kamalani), the best on the island. Overall, it's a nice place for keiki. Also check out **Salt Pond Beach Park** in Hanapepe and **Baby Beach**, both in BEACHES. **Po'ipu Beach Park** in Po'ipu is popular with local parents, as well as visitors. These are considered the best places for children except during periods of high surf. Obviously surf and keiki don't go well together.

During calm summer surf, **Kalihiwai Beach** can be a pleasant place to bring kids. While not as protected as Lydgate or Salt Pond, it's picturesque, and your kids will make many new local friends.

Train lovers might want to check out **Kaua'i Plantation Railway** (245–7245). They cruise through 2½ miles of the Kilohana Plantation in Lihu'e. You'll stop and feed pigs along the way, which the kids go crazy over.

Kaua'i Miniature Golf (828–2118) is a pretty good putt-putt. Built in 2011 (not all the plants are mature yet), it's all about the water hazards here. (You're going in the water at some point, so deal with it.) Some snacks and ice cream for sale, and the price is only $15 for adults (who will enjoy it) and $10 for keiki. Easy to rec-

ommend. Only complaint is the closeness to the highway there in Kilauea.

THE PEOPLE

The people of Kaua'i are the friendliest people in the entire country. "Oh, come on!" you might say. But this is not the admittedly biased opinion of someone who lives here. This conclusion was reached by the participants in the *Condé Nast Readers' Choice Awards*. This is a sophisticated and savvy lot. *Condé Nast* is the magazine of choice for world travelers. When asked in their yearly poll, readers rate Kaua'i at or near the top of the list in friendliness nearly every year.

What does this mean? Well, you will notice that people smile here more than other places. Drivers wave at complete strangers (without any particular fingers leading the way). If you try to analyze the reason, it probably comes down to a matter of happiness. People are happy here, and happy people are friendly people. It's just that simple. Some people compare a trip to Kaua'i with a trip back in time, when smiles weren't rare, and politeness and courtesy were the order of the day.

Some Terms

If you are confused regarding terms in Hawai'i, this should help. A person of Hawaiian blood is **Hawaiian**. That is a racial term, not a geographic one, so only people of the Hawaiian race are called Hawaiian. They are also called **Kanaka Maoli**, but only another Hawaiian can use this term. Anybody who was born here, regardless of race (except whites) is called a **local**. If you were born elsewhere but have lived here a while, you are called a **kama'aina**. If you are white, you are a **haole**. It doesn't matter if you have been here a day or your family has been here for over a century, you will always be a **haole**. The term comes from the time when westerners first encountered these islands. Its precise meaning has been lost, but it is thought to refer to people with no background (since westerners could not chant the kanaenae of their ancestors).

The continental United States is called the **mainland**. If you are returning home, you are not "going back to the states" (we *are* a state). When somebody leaves the island, they are **off-island**.

Ethnic Breakdown

Kaua'i has an ethnic mix that is as diversified as any you will find. Here, *everyone* is a minority; there are no majorities. The last census count revealed the ethnic makeup below.

White	33%
Asian	31%
Hawaiian or other Pacific Islander	9%
Hispanic	9%
Black	0.5%
Native American or Alaska Native	0.5%
Mixed or didn't respond	17%
Total population	**67,091**

Hawaiian Time

One aspect of Hawaiian culture you may have heard of is Hawaiian Time. The stereotype is that everyone in Hawai'i moves just a little bit more slowly than on the mainland. We are supposed to be more laid back and don't let things get to us as easily as people on the mainland. This is the stereotype...OK, it's *not* a stereotype. It's real. During your visit, if you get in the rhythm, you'll notice that this feeling infects *you* as well. You might find yourself letting another driver cut in front of you in circumstances that would incur your wrath back home. You might find yourself willing to wait for a red light without feeling like you're going to explode. The whole reason for coming to Hawai'i is to experience beauty and a sense of peace, so let it happen. If someone else is moving a bit slower than you would like, just go with it.

THE HAWAIIAN LANGUAGE

The Hawaiian language is a beautiful, gentle and melodious language that flows smoothly off the tongue. Just the

Your keiki doesn't swim, you say? No problem. Teach her how to boogie board out at the dunes of Polihale.

Visitors are prohibited by law from bringing their worries to Kaua'i.

sounds of the words conjure up trees gently swaying in the breeze and the sound of the surf. Most Polynesian languages share the same roots and many have common words. Today, Hawaiian is spoken *as an everyday language* only on the privately owned island of Ni'ihau, 17 miles off the coast of Kaua'i (see INTRODUCTION chapter). Visitors are often intimidated by Hawaiian. With a few ground rules you'll come to realize that pronunciation is not as tough as you might think.

When missionaries discovered that the Hawaiians had no written language, they sat down and created an alphabet. This Hawaiian alphabet has only 12 letters. Five vowels: A, E, I, O and U, as well as seven consonants: H, K, L, M, N, P and W.

The consonants are pronounced just as they are in English, with the exception of W. It is often pronounced as a V. Vowels are pronounced as follows:

A—pronounced as in *Ah* if stressed or
   above if not stressed.
E—pronounced as in *say* if stressed or
   dent if not stressed.
I—pronounced as in *bee*.
O—pronounced as in *no*.
U—pronounced as in *boo*.

One thing you will notice in this book are glottal stops. These are represented by an upside-down apostrophe ' and are meant to convey a hard stop in the pronunciation (and are quite awkward to type). So if we are talking about the type of lava called 'a'a, it is pronounced as two separate As (AH-AH).

Another feature you will encounter are diphthongs (no, that's not a type of bathing suit), where two letters glide together. They are ae, ai, ao, au, ei, eu, oi and ou. Unlike many English diphthongs, the second vowel is always pronounced. One word you will read in this book, referring to Hawaiian temples, is heiau (HEY-YOW). The e and i flow together as a single sound, then the a and u flow together as a single sound. The Y sound binds the two sounds, making the whole word flow together.

If you examine long Hawaiian words, you will see that most have repeating syllables, making them easier to remember and pronounce.

Let's take a word that might seem impossible to pronounce. When you see how easy this word is, the rest will seem like a snap. The Hawai'i state fish is the humuhumunukunukuapua'a. At first glance it seems like a nightmare. But if you read the word slowly, it is pronounced just like it looks and isn't nearly as horrifying as it appears. Try it. Humu (hoo-moo) is pronounced twice. Nuku (noo-koo) is pronounced twice. A (ah) is pronounced once. Pu (poo) is pronounced once. A'a (ah-ah) is the ah sound pronounced twice, the glottal stop indicating a hard stop between sounds. Now you should try it again.

Humuhumunukunukuapua'a.
Now, wasn't that easy? OK, so it's not easy, but it's not impossible either.

Below are some words that you might hear during your visit.

'Aina (LYE-na)—Land.
Akamai (AH-ka-MY)—Wise or shrewd.
Ali'i (ah-LEE-ee)—A Hawaiian chief; a member of the chiefly class.
Aloha (ah-LO-ha)—Hello, goodbye, or a feeling or the spirit of love, affection or kindness.
Hala (HA-la)—Pandanus tree.
Hale (HA-leh)—House or building.
Hana (HA-na)—Work.
Hana hou (HA-na-HO)—To do again.
Haole (HOW-leh)—Originally foreigner, now means Caucasian.
Heiau (HEY-YOW)—Hawaiian temple.
Hula (HOO-la)—The story-telling dance of Hawai'i.
Imu (EE-moo)—An underground oven.
'Iniki (ee-NEE-key)—Sharp and piercing wind (as in Hurricane 'Iniki).
Kahuna (ka-HOO-na)—A priest or minister; someone who is an expert in a profession.
Kai (kigh)—The sea.
Kalua (KA-LOO-ah)—Cooking food underground.
Kama'aina (KA-ma-EYE-na)—Long-time Hawai'i resident.
Kane (KA-neh)—Boy or man.
Kapu (KA-poo)—Forbidden, taboo; keep out.
Keiki (KAY-key)—Child or children.
Kokua (KO-KOO-ah)—Help.

Kona (KO-na)—Leeward side of the island; wind blowing from the south, southwest direction.
Kuleana (KOO-leh-AH-na)—Concern, responsibility or jurisdiction.
Lanai (LA-NIGH)—Porch, veranda, patio.
Lani (LA-nee)—Sky or heaven.
Lei (lay)—Necklace of flowers, shells or feathers. The mokihana is the official flower of Kaua'i.
Liliko'i (LEE-lee-KO-ee)—Passion fruit.
Limu (LEE-moo)—Edible seaweed.
Lomi (LOW-me)—To rub or massage; lomi salmon is raw salmon rubbed with salt and spices.
Lu'au (LOO-OW)—Hawaiian feast; literally means taro leaves.
Mahalo (ma-HA-low)—Thank you.
Makai (ma-KIGH)—Toward the sea.
Malihini (MA-lee-HEE-nee)—A newcomer, visitor or guest.
Mauka (MOW-ka)—Toward the mountain.
Moana (mo-AH-na)—Ocean.
Mo'o (MO-oh)—Lizard.
Nani (NA-nee)—Beautiful, pretty.
Nui (NEW-ee)—Big, important, great.
'Ohana (oh-HA-na)—Family.
'Okole (OH-KO-leh)—Derrière.
'Ono (OH-no)—Delicious, the best.
Pakalolo (pa-ka-LO-LO)—Marijuana.
Pali (PA-lee)—A cliff.
Paniolo (PA-nee-OH-lo)—Hawaiian cowboy.
Pau (pow)—Finish, end; pau hana means quitting time from work.
Poi (poy)—Pounded kalo (taro) root that forms a paste.
Pono (PO-no)—Goodness, excellence, correct, proper.
Pua (POO-ah)—Flower.
Puka (POO-ka)—Hole.
Pupu (POO-POO)—Appetizer, snacks or finger food.
Wahine (vah-HEE-neh)—Woman.
Wai (why)—Fresh water.
Wikiwiki (WEE-kee-WEE-kee)—To hurry up, very quick.

Quick Pidgin Lesson

Hawaiian pidgin is fun to listen to. It's like ear candy. It is colorful, rhythmic and sways in the wind. Below is a list of some of the words and phrases you might hear on your visit. It's tempting to read some of these and try to use them. If you do, the odds are you will simply look foolish. These words and phrases are used in certain ways and with certain inflections. People who have spent years living in the islands still feel uncomfortable using them. Thick pidgin can be incomprehensible to the untrained ear (that's the idea). If you are someplace and hear two people engaged in a discussion in pidgin, stop and eavesdrop for a bit. You won't forget it.

Pidgin Words & Phrases

An' den—And then? So?
Any kine—Anything; any kind.
Ass right—That's right.
Ass why—That's why.
Beef—Fight.
Brah—Bruddah; friend; brother.
Brok' da mouf—Delicious.
Buggah—That's the one; it is difficult.
Bus laugh—To laugh out loud.
Bus nose—How one reacts to a bad smell.
Chicken skin kine—Something that gives you goosebumps.
Choke—Plenty; a lot.
Cockaroach—Steal; rip off.
Da kine—A noun or verb used in place of whatever the speaker wishes. Heard constantly.
Fo days—plenty; "He got hair fo days."
Geevum—Go for it! Give 'em hell!
Grind—To eat.
Grinds—Food.
Hold ass—A close call when driving your new car.
How you figga?—How do you figure that? It makes no sense.
Howzit?—How is it going? How are you? Also, Howzit o wot?

I owe you money or wot?—What to say when someone is staring at you.
Mek ass—Make a fool of yourself.
Mek house—Make yourself at home.
Mek plate—Grab some food.
Mo' bettah—This is better.
Moke—A large, tough local male. (Don't say it unless you *like beef*.)
No can—Cannot; I cannot do it.
No mek lidat—Stop doing that.
No, yeah?—No, or is "no" correct?
'Okole squeezer—Something that suddenly frightens you ('okole meaning derrière).
O wot?—Or what?
Pau hana—Quit work. (A time of daily, intense celebration in the islands.)
Poi dog—A mutt.
Shahkbait—Shark bait, meaning pale, untanned people.
Shaka—Great! All right!
Shredding—Riding a gnarly wave.
Sleepahs—Flip-flops, thongs, zoris.
Stink eye—Dirty looks; facial expression denoting displeasure.
Suck rocks—Buzz off, or pound sand.
Talk stink—Speak bad about somebody.
Talk story—Shooting the breeze; to rap.
Tanks eh?—Thank you.
Tita—A female moke. Same *beef* results.
Yeah?—Used at the end of sentences.

MUSIC

Hawaiian music is far more diverse than most people think. Many often picture Hawaiian music as someone twanging away on an 'ukulele (pronounced OO-KOO-LAY-LAY, not YOU-KA-LAY-LEE) with his voice slipping and sliding all over the place, as though he has an ice cube down his back. In reality, the music here can be outstanding. There is the melodic sound of the more traditional music. There are young local bands putting out modern music with a Hawaiian beat. There is even Hawaiian reggae and hip hop. If you get a chance, check out iTunes or stop by **Walmart** (246–1599) in Lihu'e. They have a good selection of Hawaiian music.

THE HULA

The hula evolved as a means of worship, later becoming a forum for telling a story with chants (called mele), hands and body movement. It can be fascinating to watch. When most people think of the hula, they picture a woman in a grass skirt swinging her hips to the strumming of an 'ukulele. But in reality there are two types of hula. The modern hula, or hula 'auana, uses musical instruments and vocals to augment the dancer. It came about after westerners first encountered the islands. Missionaries found the hula distasteful, and the old style was driven underground. The modern type came about as a form of entertainment and was practiced in places where missionaries had no influence. Ancient Hawaiians didn't even use grass skirts. They were brought in later by Gilbert Islanders.

The old style of hula is called hula kahiko (also called 'olapa). It consists of chants and is accompanied only by percussion and takes years of training. It can be exciting to watch as performers work together in synchronous harmony. Both men and women participate, with women's hula somewhat softer (though no less disciplined) and men's hula more active. This type of hula is physically demanding and requires strong concentration. Keiki (children's) hula can be charming to watch as well.

Kaua'i was the home of the most prestigious hula school in all the islands. People came from every part of the island chain to learn the hula at the Ka-ulu-Paoa. Great discipline was required, and the teachers could be very strict. The remains of this school are still evident at a plateau above Ke'e Beach.

The lu'au around the island usually have entertaining hula shows, though not as "authentic" as some of the festival demonstrations seen on occasion. Some

. . . .

Viewers struggle to get as close as possible to a classic fleeting tropical sunset.

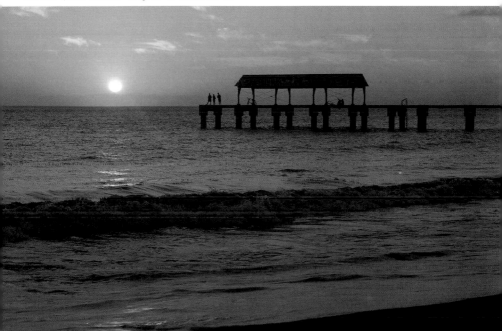

resorts and shopping centers also have hula shows on occasion.

FARMER'S MARKETS

Called Sunshine Markets locally, you'll find one every day of the week and it's a great place to pick up locally grown fruits and produce. Get there before they open, because things go fast. Below is a list; each is also shown on the maps.

Monday—In Lihu'e at Kukui Grove Shopping Center off Nawiliwili Road at 3 p.m., and Koloa Ball Park on Maluhia Road at noon.

Tuesday—In Kapa'a at Wailua Homesteads Park on Kamalu Road at 3 p.m., and in Kalaheo at the Kalaheo Neighborhood Center on Papalina Road off the Hwy at 3 p.m.

Wednesday—In Kapa'a at the Kapa'a New Town Park on Kahau Street at 3 p.m.

Thursday—In Hanapepe at Hanapepe Park at 3 p.m., and in Kilauea at the Kilauea Neighborhood Center on Keneke off Lighthouse Road at 4:30 p.m.

Friday—In Lihu'e at Vidinha Stadium on Hoolako Road at 3 p.m.

Saturday—In Kekaha at Kekaha Neighborhood Center on Elepaio Road at 9 a.m. Also a large private farmer's market in Hanalei at 9:30 a.m. at the Hanalei Neighborhood Center and Ballpark just past the post office, mauka side of the highway.

BOOKS

There is an astonishing variety of books available about Hawai'i and Kaua'i. Everything from history, legends, geology, children's stories and just plain ol' novels. In Hanapepe, **Talk Story Bookstore** (335–6469) has a very nice selection, as well as hard-to-find used books. And don't forget the **Kaua'i Museum** (246–2470) in Lihu'e. They, too, have interesting and hard-to-find books.

A NOTE ON PERSONAL RESPONSIBILITY

In past editions we've had the sad task of removing places that you can no longer visit. The reason, universally cited, is *liability*. Although Hawai'i has a statute indemnifying landowners, the mere threat is often enough to get something closed. Because we, more than any other publication, have exposed heretofore unknown attractions, we feel the need to pass this along.

You need to assess what kind of traveler you are. We've been accused of leaning a bit toward the adventurous side, so you should take that into account when deciding if something's right for you. To paraphrase from the movie *Top Gun*, "Don't let your ego write checks your body can't cash."

Please remember that this isn't Disneyland—it's nature. Mother Nature is hard, slippery, sharp and unpredictable. If you go exploring and get into trouble, whether it's your ego that's bruised or something more tangible, please remember that neither the state, the private landowner nor this publication *told* you to go. You *chose* to explore, which is what life, and this book, are all about. And if you complain to or threaten someone controlling land, they'll rarely fix the problem you identified. They'll simply close it... and it will be gone for good.

Sometimes even good intentions can lead to disaster. At one adventure, a trailhead led hikers to the base of a wonderful waterfall. There was only *one* trail, to the left at the parking lot, that a person could take. Neither we, other guides nor websites ever said, "Stay on the trail to the left," because at the time there was only one trail to take. The state (in their zeal to protect themselves from liability at an unmaintained trail) came along and put up a DANGER KEEP OUT sign at the trailhead. Travelers encountering the sign assumed they were on the wrong trail and started to beat a path to the right instead. But that direction started sloping downward and ended abruptly at a 150-foot-high cliff. Hikers retreated and in a short time a previously non-existent trail to the right became as prominent as the correct (and heretofore *only*) path to the left. Not long after the state's well-intentioned sign went up, an unwitting pair of hikers took the new, incorrect trail to the right and fell to their deaths. They died because they had been dissuaded from taking the correct trail by a state sign theoretically erected to keep people safe. The result? You'll now see more warning signs than ever in Hawai'i.

Our point is that nothing is static and nothing can take the place of your own observations and good judgment. If you're doing one of the activities you read about in our book or someplace else and your instinct tells you something is wrong, *trust your judgment* and go do another activity. There are lots of wonderful things to do on the island, and we want you safe and happy.

And also remember to always leave the island the same way you found it.

A NOTE ABOUT ACCESS

If a lawful landowner posts a No Trespassing sign on their land, you need to respect their wishes. That seems simple enough. But here's where it gets tricky.

It's common in Hawai'i for someone who doesn't own or control land to erect No Trespassing, Keep Out and Road Closed signs. Picture a shoreline fisherman who doesn't want anyone else near his cherished spot, putting up a store-bought sign to protect his solitude. Or a neighbor on a dirt road who hates the dust from cars driving by, so he puts up a sign that he knows locals will ignore, but it might dissuade unwary visitors.

In the past we did our best to try to ferret out when No Trespassing signs were valid and when they were not, and we took *a lot* of heat from residents who mistakenly thought we were encouraging trespassing when we weren't. But the current environment doesn't permit us to do that anymore. So if you're heading to one of the places we describe and you encounter a No Trespassing sign, even if you think it's not authorized by the landowner (and even if it's on *public* land), we have to advise you to turn around and heed the sign. All descriptions in our book come with the explicit assumption that you have obtained the permission of the legal landowner, and unfortunately, it'll usually be up to you to determine who that is and how to get it. But please, under no circumstances are we suggesting that you trespass. Plain and clear. Don't trespass...ever...for any reason...period.

MISCELLANEOUS INFORMATION

Kaua'i has no distinct **visitor season**. People come here year round to enjoy the island's blessings. However, certain times of the year are more popular than others. Christmas is always a particularly busy time, and you may have trouble getting a room if you are determined to stay at a particular resort. The graph below illustrates typical visitor distribution here. The island never feels crowded the way other destinations can feel. This might sound surprising, given poll

Visitors Per Month

results. When pollsters ask people where they would like to go, Kaua'i is always in the top 10.

If you're looking to dump your **digital images** onto a CD, **Walmart** (246–1599) on Hwy 56 in Lihu'e has good prices or, if you're member, try **Costco** (241–4000) near Kukui Grove Shopping Center in Lihu'e.

Travelers' checks are usually accepted, but you should be aware that some merchants might look at you like you just tried to offer them Mongolian money. You should also know that the American Express Card seems to be less welcome here than at some destinations. A number of places will not accept it.

The **area code** for the entire state is 808.

If you are planning to see either the **National Tropical Botanical Garden** or the **Grove Farm Museum**, make your reservations before you get here to assure admittance. Campers should also obtain their permits before they arrive, especially for the Na Pali Coast. See CAMPING in the ACTIVITIES chapter.

If you have an **early checkout** (or **late flight**) and need a place to freshen up before your flight, consider the bathrooms at Lydgate State Park, several miles north of the airport, which have some showers. Upon entering the road to Lydgate, the showers to the right on Nehe Street are a bit more private.

If you wear **sunglasses**, *polarized* lenses are highly recommended. Not only are colors more brilliant here, but the lower latitudes of Hawai'i make polarized lenses particularly effective.

It is customary on Kaua'i for *everyone* to remove their shoes upon entering someone's house (sometimes their office). Kaua'i's red dirt can be particularly pernicious, and nobody wants to spend their day cleaning floors.

Daylight saving time isn't observed here.

If you are going to spend any time at the beach (and you really should), woven bamboo beach mats can be found all over the island for $1 or $2. Some roll up, some can be folded. The sand comes off these more easily than it comes off towels.

If you want to arrange a **flower lei** for you or your honey as you arrive at the airport on a direct flight (no interisland flights), call **Greeters of Hawai'i** (800–366–8559) or **Honolulu Lei Greetings** (800–665–7959) before you arrive. For $25 and up, it's a pretty romantic way to start your trip, huh? While on island, **JC's Flowers** (822–5961) in Kapa'a across from Kinipopo Shopping Center has nice leis for reasonable prices. A plumeria lei is $7 and up, and they're gorgeous. (Not bad!)

THE INTERNET

Our website, **www.wizardpub.com**, has recent changes, links to cool sites, the latest satellite weather shots and more. We've posted our own aerial photos of nearly every resort on the island—so you'll *know* if oceanfront *really* means oceanfront. The site also has links to every company listed in the book that has a site—including those we like and those we recommend against. For the record, we don't charge a cent for links (it would be a conflict of interest), and there are no advertisements on the site. (Well...except for our own books, of course.) Some books and magazines print all the URL addresses, but it seems pretty mean to make you type in all those long, clumsy URLs. Besides, they change too often. Posting them as links from our site allows us to keep those Internet addresses current. (And they look downright ugly in print anyway.)

In earlier editions we had a **Calendar of Events** mentioning festivals, island celebrations and special events.

Waste of time! Organizers make changes so often (including days before scheduled events) that it wasn't reliable enough to continue printing it in advance. But the Internet is perfect for that. So the website has updated listings of island events.

If you're on-island and need **Web access** (to check your mail, etc.), most of the big resorts have business services available for around $20 an hour. Many other places have computers for about $6 per hour. On the north shore in Hanalei, try **Java Kai** (826–6717). On the east shore in Kapa'a, try **Business Support Services** (822–5195). On the south shore, the **Koloa Public Library** (742–8455) has a 3-month visitor card available for $10 that allows you access to the computers in any library in the state.

If you're just looking for a Wi-Fi signal, try Small Town Coffee or Java Kai in Kapa'a. In Lihu'e use the lobby area of Harbor Mall or the Kukui Grove Shopping Center. Kalaheo Café or the Shops at Kukui'ula are places on the south shore. In Princeville, try the Princeville Center.

IPHONE APP

OK, we have to toot our own horn here. If you have an iPhone and want a version of this book that is *geo-aware* (a book that knows where its at) visit the iTunes store and check us out. (Works on the iPod Touch, too, but it may not have GPS chips.) We have literally reGPSed the island (not relying on existing public domain maps) and created an interactive version of this book. (You haven't really lived until you've spent a whole day *GPSing all the mile markers on the island* so they will be precise on the moving map. Or spending seven days in Waimea Canyon getting all the trails precise and correct.) Just tap the map and everything we describe in the book appears along with the distance to your current location.

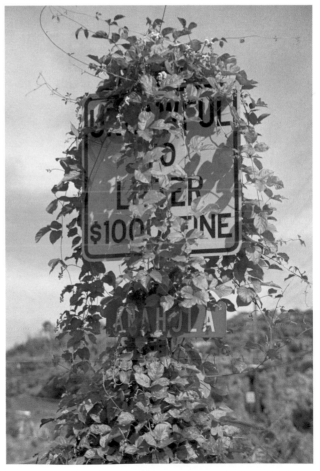

The bountiful lushness of the Garden Island presents itself in many ways.

Swimmers enjoying a giant tide-pool called Queen's Bath, a north shore summertime-only gem.

Kaua'i's north shore...where lushness takes on a whole new meaning. Every shade of green imaginable is represented in its myriad plant life. Its beaches are exquisite and its mountains unmatched in their sheer majesty. After a heavy rain, you will literally be unable to count the number of waterfalls etched into the sides of north shore mountains.

For the sake of clarity, we will identify the north shore as everything north of Kapa'a. (Look at the fold-out back cover map to orient yourself.) While this description includes Anahola (which some may consider east shore), it is easier to re-

member it this way, and anyone driving north of Kapa'a is usually going to the north shore anyway. The main highway, which stretches around the island, occasionally changing its name, has mile markers every mile. These little green signs can be a big help in knowing where you are at any given time. Therefore, we have placed them on the maps represented as a number inside a small box 16 . We will often describe a certain feature or unmarked road as being "⁴⁄₁₀ miles past the 16 mile marker." We hope this helps.

Everything is either on the *mauka* side of the highway (toward the mountains) or *makai* (toward the ocean). Since people get these confused, we'll refer to them as *mauka side* and *ocean side*.

All beaches we mention are described in detail in the chapter on BEACHES.

Driving north of Kapa'a, you'll see **Kealia Beach** on your right, just past the 10 mile marker. This is a popular boogie boarding beach. At this beach you can often see water spitting into the air from the collision of an incoming and outgoing wave, called *clapotis* for the trivia-minded. (Doesn't that sound more like something a sailor might pick up while on shore leave?)

ANAHOLA

Next, comes the town of Anahola. This area is designated Hawaiian Homelands, meaning it is available to persons of Hawaiian descent. The spike-shaped mountain you see on the *mauka* side is **Kalalea Mountain**, also called **King Kong's Profile**. As you drive north of Anahola, look back, and you will see the striking resemblance to King Kong. To the right of the profile is a small hole in the mountain called (this is clever) **Hole-in-the-Mountain**. It used to be bigger, but a landslide in the early 1980s closed off most of it. You can see it best between the 15 and 16 mile markers. One legend says that a supernatural bird named Hulu pecked the hole

in order to see Anahola on the other side. Geologists say that there was once a long lava tube stretching from Wai'ale'ale to the sea. The mountain mass on either side of the ridge has been removed by ceaseless erosion, leaving only the ridge and its ghost of a lava tube.

Duane's Ono-Char Burger is in Anahola. This is a good place for burgers and shakes if you're hungry but not in a hurry.

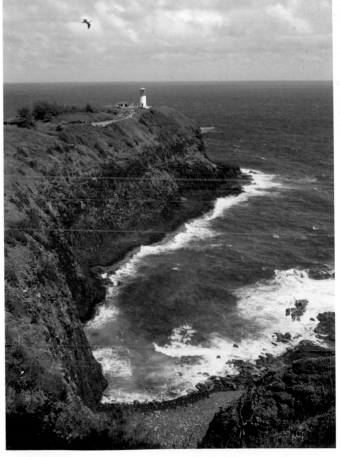

Perched on a bluff overlooking the vast Pacific Ocean, the Kilauea Lighthouse stands as a silent sentry.

Wyllie 'Anini Channel
Beach

Moku'ae'ae Island   Kilauea
Kilauea Pt. National   Lighthouse
Secret Lava Pools   Wildlife Refuge   Kahili Beach
22°13.420   (Rock Quarry)
Kalihiwai   159°25.367
'Anini Beach   Bay   Makapili   Pools of
Kalihiwai   Secret Beach   Rock   Mokolea
'Anini Rd   Beach   Crater   Kilauea
2nd Kalihiwai Rd   1st Kalihiwai   Hill   Bay
Rd   Na 'Aina Kai
The Prince   Kong Lung   Botanical
Golf Course   Center   Kilauea   Garden
Princeville   24   Farmer's Mkt
Airport   25   Thurs. 4:30 p.m.
Stop   Unnamed   Keneke Rd
kayaking   Twin Falls   Oka St.
here   Kolo Rd
Kalihiwai Falls   23
56   (Visible from   Ho'okui Rd
27   bridge, accessible   Kilauea Falls is also
Stop kayaking   by kayak or   privately owned and
here   horseback)   only accessible by kayak
(and even this is contested!).

Map continued
on page 49

Kapa ka Rd

Kilauea Slippery
Slide is privately
owned, closed and
not accessible
to the public.

Powerline Trail

Kalihiwai River

Kahihiholo

Kilauea Stream

Hanalei River

2,814'   Mt. Namahana

Power poles are
marked to serve as
a navigational aid.

	Indicates Foot Trails
	Kapa'a Bike Path
18	Roadside Mile Marker
	Unpaved Roads
	Public Access
⛺	Campsite

0   1 Mile
0   1 Kilometer

The reef edges are denoted by ·························· and come directly from government topographic maps. The task of verifying the precise location of all underwater reefs would be herculean and has not been attempted by us.

Waiakalua Beaches

Pila'a Beach

Arch

Pakala Channel
(which you won't swim in...right?)

White Tank

N. Waiakalua Rd

Larsen's Beach

1

56

20

Ko'olau Rd

19

Moloa'a Bay

Moloa'a Rd

18

17

Ko'olau Rd

16

Papa'a Bay

Papa'a Rd

'Aliomanu Beach

15 Aliomanu Road
(Broken Loop)

King Kong's Profile & Hole-in-the-Mountain

Anahola Beach Park

Kahala Point

14

Anahola
Anahola

Kukuihale

Anahola Stream

Kealia Rd

Gate

Secluded Cove

12

Spalding Monument
A monument built by a long-dead sugar baron to himself, now in disrepair. Kind of embarrassing when you think about it.

Haua'ala Rd
4WD

Kealia Rd

56

11

Donkey Beach

Map continued on page 59

There are several secluded beaches north of Anahola that require walks of various lengths, including **Larsen's Beach** and **Waiakalua Beach**. See map on the previous page and the BEACHES chapter.

Near the 17 mile marker is the **Moloa'a Sunrise Fruit Stand**. They have one of the best selections of fruit available on the island, as well as good (if a bit pricey) sandwiches.

At the end of Wailapa Road (on the ocean side of the highway between the 21 and 22 mile markers) are the **Na 'Aina Kai Botanical Gardens** (828–0525). This is what happens when you have someone with obvious big bucks (in this case the first wife of the late *Peanuts* creator Charles Schulz) with a dream and vision to create 240 acres of tropical gardens, sculptures, a teak wood plantation, a desert garden, secluded beach and stream, all scrupulously maintained. Guided tours are expensive—$35 for the recommended 1½-hour tour—but it's such an exceptionally beautiful area that it's worth it. Arrange in advance. Other guided tours of different lengths also available.

KILAUEA

The former plantation town of **Kilauea** is just past the 23 mile marker and is accessible off Kolo Road. It is known for the **Kilauea Lighthouse** (828–1413). This is a postcard-perfect landmark perched on a bluff and represents the northernmost point of the main Hawaiian Islands. When it was built in 1913, it had the largest clamshell lens in existence and was used until the mid '70s when it was replaced by a beacon. Directly offshore is **Moku'ae'ae Island**, a bird sanctuary. Self-guided tours of the lighthouse area are available, though you can't go upstairs and visit the light itself. The view from the bluff is smashing and worth your time. Open 10 a.m. to 4 p.m., it's $5 per person to get in. Take Kilauea Road.

Kilauea has also become a high-priced refuge for the super rich. Many exotic

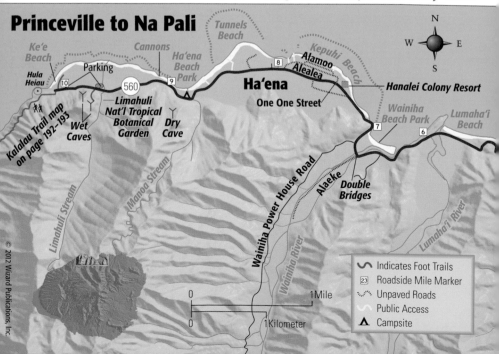

Princeville to Na Pali

Ke'e Beach
Cannons
Tunnels Beach
Ha'ena Beach Park
Parking
Kepuhi Beach
Alamoo
Alealea
Hula Heiau
10
560
9
Ha'ena
One One Street
Hanalei Colony Resort
Kalalau Trail map on page 192–193
Wet Caves
Limahuli Nat'l Tropical Botanical Garden
Dry Cave
Wainiha Beach Park
Lumaha'i Beach
7
6
Limahuli Stream
Manoa Stream
Wainiha Power House Road
Alaeke
Double Bridges
Wainiha River
Lumaha'i River

N
W E
S

0   1 Mile
0   1 Kilometer

⌣ Indicates Foot Trails
23 Roadside Mile Marker
⋰⋱ Unpaved Roads
∿ Public Access
▲ Campsite

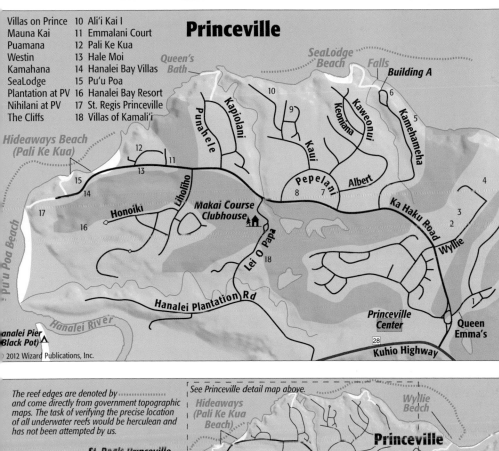

Princeville

Villas on Prince
Mauna Kai
Puamana
Westin
Kamahana
SeaLodge
Plantation at PV
Nihilani at PV
The Cliffs

10 Ali'i Kai I
11 Emmalani Court
12 Pali Ke Kua
13 Hale Moi
14 Hanalei Bay Villas
15 Pu'u Poa
16 Hanalei Bay Resort
17 St. Regis Princeville
18 Villas of Kamali'i

Queen's Bath
SeaLodge Beach
Falls
Building A

Hideaways Beach
(Pali Ke Kua)

Punahele
Kapiolani
Keoniana
Kaweonui
Kamehameha
Kaui
Pepelani
Albert
Liholiho
Honoiki
Makai Course Clubhouse
Lei O Papa
Ka Haku Road
Wyllie

Pu'u Poa Beach

Hanalei Plantation Rd

Princeville Center

Queen Emma's

Hanalei River

analei Pier (Black Pot)

© 2012 Wizard Publications, Inc.

Kuhio Highway
28

The reef edges are denoted by .... and come directly from government topographic maps. The task of verifying the precise location of all underwater reefs would be herculean and has not been attempted by us.

See Princeville detail map above.

Hideaways (Pali Ke Kua Beach)

Wyllie Beach

Princeville

St. Regis Princeville

Pu'u Poa Beach

Makai Course

Prince Course

Kahalahala portion of Lumaha'i

Hanalei Bay

Hanalei Plantation Rd

Grocery Store

Last Gas on North Shore

Hanalei Pier (Black Pot)

560 28 56

Hanalei River

Waikoko Beach

Wai'oli Beach Park

Pine Trees

Waipa Beach

Weke

Aku

Hanalei Bridge

Parking Lot

Hanalei Center

Ching Young Village

Hanalei

Kumu

Hanalei Inn

Farmer's Market Sat. 9:30 p.m.

Okolehao Trail

Stop kayaking here

Map continued on page 46

compounds are sprinkled about the area, just beyond sight.

Just north of Kilauea, on the *mauka* side, is **Banana Joe's** fruit stand. They also carry numerous locally made products. The frosties are excellent. (Frozen bananas ground through a Champion Juicer, which creates a consistency similar to ice cream.) Nearby is **Kaua'i Miniature Golf** (828–2118). See TRAVELING WITH CHILDREN on page 34 if you're in a putting mood. It's a pretty nice putt putt.

KALIHIWAI

After Kilauea you will notice two Kalihiwai Roads on the map. It used to be a loop connected at the bottom via a bridge. The bridge was erased by a tsunami in 1957, and the state hasn't replaced it yet. (Give 'em time; they're still debating whether smart phones are just another passing fad.) The first Kalihiwai Road leads to a beautiful little bay, **Kalihiwai Bay**. (Keep an eye out for a small, pretty hidden falls on your right after a bridge.) Kalihiwai is a good place to stretch your legs and enjoy the scenery. Also off the first Kalihiwai Road is a dirt road that leads to the public access of **Secret Beach** and the **Secret Lava Pools**. It requires a hike and is described under HIKING on page 152.

Back on the highway, there's a road ½-mile past the 24 mile marker called Kahiliholo Road. It's the only place you can park to walk to an **unnamed falls** ½-mile farther up the road on the left. (The falls are sometimes used by people to rinse off saltwater after they've been to **Secret Beach**.) The stream flows under the road and falls again into the valley. The long bridge past the falls has a narrow walkway. Visible on the *mauka* side is **Kalihiwai Falls**, a gorgeous, two-tiered falls. The cars on this bridge *seem* to go by at 110 mph, so be careful. You might see the remains of a vehicle turnout right at the bridge. The state closed it because of our old buddy, *liability*.

As you continue, take the second Kalihiwai Road to 'Anini Road, which leads to **'Anini Beach**, where many of the rich and famous choose to build their homes. This is one of the safest places on the north shore to swim and is protected by a long, fringing reef.

PRINCEVILLE

Continuing on Highway 56, the resort area of **Princeville** beckons. It was named after Prince Albert, the visiting 2-year-old son of King Kamehameha IV. Although the young lad died two years later, the name stuck. The resort is renowned for its ocean bluff condominiums and its golf. In fact, the best course on the island is **The Prince Course** located on your right after the 26 mile marker. This is the sort of course that makes the non-golfer want to learn.

Past the 27 mile marker is Kapa Ka Road. The end of this road is one end of the **Powerline Trail**—10¼ miles of outstanding views. See HIKING on page 156.

Princeville's cliffs lead many to think that it has no beaches to offer. *Au contraire*, beaches don't get much better than **Hideaways**, a very pleasant little pocket of coarse sand. The catch is that you need to hike down about 5–10 minutes to it. Another gem (in the summer) is **Queen's Bath**. This is a natural pool located on a lava bench. See BEACHES on page 102. The **St. Regis Princeville** is a good place to dine, shop or just gawk. If you are staying in Princeville, you may choke over the prices at Foodland or Big Save in Hanalei. Consider stocking up on food in Kapa'a where it's *somewhat* cheaper.

A REAL GEM

As you leave Princeville, note that the highway changes names again and the mile markers start at 0. The gas station here is the last place to get gas on the north shore (and they have the prices to prove it!). Across the street is the **Hanalei Lookout**. Many postcards have been sold featuring this view. This valley is where most of the taro in Hawai'i is grown. Taro corm (the root portion) is pounded to make poi. This is the stuff everyone told you not to eat when you came to Hawai'i. If you go to a lu'au, try it anyway. Then you can badmouth it with authority.

HANALEI

Going down the road, you come to the old-style **Hanalei Bridge**. Its wood planks are slippery when wet. This is a good time to tell you about Kaua'i's one-lane bridge etiquette. All vehicles (up to 7 or 8) on one side proceed, so if the car directly in front of you goes, you go. Otherwise, stop and wait for the other side to go first. All bridges from here on have one lane. Hanalei Bridge has a 15-ton weight limit, so you won't see big tour buses past this point. One bridge, called the Waipa Bridge, was built in 1912 for $4,000. It's so sturdy that it has *never* needed a major repair. The state found this intolerable and planned to replace it with a $5 million bridge that would hopefully require *lots* of maintenance. Local residents banded together in the late '90s and successfully fought 'em off.

The area around **Hanalei** (meaning wreath-shaped or crescent-shaped) **Bay** is a pretty little community. The surfing here is famous throughout the islands for its challenging nature during the winter. The entire bay is ringed by beach. A wide assortment of people live in Hanalei, including long-time locals, itinerant surfers, new age types, celebrities and every other type of individual you can imagine. You're as likely to see locals driving a Mercedes or Hummer as you are a car held together with bungee cords and duct tape.

After Hanalei, you ascend the road to a turnout overlooking **Lumaha'i Beach** (if the vegetation next to the turnout is

The Hanalei Lookout is a postcard waiting to happen...

not overgrown). This is a fantastic-looking beach made famous when Mitzi Gaynor washed that man right out of her hair in the classic Kaua'i-made movie *South Pacific* in 1957. (If you haven't seen the movie, that last statement must sound awfully stupid.) The eastern portion is the best but requires a hike down. Otherwise, you can walk right onto it just before the Lumaha'i Stream.

Notice how lush everything looks from here on? This part of the island gets the perfect amount of rain and sunshine, making anything green very happy.

HA'ENA

Wainiha Beach Park, past the 6 mile marker, is often a great place to beachcomb, but the swimming is not good.

One of the best **snorkel** and shore SCUBA spots on the island, **Tunnels Beach**, is past the 8 mile marker. See BEACHES chapter. Before you get to the 9 mile marker, the road dips at **Manoa Stream**. The stream flows over the road and is always creating potholes. It often creates a hole big and deep enough to

pop your tire, so look for it as you cross. You are now at **Ha'ena Beach Park**. Camping is allowed with a county permit, and the beach is lovely year round (but the *swimming* isn't always lovely; see BEACHES chapter). Across the street is the **Manini-holo Dry Cave**. Manini-holo was said to be the chief fisherman for the Menehune. He and other Menehune dug the cave looking for supernatural beasts called akua who had been stealing their fish, but they didn't find *da buggah*.

Below the 9 mile marker is a pile of rocks, all that remains of a heiau that was destroyed when they built the road. Called **Hale Pohaku**, it was where they raised small white dogs that served two purposes. One was food for the chiefs. The other was for chiefesses who gave birth. Often times children born to important chiefesses were removed and raised by others. So the small dogs would have their teeth pulled so they could nurse from the chiefesses to relieve the pressure in their breasts from the milk. If you look around, you'll find that one of the rocks has a petroglyph of a dog still on it.

Shave Ice: An Island Delicacy

One treat everyone should try is shave ice. Lest you be confused, shave ice is not a snow cone. Snow cones are made from crushed ice with a little fruit syrup sprinkled on. True shave ice (that's shave, not shaved) uses a sharp blade to literally "shave" a large block of ice, creating an infinitely fine powder. (Keeping the blade sharp is vital.) Add to this copious amounts of exotic fruit flavors, put it all on top of a big scoop of ice cream, and you have an island delight that is truly broke da mouf. In our constant quest to provide as thorough a review as possible, we have unselfishly tried nearly every combination of shave ice. The result: We recommend the rainbow shave ice with macadamia nut ice cream. But by all means, engage in research of your own to see if you can come up with a better combination. The best shave ice on the island is at Hee Fat General Store in Kapa'a, Jo-Jo's Clubhouse in Waimea and Halo Halo Shave Ice in Lihu'e. These can be found in the ISLAND DINING chapter. North Shore shave ice quality seems to have slipped as of late.

Past the 9 mile marker you will come to **Limahuli Stream**. Many people (including us) use this stream to rinse off the saltwater after their day at **Ke'e Beach**, which is still ahead, or use it to rinse SCUBA gear after a dive at Tunnels.

Above Limahuli Stream is the **Limahuli Garden** (826–1053). It is part of the National Tropical Botanical Garden. They have guided tours (by reservation only) of the gardens for $30, self-guided tours for $15. The variety of endangered plants is refreshing. A real treat is the ancient terrace system, crafted by some of the earliest Hawaiians, estimated to be 700 years old and in fantastic condition.

Just past the Limahuli Stream are the **Wet Caves**, called **Waikapala'e Cave** (reachable by a short trail) and **Waikanaloa Cave** (right there on the road). The upper **Waikapala'e Cave** contains a clean, freshwater pool. Until a few years ago the back portion of the cave (reachable only by swimming in the cold water) hid a phenomenon called the **Blue Room** (a chamber where the light turned everything blue). But the

water level is now too low, and too much light has erased the blue from the blue room. The wet and dry caves are former sea caves, gouged by waves when the sea level was higher than it is today. We were silly enough to SCUBA dive the upper cave and can report that there is not much to see, but it was kind of fun anyway (and spooky when we swam past where you could see the light entering the cave). Hawaiian legend has it that these caves were dug by the fire goddess Pele. She dug them for her lover but left them when they became filled with water.

At the 10 mile marker, you have gone as far as you can go by car. This is **Ke'e**

A REAL GEM

Beach, marked by a fabulous lagoon that offers great swimming and snorkeling when it's calm. The well known **Kalalau Trail** begins here. Eleven miles of hills and switchbacks culminate in a glorious beach setting, complete with a waterfall. The first leg of the hike leads to **Hanakapi'ai Beach** with a side trip to **Hanakapi'ai**

Falls. You sure ain't gonna do this trail on a whim, so for more on the **Kalalau Trail**, see ADVENTURES on page 191.

Keʻe is where **Na Pali Coast** begins. You can see its edges from here. Numerous movies have been filmed scenes at this location. If you walk past Keʻe Beach on the shoreline trail beside the rocks (when seas aren't raging), you'll get an enticing look at the rugged **Na Pali coastline**. Look up toward the mountains and you'll see **Bali Hai** (Hawaiian name **Makana Peak**). Clever photography turned the peak into the mystical island of Bali Hai in the movie *South Pacific*. As you stare at this peak with its incredibly steep sides, picture the following scene that took place in ancient times.

Men would climb the 1,600-foot peak carrying special spears made of hau and papala. The trail was so difficult in spots that they had to cling to the side of the mountain for dear life. When it got dark, they would light the spears and hurl them as hard as they could toward the ocean below. The spears were designed to leave a fire trail behind and were light enough to get caught in the updrafts. The light show was immensely popular.

From the end of Keʻe Beach, a trail cuts through the jungle up to the **Ka-ulu-Paoa Heiau**, still visible by the pavement of stones outlining its foundations next to a lava cliff. All the land here is state or county, even the rundown house in the jungle. (Despite an oddly out of place PRIVATE PROPERTY sign on land deeded to the county *decades* ago.) But nearby residents—and sometimes bullhorn-equipped lifeguards—often dissuade people from walking on this public land to the heiau due to its sacred nature. Whether they have the authority or not, if you are dissuaded, you should respect their wishes.

Walk the shoreline trail past Keʻe Beach for a great view of Na Pali.

Kauaʻi's north shore is where the majority of the state's taro is grown. This field, in the Hanalei Valley, was planted with rice to look like Vietnam in the movie Uncommon Valor.

For over 1,000 years this heiau served as the most important and prestigious school for hula in the islands. Would-be students came from around the island chain to learn from the *kumu hula,* or hula master. Please don't disturb any rocks lying about. Just past the heiau a short trail leads to a small waterfall (which is merely a trickle during dry times). *Fifty* generations of hot, thirsty students came to this tiny waterfall, sat on these very rocks and talked about their lives, hopes, fears and dreams. It's humbling to share these rocks with their spirits. It's as if you can still hear the echo of their lives in the sound of the gurgling water.

Just east of Keʻe is where the infamous **Taylor Camp** used to be. This is where Howard Taylor, brother of the late Elizabeth Taylor, owned a piece of land in the 1960s and encouraged other "hippies" to come and live off the land. The camp swelled to more than 100 people who mostly ended up living off residents or the government. Before the state condemned the property in 1977, camp residents began what would become the national *puka shell* craze when one of the residents fashioned a necklace of shells and gave it to Howard, who in turn gave it to his famous sister Liz.

NORTH SHORE SHOPPING

Across from mile marker 20 on the way north to Kilauea is **Hawaiian Hardwoods** for mostly large furniture pieces, following the natural forms found in the original wood. In Kilauea at Kong Lung Center try **Kong Lung Co.** for outstanding Japanese ceramics, housewares, toys and other items. Also in the same building don't miss **Banana Patch Gallery** for Hawaiian style ceramics and other island items for the home. In the back is **Cake**, a women's boutique with some unique clothing and accessories. Outside at the back of the center is **Coconut Style**, if your bedding could use some bright original island batik designs. **Island Soap & Candle** has just what the name implies, all made locally. And for jewelry, stop in at Lotus Gallery. Next to the Center pick up some fine wines and gourmet foodstuffs at Kilauea Town Market.

In the Princeville Shopping Center, Magic Dragon Toy & Art Supply has many options to keep the young and old entertained, including books, games, puzzles and of course, dragons. Walking in Paradise has all kinds of sandals from fancy to functional. Also stop in at Nani Kaua'i Gallery where we especially like their custom-order "vintage" Hawaiian signs. The Princeville Wine Market has a small but discerning selection of wines and spirits, as well as a chill barrel outside for your convenience.

As you approach Hanalei, the north shore's shopping mecca, stop at Hanalei Dolphin Center and have a look at Ola's for fine arts and some pretty unusual gifts. Also in the center is The Black Pearl for…well, pearls. Also check out Kim McDonald Art Gallery. On the same side of the road is the green Halele'a Building where Titus Kinimaka Kai Kane has some good buys on surf-wear. On the main highway before Ching Young Village, don't pass up some of the shops behind the main road in Kauhale Center, such as the The Root, for women's clothes and Crystals & Gems Gallery, which has some unusual handcrafted jewelry. Back on the main highway Kokonut Kids has adorable children's island wear and some toys. Browse Artists Gallery of Kaua'i (aka Evolve Love Gallery) for art, jewelry and clothing all made by local artists. One of our favorite shops is On The Road To Hanalei next door for Asian-inspired housewares, pottery and jewelry.

In Ching Young Village there are many shops and places to eat. Pedal 'n Paddle has great outdoor gear for sale and rent, and if your shoes have taken a beating on your trip, this is a great place to pick up island-friendly surf and turf footwear. Spin-

ning Dolphin will print Hawaiian design T-shirts while you wait. Hanalei Music's Strings & Things has a small selection of Hawaiian music and 'ukulele. Robin Savage Gifts and Gourmet Hanalei is a great stop for housewares and Hawaiian foodstuffs.

Across the street in Hanalei Center be sure to walk behind the building and see Hula Beach for hip island clothing for the whole family. Havaiki Oceanic and Tribal Art has extensive and unique artworks from all over the pacific islands and is not to be missed. Yellowfish Trading Co. carries vintage Hawaiiana, antiques and collectables. Tropical Tantrum has batik print clothing; Sand People also has women's clothes and island-style items for your home. Hanalei Surf Co. has surfer gear and clothes. Jewel of Paradise has some unusual glass paperweights of celestial bodies that are worth a look. If you are heading up to Ha'ena, stop in at the Hanalei Colony Resort and check out Na Pali Art Gallery & Coffee House.

NORTH SHORE BEST BETS

Best Beach—Ke'e or Hideaways
Best Snorkeling—Tunnels, Hideaways or Ke'e
Best Treat—Apple Cobbler at Village Snack & Bakery or any flavor at Kaua'i Nut Roasters
Best Lava Swimming Pool—Queen's Bath or Secret Lava Pools
Best Secluded Beach—Waiakalua
Best Swimming When Calm—Ke'e
Best Shore SCUBA Dive—Tunnels Beach
Best Beachcombing—Wainiha Beach
Best View—Sunset from Ke'e Overlooking Na Pali, or from Kalalau Trail
Best Parking Spot—One of the Few Available at Tunnels
Best Place to be Glad You're Wearing Comfortable Shoes—The End of the 11-Mile Long Kalalau Trail

Wailua is known as the coconut coast—can you guess why?

Kaua'i's east shore is where the majority of the population resides. The kings of yesteryear chose the Wailua River area to live, making it forever royal ground. All members of Kaua'i royalty were born in this area. Kuamo'o Road, designated as 580 on the maps, is also called the King's Highway. In ancient times only the king could walk along the spine of this ridge (Kuamo'o means the lizard's spine.)

Today, the east shore is often referred to as the Coconut Coast. One drive through Wailua and it's obvious why: thousands of coconut trees planted over a century ago by an idealistic young German immigrant who dreamed of oversee-ing a giant copra (dried coconut) empire. Unfortunately, nobody told him how long coconut trees took to mature, and the plantation was not economically successful, but his legacy lives on in the form of a gigantic coconut grove. The resort across from Wailua Beach ensconced in all those coconut trees was called **Coco Palms**. It got whacked by a hurricane on Sept. 11, 1992 and has been closed ever since. Even with its rich Hawaiian history (and even though Elvis Presley filmed *Blue Hawai'i* there), none of its subsequent owners has been able to figure out a way to reopen it.

For our description, the east shore means the Wailua/Kapa'a area to Lihu'e.

58

Detailed map on page 197

Kahuna Rd

Kawaihau Rd

Moalepe Trail

Kainahola Rd

Bridge — Intersection of Moalepe & Kuilau Trails

Waipouli Rd

Ignore.

1,000'

Kuilau Ridge Trail

Powerline Trail

'Olohena

Puuopae

Keahua Arboretum

600

520'

Kamalu

Wailua Reservoir

Kaua'i Research Station

4 (Again)

Farmer's Market Tues. 3 p.m.

581

5

'Opaeka'a

Kuamo'o Rd

Kaua'i's Hindu Monastery

580

4

Kuamo'o-Nounou Trail

Wailua Forest Management Rd

Electrical Substation

3 5

Kuamo'o Rd

280'

2

North Fork Wailua River

Secret Falls
22°02.951
159°22.369

Map continued on page 201

Private

Indicates Foot Trails
Kapa'a Bike Path
18 Roadside Mile Marker
Unpaved Roads
Public Access
Heiau (Temple)

South Fork Wailua River

Kayak Landing
22°02.486
159°21.837

Wailua Falls

Rope Swing (maybe)
22°02.209
159°21.753

Trails to bottom

583

Ma'alo Rd

© 2012 Wizard Publications, Inc.

Detailed map on page 156

Map continued on page 47

2 Miles ↑ To Anahola

11

Kapa'a Stream

Kahuna Rd

Kealia Rd

56

Kapahi Rd

Falls

Kawaihau Rd

Hauaala Rd

Kaehulua Rd

Ka-apuna Rd

Kealia Beach

10

Hauiki Rd

Moikeha Stream

Kawaihau Rd

Mailihuna

Lookout

'Olohena Rd

581

Farmer's Market Wed. 3 p.m.

9

Walking / Biking Path

Road

Kaiau

Lehua

Kapa'a Beach Park

Lokelani

Nounou (Sleeping Giant)

Kukui St

Roxy Square

400'

Nounou Mt Trail

Kapa'a Shopping Center

8

3

Lihi Boat Ramp

Cook Island Pine Trees

1,241'

200'

"Temporary" Kapa'a Bypass

Kaua'i Village Shopping Center (Whale Mural)

Waipouli Complex

Waipouli Plaza

Moanakai Rd

Waipouli Beach Park

Haleilio Rd

Waipouli Town Center

4

Kapa'a

56

1   Kaua'i International Hostel
2   Hotel Coral Reef Resort
3   Pono Kai Resort
4   Waipouli Beach Resort & Spa
5   Courtyard Kaua'i Coconut Beach
6   Plantation Hale (Best Western)
7   Kaua'i Coast Resort
8   Islander on the Beach
9   Kaua'i Sands Hotel
10 Lae Nani
11 Lanikai
12 Kapa'a Sands Resort
13 Wailua Bayview
14 Coco Palms Resort *(Still closed)*
15 Aloha Beach Hotel
16 Kaha Lani

Kinipopo Shopping Center

7

5

Aleka Loop

7

Wailua

Kuamo'o Rd

580

14

Papaloa

6

13 12 11 10 9 8

Coconut Marketplace

Waipouli Beach

'Opaeka'a Falls

1

Smith's Tropical Paradise

Wailua

Wailua Bay

Kamokila Hawaiian Village

683'

Lydgate Beach Park

15

Leho Dr

16

Playgrounds

Fern Grotto

5

N
W   E
S

Kalepa Ridge

Kuhio Highway

Wailua Golf Course

Nukali'i Beach (Kitchens)

707'

0   1 Mile

0   1 Kilometer

4

Map continued on page 65

56

Wailua & Kapa'a

(Take a look at the fold-out back cover map to orient yourself.) Both areas are heavily populated. (This is a relative term; together they have about 25,000 residents.)

The same descriptive ground rules that we discussed at the beginning of NORTH SHORE SIGHTS apply here.

Unlike other areas of the island where a single road dominates your tour, this area has many significant sights located off the main road. Therefore, we will describe them in a more scattershot manner and generally work our way from north to south.

WAILUA/KAPA'A

In the extreme northern part of Kapa'a is a delightful waterfall called Ho'opi'i Falls, which you can hike to. See HIKING on page 157.

While we are up the road off the main highway, there are several hikes in this area that provide excellent views. The Nounou Mountain Trail (also called the Sleeping Giant), the Kuilau Ridge Trail, the Jungle Hike and the Secret Tunnel to the North Shore Hike are all located inland and all are worthy of consideration. (See HIKING in the ACTIVITIES chapter for more information.)

One aspect of ancient Hawaiian culture that can be seen to this day is the heiau, a structure carefully built from lava rocks and used for religious purposes. There are seven heiau stretching from the mouth of the Wailua River to the top of Mount Wai'ale'ale. All except the Wai'ale'ale heiau are marked on the map on the previous page. The mouth of the Wailua River was well known, not only throughout the Hawaiian Islands, but also in parts of central Polynesia as well. Ancient Polynesians are thought to have come all the way from Tahiti to visit it.

Wailua is also known for ghosts and spirits. It was thought that during a certain phase of the moon, spirits of those who died recently would paddle down the river in large numbers and work their way around the island to a cliff at Polihale (described on page 88) where they would leap to the next life. Known as night marchers, these ghosts are still believed by many Hawaiians to exist, and sightings are most prevalent along the highway between Wailua and Lihu'e. Interestingly, this stretch of road has also been responsible for many bad car accidents. Of course, police blame the wrecks on another type of spirit—the kind that comes in a bottle.

The first heiau, near the mouth of the Wailua River on the southern side, is called Hauola, City of Refuge. It is part of what was a larger structure called Hikina-akala, meaning the rising of the sun. If a person committed an offense worthy of execution (such as allowing his shadow to touch the shadow of a chief or interrupting an important person), he would attempt to elude his executioners by coming here. By staying at the site and performing certain rites prescribed by the priest, he would earn the right to leave without harm.

The second temple is on the mauka side of the highway between the north end of Leho Road and the road to Smith's Tropical Paradise. This is called Malae and at 273 x 324 feet, it is the largest heiau on Kaua'i. Legend states that it was built by Menehune. There is not a lot to see. If you decide to visit it, be wary of your footing.

The third heiau is just up Kuamo'o Road (580) on the left side. This area had several names and several functions. The first portion that you see is called Holoholoku. Some archeologists say

Throw-net fishing was introduced to Hawai'i by Japanese immigrants. The native Hawaiians quickly embraced this method, and today it is considered an island tradition.

that this area was used for human sacrifice. Most of the time those sacrificed were prisoners of war. If none could be found, however, the kahuna would select a commoner and have the executioner strangle him secretly at night. Some archaeologists find this interpretation of Hawaiian history in spiritual bad taste, given its very close proximity to the **Birthstones**, described below, and assume that the area was used for animal sacrifices. The heiau was later purposely desecrated and used as a pigpen by the wife of the last king of Kaua'i, who did so as a signal that the ancient religious ways should be abandoned in favor of Christianity.

Just a few dozen feet up the road from **Holoholoku** is the **Birthstone**. It was essential that all kings of Kaua'i be born here, even if they were not of chiefly origin. One of the two stones supported the back of the mother-to-be while the other was where she placed her legs while giving birth. The outline of stones near here indicates where a grass shack once stood, where the pregnant mother stayed until it was time to give birth. The flat slab of sandstone that you

see on the ground covered the remains of a sacrificed dog, indicating that the place was kapu, or forbidden to commoners. The giant crack in the rock wall was where the umbilical cord of the newborn was placed. If a rat came and took the cord, it was a sign that the child would grow up to be a thief (or worse, a tax collector); otherwise, all was well.

Continuing up 580, a short way past the 1 mile marker, there's a dirt road angling back toward the ocean. (You're allowed to walk around the yellow gate.) Located at the end of the road are two large boulders. Though few residents are aware of it, the rocks' position is no accident and dates back over 1,000 years.

The ancient Hawaiians didn't live in a world of well-defined seasons. They didn't even measure their own lives in years, but rather stages of life. But they did need to keep track of the passage of the sun for planting and religious reasons. These two multi-ton rounded and shaped **solstice rocks** are perfectly offset so that if you align yourself with them so they appear to touch with the right one closer to you, the sun will rise from the intersection on the summer solstice.

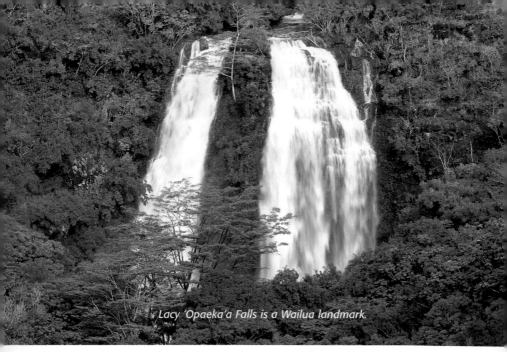
Lacy 'Opaeka'a Falls is a Wailua landmark.

(Winter solstice involves aligning the right side of the left boulder with the thumb-like hill on Sleeping Giant behind you.) Imagine the importance they must have attributed to this task by considering the difficulty of hauling these boulders up from the Wailua River, perhaps one boulder from each fork for symmetry. (Hawaiians *loved* symmetry.)

From those boulders, if you walk down the path about 100 feet past the guardrail, you will see several large stones. One of them was known as the **Bellstone** and, if thwacked properly, can produce a metallic clank (not the gong we have come to expect from metal bells). This sound supposedly carried throughout the entire Wailua Valley. The stone was struck in ancient times to signal the birth of what would be a new chief. Unfortunately, at press time, the state had effectively vandalized this area by dumping tons of rocks and construction debris all over the road and allowed vegetation to swallow up the solstice rocks and Bellstone.

Still on 580 just before you get to the 'Opaeka'a Falls turnout is the last heiau

you will see. Called **Poli'ahu**, this is a rather mysterious heiau. Legend states that it was built by Menehune, the legendary people of small stature, and was devoted to the interests and activities of the gods, demigods and high ali'i. Look for lots of native and Polynesian-introduced plant species in the area. There is also a nice **Wailua River Lookout** here.

The actual final heiau in this chain rests atop the rain-soaked plateau of Wai'ale'ale. The remnants of this most sacred heiau are still visible today. Called **Ka'awako**, the altar itself stood 2 feet high, 5 feet wide and 7 feet long. Toward the rear, standing on one end was a phallic stone. It is located on the wettest spot in the entire world. According to the USGS, this spot receives 432 inches of rain per year. (You read a lot of numbers about the annual rainfall on Wai'ale'ale—this number comes straight from the people who read the rain gauges. The original gauge is in the Kaua'i Museum.)

The ancient Hawaiians were bothered that the small, sacred pool on top of

Wai'ale'ale didn't feed their most sacred river, the Wailua. Not to worry. In a project that would make the Army Corps of Engineers proud, they cut a trench at the top of the mountain from the small pool to the edge of the cliff so the water would add to the waterfalls that feed the Wailua River. Then they could say the most sacred pool fed the most sacred river.

While on Kuamo'o Road *(a well-known speed trap)*, stop by the **'Opaeka'a Falls Lookout**. These lacy 151-foot falls flow year round. Late morning light is best, around 10:30 a.m. There is another **Wailua River Lookout** across from the 'Opaeka'a Lookout.

NOT TO BE MISSED!

Kamokila Hawaiian Village (823–0559) is across the street from 'Opaeka'a Falls. It's 3 acres of private land with numerous huts scattered about. Some might find it interesting; others might get antsy. It's not exactly lavishly maintained, but it's only $5 per person to get in and wander around. It'll probably take 40 minutes to see it, and it's certainly *not* indispensable. You can also do a canoe or kayak trip to Secret Falls from here (see KAYAKING on page 164) for $30.

Further up Kuamo'o Road, past some hairpin turns, is a road on the left called Kaholalele. At the end is **Kaua'i's Hindu Monastery** (888–735–1619). This is an *incredible* place, but they only give free tours by reservation once a week from 9 a.m. to noon. (It varies depending on the Hindu calender—call for dates.) It's set in an absolutely idyllic environment next to the Wailua River. This temple is built entirely of hand-carved stones from India. Some stones take as long as 7 years to carve, and there are 4,000 of them. And their special Roman-inspired fly ash concrete founda-

tion is designed to be crack-free for a thousand years. (When we had our driveway paved, they guaranteed it *would* crack within a month—and it did.) They say it's the only pure stone temple being built anywhere in the world and should be complete in 2017, but their narrative, details and completion date seem to change with every visit. They have a strict dress code, so wear long pants and shirts with short or long sleeves. If you get a chance, a tour is highly recommended. Bring mosquito repellent.

Continuing several miles up Kuamo'o Road, the road eventually crosses *under* a stream and becomes unpaved. It occasionally flows too heavily over the road to cross in your car. See the detailed map of this area on page 201. A 4WD is a dream back here, but regular cars are often OK, depending on the maintenance cycle of the road and the weather. (Sometimes the wimpiest Neon can make it; other times pre-maintenance ruts become too much for some 4WDs.) Large puddles are usually lined with small rocks, not mud. Several trailheads are in this region. A pretty one, before the road becomes unpaved, is the **Kuilau Ridge Trail**. The **Keahua Arboretum** is located near here, but it's been rather unkempt for years, so don't knock yourself out to see it.

The unpaved section of this road is Waikoko Forest Management Road. The area feels like a giant oxygen factory. Take a big whiff and you'll almost get a buzz from the purity of the air. The **Jungle Hike** on page 155 and the **Secret Tunnel to the North Shore** in ADVENTURES are back here, as well as stunning forests. This area is excellent for mountain biking.

Back on the main highway, you'll find that traffic in downtown Kapa'a (on the

Lihu'e & Puhi

1 Mile to
Wailua Falls

*Kilohana
Crater*

Indicates Foot Trails
23 Roadside Mile Marker
Unpaved Roads
Public Access

0   1 Mile
0   1 Kilometer

Map continued on page 75

Kukui Grove
Shopping Center
(Farmer's Mkt
Mon. 3 pm)

Kilohana

Kaua'i
Community
College

Kaumuali'i Hwy

58

1

50

Puhi

Nuhou

Costco

Kalepa

Pi

Kaumuali'i Hwy

2

50

3

← 9 Miles
to Po'ipu

Puhi Rd

Hanalima

Puakea
Golf Course

Kipu Rd

(Puhi Bypass)

Haleukama

Halehaka Rd

Kipu Rd

Hulemalu Rd

Bridge

Papakolea
Stream

Hulemalu Rd

Kipu Falls

Falls

(Puhi Bypass)

Cook
Island
Pines

Hule'ia Stream

As far as you can go by kayak.
21°56.588
159°23.719

Falls

Kipu Ranch

Map continued on page 59

Kaua'i Beach Villas

Kauai Beach Dr.

Kaua'i Beach Resort

Kuhio Hwy

N
W · E
S

583

Kalepa Ridge

Ma'alo Rd

To Wailua Falls

Traffic bottleneck at pau hana (quit work) time

56

3

51

Hanamaulu

Hehi

Ahukini Pier

Hanama'ulu

Hanama'ulu

During traffic, avoid Hanama'ulu by taking Ahukini Road & Hwy 51. Still slow, but faster than Hanama'ulu.

Hanama'ulu Bay

Kuhio Hwy

Kapule Hwy

✚ Wilcox Hospital

51

Tip Top Motel

Wal-Mart

Coconut Corner

2

Rentals

Inter-island   Commuter

56

Ahukini Rd

570

Kaua'i Museum

50

'Akahi   'Elua   'Umi
'Umi   Ewa   Palai

Lihu'e

Kapule Hwy

✈

Lihu'e Airport

0

Haleko

Ewalu

Kress   5   6
St   Hardy St

Farmer's Market Fri. 3 p.m.

Ho'olako
Vidinha Stadium

Rice St

1

Kaua'i Lagoons Golf Course

Grove Farm Homestead

Nawiliwili Stream

51

Kaua'i Marriott Resort

Nawiliwili Rd

1

Harbor Mall

2

Ninini Beach (Running Waters)

Nawiliwili

Kalapaki Beach

Anchor Cove Mall

Kuku'i Pt. & Lighthouse

Ninini Point & Lighthouse

58

4   3

Hulemalu Rd (Puhi Bypass)

Kayak put-in

Niumalu   Waapa   Wilcox

Nawiliwili Bay

Menehune Fishpond

7

Nawiliwili Harbor

Niumalu Beach

1   Marriott's Kalanipu'u
2   Kaua'i Marriott Resort
3   Garden Island Inn
4   Banyan Harbor
5   Kaua'i Palms Hotel
6   Motel Lani
7   Kaua'i Inn

Ha'upu Range

© 2012 Wizard Publications, Inc.

highway) can get congested at times, *especially* going south. The county opened up a "temporary" bypass road across from Coconut Marketplace on the south end, and up mauka from the ABC store at the north end. (See map.) The "permanent" bypass road is scheduled to be completed sometime during the next ice age. All the land around the bypass area was for sale some years back. Kaua'i residents were worried that someone would buy the 1,400 acres and develop it, connecting Kapa'a to Wailua and creating a big-city feel. Entertainer Bette Midler (a part-time resident) bought it instead and promised never to put anything other than trees on it.

One of Kapa'a's notable views is the **Sleeping Giant**. The best angle is from the small turnout kitty-corner from the Chevron station (on the main highway). Look *mauka* and you will see the outline of a giant. (This is your *ink blot* test for the day.) According to legend, the giant you see (you *do* see it, don't you?) was a friendly sort who flattened areas where he sat. Local villagers liked this and also

planted bananas in his footsteps. One day the chief ordered a heiau to be built. Villagers were too busy, so the giant volunteered. It took two weeks and he did a great job. Villagers threw a party to celebrate, and the giant ate a bit too much. (If you've been to a lu'au, you can relate.) He fell asleep and has not been roused since, but is expected to wake up any time (maybe during your visit).

Local folklore says that if Kaua'i's people learned of an attempt to invade their island, they would light fires behind the **Sleeping Giant** in order to illuminate his profile at night. This would frighten invading warriors into thinking that Kaua'i had some really big dudes and that intruders should rethink their invasion plans.

While you are in Wailua, riverboat trips up the **Wailua River** can take you to the **Fern Grotto** for $18 per person. This is a natural amphitheater filled with ferns and is a popular place for weddings. See RIVER TRIPS in the ACTIVITIES chapter. The **Wailua River** is usually called the only navigable river in all Hawai'i, but that depends on your definition of navigable. The mouth of the river has several stones with ancient **petroglyphs** carved in them. After heavy rains, the river sometimes washes away

These petroglyphs are usually submerged in the mouth of the Wailua River, but they can appear after heavy rains.

large amounts of sand, revealing these stones for a short period of time. The mouth itself is always changing, and watching it wash over its banks after a heavy rain can be wild. The river mouth can go from not flowing at all to carving up the mouth in a matter of hours.

There is a paved beachside walking path behind the Courtyard Kaua'i at Coconut Beach, and a longer path from Kapaʻa Beach Park north to Donkey Beach. They are great for a stroll or to ride a bike. A good place to take a *sandy* beach walk is from **Lydgate Beach Park** south as far as the Kauaʻi Beach Resort. The sand is continuous almost the whole way.

Lydgate Beach Park is the best place on the island to learn snorkeling. It has a boulder-enclosed pond that allows water and fish in, but keeps out the ocean's force. See SNORKELING on page 178 and BEACHES on page 110. There is even a keiki (kid) pond, which is shallower. Add to this showers, restrooms and two playgrounds, and you have a nice little park for a day at the beach.

On the southern side of the Wailua River is **Smith's Tropical Paradise**. Here you will find a nice garden (not in the same league as other nicer island gardens) in which to stroll, filled with tropical plants and wailing peacocks (which sound like cats being tortured). Entrance is $6 per person. They also hold a pretty good luʻau here. See ISLAND DINING chapter for more information.

As you pass the **Wailua Municipal Golf Course** going south toward Lihuʻe, realize that the entire coast fronting the course is a sandy beach. Called **Nukoliʻi Beach**, there are rarely more than a few people on it.

LIHUʻE

Coming from Kapaʻa and just before you enter Lihuʻe from Highway 56, you see Maʻalo Road (583) on the *mauka* side. This leads to **Wailua Falls**. In ancient (and occasionally modern) times, men would jump off the top of the falls to prove their manhood (which was often left on the rocks below). This test was often fatal. Government maps list

the falls' height at 80 feet. It always bothered us because it sure *looks* taller. So, a few years ago we dropped a fishing line and sinker to the bottom from the lip of the falls (boy, did *we* look stupid) and measured it. To our amazement, it was 173 feet of solid drop. (We measured it *twice* to be sure.) That's actually taller than Niagara Falls (though the latter has a tad more water flowing).

You might see people splashing about in the pool below the falls. It's a wonderful scene and lots of fun. They either took the steep trail (if it's dry) about 100 feet before the metal guard-rail ends at the lookout, or the less steep trail 3/10 mile back down the road from the end of the turn-around. (See map on page 58.) The latter requires a much longer walk, is not as steep but includes river walking. Neither are professionally maintained, and both can be slippery when wet. The state, in their paranoia about liability, has erected signs telling you not to take the trails to the bottom. They even cut the ropes once (but users keep replacing them) that had been strung to make it safer and easier. (Making it *less* safe apparently makes some bureaucrat *feel* safer.) You may see people ignoring the signs—and the fences erected by the state are promptly vandalized by local residents who have played at the bottom of the falls for generations—but state bureaucrats don't want you down there, so you should stay on top.

The falls plunge into a pool that's 33 feet deep. Why so exact? Because in one of those *just because* moods (before the state put up the signs), we hiked down with some friends, hauling SCUBA gear (gee, those ropes sure did help), and SCUBA-dived the pool. There we found 14-inch long small-mouthed bass and some giant shrimp (isn't that an oxymoron?) with bodies over 8 inches long, plus arms. Lingering beneath the falls, the scene is like an upside-down battlefield with explosions of white that will cause percussive waves to sweep through your entire body, your air-filled chest shuddering from the blasts. We also found rental car keys (perhaps tossed by an irate but shortsighted spouse), bolt cutters, a cane knife, and other odds and ends.

Back on the highway, if we're just trying to get *through* Lihu'e during traffic, we usually take 51 to 570 (Ahukini Road) to Hwy 56. (See map on page 65 for this to make sense.) It bypasses Hanama'ulu and much of Lihu'e.

In Lihu'e, one place worth stopping for is the **Kaua'i Museum** (245–6931) on Rice Street. They have an interesting display of Hawaiian artifacts and a permanent display called *The Story of Kaua'i* and other rotating displays. Their gift shop is well stocked with books, maps and assorted items. If you are looking for topographic maps of the various areas (serious hikers prefer these as traveling companions) or just an obscure book on Kaua'i or Hawai'i, this is a good place to stop. This isn't exactly the Smithsonian, but admission is only $10 per person unless you are going to the gift shop, which is free.

If you need camping permits or other county or state items, their buildings are behind the museum on Eiwa Street.

While you are in the area, there is a dumpy little place on Kress Street called **Halo Halo Shave Ice** inside Hamura Saimin that serves good shave ice (when they feel like serving it). Have them put ice cream on the bottom for a real treat.

Taking Rice Street east leads you to Nawiliwili Harbor. There are two shopping centers here called **Harbor Mall** and **Anchor Cove Shopping Center**.

Kalapaki Beach, behind Anchor Cove, is a good place to watch sailboats, outrigger canoes and cruise ships, in addition to the beach's other attributes.

On Rice Street, you will pass the main entrance to the **Kaua'i Marriott**. Its other entrance is off Kapule Highway (51) and leads through **Kaua'i Lagoons** to either **Ninini/Running Waters Beach** or the **Ninini Lighthouse**. The lighthouse uses a 4.7 million candlepower light. We remember how that sounded like *a lot* the first time we heard it, until we realized you can go to the store and buy *15 million* candlepower flashlights for $30. To get to the lighthouse, you pass a golf course.

Rice Street loops around and becomes Nawiliwili Road. It is here that you will find **Grove Farm Homestead Museum** (245–3202). This was the private home of George N. Wilcox and his nieces. It was turned into a museum by Mabel Wilcox shortly before her death in 1978. With 80 acres and several buildings to browse through, it is quite popular. (And they make an awesome sugar cookie here.) Groups of about six are escorted around the grounds and house for 2 hours for $10 per person. Even if this isn't normally your cup of tea, you will probably find it interesting. It's the story of an incredible family's rise to prominence in the old, sugar-dominated Kaua'i. Reservations are required. Tours on Mondays, Wednesdays and Thursdays.

Off Nawiliwili Road is Wa'apa Road. Take this road to Hulemalu Road, and you will come to an overlook for the **Menehune (Alekoko) Fishpond**. This is a large, impressive fishpond adjacent to the **Hule'ia Stream**. According to legend, it was built in one night by the Menehune as a gift for a princess and her brother. Estimates of its age range as high as 1,000 years. Today, it is private-

ly owned and has fallen into disrepair as a fishpond. Nonetheless, it is a remarkable landmark that is worth a look.

Back on the main highway (which has changed its name to Hwy 50, the Kaumuali'i Hwy), you'll find yourself heading south. Before the 1 mile marker is **Kukui Grove Shopping Center**, the biggest shopping center on the island. It's more geared toward locals but might have something to offer you. Past it is our island **Costco**.

Past the 1 mile marker you will see **Kilohana** (245–5608) on your right. This was the home of Gaylord and Ethel Wilcox and has been lovingly restored to its former glory. Gaylord Wilcox was manager of the Grove Farm Plantation. Walk through the door of this 16,000-square-foot mansion and you get a sense of Kaua'i in days past. The furniture, fittings and motif all harken back to a simpler day when sugar was king. Inside is a good restaurant called **22° North**, as well

as several shops, galleries, a lu'au and the tasting room for **Koloa Rum**, distilled here on the island. Their spiced rum is the best we've ever tried. They also have a train ride for $18 that kids might enjoy. See BASICS on page 34 for more.

Across from the 3 mile marker on the main highway is Kipu Road, which also acts as a bypass road. Located off this road is a glorious little waterfall called Kipu Falls. Though people have been swinging off a rope swing and jumping into the pool here for over a century, and though you may read about it elsewhere, the current landowner does *not* allow access. At press time there were no signs telling you to keep out, but trust me— they *don't* want you here due to safety and liability concerns. In 2011 these falls became notorious in the islands when a bill passed though the state house that would have effectively *ended all travel writing of any kind* to Hawai'i because of controversy (in part) over access to

Baby Beach in Kapa'a has a natural sandstone breakwater that is a hit with little kids.

these falls. So do everyone a favor: Keep the peace and stay away from Kipu Falls.

If you were to continue on Kipu Road, you would quickly come to a magnificent strand of Cook Island pines. These trees were highly valued as ship's masts in the Age of Discovery. This entire area is called **Kipu** and is currently leased to the Rice family and the Waterhouse Trust. William Hyde Rice was a cattle rancher, and a monument to him was erected here by his Japanese workers. Behind Ha'upu mountain is the fabulous beach called **Kipu Kai**. This long crescent of sand is a beachgoer's dream. Unfortunately, the only way to reach it is by boat or over the private road owned by Kipu Ranch and the Waterhouse Trust. This road is closed to the public, though you can get a glimpse of Kipu Kai from the ATV tour on page 121. John Waterhouse ordered that the 1,096 acres of leased state land revert to the state at the time of death of the last of his nieces (all in their 70s). We've tried walking to Kipu Kai from Ha'ula Beach. The horse path up and over the tall mountain is riddled with evil plants with thorns that turned our exposed legs to hamburger.

EAST SHORE SHOPPING

The east shore is a shopper's paradise. Starting in northern Kapa'a, there's the **Kaua'i Products Fair**. Most of the products, ironically, are *not* made on Kaua'i— so ask—but a few are and may be worth a look. The **Red Dirt Store** is inside the fair with red dirt T-shirts.

In downtown Kapa'a, try **The Root, Island Hemp & Cotton** and **Tropical Tantrum** for clothing. A great find, but easy to miss, is **a.ell atelier** for unique men's Hawaiian shirts and *outstanding* one-of-a-kind formal gowns, as well as casual clothes made on the premises, some

gifts and art. Look for vintage-style Hawaiian clothing and gifts at **Hula Girl**. A charming shop is **Serendipity: A Vintage Boutique** for stuff you wish you'd find at a garage sale, but never do. **Larry's Music Boutique** has a vast selection of 'ukulele. Next to Roxy Square, manly jewelry and accessories abound at **Men's Hardwear**. Pick up some fresh baked goods at **Country Moon Rising Bakery**. There are also some small galleries worth a stop sprinkled around town. Our favorites are **Earth & Sea Gallery, Kerry Oda Fine Art Photography**, both in the Dragon Building, and **Alley Kat Art** for recycled glass pieces and other artworks. **Kela's A Glass Gallery** has amazing glass art and decorative items. Fantastic, though ultra-pricey, but worth a look even if it's not in the budget. Across the street in Roxy Square, **The Glass Shack** has hand-blown glass you can watch being made at prices for the rest of us. A few doors north of Highway 581, **Ship Store Galleries** has art and antiques *mostly* with a nautical theme. **Orchid Alley** will ship any of their plants to the mainland.

Continuing south just before the whale mural, **Sweet Bikinis** behind the Lemongrass Restaurant offers great bikinis and cover-ups. **Marta's Boat** is women's boutique (across the street from the Foodland). Plan to shop here in the afternoons to be sure they're open.

In Kaua'i Village Shopping Center, if you enjoy making your own jewelry, visit **Divine Planet** for a huge selection of beads, as well as textiles for the home.

Coconut Marketplace is a mall that was looking pretty gloomy at press time, and it's kind of hard to shop here without getting depressed.

At Kinipopo Shopping Village across from Haleilio Road in Kapa'a, stop by **Style World** for women's clothes in natural fabrics. **Goldsmiths Kauai** has been around for more than 30 years and designs their own jewelry. We really like the fireball pearls here.

Before or after your visit to Wailua Falls, stop by **Kapaia Stitchery**. In addition to the *unrivaled* Hawaiian print and Batik fabric selection, they also have beautiful Japanese kimonos and everything any quilter could need. Koa wood items can be seen at **William & Zimmer Woodworkers** next door.

In Lihu'e, many visitors stop at **Walmart** or **Hilo Hattie** (on Hwy 56 near Ahukini) before that last rush to the airport. Always something here for everyone. Walmart is also a good first stop on the island for tabis, water shoes and all kinds of outdoor gear, Hawaiian music CDs, flower leis, Hawaiian coffee and macadamia nuts.

Kukui Grove Shopping Center at the corner of Hwy 50 and Nawiliwili Road is a sprawling mall in two large sections. One section contains **Kmart**, and the other portion has some good places to grab a treat or a sandwich while shopping at **Macy's**, **Sears** or any of the other specialty stores. There are also **Longs Drugs**, **Starbucks** and **Jamba Juice**.

Heading south on the highway, you'll come to **Kilohana Plantation**, a former plantation manager's private home. The pottery at **Clayworks of Kilohana** (behind the main house) is worth a stop, and you or your young one can make a keepsake of your own to take home or have shipped. **Koloa Rum** is where you'll find the best rum made in the islands, and their tasting room is beautiful. *Love* their spiced rum. **Grande's Gems**, above the restaurant, has some of the most beautiful fine gemstone jewelry on the island. There are also other galleries in the main house worth a browse.

Puhi Village Plaza at the stoplight in Puhi has specialty wines (including Hawaiian), liquors and champagne at **The Wine Garden**. They also carry Kaua'i Cigars—at least the tobacco comes from Kaua'i. They're not bad, but smoke a bit young and simple, and they are pretty pricey, too.

If you'd like to arrange a shipment of tropical flowers or a plant grown on lava rock, try **Kaua'i Nursery & Landscape** (245–7747) on the left side as you head toward Po'ipu.

EAST SHORE BEST BETS

Best Beach Walk—Lydgate Beach Park to Kaua'i Beach Resort

Best View—From the Top of Sleeping Giant for Hikers; Sunrise over Lydgate for Non-Hikers

Best Place for Novice Snorkelers, Fish Feeding or to Let Children Swim— Lydgate State Park

Best Treat—Apple Turnover at Kaua'i Bakery

Best Hidden Gem—Ho'opi'i Falls

Best Uncrowded Beach—In front of Wailua Golf Course

Best Playground—Kamalani Playground at Lydgate Park

Best Boogie Boarding—Kealia Beach

Best Evening Stroll—Paved Beach Path between Kapa'a Beach Park and Kealia)

Best Lu'au—Smith's Tropical Paradise or Kalamaku at Kilohana

Best Way to Spend 7 Years—Carving One Stone for the Kaua'i Hindu Monastery

Best Place to Grab a Drink and Head to the Beach—Poolside Bar at the Kaua'i Coast Resort

Best Place to Make Your Pupils Big— Mile-Long Secret Tunnel to the North Shore

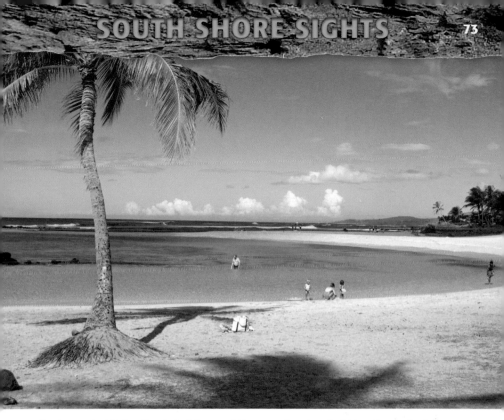

Semi-protected Po'ipu Beach Park is one of the many beaches that bless the south shore.

The sunny south shore... where rainfall is less frequent and sunshine is abundant. Many people prefer the sunnier quality of the south shore to the lushness of the north shore. Fortunately, you can have it all.

For the sake of this discussion, we will consider the south shore as everything past Puhi to Kalaheo. (Look at the fold-out back cover map to orient yourself.) Past Kalaheo, the character of the island changes again, and we will cover that in the WEST SHORE SIGHTS chapter.

The same descriptive ground rules that we discussed at the beginning of NORTH SHORE SIGHTS chapter apply here.

All beaches we mention are described in detail in the chapter on BEACHES.

Driving to Po'ipu from Lihu'e along the main highway, you will pass through the **Knudsen Gap** between the 6 and 8 mile markers. A century ago this was the scariest part of the island. The small gap between the mountains was the only route you could take to the south shore and was a perfect place for an ambush. Even the local sheriff always dreaded going through the Knudsen Gap.

Past the 6 mile marker you will come to Hwy 520, or Maluhia Road. This road to Koloa and Po'ipu is called the **Tree Tunnel**. When Walter Duncan McBryde was

Koloa, Po'ipu & Kalaheo

1. Prince Kuhio
2. Kuhio Shores
3. Whalers Cove
4. Waikomo Stream Villas
5. Koloa Landing at Po'ipu Beach
6. Alihi Lani
7. Po'ipu Kapili
8. Sheraton Kaua'i Resort
9. Kiahuna Plantation Resort
10. Ko'a Kea Hotel & Resort
11. Marriott's Waioha'i Beach Club
12. Regency II & Villas
13. Po'ipu Kai Resort
14. Cottages at Po'ipu Kai
15. Villas at Po'ipu Kai & Regency Villas
16. Hideaway Cove Villas
17. Nihi Kai Villas
18. Po'ipu Plantation
19. Po'ipu Shores
20. Sunset Kahili
21. Po'ipu Crater Resort
22. Po'ipu Palms
23. Po'ipu Makai
24. Makahu'ena
25. Point at Po'ipu
26. Grand Hyatt

Indicates Foot Trails
Roadside Mile Marker
Unpaved Roads
Public Access

Alexander Reservoir

Map continued on page 85

Farmer's Market Tues. 3 p.m.

5 Miles to Hanapepe, 'Ele'ele & Port Allen

Kalaheo

Kalaheo Inn

Lawa'i

Papalina Road

Puu Rd

Kukuiolono Park & Golf Course

Lauoho

Waha Rd

Papalina

Hailima

Koloa Road

Gate

Omao Road

Lawa'i Stream

Niukapu Heiau

National Tropical Botanical Garden

NTBG Visitor Center

Shops at Kukui'ula

Hoona Rd

Prince Kuhio Park

Blowhole

Lawa'i Bay

Spouting Horn

Lawa'i Rd

Nomilu Fishpond

Palama Beach

Kukui'ula Small Boat Harbor

Keiki Cove

Lawa'i Beach

PK's Baby Beach

Palama Buoy

N
W   E
S

0   1 Mile

0   1 Kilometer

Halfway Bridge

Kaumuali'i Highway

To Puhi

50

5

4

3

50

Knudsen Gap

6

50

A'akukui Road

Kipu Road

Puhi Bypass

Hulemalu

Bridge

Cook Island Pines

Kipu Falls

Huleia

Stream

7

0

(Tree Tunnel)

520

1

Ha'upu Tunnel

Map continued on page 64

Private Road–Gated

Ha'upu 2,297'

Maluhia Road

Private Road–Gated

Waita Reservoir

Anne Knudsen Park (Farmer's Mkt. Mon. Noon)

Note: Since none of the cane roads in this area have street signs, relevant telephone poles are indicated on the map to assist in navigating the roads if they are unlocked.

520

Koloa

Ala Kinoiki

3

Grocery Store

530

Koloa Road

Weliweli

Waikomo

Old Koloa Sugar Mill

Maha'ulepu Beaches

Ha'ula Beach

Telephone Poles

Lithified Cliffs

Po'ipu Rd

4

Koloa-Po'ipu Bypass

Guard Shack

Cliff Cracks

Kiahuna Golf Course

Po'ipu

Kiahuna Plantation Dr.

Gate (closes at 6 p.m.)

Cave

Gillin's Beach

Kawailoa Bay

Dry Blowhole

Ala Kinoiki

Po'ipu Rd

CJM Stables

Po'ipu Bay Resort Golf Course

Lithified Cliffs

Po'ipu Rd

5

Kapili

Poipu Shopping Village

4

Hoonani

6 7

8 9

10 11

Hoowili

Hoone

12 14 15 19 16 17 18 20 13 21 22 23 24

Pe'e

26

25

Makewehi Lithified Cliffs

Shipwreck Beach

Koloa Landing

Kiahuna Beach

Po'ipu Beach Park

Sheraton Caverns

Brennecke Beach

Makahu'ena Arch
21°52.124
159°26.697

The reef edges are denoted by ·········· and come directly from government topographic maps. The task of verifying the precise location of all underwater reefs would be herculean and has not been attempted by us.

© 2012 Wizard Publications, Inc.

landscaping his home in the early 1900s, he found that he had over 500 eucalyptus trees *left over*. He donated these trees, called swamp mahogany, to the county. Many residents showed up to help plant the trees. The result is the Tree Tunnel. (Part of it was torn down in the '50s when they rerouted the highway.) Today it should more aptly be called the "tree corridor." Though still beautiful, the trees don't intertwine at the top the way they did before either Hurricane 'Iwa in 1982 or 'Iniki on Sept. 11, 1992.

KOLOA

Driving down Hwy 520 you come to the town of Koloa, sometimes called Old Koloa Town. This was the first sugar plantation town in all the islands when Kamehameha III leased the land to Ladd and Company in 1835. The town has much charm and is worth a stop. Next to Crazy Shirts Store there is a marvelous monkeypod tree whose branches seem to meander forever.

Across the street (kitty-corner) from the shops are the remnants of an old sugar mill built over 170 years ago. There you will also find a plaque dedicated to the sugar plantation workers and a good (if somewhat dated) synopsis of sugar history on the island.

Looking at the map, you will see a dirt road leading to Waita Reservoir and Ha'upu Range Tunnel. They are gated and not available to visit unless you book an ATV tour. We used to think these gates were a relatively modern annoyance until we stumbled across an old local newspaper from 1934. In a letter to the editor the writer warned people not to accept an invitation from a well-known plantation manager when he said he "wanted to show you something interesting." Apparently the crafty manager did this whenever he had a long way to drive and wanted to have somebody along to open and close all the gates.

PO'IPU

Continuing to Po'ipu on Hwy 520 and doglegging onto Po'ipu Road, watch your speed. This is a notorious speed trap and sobriety checkpoint area, and the limit is 25 mph, 15 mph near the school. (The Po'ipu Bypass shown on the map is an even more effective speed trap because you are easily lulled into going over 40 mph.)

Past the 4 mile marker as you approach Po'ipu, the offshoot on the far side of the traffic circle instead takes you onto Lawai Road where you'll come to Prince Kuhio Park. There you will find a monument to Prince Kuhio, the last royally designated heir to the Hawaiian throne. He went on to become a delegate to Congress until the early 1920s. In this park you will also find the Ho'ai Heiau, impressive in its perfection and almost chiseled appearance. The entrance is toward the rear on the left side.

Continuing along Lawa'i Road, you will come to Spouting Horn Beach Park. This wonderful delight is a small lava shelf where water from waves is thrust through an opening, causing water and air to squirt out a blowhole. This particular site distinguishes itself from other blowholes around Hawai'i in that it has an additional hole that blows only air, causing a loud moaning and gasping sound. Legend has it that the entire coastline in this area was once guarded by a giant female lizard called a mo'o. She would eat anyone who tried to swim or fish in the area. One day a man named Liko went fishing. The mo'o went to attack Liko, who threw a spear into the mo'o's mouth. The angry mo'o chased Liko into the lava tube. Liko escaped, but the mo'o became trapped in what we now call Spouting Horn, where its cries of hunger and pain can be heard to this day.

The Spouting Horn was formerly dwarfed by an adjacent blowhole called the Kukui'ula Seaplume. That

NOT TO BE MISSED!

seaplume would shoot much higher—as high as 200 feet into the air. But on an early Sunday morning back in the 1920s a sugar company manager ordered one of his workers to drop blasting powder into the hole to widen it so the plume wouldn't shoot into the air. The reason? The salt spray from the geyser was stunting the growth of 10 acres of cane (among the company's many thousands of acres), and the manager would not stand for that. From down on the lava shelf you can see its remains in the form

Spouting Horn is often more dramatic at high tide.

Watch your step around these ficus roots at the Allerton Garden in Lawa'i. This tree is where they found the dinosaur eggs in the movie Jurassic Park.

of a large rectangular aperture to the left of the current blowhole opening.

The view from the guard-rail is quite interesting. Many people walk down and view the Horn and some of the other delightful offerings from the lava area itself. The power and forces in this area can only be experienced from this vantage point. Be forewarned, however, that while the experience is far more rewarding than the view from the guard-rails, it can be dangerous. There have been incidents where people have been swept to their deaths into the Horn. Unexpectedly large waves can even wash over the entire shelf, dragging you into the hole or over the edge into the open ocean.

There may be signs suggesting that you not go down, although county personnel we spoke with said it wasn't illegal. Use caution and common sense. If you go onto the bench, you do so at your own

risk. (For some odd reason, tour bus drivers sometimes authoritatively yell at people on the bench, but hey...they're just tour bus drivers.) In any event, *never* stand between the hole and the ocean. A very large wave would have no difficulty dragging you in. Some years ago two visitors from San Francisco were knocked in while they stood between the hole and the ocean. One was *on crutches* at the time. They were lucky—rather than being crushed inside the hole, they were immediately sucked out of the blowhole and into the open ocean where they were rescued by some phone workers on their break.

Just before Spouting Horn is the entrance to the National Tropical Botanical Garden. This incredibly beautiful garden consists of 252 acres called the McBryde Garden and 80 acres called the Allerton Garden (742–2623). Even if you normally wouldn't visit a garden, you'll probably like this one. See LAND TOURS on page 166.

Going back the way you came, just before the fork is a road leading to Koloa Landing. This is a popular SCUBA shore dive. Until the 1900s this was Kaua'i's main port. Whaling ships used to winter here, and all goods brought to Kaua'i came through either Koloa Landing or Waimea.

Going back to the traffic circle, take the branch toward Po'ipu, which is turtle country. Look out at the water for any reasonable length of time, and you'll see green sea turtles swimming nearby. This area was developed in the '70s and '80s and has become a much sought after visitor destination. Swanky hotels and condominium resorts line the road. (See WHERE TO STAY chapter for more information.) The beaches in this area are fantastic, with the best of the best located past the resorts at a place called Maha'ulepu. This beach (see BEACHES chapter) sports lots of places to walk and **A REAL GEM** some incredible sandstone cliffs. The dirt roads around here can be good places to ride mountain bikes. Horseback riding, snorkeling, fishing and more are all available in this area. The lithified cliffs from Maha'ulepu to Shipwreck Beach offer delicious shoreline hikes. See HIKING in the ACTIVITIES chapter.

One thing that totally escaped our attention until an alert reader pointed it out to us was the presence of a cool-looking lava arch at the shoreline between the Point at Po'ipu Resort and Makahu'ena at the southern tip of the island. Park at the Point and walk along the shoreline until you see a light beacon. The

chain link fence from Makahu'ena points toward the arch. Don't let the ocean smack you around here.

There's lots of cactus along this part of the island. It was imported in the 1800s because it made a perfect natural cattle fence—and you don't even need to repair it.

KALAHEO

After Lawa'i comes Kalaheo (which has the best pizza on the island—see ISLAND DINING). One of Kalaheo's lesser known gems is the Kukuiolono Park and Golf Course (see GOLFING in the ACTIVITIES chapter). This is the private course and garden donated by Walter

These lithified sand dunes of Maha'ulepu are a stunning testament to the power of the ocean.

McBryde to the people of Kaua'i. If you want to try your hand at golf, this is the place to learn. The price is $9 *per day*. The small Japanese garden located on the course was Mr. McBryde's pride and joy. This is where he chose to be buried, near the 8th tee.

Although it was sugar that drove the economy along here for over a century, it was phased out in the 1990s to grow coffee, on the assumption it would be more profitable. It struggled for years, and the company was sold in 2011 to the same Italian coffee conglomerate that owns Hills Bros. The Kaua'i Coffee Company, has 3,100 acres under cultivation. To be honest, it's not very good coffee. Most of the trees are an unimpressive breed called *yellow catuai*. Don't confuse it with the *far* superior coffee grown on the Kona coast of the Big Island where the coffee-grow-ing environment is ideal. Also, most Kaua'i coffee is machine-picked, so beans slightly under and over their peak get picked in the process. Kaua'i Coffee has smaller fields of *blue mountain*, and *red catuai*, which is better, but it's expensive, and we've only found this coffee at their visitor center located on Hwy 540 just past the 12 mile marker on Hwy 50. That 4-mile-long road, sometimes called the Coffee Highway, cuts through much of the coffee plantation. The visitor center is popular with tour buses but is only marginally interesting, and their museum is particularly scant. Only for hard-core coffee groupies.

Incidentally, any fixed-wing pilot on the island will tell you they *love* coffee trees. Their leaves are dark and dense, which capture the sun and heat the air around them. This makes them exceptional gen-

The alien landscape of the tortured sandstone cliffs between Maha'ulepu and the Hyatt.

erators of thermal currents, providing free lift when the heated air rises.

Just after the 14 mile marker you will come to the Hanapepe Valley Lookout. As you gaze over the peaceful vista, it's hard to believe that this was the scene of the bloodiest and most savage battle known to have taken place on Kaua'i. The embittered son of Kaua'i's last king started a revolt against government rule. Remember that Kaua'i had never been conquered by Kamehameha the Great. Both of his invasion attempts had been costly in terms of men, and neither had even reached Kaua'i in large numbers. Even though Kaua'i's last king voluntarily accepted Kamehameha's rule, it forever stuck in the royal craw that Kaua'i had not been *forced* into submission. So when this revolt occurred, it was a perfect excuse to send Hawai'i troops over to show those Kauaians who was boss. Government troops sent to put down the revolt were unimaginably brutal, and their methods were reviled even among their supporters. Men, women and children were needlessly slaughtered, and the wanton killing continued for 10 days.

Everything past here is covered in the WEST SHORE SIGHTS chapter.

SOUTH SHORE SHOPPING

In Kalaheo, if you have decided to take up the 'ukulele, hit Scotty's Music on the main highway. Real Dirt Hawaii has red dirt shirts that are a better value than other locations and manufacturers. Visit Maile Organics (next to Kalaheo Café)—they only use indigenous flora to create their spa and beauty products.

Just off Highway 50 in Lawa'i on Koloa Road is Hawaiian Trading Post, which has the largest selection of Ni'ihau shell leis and Tahitian Black Pearls on the island, as well as other jewelry and gift items.

If you are out by Spouting Horn, check out the jewelry vendor stalls there, especially for pearls.

Following Koloa Road will take you right into Koloa Town, where there are many shops and galleries to browse. Among the more interesting, starting from the east end of Koloa Road, is The Wine Shop, which has a great selection of wines, spirits and gourmet foodstuffs. At Island Soap & Candle Works, you can watch the items for sale being made. The many scents can become overwhelming, but small bowls of coffee beans placed around the store will help your nasal palate stay clear. Behind their store is Discount Variety for reasonably priced beach mats, etc. Jungle Girl carries some funky island fashions for women. Christian Riso Fine Art is our favorite art gallery in town. The 'Ukulele Store has a wonderful selection and knowledgable staff. On down Poipu Road Pohaku T's carries only locally made items and has a huge selection of T-shirts, all designed and printed on Kaua'i.

Continuing on Poipu Road toward Po'ipu, is Poipu Shopping Village. You will find many boutique fashions from $3 flip-flops to $30,000 pearl necklaces. If you forget your swimsuit or just want to look more island-style, try Making Waves for women and keiki or Overboard for men. For kids' fashions, you can't beat Blue Ginger or Sand Kids, where they also have lots of toys to entertain your keiki. Po'ipu Fine Arts is one of the better art galleries. Black Pearls Kaua'i has stunning pearls (not just black ones).

Farther along are The Shops at Kukui'ula with a nice mix of restaurants, shops and galleries. We like Scott Hanft Photography and Galerie 103 galleries.

The latter has rotating exhibits. Other outstanding shops here are Palm Palm for women's accessories, Red Koi for artworks and housewares, and Bungalow 9 for modern island home decor and accessories. Ocean Opulent Jewelry has some outstanding and unusual pieces. For clothes try, Tommy Bahamas, Quicksilver or Hawaiian Salt for T-shirts. There is also Living Foods Market & Café that sells local produce, foodstuffs and a large selection of wines and beers.

SOUTH SHORE BEST BETS

Best Strolling Beach—Maha'ulepu
Best Short Cliff Stroll—To the Left of Shipwreck Beach near Hyatt
Best Snorkeling—Around the sandy point at Po'ipu Beach Park
Best Sunset View—At Spouting Horn
Best Hot Dog—Puka Dogs
Best Treat—Baked Chocolate Soufflé at Roy's Po'ipu Bar & Grill
Best Place To Watch Fools Jump Off A Cliff—Shipwreck Beach in Front of the Hyatt Po'ipu
Best Secluded Beach—Ha'ula Beach
Best Swimming—Po'ipu Beach Park
Best Pizza—Brick Oven Pizza
Best Beachcombing—Kawailoa Bay
Best Golf—Po'ipu Bay Resort
Best Hotel Grounds—Grand Hyatt
Best Chance of Seeing a Beached Monk Seal—Po'ipu Beach Park
Best Lasagna—Pomodoro
Best Romantic Restaurant—Tidepools at Grand Hyatt or Beach House at Sunset
Best Place for a Sunset Cocktail—The Sheraton Kaua'i Resort

Ni'ihau Shell Leis

The women of Ni'ihau carry on a tradition dating back centuries. With indescribable patience, they collect tiny Ni'ihau shells, then clean, drill, string and pack them with fiber, creating fabulous leis. This is no easy task. An entire day's labor often reaps only four or five useable shells. And it requires thousands of shells to make a lei. Some women only search for shells at night, believing that the sunlight dulls the shell's luster. While costing from several hundred to several thousand dollars each, this is a relative bargain given the amount of labor that goes into one. It can take several years to complete the more ornate leis. The result is a perfect, handcrafted and tightly packed lei representing one of the last truly Hawaiian art forms. There are fewer and fewer people on Ni'ihau who are willing to participate in this process, and many consider it a matter of time before this art form will be lost.

If you purchase one, the best selection on the island is at the Hawaiian Trading Post on the corner of Highways 50 and 530 (Koloa Road) in Lawa'i. Make sure it was actually made on Ni'ihau, and not a copycat made on Kaua'i.

One last caveat: If you buy one, do it for yourself. It would be crushing to spend all that money only to show your lei to someone and have 'em say, "Oh, yeah, I got one for free at Hilo Hattie's." While Ni'ihau shell leis are infinitely more beautiful, some might not appreciate the difference.

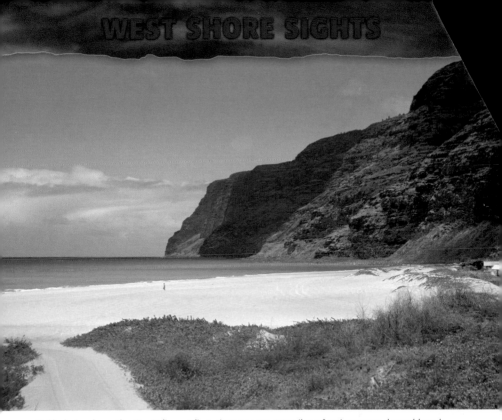

WEST SHORE SIGHTS

Polihale is where the Na Pali coastline gives way to 17 miles of uninterrupted sand beach.

If the south shore is called the sunny south shore, western Kaua'i should be called the *very* sunny west shore. That's because rain is very scant indeed, and the temperature is 3 to 4 degrees hotter than most of the rest of the island. The first two things visitors notice on this side of the island are the relative aridity of the land and the deep red color of the soil. Trade winds coming from the northeast lose the bulk of their rain on Mount Wai'ale'ale, creating a rain shadow on the west side. Unless there are Kona winds (meaning from the south or west), you can pretty much be assured that it will be dry and sunny on the west side.

This part of the island is dominated by two attractions: the 17-mile long sand beach stretching from Waimea to Polihale and the incredible Waimea Canyon in the interior.

HANAPEPE

As you drive along the main highway leaving Kalaheo, you will come to the **Hanapepe Valley Lookout**, described in SOUTH SHORE SIGHTS chapter. After you go through 'Ele'ele (where many of the boat tours leave from), you come to Hanapepe. Called Kaua'i's "Biggest Little Town," Hanapepe is but a shadow of its former self. It was founded by Chinese rice farmers in the mid to late 1800s. They were opium-smoking

hore &
Canyon

Kalalau Beach

Honopu Beach & Arch

Kalalau Valley

Nu'alolo Kai

Miloli'i

Kalalau Lookout

Awa-'awapuhi Trail

Detailed map of Koke'e on page 140–141

18

Pu'u o Kila Lookout (better)

Koke'e Lodge & Museum

Makaha Ridge Tracking Station

Miloli'i Ridge Rd

Nu'alolo Trail

Don't go past here in the rain.

17

16

Koke'e Rd

2000 ft. Descent–Watch Your Brakes

22°07.589
159°41.343

15

Koke'e Ditch

Pine Forest Drive & Picnic Area

Makaha Ridge Rd

14

Pu'u Hinahina Viewpoint

Ka-uhao Ridge Rd

Ka'aweiki Ridge Rd

Waipo'o Falls

Po'omau Canyon

Polihale Ridge Rd

13

Pu'u Ka Pele Lookout

Contour Rd

12

Waimea Canyon

Koai'e Canyon

Lonomea Camp

Soft, sandy spot in road

Ha'ele'ele Ridge Rd

550

Kaluahaulu-Wai'alae Trail

Queen's Pond

Ancient Hawaiian jumping off point for spirits

Pu'u Lua Reservoir

Hipalau Camp

Nohili Point

Polihale State Park

11

Waimea Canyon Lookout

Kaluahaulu Camp

Kukui Trail

Monkeypod Tree

Kolo Ridge Rd

10

Wiliwili Camp

Poachers Camp

Barking Sands

Mana Ridge Rd

Picnic Area

9

Military Boundary

Kahelu Ridge Rd

8

32 (Again)

These ridge roads are hunter roads and only open to vehicles on most weekends and holidays. The state's web site implies you can hike at any time. The views from the ends of these ridge roads (especially Polihale and Ka-uhao) are extraordinary.

Hunter Check-in Station

7

Waimea Canyon Trail

33

Mana (gone)

Ka-boom Mountain

32

6

Waimea River

31

5

30

Waimea Canyon Dr

Pu'u Ki Wai'alae

Major's Bay

Pacific Missile Range Facility

29

552

4

Waimea Canyon Plaza

Koke'e Rd

28

Kokole Point

27

Kekaha

1

Menehune Ditch & Waimea Swinging Bridge

Mana Drag Strip

Farmer's Market Sat. 9 a.m.

26

25

550

In Waimea, check your gas gauge before going up to the canyon.

Kekaha Beach Park

24

Waimea

Kikiaola Small Boat Harbor

Waimea Plantation Cottages

23

22

Beach access is usually obvious along this part of the island. Only Pakala Beach needs to be pointed out.

Lucy Wright Beach Park

Russian Fort Elizabeth

Pakala Beach (Infinities)

21

The reef edges are denoted by ···· and come directly from government topographic maps. The task of verifying the precise location of all underwater reefs would be herculean and has not been attempted by us.

20

Gay & Robinson Sugar Mill (now closed)

19

Hanapepe/ 'Ele'ele

18

50

17

South Shore map on page 74

0   5 Miles

0   5 Kilometers

Salt Pond Beach Park

Port Allen Airport (Burns Field)

Glass Beach

© 2012 Wizard Publications, Inc.

bachelors, and underground opium shops could be found there as recently as the 1930s. Hanapepe was the only non-plantation town on the island, and it gained a reputation as Kaua'i's wildest spot. In 1924 they had a riot that killed 16 Filipino workers and four police officers. This was a violent and flamboyant town that had as many bars as churches. It began to decline in the late '70s. The 1982 opening of Kukui Grove Shopping Center in Lihu'e marked the end of an era for Hanapepe's business community.

A good analogy for Hanapepe today is that of an old chair. While some people look at an old stick of furniture and see a priceless antique, others see it as an old, used item to be replaced by a newer one. Depending on your outlook, you will either find downtown Hanapepe charming or a quasi-ghost town. Although we probably agree with the ghost town description, improvements *are* taking place and a certain amount of rehabilitation is occurring, so Hanapepe is sort of a moving target. If you have a couple minutes to spare, you might want to blow through downtown just to decide for yourself. There are several shops and galleries that might be worth exploring. Friday night is *art night,* and it's really starting to become a draw. Check out some of the galleries we mention on page 93. There's a **swinging footbridge** over the Hanapepe River. It replaced the old bridge that swung off during the 1992 hurricane.

This area is where most of our power is generated. People assume that, living on a tropical island, we must have some exotic way of making

our electricity. Sorry to burst your bubble, but we burn oil—it's just that simple—and we have the electricity bills to prove it! In a few years we hope to burn wood chips from local tree farms to help supplement that.

If you take Lele Road (Hwy 543), you come to **Salt Pond Beach Park**. This is where they continue to make salt out of seawater (see BEACHES chapter). This park usually offers very safe swimming as well as **restrooms**. (Hard to find in this area.)

Before you get to Waimea, you will see a road to **Fort Elizabeth** just past the 22 mile marker. (The sign is misspelled.) Here are the vague remains of a Russian fort built in 1816 by George Scheffer.

Scheffer was a German-born doctor working for a Russian company. A difficult, quarrelsome and conceited man, he had a habit of eventually alienating most people he met. (Know the type?) He did make a good *first* impression, however, and managed to sufficiently impress a Russian official, who sent Scheffer to

© 2012 Wizard Publications, Inc.

Hawai'i to ingratiate himself with King Kamehameha and recover a lost ship's cargo. When Kamehameha eventually became suspicious of Scheffer, the German moved on to Kaua'i. There he found a receptive King Kaumuali'i who, although he had officially given his kingdom to Kamehameha, still resisted offshore rule. Kaua'i's king-in-name-only saw a chance to get the Russians involved and perhaps restore his power. The two men realized how much they could help each other and soon hatched plans to conquer the other islands using Russian ships. By this time Scheffer had become intoxicated by his status on Kaua'i and lost sight of the fact that he could not deliver on any of the promises he was making to Kaua'i's king. He even renamed Hanalei Valley, calling it Schefferthal, with the king's blessing.

As Scheffer began building the Russian Fort in honor of Elizabeth, a Russian consort, his sponsors back in Russia were beginning to get a hint of Scheffer's tactics. They sent a ship to Hawai'i to tell Scheffer that he was to pack and leave the island. Scheffer ignored the message and continued building the fort. By this time Kaua'i's king was becoming suspicious,

and a group of American businessmen saw an opportunity to rid the island of Scheffer and Russia. They started the rumor that Russia and America were at war. Kaua'i's king abandoned Scheffer, who fled the island in a leaky old ship and set sail for O'ahu. Once there, Scheffer was told he would be taken prisoner. He fled to Brazil where he changed his name to Count von Frankenthal and tried to lure colonists to his estate of the same name.

Why are we telling you all this? Because the story's more interesting than the actual site—little more than a perimeter of rocks from the foundation. (By the way, there are lots of bees here.)

If you drive through Fort Elizabeth and take the dirt road, you'll come to the **mouth of the Waimea River**. This can be a beautiful area to linger and watch the interaction of the ocean with the river, especially when the river flow is low. The dark, rich sand separating the ocean from the river is saturated with water from the river. White waves sometimes gently lap up and down the sand without sinking in, creating a delicate show of contrasts. You'll notice an olive green tint to the sand here. This is from

The dark sand at the mouth of the Waimea River beautifully contrasts the ocean foam slithering into the river.

a semi-precious gem called olivine, which the Waimea River tirelessly mines from its lava bed along with black flecks of lava, making the floor of the Waimea Canyon lower and lower in the process.

WAIMEA

Back on the main highway you come to the town of Waimea. This part of the island usually looks best (and greenest) in the winter. Off to your right you will see the **Captain Cook Monument**. It was in Waimea that the great explorer first set foot in Hawai'i in January 1778. (He was later killed on the Big Island in a petty dispute over a stolen rowboat.)

Travel 1⅓ mile up Menehune Road on the *mauka* side of the highway to see the **Menehune Ditch**, a smooth, lined irrigation ditch designed to bring water from the Waimea River to the taro fields. Only the top of a tiny section is now visible. It's mostly buried and not visually striking. But it's impressive to think that the rocks used for its construction came from a quarry more than 6 miles away. This is one of the few Hawaiian relics that almost certainly wasn't created by the current race of Hawaiians who came from Tahiti around 1,000 AD. *That* group didn't cut and dress stones—as is the case at Menehune Ditch—they simply stacked them. This irrigation ditch is much older and was probably built by the initial inhabitants—the original "native Hawaiians"—who came from the Marquesas Islands around 300 AD. These first settlers lived a peaceful though less structured life until the Tahitian invaders displaced them and their culture 700 years later, establishing the Hawaiian culture we know today.

Across from the ditch is the **Waimea Swinging Bridge**. Like the one in Hanapepe, it, too, is a replacement for the old one blown away in 1992.

The **Waimea** (meaning red water) **River** is full of sediment that dyes the water red. All the beaches in the vicinity of the river are murky due to river runoff, and the swimming is correspondingly poor. (In fact, you can see the runoff from the Space Shuttle photo on the cover.) According to legend, there was a beautiful chief's daughter named Komali'u who was sought after by many men in the village. One day a man named Mano asked her to marry him. When she refused, he killed her at a waterfall where her blood ran into the river. The chief named the village, canyon and river Waimea in memory of his daughter.

While in Waimea, **Jo-Jo's Clubhouse** (across from the 23 mile marker and not to be confused with Jo-Jo's Anuenue) serves some of the best shave ice on the island. (Yes—we've tried it everywhere else. It's our duty.) They offer a staggering 60 flavors and big portions at a cheap price. Only problem is the sometimes *slooooow* service.

KEKAHA

From Waimea, most people go up the road to the Waimea Canyon, but we will get to that later. Assuming you are continuing along the coast, you arrive in Kekaha. This is the last town on this side of the island. Past the 25 mile marker the highway hugs the beach for 2 miles. It's a nice place to stop and enjoy views of Ni'ihau past the 26 mile marker, and beach access here is accomplished by simply falling out of your car onto the sand.

Waimea Canyon Plaza is the last area with food along here. The **Menehune Food Mart** has sandwiches and hot dogs. Things aren't as hideously expensive there as you'd expect given the remoteness of the location.

While driving along the west side past Waimea, take note of the cliffs to your right. Those are former sea cliffs cut off from the sea. The land you are driving on is different than most other land in the island chain. It's not technically volcanic. When the massive Waimea Canyon (described later) was formed, the river carried the rock and soil out of the canyon where the ocean's current drove it along the shore to the northwest (as it still does today). Much of it washed up on shore, forming the large plain you see today. It's an odd cocktail of fine sediment, the remains of a gigantic, now drained, fringing marshy lagoon, sand, the shells of countless sea creatures and plant remains. The result is one kickin' place to grow sugar—just ask the Robinsons, who grew thousands of acres of it here until 2009. In that year they shut down the island's last sugar mill, though some of the remaining sugar cane under cultivation is used by the **Koloa Rum Company** to make Kaua'i rum. The Robinsons, along with the state of Hawai'i, now lease 12,000 acres to several mainland seed companies that take advantage of the perfect year-round growing conditions to grow mostly GMO (genetically modified) seed corn and soybeans in the various former sugar cane fields.

Many maps list a town farther north called **Mana**. It was once a thriving little community until the mid-1900s. This area was formerly marshy and famous for its mirages. Now the town of **Mana** is a mirage, nothing more than two mango trees and a mule. Some of its homes were moved and are now part of Waimea Plantation Cottages Resort. You can tell a former Mana cottage because it always had a door facing north and one facing south so passing spirits wouldn't get stuck inside.

From here on the coastline is pure sand. There's a great opportunity to have a huge stretch of sand to yourself along here. See Kokole Point on page 118.

You will pass the **Pacific Missile Range Facility**. About every two months they do a Star Wars missile test. (When they fire missiles, rather than move the rockets, they literally move the building out of the way.) Offshore, submarine hunting exercises take place almost continuously. This is a repository for some of the most sophisticated sensing equipment in the world, and they are capable of detecting a bottle bobbing up and down in the choppy water. (But for some reason, when a fishing boat is missing in the area, they seem incapable of finding it.) Fronting part of the base is **Barking Sands Beach**. The sand grains at this beach have a thin coating of silica and are supposed to make a barking sound if you walk on them when conditions are right (see BEACHES). Access is a problem, though. See BEACHES chapter for more.

A well-known surf site here is **Major's Bay**, so called because it's off the old commanding officer's quarters. *Hey, wait a minute. This is a navy base. Isn't major an army rank?* True, but it *used* to be an army base, and the name stuck.

POLIHALE

Looking at the map, you'll notice that the highway ends after the first 32 mile marker. Follow the map, and the first dirt road will take you to **Polihale**. (It's a public access, misleading signs notwithstanding.) On the very rare occasions that it rains heavily here, the road to Polihale can get pretty sloppy. (It also gets potholed at times, and officials at State Parks like to close it once in a while as they wait to re-scrape it.) From the extreme northern end of the beach, the magnificent cliffs of **Na Pali** beckon you with their sheer majesty. The **dunes of Polihale** are up to 100 feet high. The BEACHES chapter provides more information on **Polihale**.

As soon as you leave Hwy 50 on your way to Polihale, look at the mountain in

A lone boat cruises Polihale on a trip up Na Pali.

front of you. It's a **military restricted area**. They've bored caves into the mountain where they store ammunition, such as bombs and bullets. With so much explosives, you're about as welcome there as a pack of matches.

If it's summer, you might see kayaks coming (or rolling) in for a surf landing. From here you could walk to the left for 17 miles in the sand. (Maybe another day, huh?) Winds are usually calm here. There are facilities, including showers, restrooms and drinking water.

The Hawaiians believed that the cliffs at the end of Polihale Beach, called **Ha'ele'ele**, were the jumping off point for spirits or 'uhane leaving this world. There they would leave this life and join their ancestors forever. If there was no 'aumakua, or family of spirits, to receive them, they would wander around the area, attaching themselves to rocks and generally causing mischief. That's why it's considered unwise to take anything, such as stones, from this area. You may bring back a wayward spirit itching to get back home.

WAIMEA CANYON

The **Waimea Canyon** is a spectacular gorge that defies description. Island legend states that when Mark Twain was

here, he dubbed it "the Grand Canyon of the Pacific." (Unfortunately, when you read his biography, you find that when he visited Hawai'i, he never set foot on Kaua'i. Oops, there goes another urban legend.) Regardless, the layers evident on the sides of the canyon are reminiscent of the grander canyon in Arizona. Each layer represents a different eruption and subsequent lava flow. The canyon is 10 miles long, 1 mile wide and more than 3,600 feet deep.

To get to the canyon, take Waimea Canyon Drive from Waimea. They *want* you to go up from Koke'e Road in Kekaha because they hope you'll buy something there, but the views are better going up from Waimea. On your return from the canyon, you can take Koke'e Road (between the 6 and 7 mile markers) down for a different view of the coast.

Before you go up the road, check your gas gauge. There are no stations up there (but restrooms at the major lookouts), and you've got a 40-mile round trip ahead of you with a 4,000-foot elevation rise. The temperature is 10–15 degrees cooler up there, and a sweater or light jacket might be wise, depending on conditions. There are more good hiking trails in this area than anywhere in Hawai'i. For more hik-

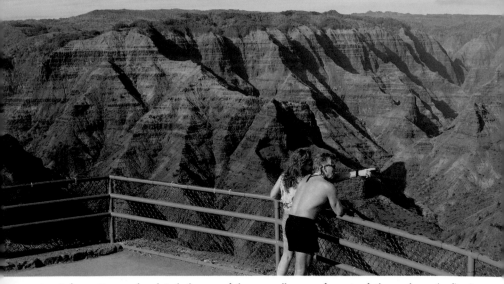

Splendid Waimea Canyon provides yet another facet of Kaua'i's personality.

ing information and a detailed map of the trails in the Waimea/Koke'e area, see HIKING on page 139.

To reach the canyon, turn *mauka* onto Waimea Canyon Drive just past the 23 mile marker near a church. The road twists and turns its way up the canyon's side. On the way, keep an eye out for **Ni'ihau**. There are some great views of that private island from up here. (Even on cloudless days there's almost always a cloud over Ni'ihau. Its land mass causes them.) Past the 10 mile marker is the **Waimea Canyon Lookout**. This is one of several vantage points and definitely worth a stop. From here on, you will probably see lots of wild chickens about. They thrive in this environment.

The canyon lookout is an awesome vista. At one time three rivers, fed from the island's center by the Alaka'i Swamp on Mt. Wai'ale'ale, all ran down the gently sloping shield volcano, emptying into the ocean at separate points like the spokes of a wheel. That's what created the now-dry valleys you see on your way out to Polihale. When a fault caused the

collapse of part of the volcano's flank, the three rivers were forced to combine as they ran down into the fault. This new, opportunistic river carved a place for itself in the splintered and fractured lava flows. The results are extraordinary.

As you drive upward, there are numerous areas along the road from which to view the canyon. From the **Pu'u Ka Pele Lookout**, the **Waipo'o Falls** are visible after a heavy rain, especially in the winter. The hike there (see HIKING in the ACTIVITIES chapter) is fabulous. The **Pu'u Hinahina Lookout**, located past the 13 mile marker, has a **Ni'ihau Viewpoint** in addition to its canyon lookout. If it's clear, the view of **Ni'ihau** is great.

Shortly after this lookout, there is a paved road on your left leading to the **Makaha Ridge Tracking Station** run by the military in conjunction with the **Pacific Missile Range Facility**. The road drops 2,000 feet over a relatively short distance and can be a real brake burner. Not far before the gate at the station you will see several dirt roads leading into a pleasant forested area with picnic tables.

NOT TO BE MISSED!

Looking at the map, you'll see that there are dirt hunter-roads all along this part of the coast. The views from the edge of the ridges are mind-boggling (it's where we took the photo on page 89), but they are only open certain weekends and are *supposed* to be used by hunters. The only one that's always open and available is Miloli'i Ridge Road. See ADVENTURES on page 198.

Past the 15 mile marker is the **Koke'e Museum** (335–9975). This is a good place to stretch your legs, and the parking lot is usually loaded with wild chickens. The museum itself has several interesting displays, and its three-dimensional map of the canyon really gives you a sense of what you are seeing. We've found the personnel there to be extremely knowledgeable. The **Koke'e Lodge** (335–6061) next door is the *best place in Koke'e* to get lunch. (It wins first place in a contest of one.)

As you ascend the road, note how different the vegetation is up here. Remember how dry it was down at the bottom near Waimea? Here it is always cool, and there is more rainfall than on the plain below.

Just past the lodge (on the opposite side of the road), driving Waineke Road to Mohihi Road makes a wonderful diversion if you happen to have a 4WD vehicle. You can drive 6 miles into the interior of Koke'e, visiting beautiful sights along the way. The map of the area is on page 140.

At the 18 mile marker is the **Kalalau Lookout** where most people stop. We suggest that you drive right past it and go to the *far* superior, but less used, **Pu'u o Kila Lookout**. You are not about to see another canyon lookout. You are **A REAL GEM** about to be treated to one of the greatest views in the Pacific. The **Kalalau Valley** is the largest valley on **Na Pali**. It was inhabited until 1919, and its beach is only reachable by an 11-mile hike or by kayak (see ADVENTURES chapter). For now, just revel in the view. Clouds are always moving in and out of the valley, so if it's cloudy, wait a while before you give up. It's well worth it. The earlier you go, the fewer clouds there tend to be. You can usually see clouds coming from the interior of the island. When they encounter the

The sometimes misty forests of Koke'e demonstrate the contrasts found on the Garden Island.

valley, they sink. Sinking air warms, and warmer air can hold more moisture. So if conditions are right, during normal trade winds, the clouds disappear into humidity in less than a minute right before your eyes. If the winds are coming from the ocean (not the norm), clouds back up in the valley, and it won't clear up.

According to historians, there used to be a *steep* trail into the valley from here leading down across a ridge called *kapea*, a Hawaiian word for scrotum. It was so-named because the trail was so steep that it made your…well, *you* figure it out.

Hawaiian geese, called **nene**, tend to hang out at the lookouts. These are endemic to Hawai'i (found nowhere else) and are what you get when you take wayward Canada geese and isolate them in the tropics for a million years. They've adapted to higher altitudes, lost most of the webbing on their feet and have no fear of cars or people, so be careful driving around at the lookout. They also try to make their living begging food from visitors. Please try to resist.

This is the end of the road. As the crow flies, Ha'ena on the north shore is less than 7 miles away, but you ain't no crow. They tried to build a road from here to Ha'ena in the '50s. Anybody who has ever hiked the **Alaka'i Swamp Trail** before they installed a boardwalk could tell you that a road in these parts is next to impossible. The results of this boondoggle are monuments in the form of heavy earthmoving equipment still stuck in the swamp where the prison work crews left them. A stroll from here down part of the **Pihea Trail** can be a pleasant diversion. This is where the road to Ha'ena was supposed to start.

In 1870, Queen Emma made a famous trek through the **Alaka'i Swamp** to the Kilohana Lookout. (As an aside, Alaka'i means "to lead," because it's impossible to get around in there without a guide.) She had a hundred people accompany her and stopped at awkward times

The Kalalau Valley is best viewed not from the Kalalau Lookout, but from the Pu'u o Kila Lookout.

to insist on hula demonstrations. Her guide vowed never to go into Alaka'i again, and the trip became legendary throughout the islands.

By not having a road completely encircling the island, Kaua'i has been able to escape the fate that has befallen O'ahu. As long as the dots aren't connected, there will always be parts of Kaua'i that are remote.

WEST SHORE SHOPPING

In Waimea, check out **Collectibles & Fine Junque** for Hawaiian collectables from artwork to vinyl record albums, china to jewelry and everything in between. **Hidden Dragon Imports** has jade, specialty teas and other items direct from China. **Aloha N' Paradise** has a nice selection of local artwork for sale. Pick up your fresh deli foods from **Ishihara Market** or **Big Save** across the street. Don't miss **Aunty Lilikoi** (near Big Save) for outstanding passionfruit products made on premises. They'll even share recipes. On the west end of town is **Kaua'i Granola/Sugar Cane Snax**. They are generous with free samples. If you like your coffee and granola in the morning, they have *Espresso Bytes,* which combines both. Try their frozen cheesecake dipped in chocolate on a stick. (Who'd a thought?) Chocolate Macaroons are also very yummy.

Hanapepe has many galleries. Some of our favorites are starting from the east are: **Kaua'i Fine Art** has historical maps and prints. **Rob Bader: Wood Sculpture/ Becky Wold: Art of Marbling** creates gorgeous wood bowls and plates carved almost paper-thin, and fine silk scarves in one-of-a-kind marbleized print designs. **Banana Patch Studio** is where artists can be seen making a multitude of pottery items for sale. They also have other artworks, jewelry and housewares. **Island Art Gallery** has spectacular modern artworks

The nene of Koke'e are accomplished beggars. This one flew off in a huff when we said no.

and jewelry from around the world. **Amy Lauren's** features contemporary Kaua'i artists. Behind them is **Puahina** for original silk-screened Hawaiian warrior T-shirts and clothing items screened with native plant motifs. Across the street is **Talk Story Bookstore** specializing in used and rare books, as well as new works by local authors. Get a custom Hawaiian shirt made at **Jacqueline on Kaua'i**. Slightly farther west of the main part of town, don't miss **Keiki Kovers** for adorable island-made clothes for babies and young kids.

WEST SHORE BEST BETS

Best Sunset View—A Couple Miles up Waimea Canyon Drive

Best Treat—Shave Ice at Jo-Jo's Clubhouse in Waimea

Best Hearty Food—Chili and Cornbread at the Koke'e Lodge

Best Place for Quiet Contemplation— To the Right of the viewing Platform at Pu'u o Kila Lookout

Best Swimming—Salt Pond Beach Park or Queen's Pond at Polihale (if calm)

Best Place to Get Away From It All and Write the Great American Novel— Waimea Plantation Cottages

Best Place to Have Good Brakes— Makaha Ridge Road

Ke'e Beach and its reef lagoon offer some of the best swimming on the north shore. This is how it looks from the Kalalau Trail.

Because Kaua'i is older than the other major Hawaiian islands, it is blessed with having more sand beaches per mile of shoreline than any other. No part of the island is without sandy beaches. Many are accessible by merely driving up and falling into the sand. Others are deliciously secluded, requiring walks of various lengths. Some are local secrets; others are unknown even to most locals. In this section we will describe virtually all of Kaua'i's beaches starting from the north shore and working our way around the island clockwise. All of these beaches are located on the maps of the various areas.

BEACH SAFETY

The beaches of Kaua'i, and Hawai'i in general, are beautiful, warm and, unfortunately, can be dangerous. The waves, currents and popularity of beachgoing have caused Hawai'i to become the drowning capital of the United States. If you're going to swim in the ocean, you need to bear several things in mind. We are not trying to be killjoys here, but there are several reasons why Hawai'i's beaches can be particularly dangerous. The waves are stronger here in the open ocean than in most other places. Rip currents can form, cease and form again with no warning. Large "rogue waves" can come ashore with no warning.

These usually occur when two or more waves fuse at sea, becoming a larger wave. Even calm seas are no guarantee of safety. Many people have been caught unaware by large waves during ostensibly "calm seas." We swam and snorkeled most of the beaches we describe in this book on at least two occasions (usually more than two). But beaches change. The underwater topography changes throughout the year. Storms can take a very safe beach and rearrange the sand, turning it into a dangerous beach. Just because we describe a beach as being in a certain condition does not mean it will be in that same condition when *you* visit it.

Consequently, you should consider the beach descriptions as a snapshot in calm times. If seas aren't calm, you probably shouldn't go in the water. If you observe a rip current, you probably shouldn't go in the water. If you get caught in a strong rip current that pulls you away from the shoreline, *don't* panic and *don't* try to fight your way back in. Swim parallel to shore and try to signal for help. If you're at a remote beach, consider asking a local person about conditions. Most will be helpful. If you aren't a comfortable swimmer, you should probably never go in the water, except at those beaches that have lifeguards and protected pools, such as Lydgate State Park. But during abnormally high seas, even these are potentially hazardous. Kaua'i averages 9 drownings per year—most of these are visitors. We don't want you to become part of that statistic. There is no way we can tell you that a certain beach will be swimmable on a certain day, and we claim no such prescience. There is no substitution for your own observations and judgment. And though it might sound obvious, one of the biggest con-

tributors to drownings is alcohol. Hey, we're not lecturing. Go ahead, *suck em up* if you like. But stay on dry land and off the roads when you do.

Sprinkled among remote island beaches are red rescue tubes. If you see someone in distress and you're a good swimmer with fins, you can grab one and take it out and possibly save a life.

In general, the north shore beaches are calmest during the summer months (meaning April–September). The south shore is calmest during the winter months (meaning October–May). North shore high surf is stronger than south shore high surf since our location in the northern hemisphere makes us closer to northern winter storms than southern hemisphere storms. But ironically, the south shore has had a surge of drownings recently, claiming 27 victims over the past decade.

A few of the standard safety tips apply. Never turn your back on the ocean. Never swim alone. Never swim in the mouth of a river. Never swim in murky water. Never swim when the seas are not calm. Don't walk too close to the shore break; a large wave can come and knock you over and pull you in. Observe ocean conditions carefully. Don't let small children play in the water unsupervised. (In fact, it's best to keep them at the protected ponds such as Lydgate.) Fins give you *far* more power and speed and are a much underappreciated safety device (besides being more fun). If you are comfortable in a mask and snorkel, they provide considerable peace of mind, in addition to opening up the underwater world. Lastly, don't let Kaua'i's idyllic environment cloud your judgment. Recognize the ocean for what it is: a powerful force that needs to be respected.

When frolicking at a beach, especially a rocky one, **water shoes** are invaluable for protecting your feet from cuts. They can turn a marginal beach into a fun beach.

People tend to get fatigued while walking in sand. The trick to making it easier is to walk with a very gentle, relaxed stride while lightly striking the sand almost flat-footed.

Beach conditions are usually best in the first half of the day. And remember that weekends—like weekends everywhere—are more popular with local beachgoers, so it's best to plan your beach activities for weekdays, if possible.

One thing you should be aware of is that in Hawai'i, all beaches are public beaches. This means that you can park yourself on any stretch of sand you like. The trick, sometimes, can be access. To get to a public beach, you might have to cross private land. The county and state have procured easements to many of the beaches. On our various maps, we have marked these public access routes in yellow. This, along with descriptions and directions, will assist you in finding the beach of your choice. But public access is an involved and often murky subject. We did our best to get it right, but there *may* be some that are marked where *somebody* may object. (E.g., "This *used* to be public access, but the county easement wasn't filed properly when the moon was full, and my attorney talked to their attorney, and together they drafted this 85-page document describing the protocols necessary when accessing every fourth Tuesday…") You get the idea. Use your best judgment.

The beaches that are *supposed* to have **lifeguards** are highlighted with this ✚ symbol. They are Ke'e, Ha'ena Beach Park, Hanalei, Kealia, Lydgate, Pine Trees, Po'ipu, Salt Pond, Lucy Wright, and Kekaha.

When we mention that a beach has **facilities**, it usually includes restrooms, showers, picnic tables and drinking water. Facilities are sometimes less than pristine.

A WORD ABOUT SHELLS

Hawai'i's creatures produce only a tiny fraction of the shells you'll find in other parts of the world, so it's illegal to take any from the beach. Once we were snorkeling at Larsen's when a visitor asked us, "How come I don't see any such and such type of shells anymore? We were here five years ago and saw lots of them. I have a whole bag of 'em back home in my garage." We told him, "Maybe we don't have much anymore because they're all in that bag of yours in the garage."

NORTH SHORE BEACHES

✚ Ke'e Beach

A REAL GEM

This is as far as you can go *by car* on the north shore. The beach here is called Ke'e (also called Ha'ena *State* Park), and it's a swimming, snorkeling and sunbathing favorite that can get crowded. The sand volume here varies tremendously. Some summers the sand fills the lagoon, creating a knee-deep sand swimming pool. During these times *on flat calm days* the snorkeling just *outside* the reef is unreal. Tons of fish, clear water and so many turtles you'll lose count as you cruise out the reef opening on the left side and head right. But calm seas are the *only* time you should consider *leaving* the lagoon. During winter months and at other times, large waves may wash over the reef, creating an excess of lagoon water. Since Ke'e has the only reef opening, this water has only one place to go to equalize the volume—out the reef opening on the left side. That's why it's important to observe ocean conditions carefully. Big waves

A beachgoer wonders if it's too late to return his snorkel gear.

mean big currents in the reef openings and big problems for you unless you stay away from the reef opening.

The park is equipped with facilities and is often crowded—too crowded—and parking is often an issue. If the showers are full, the stream you crossed 3/10 mile back makes an ideal place to rinse off the saltwater, but be careful—the rocks can be slippery.

The highway's end is also where the Kalalau Trail begins. It leads to **Hanakapi'ai Beach** and **Kalalau Beach**, which are described in the ADVENTURES chapter.

⊕ Ha'ena Beach Park

This very pretty beach has complete facilities and lifeguard. It is located across from the **Dry Cave**. Plenty of parking near the beach. Sand is very coarse (and therefore, comes off very easily). Although you might see people swimming here, the shore is totally exposed, lacking any reef protection. The smallest of waves has a surprising amount of force. A popular surf spot off to the left of the beach is called **Cannons**. Since the beach is very steep, a small wave could knock you over and

the backwash could pull you in; therefore, swimming is hazardous except during very calm seas. Camping with county permit.

❖ Tunnels Beach / Makua Beach

A REAL GEM

One of Kaua'i's snorkeling nirvanas. This superb beach has a wide-fringing reef that is so large it can be seen from space. (Don't believe me? Locate it on the map, then look at the cover of this book. The reef is very prominent in this shot taken from the space shuttle.) There is often a lateral rip current, but it's *normally* quite weak, making Tunnels a good snorkeling spot most of the time. The beach is quite popular, and you will often see SCUBA divers here, as well as surfers and windsurfers. All this makes it sound crowded, but a lack of street parking keeps the numbers relatively low. The kaleidoscope of underwater life is usually profuse and definitely worth your time to explore. See section on SNORKELING on page 178 for some useful tips. See also the SCUBA section; both are in the chapter called ACTIVITIES. Public access is by either of two short dirt roads past the 8 mile marker on Hwy 560. The first (and best if you're snorkeling) one is 4/10 mile past the 8 mile marker. It is actually privately owned (by the seven surrounding landowners) and they don't want you parking on it. Fortunately, one of the nearby landowners wrote to us pointing out that the deed to the road says, "There is an easement in favor of the county of Kauai." Perhaps this is why the county has listed it as a public access. The second one is almost 6/10 mile past the 8 mile marker and, although it has shorter access to the sand, you may have to scramble down some tree roots, which might be difficult for some. Get there early to assure a parking spot. If they're full, park at Ha'ena Beach Park and walk to the right. You could also take Alealea Street before the 8 mile marker, park near the sand, and walk to the left along the beach. (It's a half-mile walk in sand that way, but it's pretty.) You should know that if you park on the highway itself, they *do* give tickets.

❖ Kepuhi Beach

The snorkeling is good here but not nearly as good as Tunnels. You'll rarely find many people on this beach, so if you're in the area and want easy access but no crowds, this is the beach for you. This long strip of sand is fronted by an even longer coral reef. The makeup of this reef causes a slightly stronger current. Check out conditions before you snorkel. Because most of it is not located directly off the main highway, it tends to be forgotten, even by locals. It is, however, still used on occasion by throw-net fishermen. Access is at the eastern end of Alamoo Road. See map on page 48.

❖ Wainiha Beach Park

Hazardous surf and its location at the mouth of the Wainiha River make it murky and unsuitable for anything other than shoreline fishing and beachcombing.

❖ Lumaha'i Beach

This is the long, wide, golden, glorious beach you see just after you've passed Hanalei Bay. Pictured on countless postcards and posters, this beach was made famous as a location for the movie *South Pacific*. This is where Mitzi Gaynor spent considerable time washing that man right out of her hair. If you're looking for a huge, picture-perfect stretch of sand on the north shore, Lumaha'i shouldn't be missed. If you're looking for safe swimming, Lumaha'i shouldn't be touched. This beach and Hanakapi'ai on the Na Pali Coast are the two most dangerous beaches on Kaua'i. Exposed to open ocean, the waves here, even small ones, are frighteningly powerful. We've come to this beach after seeing it absolutely flat at Ha'ena Beach Park, a few miles away, only to be utterly assaulted by Lumaha'i's waves. Put simply, most of Lumaha'i is almost never safe to swim. The waves, currents and backwash are not to be underestimated. Lumaha'i Stream on the left side is sometimes crossable during calm seas and low stream flow. It serves as an estuary for 'o'opu during the summer when the shifting sands tend to cut off the river from the ocean. During this time, the closed river mouth is sometimes safe to swim. But absent these conditions, swimming in Lumaha'i Stream has caused numerous individuals to be swept out to sea. Surfers and boogie boarders often use the left side of the beach near the rocks, but unless you're an expert on Hawaiian surf, this should not be attempted.

Separated by lava rock to the right (east) of Lumaha'i is **Kahalahala Beach** (technically part of Lumaha'i, but who's quibbling?). Swimming here is a different

The Hawaiian Monk Seal

The endangered Hawaiian monk seal occasionally comes ashore after a heavy meal or to avoid a predator. Many people assume the seals are sick or injured and attempt to coax them back into the water. If you are lucky enough to encounter one, please leave it alone. Beaching is perfectly normal. The fines for disturbing one can range as high as $25,000. The seals dive as deep as 400 feet to feed and are considered the most primitive seals in the world with ancient social behavior. Unlike other seals, they don't come ashore in large numbers.

A monk seal snoozes at a Kapa'a beach, oblivious to the kite surfers just offshore. Then again, this photographer watched the same kite surfers for over 5 minutes, oblivious to the monk seal 10 feet away.

If you can negotiate the steps and path on the right side coming down to the sand, Hideaways delivers the right ingredients that make a great beach. And in the summer it's twice as long as this.

story. You access it from a marvelous 3–4 minute walk down through lush jungle to the beach 100 feet below. During calm summer days the water here can be like a crystal-clear swimming pool. There's a tide-pool for keiki to splash about, a fair amount of shade and a tall rock that some people love jumping off. (Our general rule is, never jump off anything you haven't checked out first.) When seas are calm here, this area is utter paradise. Big surf, however, which is not uncommon in the winter, makes this part of the beach nearly as dangerous as the rest of Lumaha'i.

Access to these beaches can be obtained either via a trail from the top of the lookout at the eastern edge of the beach *before* the 5 mile marker on Hwy 560 (this gets you to the eastern part, which is the best part), or from the parking area just before you get to the Lumaha'i River. See map on page 48.

❖ Hanalei Bay

The four beaches described below are all part of Hanalei Bay. With its single long crescent of sand, the bay is beautiful to look at but not great to swim in. Pounding shore break, backwash and rip currents, especially during the winter months, make Hanalei Bay less than ideal as a swimming beach. But that doesn't make it any less pretty. Large surfing waves make Hanalei Bay very popular with surfers, who come from other islands to experience the extremely long-lasting waves.

❖ Waikoko Beach

Easy access and good reef protection at this one portion of Hanalei Bay make this a popular beach during moderate surf periods, but the water is shallow, which makes for marginal swimming conditions. The snorkeling is better than the swimming if stream flow isn't high. Located between the 4 and 5 mile markers as the road begins to ascend. Access is near the 15 MPH sign. See map on page 49.

⊕ Wai'oli Beach Park

Located at the end of either He'e or 'Ama'ama Roads in Hanalei and often referred to as **Pine Trees** (though there are no pine trees there—only ironwood trees). The underwater topography focuses more of the ocean's force here, making the swimming hazardous except during very calm seas. Access is from Weke Road in Hanalei. A reader pointed out (and we verified) that this beach has particularly good sand for building **sand castles**. The stuff sticks together like cement.

⊕ Hanalei Pavilion Beach Park

Also located on Weke Road in Hanalei, it includes facilities and a lifeguard. Popular with boogie boarders and surfers, the shore break and backwash make for less-than-ideal swimming conditions most of the time.

❖ Black Pot

Located near the mouth of the Hanalei River, swimming conditions are marginal. During calm summer surf, boogie boarding is possible near the pier area. Black Pot refers to a large black cooking pot residents used to keep at the beach. This is the area where kayakers put in to paddle up the Hanalei River. The picturesque pier here makes a good sunset photo. Facilities available at beach. Camping with county permit.

❖ Pu'u Poa Beach

Located next to the St. Regis in Princeville, the beach has a fringing reef and offers good snorkeling possibilities during calm seas. During the winter, the waters off the outer edge of the reef offer some of the best and most challenging surfing in the state (for experts only). Access is through a cement path starting just to the left of the gate house at the St. Regis. Getting to the beach necessitates negotiating 191 steps. (Yes, we counted...it was a slow day.) From here you can walk all the way to the mouth of the Hanalei River. The other access is to come from Black Pot Beach and wade across the usually shallow water at the mouth of the Hanalei River.

❖ Pali Ke Kua (Hideaways)

A REAL GEM

Fifty feet before the St. Regis in Princeville gate house is a corridor off to the right (next to the Pu'u Poa tennis courts). This path leads *down* (120 feet below) to Pali Ke Kua Beach, also called Hideaways. Parking is pretty limited. The first half of the descent consists of stairs and a railing. The remainder is trail. All told, it takes 5–10 minutes to get there. There are actually two beaches here, with the second one off to the right separated by a rocky point. Both offer excellent snorkeling during calm seas. The salient underwater features are good relief and a diverse fish community punctuated by the occasional turtle. With marvelous coarse sand, large false kamani trees for shade and good snorkeling when calm, this beach is a wonderful place to spend the day. You won't usually find too many people here since it's still poorly marked, and parking near the trailhead corridor is limited.

While the beach can be a nice place to bring the kids, some may have trouble negotiating their way down the path. (In fact, *you* might have trouble, too, if it has been raining and the path below the steps is muddy. Ropes might be there to help, if that's the case.) When seas aren't calm, rip currents can form. Check ocean conditions carefully. Unusually high surf has been known to generate waves that can sweep across the entire beach. The *other* part of Pali Ke Kua beach can be reached by swimming to the right from Hideaways or by walking a paved trail leading down from

The 2-mile long fringing reef at 'Anini usually gives this beach the calmest water on the north shore.

the Pali Ke Kua condominiums. That *other* path is a private trail available only to guests at Pali Ke Kua.

❖ Queen's Bath

A REAL GEM

Queen's Bath is actually a large pool the size of several swimming pools carved by nature into a lava shelf with an inlet from the ocean for fresh seawater to flow. (Shown on page 24.) If the surf is too high, you would never recognize this place as anything special. But *during calm seas*, Queen's Bath is a marvelous pool to swim in. Fish get in through the inlet, making it all the more charming. (Bring your mask; no fins needed.) It's a great place to take your underwater camera. During mid-summer, if the ocean is *too* calm, the water is not refreshed as much as it should be. During high surf, it's dangerous as the water flows in and out of the pond. Queen's Bath has claimed numerous lives because people got nailed by large waves during times that they should not have gone. During winter

months (generally October–April), high surf assaults the area, and you should always stay away. Even when the ocean appears calm, it's always possible for a rogue wave to snap at this part of the shoreline, knocking people around, maybe even dragging them back into the open ocean. Some people think we shouldn't even mention this attraction. But this is the information age—you're *gonna* hear about it—and we'd rather you know about the safety issues than leave you with no information at all. And it *is* a GEM—just one to experience during calm seas only. To get there, follow the trail off Kapiolani Road near Punahele Road in Princeville. See map on page 49. The trail (slippery when wet) passes a marvelous seasonal waterfall on your right after a few minutes. (Good for rinsing off the salt when you're done.) After dropping 120 feet, the trail encounters the ocean at the lava shoreline where a small waterfall drops directly into the ocean. Go to the *left* along the lava for 260 yards. (It'll seem like more.) Queen's Bath is recessed in the rock and is part of a horseshoe-shaped lava cut. Use the photo on page 44 or the inside cover to identify it. If you can't find it, the ocean probably isn't cooperating.

❖ SeaLodge Beach

A REAL GEM

This wonderful pocket of sand is set in an indentation in the cliff. With plenty of shade courtesy of false kamani trees and heavenly coarse sand (the kind that won't stick to you with the tenacity of a barnacle), SeaLodge Beach is a real find. This beach is sometimes empty of people because most don't know it's there. During the summer in particular, it's an ideal secluded beach. Access is from a trail at *Building A* at the SeaLodge Resort, which is at the end of Kamehameha Road in Princeville. See map on page 49. Where the trail encounters the ocean, it veers to the left. Look for turtles in the water here. The snorkeling can be outstanding during very calm seas, but entry and currents need to be respected. Depending on the weather, the trail can be slippery and a bit tricky in areas. During periods of unusually high surf, waves have been known to travel all the way to the base of the cliff. Don't come here if this is the case. The entire picturesque hike should take between 10 and 15 minutes and is well worth it. (If you had taken a right at the ocean instead, a short hike along the coastline would bring you to small, pretty waterfall.)

❖ 'Anini Beach Park

A REAL GEM

Protected by a *long* fringing reef, 'Anini Beach has become a popular place for the rich and famous to build homes. The water can be very shallow, and the snorkeling *can* be good in many areas when visibility cooperates though it seems to have been overfished. The swimming is among the safest you'll find on the north shore. The channel at the western end of the beach is where the water flows out, so stay away from this part. (See the left side of

Local children often play in the shallow stream at Kalihiwai Bay.

the map on page 46.) There are numerous areas along this stretch of sand to swim, snorkel or just frolic. There is a polo field across from the beach; check it out if you're there during summer. 'Anini Beach is a good place to learn windsurfing. Camping with county permit, facilities at the pavilion. The name used to be *Wanini Beach,* but the "W" was blasted away with a shotgun by an irate resident who felt it had been misspelled. Other residents assumed the gun-toting spell-checker must have corrected a mistake and the "new" name stuck. (*That's* typical Hawai'i.) Take the northern Kalihiwai Road (between the 25 and 26 mile markers) and stay to the left on 'Anini Road.

The far (west) end of the beach, on the other side of the channel, is known as **Wyllie Beach**. Residents of Princeville access it by taking a ¼ mile-long trail from the end of Wyllie Road, which drops 20 stories. The easier way is to park near the channel on 'Anini Road and wade across the stream. Wyllie Beach is a thin ribbon of sand with lots of shade from false kamani trees (whose fallen leaves turn yellow, red, orange and brown). It makes a very nice stroll as the ocean gently laps at your feet (though the sand can disappear during high tide and surf). There is a touch more sand in nearshore waters (though still plenty of rocks) than at other parts of 'Anini. Be aware that when the surf is breaking over the reef offshore, a rip current can form leading to the channel.

❖ **Kalihiwai Beach**

Located at the mouth of Kalihiwai Stream, you drive down from either Kalihiwai Road. (It used to be a loop, but the bridge was knocked out by a tsunami in 1957, and they haven't rebuilt it.) At the bottom of the road, you encounter a picturesque bay with a wide sand beach lined with ironwood trees to park under. There are houses on the other side of the road. The beach is popular with boogie boarders in the summer and is a good place to see local keiki learning to ride waves. It's also a good place to just enjoy the water during the summer. During the winter, surfers ride the large waves under the cliff area. The eastern (first) Kalihiwai Road is the best road to take to the beach. The only ding is that local dogs occasionally roam free, leaving—well, *you* know what they leave behind.

❖ **Secret Beach**

A REAL GEM

Also known as Kauapea Beach and known to most locals by the more enticing name of Secret Beach, this is a stunningly beautiful beach only accessible via a 10–15 minute hike. This fact, along with its former anonymity, caused it to become Kaua'i's premier nude beach. For the record, public nudity is illegal in Hawai'i, and police issue tickets there, so it's not as prevalent as it once was. This long, golden sand beach is not swimmable during the winter, but on calm summer days it can be a delight for swimming and offers good snorkeling. It's worth the trip year-round just to see its exceptional scenic beauty. There is usually a small waterfall to rinse off your gear and a few places where water squirts from the side of the cliff. The island off to your right is Moku'ae'ae Island, a bird sanctuary. To get to Secret Beach, turn right off the first (eastern) Kalihiwai Road, then right on the first dirt road you encounter. (See map on page 46.) Take the trail to the bottom. (It's real slippery when it's raining.) Make a mental note of where it encounters the beach for your return. If you go to the *left* at the bottom of the trail, the shore-

Larsen's Beach has an excellent reef, but stay away from the channel near the top left of the photo.

line leads to the **Secret Lava Pools** described on page 155.

❖ Kahili Quarry Beach

Where Kilauea Stream encounters the ocean is a beach sometimes called Rock Quarry Beach. There is good swimming on the left (western) side and good snorkeling on the right side during calm seas. Since this is a river mouth, the water can get murky at times. (Sharks, which like murky water, have been sighted here during periods of heavy stream flow.) This is a popular boogie boarding and surfing site. The river mouth can cause rip currents. Easiest access is from a dirt road off N. Wailapa Road. See map on page 46. A good hike near here is described under HIKING on page 150.

❖ Waiakalua Beach

A marvelous and undiscovered north shore beach. Although from your car it requires a steep, 5–10 minute walk to the beach 160 feet below, Waiakalua is an undisturbed, serene place to spend the afternoon. Medium coarse sand, a long, fringing reef, numerous pockets of shade and a freshwater spring at the far end add to the charm. Observe the reef from up on the bluff. Calm summer snorkeling can be interesting but shallow; watch out for rip currents. During other times, swimming can be hazardous. At the far end of the beach is a rocky point separating the two halves of the beach. The snorkeling around this point is exciting, featuring clear water teeming with big life. However, the rips, surges and surf make this area tricky—only advanced snorkelers need apply. Otherwise, just enjoy the beach. The cool spring at the far end offers sweet, fresh water. Bring an empty container and some way to filter the water treatment—all fresh water obtained anywhere in nature should be treated to prevent bacterial disease. (It barely trickles during dry months.) To get to Waiakalua, turn onto North Waiakalua Road and take the dirt road on the left side just before the end of the road. Park when you can't drive any more, and take the trail off to the left. The beach on your

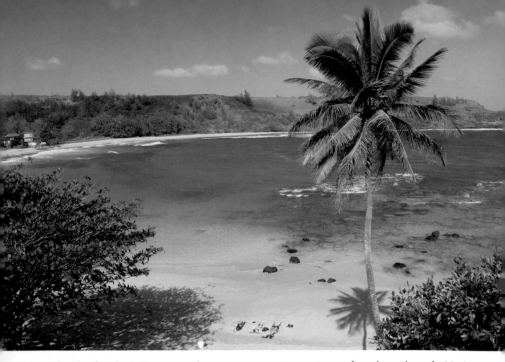

The south side of Moloa'a Bay on a calm, sunny day is paradise found.

left at the bottom is Waiakalua Beach. The path off to your right leads to **Pila'a Beach**. It can take 10–30 minutes to reach **Pila'a Beach**, depending on your boulder-hopping prowess. Otherwise, just stay at Waiakalua Beach. You'll probably have either one all to yourself. See map on page 47.

❖ Larsen's Beach / Lepe'uli Beach

A REAL GEM

This has crystal-clear water, lots of beachcombing and seclusion. The beach is named after a former manager at Kilauea Plantation named L. David Larsen (the rascal who introduced the hated blackberries to Koke'e). This beach is splendidly isolated but can be accessed by walking down a county access trail. Off to the right are a bunch of lava rocks that make for good snorkeling if conditions are right. To the left is a long crescent of sand broken by occasional outcroppings of rock and reef. Underwater topography creates good conditions for beachcombing. Pakala Point is on the left side where the first beach ends and lava rock protrudes out into the ocean. Just before these rocks is **Pakala Channel**. (Shown near the top of the photo and on the inside back cover.) Most of the water you see breaking over the reef drains through this channel; therefore, *don't swim in or near the channel*. The water leading just up to the channel moves so swiftly at times that it seems more like rapids than a rip current. If the ocean is calm and you stay away from the channel, if the tide is right and you have some experience snorkeling, this place can be a snorkeler's paradise. Lots of coral and fish in shallow, crystal-clear water greet the eye. Relatively few beach-goers use this beach during the week. This beach is *not* a swimming beach, just for snorkeling, due to the sharp reefs and shallow water.

One thing that can be *very cool*—if you're careful—is to get in the water at the southeast end (where the trailhead is) and let the current take you toward (but not into!) the Pakala Channel. Then get out and walk back.

The end of summer is when water at reef-fringed beaches like Larsen's has the poorest visibility because it has usually been many months since it has had a good flushing by the high surf.

During periods of high surf, waves *tower* above the reef, breaking on the edge, which can be quite a spectacle.

On the opposite side of Pakala Point are two pockets of sand that are even more secluded and offer good snorkeling and a chance of spotting a monk seal. Larsen's is about 20 minutes north of Kapa'a; take the *north* end of Ko'olau Road (the second Ko'olau if you're coming from Kapa'a) just before the 20 mile marker. 1²/₁₀ miles from the north end of Ko'olau Road, take the left Beach Access road all the way until it ends—it looks like a driveway at the beginning. (See map on page 47.) Follow the steeper trail to the bottom, which is 140 feet below you. (The easier path to the left is private property.) The beach is a 5–10 minute walk down the hill. Note where the trail hits the beach for your return. We've noticed that the beach sometimes attracts nudists.

❖ Moloa'a Beach

A REAL GEM

A wonderful beach on calm days. The right (southeast) side is much nicer than the northwest side. Very pretty beach, but not a great swimming beach when seas aren't calm. It's off the main highway and not as well known as other beaches. Take the first (southeastern) Ko'olau Road (before the 17 mile marker and next to a large fruit stand) to Moloa'a Road. The public access is near the end of Moloa'a Road. Parking is *very* limited. There are a few stalls toward the end of the road; other-

wise, park where there are *no* NO PARKING signs to dissuade you. You might have to walk a ways to the beach, but it's worth it. To get to the southeast side, you'll have to walk 100 yards along the beach. There you'll find the wading, swimming and boogie boarding the best, and shade is plentiful. See map on page 47. Turn at the Moloa'a Fruit Stand.

❖ Papa'a Bay

Very picturesque. The beach access involves a 5-minute trail through the brush down to some rocks below. After that you'll have to boulder-hop about a hundred yards. You need to use the access to North 'Aliomanu Beach (see map on page 47) and look for a beach access when the road turns to the right. In addition, it is one of the few beaches on Kaua'i where you may detect a fishy smell. When the producer of the movie *Six Days/Seven Nights* was here to film the plane crash scene, he apparently liked the location so much, he purchased all *174 acres* around the bay for $7.2 million and built quite a compound, which sold in 2009 for $28 million (down from the asking price of $46.5 million.) Although the land and house around the bay are private, the *beach* is public.

❖ 'Aliomanu Beach

This is really two beaches with different access points. The long, fringing reef offshore of the south beach is used heavily by locals for throw-net fishing, octopus hunting, pole fishing, torch fishing and limu harvesting. This beach, along with Pila'a and Larsen's, attracts families who have been limu (an edible seaweed) harvesting on the outer parts of the reef for generations. They pick the top part of the plant, leaving the roots to regenerate.

The northern (and better) beach is accessed from a parking lot 80 feet above the beach, requiring a 5-minute walk. (See map on page 47.) Although the nearshore waters are rocky, the beach is sandy and very pretty.

⊕ Anahola Beach Park

The area around Anahola is designated Hawaiian Homelands, and most of the beach users are Hawaiian. Visitors aren't common but are certainly welcome. Swimming is safest where it is protected on the right (eastern) side of the bay to just before Kahala Point. Watch for rip currents near the remains of a pier. Also nice is the northern end, which is lightly used and can be accessed from the first Aliomanu Road.

EAST SHORE BEACHES

❖ Donkey Beach / Paliku Beach

So named by drifters in the '60s who observed burros and mules being used by the sugar company to haul seed cane to the fields nearby. Donkey Beach has been

A REAL GEM

a popular nudist beach on Kaua'i due to its location, but the land's current owners are doing much to end this practice. (After purchasing the land from a defunct sugar company and selling house lots for $2 million plus, they're not too thrilled with the idea of naked beachgoers.) This long stretch of sand is also popular with surfers. Interestingly, surfing in ancient times was usually done nude. (I wonder if that's where the term *hang loose* came from...)

Access is ½ mile north of the 11 mile marker, north of Kapa'a. Look for a hiking sign guiding you to the parking lot with facilities. The uncrowded beach is very attractive, with a convenient tree in the middle for shade. The foreshore at the beach is steep, creating a pounding shore break and strong backwash. Swimming is often hazardous. It's about a 10-minute (550 yard) walk on the

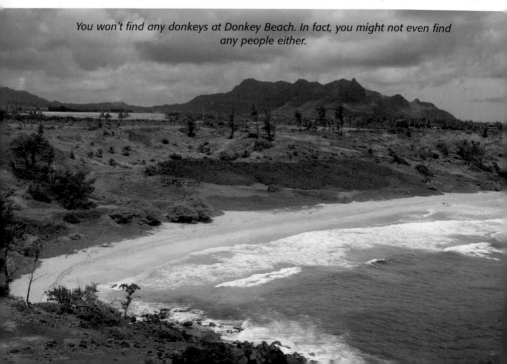

You won't find any donkeys at Donkey Beach. In fact, you might not even find any people either.

paved path to the beach. As you near the shoreline, veer to the right for the beach. To the left (north) past the stream and over the small hill is a secluded cove (cleverly labeled "secluded cove" on our map) where the snorkeling can be very good at times. You will probably have that cove all to yourself. During rainy times, there might be a small waterfall and swimming hole behind the cove.

⊕ Kealia Beach

Drive north of Kapa'a and you will often see lots of boogie boarders and surfers in the water here. (See map on page 59.) The powerful waves are fantastic but can be treacherous. The currents and backwash are sometimes ferocious. The northern end of the beach is more protected by a breakwater and can be good for wading and occasionally snorkeling on a calm day. If you have never ridden waves, be very careful here or you might get drilled into the ground. If the surf is high, definitely leave it for the big boys. Lifeguard and facilities.

❖ Kapa'a Beach Park

Located in the heart of Kapa'a, this is heavily used by locals. Like any beach located close to a population center, Kapa'a Beach Park is not as pristine as other beaches you will find. That said, the northern section (the part just before the lookout as you leave Kapa'a going north) offers interesting but shallow snorkeling. Check for currents. The rest of the park is not as memorable. It is, however, a good place for a beach stroll or to watch the sunrise. There are a few large sand pockets along the beach that are swimmable when the surf isn't high. Regular facilities here plus a swimming pool. The best thing about Kapa'a Beach Park is watching the kite surfers on a windy day.

❖ Waipouli Beach

Pretty, but not a good swimming beach. There are a few small pockets along the southern portion of the beach that are relatively safe for swimming during calm periods, but be cautious. The area seaward of the beachrock fronting the beach is subject to strong currents year-round. This is normally considered a dangerous beach. There is a paved shoreline trail along much of this beach, which is perfect for jogging or a leisurely stroll.

Just north of Waipouli Beach is **Waipouli Beach Park**, also called **Fuji Beach** and sometimes **Baby Beach**. Conditions there are different. This can be a nice place to let keiki splash around in the ocean. Part of it (on Moanakai Street between Pahihi and Makana) is often protected by a long, natural sandstone breakwater. Only when the tide or surf are high does water flow over the sandstone and form a slight current to the left. Otherwise, it's usually flat calm. The sand is coarse, so you'll sink a bit more into it. Check to make sure the ocean isn't making a liar out of us and that it's clean enough. Since it's located in the middle of town, it sometimes gets a little dirty.

❖ Wailua Beach

Across from the closed Coco Palms Resort, from the mouth of the Wailua River to a rocky point to the north, this is an easily accessible beach. Just drive right up. It is popular with surfers and boogie boarders who appreciate the unprotected waves. Winter swells sometimes keep even these users out of the water. Swimmers should be aware of rip currents in several areas along the beach and pounding shore break during high seas. The river itself, which is crossable only during periods of *low flow*, can cause tricky water conditions, so caution is advised. The ocean and the river are constantly battling for supremacy, and the struggle can be dramatic. The ocean builds up a sand bar, and the river attempts to erode it. Sometimes the river is completely stopped up. When it finally breaks through the sand bar, it can be fascinating. The sand bar can erode in a matter of an hour or two, taking large amounts of sand with it. For a short time thereafter, ancient Hawaiian petroglyphs are exposed on rocks in the river mouth.

➊ Lydgate Beach Park

A REAL GEM

Located just south of the Wailua River, Lydgate is composed of a picnic area, a large patch of grass, restrooms, two nice playgrounds, showers, lifeguard and two marvelous, boulder-enclosed ponds. These ponds are nearly always safe to swim, with the smaller one meant for the keiki (kids). These ponds were created to allow fresh seawater and fish into the pond, while protecting you from the ocean's force. And they work quite well. Lydgate is the most popular fish feeding place on the island. Mornings are the best times. Some chips, bread or rabbit food sparingly squeezed through a hole in a plastic baggie will usually win you lots of new underwater friends. If you are having trouble attracting a crowd, keep swimming slowly while staying reasonably close to the rocks. Fish like the rocks since they offer protection from predators. Once a few start eating, continue to swim slowly to attract the maximum crowd. For more tips on feeding the fish, see page 181. Please be careful to take the plastic baggie out with you. There are plenty of turtles in the area that can choke on the plastic. Access is just off Leho Drive in Wailua. (See map on page 59.) Note that if Portuguese man-o-wars happen to be present, they're usually near the rocks at far right end.

❖ Nukoli'i Beach Park

From Lydgate to the far end of the Kaua'i Beach Resort is a long sand beach called Nukoli'i Beach. This beach includes the area fronting the Wailua Golf Course. This entire stretch of sand, more than 2 miles long, is never crowded, often deserted. This is surprising given its proximity to Kapa'a, but good for you. There is a road fronting much of the golf course, until it erodes at the very end. If you just want to easily claim a large spot of beach for yourself, this is as good a place as any. The swimming conditions vary along the beach but are usually marginal. Currents and surf are the usual villains. The area in front of the golf course is the only part worth considering for swimming purposes. The snorkeling can be good when it's calm, and it's fun to hunt for golf balls in the water. You might even find a club hurled by someone having an off day. Access? Just drive right up from the dirt road between the golf course and the resort entrance (not far from the 4 mile marker). Or take the Kaua'i Beach Resort entrance to access the southern portion of the beach. Facilities near the resort. One caveat: Natural currents often bring to this beach flotsam, such as netting and ropes from passing ships.

❖ Hanama'ulu Beach Park

Water is usually murky (and sometimes so are its beachgoers) due to the Hanama'ulu Stream. Sharks are often seen in the area. The waters around Ahukini Pier can offer interesting snorkeling when it's very calm. In general, a mediocre beach with fairly good park facilities—usually used by...long-term campers—such as BBQ grills next to the picnic tables and a pavilion.

❖ Ninini Beach / Running Waters
Located below the golf course near the Marriott, there's good snorkeling off to the left in front of the rocks on a calm day. However, even then it can be surgy and a bit tricky. Access via a walk along a golf course fairway, then a right turn before the beach turning into a steeper dirt trail to the water; see map on page 65.

❖ Kalapaki Beach
With a gently sloping sand bottom and partial protection from the open ocean, Kalapaki is popular with visitors and locals alike. Swimming, bodysurfing, windsurfing (no kite surfing because of the nearby airport), beginner surfing and boogie boarding conditions are usually good except during periods of high surf.

Adjacent Nawiliwili Park behind the Anchor Cove Shopping Center is a popular picnic spot. Canoes and twin-hulled sailing catamarans often come ashore here. Facilities near Anchor Cove Shopping Center. Access is by a road behind the shopping center or through the Marriott. See map on page 65. This is a good place to be when a cruise ship goes by. Because it's at Nawiliwili Bay (where the Hule'ia and Nawiliwili streams empty), the water won't be as clear as other water around the island. When calm (which is most of the time), it's a good place to teach your little one how to ride a boogie board.

❖ Niumalu Beach Park
Good place to launch kayaks for trips up the Hule'ia Stream (where the opening scenes from *Raiders of the Lost Ark* were filmed). Camping by county permit but you wouldn't want to. Other water activities are lousy due to its location so far up the river.

Kawailoa Bay at Maha'ulepu is a great place to spend a beach day.

The water is nice, but entry can be a bit awkward from this spot. Shipwreck Beach can be a good place to sit and watch frustrated fishermen cast off (literally).

SOUTH SHORE BEACHES

❖ Maha'ulepu Beaches

A REAL GEM This marvelous coastline is wild and undeveloped, actually consisting of three separate areas known as **Gillin's Beach, Kawailoa Bay** and **Ha'ula Beach.**

The whole of Maha'ulepu makes for fantastic exploring and beach walking, hence the gem. The swimming can be hazardous, and seas here are often choppy. Winter is best. Ocean entry is difficult in many places. There is an abandoned guard shack on the road to the beaches, and they close off access between sunset and sunrise. Please take everything out that you bring in. The land company can close this access down any time they wish, so locals are bending over backward not to give 'em a reason.

Maha'ulepu is located past the Hyatt on Po'ipu Road after the road becomes dirt. Turn right when the road ends and drive past an old guard shack. See map on page 75.

To get to **Gillin's Beach**, park at the lot where the road otherwise continues to the left. A short trail from the right side of the lot takes you to the beach. (See map.) This beach is named after the late Elbert Gillin whose rebuilt house (now a pricey vacation rental) is on the beach just off to your right. If you walk past it, you'll see a stream that may or may not reach the ocean. Take the trail *before* the stream and look for an off-shoot to the left that has a bridge. (Generously built by the makers of *Pirates of the Caribbean 4*.) Upstream you'll see a small, triangle-shaped opening off to your left. This is an ancient, open-roofed sandstone sinkhole with some cool features. Seven thousand years of protected sediment in one corner of the cave acts as a time machine and hides the bones of extinct birds, now-vanished palm tree species and evidence of a large pre-contact tsunami.

Local paleoecologists have been doing some studies here and sometimes have it gated off. This area is identified as a cave on the map rather than as an amphitheater because we didn't want the casual map reader to think that rock concerts were held there. If the cave is locked, there's a trail to the left that overlooks the amphitheater from above.

To get to **Kawailoa Bay**, continue on the dirt road until it is directly next to the beach. Kitesurfing is popular from here to **Gillin's Beach**. They ride the waves faster than the wind, and it is a real treat to watch.

The trail to **Ha'ula Beach** (see map on page 75) requires a walk along an elevated field of lithified sand. (The trail starts where a fence ends at the cliff's edge.) The constant assault from sea spray has caused the sandstone to erode into short but fantastically sharp and strangely shaped pinnacles. This is a great place to observe the power of the ocean as it smashes into the cliff. Local fishermen drop their lines into the water from here since they can see their prey before they cast. When you reach **Ha'ula Beach** (about a 10–15 minute walk), you will almost certainly have it all to yourself. The beach is backed by high sand dunes. Behind one you will find an old picnic table. The beach is rarely visited except by occasional horseback tours from CJM Stables. The swimming isn't very good; in fact, it can be quite hazardous depending on conditions. But the beach is a beautiful place to enjoy your solitude. Over the ridge to the northeast is **Kipu Kai Beach**. Totally isolated, the only way to get to it is by sea or over that ridge. And the horse trails over the ridge are generously sprinkled with evil, spiked stickers. Bring your Kevlar pants.

The area between **Ha'ula Beach** and **Kawailoa Bay** contains other lithified sand dunes as well. Fishing from the top (labeled Cliff Cracks on the map) is incredible, but be careful—the dunes can be brittle, so don't fall in. The beach area just north of these lithified dunes often provides lots of goodies for the beachcomber. Check out the dry, sometimes gasping blowhole near the shoreline at the eastern edge of Kawailoa Bay.

Maha'ulepu was the scene of a terrific slaughter in the spring of 1796. When King Kamehameha launched the first of two invasion attempts, he and his fleet of 1,200 canoes carrying 10,000 soldiers left O'ahu at midnight, hoping to reach Wailua on Kaua'i by daybreak. They were in the middle of the treacherous Kaua'i Channel when the wind and seas picked up. Many of his canoes were swamped. Reluctantly, Kamehameha ordered a retreat, but too late to stop some of his advance canoes. When they landed at Maha'ulepu, they were exhausted. They awoke to the sound of enemy troops who proceeded to kill all but a few escapees. The last thing these escapees wanted to do was go back to O'ahu and tell their boss what happened. So they bolted all the way to the Big Island and kept their mouths shut.

❖ Shipwreck Beach

This beach was named for an old, unidentified wooden shipwreck now long gone. Also called **Keoniloa Beach**, it fronts the Hyatt. The public access road is between the Hyatt and the Po'ipu Bay Resort Golf Course. The beach is used mostly by surfers, boogie boarders, body surfers and people staying at the Hyatt. High surf can create very unfavorable conditions. Even during calm seas, swimming is sometimes difficult.

The Hyatt erects colored flags to signal ocean conditions—green meaning safe. (Though we've *never* seen a green flag. Their lawyer probably confiscated it.) The cliff off to your left is called Makawehi Point and is a popular place for pole fishermen. You will often see foolhardy young men jumping off the cliff into the waters below. (As did Harrison Ford and Anne Heche—or at least their stunt doubles—in the movie *Six Days/Seven Nights*.) The cliffs are a fascinating place to hike and are described in HIKING on page 159. The Hyatt has some outdoor showers near the beach area to rinse off, but they are technically only for the guests.

❖ **Brennecke Beach**

Great boogie boarding and lots of turtles. Since it is so small, surfboards are not allowed near the shore. The waves are usually great and tend to break both far away and close to shore—perfect for both beginners and advanced. You can rent boogie boards across the street at Nukumoi Surf Co. Observe conditions carefully before you go in. Since this beach is more susceptible to change than most island beaches, you'll have to evaluate its boogie viability. Be careful bodysurfing here. The local ER nickname is Break Neck Beach since body surfers sometimes get drilled into the sand.

➊ **Po'ipu Beach Park**

A REAL GEM This is the major center of beach activity on the south shore. The swimming is nearly always safe just to the left of the tombolo/sandbar. Snorkeling around the right side can be fantastic. Park facilities and lifeguard are present. To the left is an area semi-protected by a breakwater. It's very popular with children. This park is a nice place to enjoy the ocean. The far right side isn't as protected but features excellent snorkeling and swimming if the surf isn't high.

❖ **Kiahuna Beach / Sheraton Beach / Po'ipu Beach**

A REAL GEM Take your pick with regard to the name. This beach fronts the Sheraton Hotel and Kiahuna Resort. It is postcard pretty and often safe to swim thanks to an offshore reef. Surfers ride waves outside the reef, but you should stay inside unless you really know your stuff. Boogie boarding and snorkeling help make this one of the most user-friendly beaches around. Access from the end of Hoonani Road. See map on page 75.

❖ **Koloa Landing**

An old boat launch used as a SCUBA spot. See SCUBA in the ACTIVITIES chapter.

❖ **Baby Beach / Kaheka Beach**

This stretch of sand is partially protected from surf by a natural breakwater of lava boulders forming a quasi-protected pool. The sand only extends a little way into the water, giving way to a lining of lava stones, so you'll be grateful for those cheap water shoes you brought with you. These same shallow stones also capture some of the sun's heat, making the water a little warmer here. A REAL GEM for people terrified of the ocean, as well as little crumb-crunchers, hence the name. Check conditions first. On Hoona (loop) Road off Lawa'i Road. See map on page 74.

❖ **PK's**

Named after the Prince Kuhio monument across the street on Lawa'i Road in **Ho'ai Bay**. Almost no sand and entry can be awkward, but snorkeling is good at times. Also used for SNUBA and SCUBA.

❖ Lawa'i Beach / Beach House

This tiny pocket of sand next to the Beach House Restaurant nearly disappears at high tide. The snorkeling in front of the restaurant is great, but the water is subject to currents during periods of high surf and needs to be respected. At other times it can be calm and a good place for the less-experienced snorkeler. SNUBA (not SCUBA) is also done here. Just stay near the shore around the restaurant.

❖ Keiki Cove

A minuscule pocket of sand just past Lawa'i Beach where the road almost clips the ocean. (A break in the low stone wall between two houses hides stairs.) It's usually protected and an excellent place to let rug-rats experience the ocean, but check it yourself first.

❖ Kukui'ula Harbor

Probably the most forgotten beach on the South Shore. When tiny little Lawa'i Beach is jammed with people, this protected harbor with a very pretty mountain backdrop is lightly used during the week and there's plenty of parking. (Weekends are more crowded with locals launching their boats.) There's plenty of sand and a huge lawn plus facilities. Snorkeling won't be great, but the swimming is often protected by the boat jetty.

❖ Lawa'i Bay

Access is the problem here. There's no way to get here by land without crossing private property. But you can kayak here from Kukui'ula Harbor, which is only a mile to the east. The beach is in a particularly lovely setting, backed by the National Tropical Botanical Garden. If you visit the beach, you're not allowed to venture into the private garden. Garden

If high surf is rockin' at other beaches, Baby Beach near Po'ipu usually provides a calm respite.

personnel say that this is one of the rare places on the island where green sea turtles nest. (Most of Hawai'i's green sea turtles are born in French Frigate Shoals, 500 miles away.)

❖ **Palama Beach**

The only way to get to this beach is to take Kaua'i Coffee's dirt road past the 4 mile marker on Po'ipu Road. From there, take one of the feeder roads to the beach. (The feeder road is on the map, but the gate's probably locked.) All this requires permission from Kaua'i Coffee, which they probably won't give. If you're still with me, the beach is quiet and nearly always deserted.

WEST SHORE BEACHES

There aren't a lot of listings under West Shore Beaches. That's because it's almost *all beach*.

❖ **Glass Beach**

If someone told you that you gotta check out the beach near an old dump, would you believe 'em? Then if they said the reason to check it out was because stuff from the dump washes ashore, would you go? Well…you should. Glass Beach makes a rotten first impression. It's in the industrial part of 'Ele'ele backed by huge, ugly tanks full of gasoline. Add to that millions of pieces of broken glass, washed in from broken bottles and auto glass. The result? A colorful tapestry of sand and multicolored glass. (Come to think of it, doesn't glass *come* from sand?) This isn't a beach to frolic at or swim in. It's a good strolling beach, especially if you want to tie in a visit here with a hike along the Swiss cheese-type of lava farther east. That hike is described on page 159. The amount of glass varies with tides and surf—sometimes there's almost none here or ultra-fine; sometimes it's everywhere. Please

Part of the longest beach on the island, Polihale is the ultimate beach stroll.

don't take any of the glass litter. (Now *there's* a bizarre statement if taken out of context.) To get to Glass Beach, drive toward Hanapepe, turn left on Waialo Road going toward Port Allen. Before the ocean, go left on Aka Ula until it's dirt. (You may want to park there.) Then take a right on the dirt to the beach. A 20-minute or so walk further east leads to **Wahi-awa Beach**, a dark sand beach where tour boats sometimes moor for lunch and kayaks visit in the winter. See map on page 85.

✪ Salt Pond Beach Park

This area is distinguished in that it has the only natural salt ponds in Hawai'i still used to make salt. Seawater is pumped into containers and allowed to evaporate. More water is added, and then it is transferred to shallower pans. The process is repeated until the water is loaded with salt. This is allowed to evaporate completely, leaving crystallized salt behind. (Excellent in kalua pig.) During the summer you'll likely see people practicing this process. The nearby park and its facilities are a popular place for locals to bring their families. The beach is separated by two rocky points. A natural ridge of rock runs between the two points, creating an area of relative calm inside. Swimming is usually safe, and children play in the semi-protected ocean water. The exception is during periods of high surf, which can make it unsafe. In Hanapepe past the 17 mile marker off Lele Road. Usually windy, especially in the afternoon. Camping with county permit, full facilities and lots of wild cats. The parking lot and restroom area may turn you off, but the beach is very nice.

❖ Pakala Beach

Those cars you might see parked on the side of the road shortly after the 21 mile marker belong to surfers carrying their boards to a very famous surfing site also known as **Infinities**, so named because the ride seems to last forever. The water is murky and only used for expert surfing.

✪ Lucy Wright Beach Park

Lucy Wright was a prominent member of the Waimea community when she died in 1931. It is a testament to how the townsfolk felt about her that the beach was named in her honor, especially in light of the more historic event that happened here. For it was at this spot that Captain James Cook first set foot in the Hawaiian Islands in January 1778. The beach itself is not a particularly good beach. The Waimea River mouth is nearby, and the silty water is less enticing than clear waters elsewhere. Some guidebooks label this a black sand beach, like the black sand beaches on the Big Island or Maui. That's not quite accurate. Though there *is* lots of black sand here—flecks of lava along with a green stone called olivine chipped from the riverbed by the Waimea River—much of the "black sand" is simply fine sediment carried by the same river. Camping by county permit, though we noticed lots of illegal long-term campers at press time. Across the river are the remains of the Russian Fort called Fort Elizabeth State Historic Park. For more information on the fort, see page 85. The best part of the beach is watching the interplay of the ocean and river mouth, described on page 86. Full facilities. The river mouth is also a popular place for beginner stand-up paddleboarding.

❖ Polihale

A REAL GEM This area consists of more than 15 *miles* of uninterrupted sand beach. There are three regions, called **Kekaha Beach Park, Pacific Missile Range Facility** and **Polihale State**

Park. Except for a few small areas, the entire stretch is unprotected, which means it is exposed to the ocean's force. During periods of high surf, waves can travel up the beach and pull you in, so be wary. When the seas are calm, you might enjoy the water. The sand can get pretty hot out on this side—hot enough to fry your feet—so watch it. Take water with you. It's available only at Kekaha Beach Park and at the other end at Polihale State Park.

➕ **Kekaha Beach Park** is the first region you encounter. High surf generates a particularly powerful rip current and waves can be unbelievably strong; stay out or ask the lifeguard unless the water is real calm.

Past Kekaha is one of the least appreciated (and used) stretches of beach on the island. **Kokole Point** marks the beginning of PMRF (below). The dirt road ⅔ mile past the 27 mile marker leads to the shoreline. 4WD drivers should read the part about driving on sand under the Polihale description below if you want to drive on the beach. At the beach here you can often walk for a mile (especially to the west) and not find a soul. Ni'ihau seems so close from here. There's no shade, and the same swimming warnings apply as Kekaha Beach Park. But it's a great place to enjoy a wide, sandy beach and awesome for a late afternoon BBQ.

Pacific Missile Range Facility (PMRF) is operated by the U.S. Navy. It is here that they train for ASW or Anti Submarine Warfare. They also conduct "Star Wars" missile tests here. Access these days for visitors is pretty hard to get. It's a long and arduous process, but you can call 335–4740 if you're determined. The beach on the northern part (adjacent to Polihale State Park) is **Barking Sands Beach**. If conditions are right, the sand dune (which has numer-

ous kiawe trees) is supposed to make a barking sound with your every step. The likely cause is a combination of uniform grain size coupled with a thin coating of silica that sticks when dry. Don't feel bad if it doesn't happen. We've jumped up and down like idiots on that sand until we were blue in the face, and we haven't even gotten it to whine. The sand needs to be *real* dry. Local legend has it that the barking sound comes from nine dogs buried in the sand. They belonged to their master, a fisherman, in the days when dogs didn't bark. (Sometimes I wish those were *still* the days.) One day, they started acting antsy after the master tied them up before he went fishing. While he was out, a storm broke and forced him off course. A god gave the dogs the power to bark so they could guide their master home. Unfortunately, the dogs were so fearful waiting for their master that they ran around the stakes they were tied to. Around and around and around they ran until they buried themselves in the sand. The fisherman was depressed when he returned and couldn't find his dogs. He would go down to the shore every day looking for them, but he never found them. The dogs remain there to this day, barking for their master, hoping he will find them. (My neighbor's dog seems to bark for the same reason.)

Polihale State Park is the end of the line. You can't go any farther north on this part of the island without a boat. This is where the Na Pali Coast starts. Rain is rare in these parts. On the few occasions that it does rain hard, the road can get pretty sloppy. Other times potholes might slow you down, but regular cars can almost always make it. The sand can get *real* hot in the summer. The four facility areas here tend to be poorly maintained but include showers, restrooms, picnic tables and drinking water (which you'll need).

The dunes of Polihale are famous throughout the islands. The beach averages 300 feet wide, and the dunes can get up to 100 feet high. Walking down a dune like that can be fun; walking up is a monster. Better to walk around unless you are training for the *Ironman Triathlon*. Locals drive their 4WD vehicles right onto the beach. If you try it, be aware that you are a *long* way from Lihu'e. The first thing a tow truck driver will probably ask you is, "Do you own your own home?" It's probably cheaper to buy a new car. And AAA won't tow a *stuck* car, only one that won't start, so yank an important-looking wire before you call them. Remember the 4WD drive trick to driving on sand is to have low air pressure in your tires (15 psi is what we use), be gentle on the gas, and *don't stop* in soft sand; let your momentum carry you. A cheap air pump from Walmart that plugs into the cigarette lighter can refill the air. Even with all that,

it's still possible to get stu... ing the carpet out of the tru... on it if you're stuck.

To get there, take Hwy 50 till it ends, veering right at the fork. (See map on page 84.) The first dirt road leads $3\frac{2}{10}$ miles to a large monkeypod tree. To the left is **Queen's Pond**. This is the one part of Polihale that often offers safe swimming. It is partially protected by a small fringing reef, and the swimming inside the reef is good except during periods of high surf.

If you go to the right at the monkeypod tree, there's a soft sandy spot in the road $4\frac{1}{2}$ miles from where you left the pavement. If you drive past it *(don't stop in the sand)*, look for the large parking lot on your left with three small pavilions and restrooms. You'll be able to fall out of your car onto the sand.

Beaches along **Na Pali** are not reachable unless you're up for an adventure. That's why they are described in the ADVENTURES chapter.

Two lovers live their sunset dream at a west side beach.

ACTIVITIES

Wet, warm and happy. Life is good...

If you want more from your Kaua'i vacation than a suntan, Kaua'i offers a multitude of activities that will keep you happy and busy. Among the more popular activities are helicopter tours, ocean tours of Na Pali, golfing, hiking, SCUBA diving and kayaking. You will find lots more to do here as well.

We've listed the activities here in alphabetical order. Beware of false claims on brochures. We've seen many fake scenes in some brochure racks. Computers have allowed photo manipulation to imply realities that don't exist (which *we* don't do).

Activities can be booked directly with the companies themselves. Ask them if they have any coupons floating around in the free publications or if there is a dis-

count for booking direct. You can also book through **activity brokers** and **booths**, which are numerous and usually have signs such as FREE MAPS or ISLAND INFORMATION. Allow me to translate: The word FREE usually means I WANT TO SELL YOU SOMETHING.

What we're about to tell you has gotten this book pulled from some shops and badmouthed in some circles, but the truth's the truth. Their objective, as is the case with many concierges, is to sell you activities for a commission. *Occasionally,* you can get better deals through activity booths or your concierge, but not often, because 25–30 percent of what you're paying is their commission (which they call a "deposit") for making the phone call. That's why calling direct can sometimes save money. Companies are so happy they don't have to give away ¼ to ⅓ of their fee to activity booths, they'll sometimes give you a discount.

Many of the activity booths strewn about the island are actually forums for selling timeshares. We are not taking a shot at timeshares. It's just that you need to know the real purpose of some of these booths. They can be very aggressive, especially with so many timeshares on the market. (To use a wilderness analogy—they are the hunters; you are the hunted. Don't let them see the fear in your eyes.)

Selling activities has become a *big* business on Kaua'i, and it's important to know *why* they're pitching a certain company. If an activity booth or desk steers you to XYZ helicopter company and assures you that it's the best, that's fine, but consider the source. That's usually the company that the booth gets the *biggest commission* from. We check up on these booths frequently. Some are reputable and honest, and some are outrageous liars. Few activity sellers have ever done any of the activities unless they got it *free* and the company *knew* who they were. On the other hand, we *pay* for everything we do and review activities *anonymously*. We have no stake in *any* activity company we recommend, and we receive *no* commission. We just want to steer you in the best direction we can. If you know who you want to go with (because you read our reviews and decided for yourself), call them direct first.

A Warning: Many of the companies listed have a 24-hour cancellation policy. Even if the weather causes you (not them) to cancel the morning of your activity, *you will be charged.* Some credit card companies will back you in a dispute if the 24-hour policy is posted, some won't. Fair? Maybe not. But that's the way it is.

Lastly, consider booking by e-mail before you come. Good companies can fill up in advance, and the Web can pave the way for your activities. Our site at **www.wizardpub.com** has links to *every* company listed here that has a site, even the ones we recommend *against*.

ATVs (also called quads) can be a fun way of seeing the back country. They are like Tonka Toys on steroids with knobby tires. The two companies here offer *very* different experiences.

Kipu Ranch Adventures (246-9288) is our favorite. The scenery is much nicer than Kaua'i ATV (below) and their guides are better and will stop often to narrate. Their tour is of Kipu Ranch, a *very* beautiful ranch. In the 3-hour tour ($125), you're treated to the lump-in-your-throat backdrop of Ha'upu Range along the pastures. They'll descend into woodsier areas, along a stream and usually end up at a viewpoint almost no one on Kaua'i *ever* gets to see—the hidden valley and beach of Kipu Kai from the road that drapes across the mountain. (Because it's private and closed, we *never* thought we'd get to see this sight.) If you choose a 2-passenger ATV, the 2nd person costs $100. The 4-hour tour ($150) omits that grand view of Kipu Kai but visits two small waterfalls. They use big bikes and run their tours well. You won't be allowed to totally cut loose on your bike, if that's what you're aiming for, and their average moving speed is slower. It's a tour, and you *will* get dusty or muddy. But it's a fun way to see exceptional scenery.

On the other hand, **Kaua'i ATV** (742-2734) in Koloa is the exact opposite in almost every way. They lack the good views of Kipu Ranch and instead concentrate on the thrill of riding an ATV. The average moving speed is 15 MPH, and you may reach 25 MPH at times; it depends on the guide. Some guides might give you more freedom to cut loose; others might be stern taskmasters who keep you on a short leash and get on your nerves with their nastiness. If you get one of them, you'll hate the whole experience. Get the right guide and it can be a hoot for those who like busting loose. If it's been raining, you're encouraged to crash through every puddle. During dry times, it's super dusty. Either way you'll get dirty. They almost never cancel due to weather. Groups are bigger (up to 24), and lunch on the longer tour is simple sandwiches. Service is scant if not downright surly at the baseyard. If it's pouring rain and you ask for a jacket, you're likely to be indifferently told you "should have bought a poncho back at the store." And the helmets are disgusting, with no obvious effort that we saw to clean them from the previous riders.

(Bring a bandanna or buy one from their shop.) Their playground is mostly old sugar cane roads plus two stops at small waterfalls and a cool trip through a ½ mile-long tunnel. Two- and four-person mud buggies (which are a blast) are also available in addition to the ATVs that set the pace. Narrations are minimal, which is good, because when they *do* talk, the information is often inaccurate. The waterfall tour is $155. It's $125 for the shorter tour.

BIKING

Bike lanes or shoulders of some kind line the main highway from Princeville all the way around to Mana on the west side (though some are narrow in spots, and some bridges force you into the traf-

Beachside biking along the east shore.

fic). Past Princeville, forget it. And for what it's worth, we find that Kaua'i drivers are more likely to crowd bikes off to the side than other islands. Don't know why, but it's true.

For mountain biking, the dirt roads in **Po'ipu,** especially near **Maha'ulepu,** can be fun, though a bit dusty. Another good place is the cane road between **Kealia Beach** and **Anahola.** (Start at Kealia Beach and pedal north; give way to ATV riders.) And the 2½-mile paved road from **Kealia Beach up to Spalding Monument** is really scenic and sparsely driven. You'll gain 400 feet of elevation in the process. The **Kuilau** and **Moalepe Trails** can be exciting. (Described under HIKING on page 154.) The roads past the end of **Kuamo'o Road** in Kapa'a leading toward Wai'ale'ale and the **Jungle Hike** described on page 155 are excellent for mountain bikes.

If you don't mind a long drive, the roads of Koke'e offer good choices. See the Koke'e map on page 140 and the west side map on page 84. Pay attention to **Mohihi-Camp 10 Road** on the Koke'e map. The **contour road** in Koke'e is always fun. You can even travel down the spine of some of the ridges, such as Kauhao and Ka'awe-iki, if you have the stones to pedal back up. The ADVENTURES chapter has a bike/hike combo.

If you're interested in renting a mountain bike, call any of these companies: **Kaua'i Cycle** (821–2115) in Kapa'a, the friendliest bike shop on the island, or **Outfitters Kaua'i** (742–9667) in Po'ipu. **Pedal 'n Paddle** (826–9069) in Hanalei has beach cruisers and hybrids only. You'll pay $20–$45 per day. Bikes with shocks are better but more expensive.

If you just want to go downhill, road trips down Waimea Canyon Drive are available. They're fun but pretty short. With **Bicycle Downhill/Outfitters Kaua'i** (742–9667) you meet at 6 a.m. or 2:30 p.m. in Po'ipu, then drive up to

the canyon in their van. Near the 12 mile marker you get out and coast downhill almost the entire way on 550 and 552, ending up in Kekaha before noon. $98. (Interestingly, one of their ads says "100% downhill" but shows a woman riding *uphill!)*

Kaua'i is in the process of spending 50 million federal dollars to construct a shoreline walking/biking path from Nawiliwili to Anahola, scheduled to be completed when Lady Gaga draws her first Social Security check. Currently the only completed section is the 5-mile section from Kapa'a to just north of Donkey Beach. The northern section is the prettiest, and the smooth concrete path is easy to ride on beach cruisers. Two shops in Kapa'a rent them. **Coconut Coasters** (822–7368) is near the north end of town and also has some mountain bikes, as well as tandems. **Hele On Kaua'i** (822–4628) is behind Ono Family Restaurant with a smaller selection, but you can get two bikes for two hours (enough for the bike path) for a cheap *$10.* **Eastside Cruisers** (821–1519) in Kapa'a's Roxy Square also has cheap prices. Otherwise, it's $10–$45 for the day.

In Princeville, **Ride On** (652–8958) rents cruisers, but Princeville is not good riding territory and you *don't* want to bike down into Hanalei and beyond.

Boogie boarding (riders are derisively referred to as *spongers* by surfers) is where you ride a wave on what is essentially a sawed-off surfboard. It can be a real blast. You need short, stubby fins to catch bigger waves (which break in deeper water), but you can snare small waves by simply standing in shallow water and lurching forward as the wave is breaking. If you've never done it before, stay away from big waves; they can drill you. Smooth-bottom (hard shell) boards work best. If you're not going to boogie board with boogie fins (which some consider difficult to learn), you should do it with water shoes or some other kind of water footwear. This allows you to scramble around in the water without fear of tearing your feet up on a rock or urchin. Shirts are *very* important, especially for men. (Women already have this aspect covered.) Sand and the board itself can rub you so raw your *da kines* will glow in the dark.

Your hotel activity desk may have boards. It should cost you $5–$9 per day, $15–$30 per week. Other places include: **North Shore**—**Hanalei Surf Co.** (826–9000), **Kayak Kaua'i** (826–9844) or **Pedal 'n Paddle** (826–9069).

East Shore—**Kayak Kaua'i** (826–9844) and **Boss Frog** (822–4334).

South Shore—**Seasport Divers** (742–9303) in Po'ipu, **Progressive Expressions** (742–6041) in Koloa or **Nukumoi Beach & Surf Shop** (742–8019) across from Po'ipu Beach.

Below are some beaches worth considering. Also check the BEACHES chapter.

- **Kealia Beach** in Kapa'a is excellent, but the waves are powerful.
- **Kalapaki Beach** in Lihu'e is a smart choice for beginners and the timid.
- **Brennecke Beach** has returned to its former glory. (For a decade it was poor after being chewed up by a hurricane.)

CAMPING

The ultimate in low-price lodging is offered by Mother Nature herself. Kaua'i is a great place to camp with 13 different areas—six state camping areas and seven county campsites. See map on next page. To camp at a state-controlled site, you need to contact the **Hawai'i DLNR, State Parks** at 3060 Eiwa St., #306, Lihu'e, HI 96766, (808) 274-3444. (Our website has a link to a page where permit applications can be filled out online.) You are *strongly* advised to get your permit before you arrive because the sites can fill up, especially during peak season (May–December). The state requires that you enter the driver's license or passport number of every adult who will be camping, as well as the names of any minors, along with your dates of travel. The permits are $18 per group per night (except Na Pali, which is $20 *per person*) and should be acquired as far in advance as you can. They recommend at least six months in advance during the busy months. *More* for Na Pali.

The state enforces permits with uncommon zeal, so when officers swoop in to check your permits, stand at attention and wipe that smile off your face.

For more on beach campsites see BEACHES chapter.

County sites require a county permit. They will send you an application or you can

Keiki shreddin 'em.

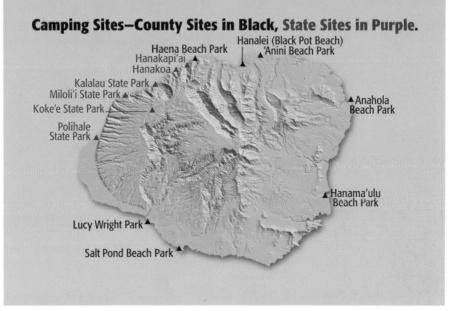

Camping Sites—County Sites in Black, State Sites in Purple.

Haena Beach Park
Hanakapi'ai
Hanakoa
Kalalau State Park
Miloli'i State Park
Koke'e State Park
Polihale State Park

Hanalei (Black Pot Beach)
'Anini Beach Park

Anahola Beach Park

Hanama'ulu Beach Park

Lucy Wright Park

Salt Pond Beach Park

get it online. The cost is $3 per adult per night. Call:

County of Kaua'i Parks & Recreation
4444 Rice St. #150
Lihu'e, HI 96766
(808) 241-4463

The county also has regional neighborhood offices for permits, but they *only* take cashier's checks or money orders—go figga.

Car camping from 4WDs at Koke'e State Park is lovely—especially Sugi Grove—and is convenient if you plan to hike much there.

If you need to rent camping or hiking gear, your best sources will be **Pedal 'n Paddle** (826-9069) in Hanalei or **Kayak Kaua'i** (826-9844) also in Hanalei.

Propane can be found at **Kmart** or **Walmart** in Lihu'e. For white gas or butane call **Gaspro** (245-6766) in Lihu'e or **Waipouli Variety**.

Good places to buy gear include: **Da Life** (246-6333) in Kalapaki Bay, **Pedal 'n Paddle** (826-9069) in Hanalei,

Waipouli Variety (822-1014) in Kapa'a and **Discount Variety** (742-9393) in Koloa. Others are **Walmart**, **Kmart** and **Costco** in Lihu'e and **Cost-U-Less** in Kapa'a for food.

Lastly, TSA can be fussy with camp stoves, even when checked. Just so you know… Readers have been enraged when stoves they bought here have been confiscated, even when they're clean.

Kaua'i's waters contain abundant fish. Of course, it's one thing to have 'em and another thing to catch 'em. Whether you want to go deep sea fishing, sit by a lake or cast off a cliff, you will be pleased to know that all are available on Kaua'i.

Deep Sea Fishing

If deep sea fishing's your game, there are several charter companies around.

They all provide the necessary gear. Tuna, wahoo (ono) and marlin, among others, are all caught in these waters. The seas around the islands can be rough if you're not used to them, and it's fairly common for someone on board (maybe you) to spend the trip feeding the fish. We advise that you take Dramamine or Bonine *before you leave*. Scopolamine patches work well but have side effects that can temporarily affect vision. (It can make close-up vision poor for a week.) Other alternatives may be available. See your doctor. (I've always wanted to say that.) Some people feel that greasy foods or citrus before or during your trip is a no-no; *many* swear by ginger tablets. Some seriously suggest putting a cherry seed in your bellybutton (and hope the fish don't laugh at you).

Most boats troll nonstop since the lure darting out of the water simulates a panicky bait fish—the favored meal for large game fish. On some boats, each person is assigned a certain reel. Experienced anglers usually vie for corner poles on the assumption that strikes coming from the sides are more likely to hit corners first.

You should know in advance that in Hawai'i, the fish belongs to the boat. What happens to the fish is entirely up to the captain, and he'll usually keep it. You may catch a 1,000-pound marlin and be told that you can't have as much as a steak from it. If this bothers you, you're out of luck. If the ono or another *relatively* small fish are striking a lot and there is a glut of them, you might be allowed to keep it— or half of it. You *may* be able to make arrangements in advance to the contrary.

Before deciding *who* to go with, decide if conditions warrant going at all. It might be calm on one side of the island and rough on another. Current ocean conditions can be obtained by calling the **National Weather Service** (245–6001) for weather, for **Hawaiian Waters Forecast** (245–3564).

Prices below do not include taxes, harbor fees or fuel surcharges or tip. Reputable charter companies are:

West Shore Charters

Na Pali Sportfishing (635–9424) has a 35-foot power cat and is based out of Kikiaola Harbor near Waimea. They are slightly cheaper than other charters, but they like to set sail at 6 a.m., which can be hard to do if you're staying in Princeville. $135 for a half day. They'll also fish off Ni'ihau for a 10–12-hour private charter.

Na Pali Explorer (338–9999) has half-day shared charters for $155 on a 41-foot Concorde.

We've had astonishingly bad experiences with **Deep Sea Fishing Kaua'i** (634–8589).

East Shore Charters

Hawaiian Style Fishing (635–7335) has a 25-foot boat that goes out of Kapa'a. Unlike most boats there's no deckhand, so it'll be a bit more hands-on (literally). If the trolling's not working, they'll bottom feed. A good, flexible outfit. $130 for a half day.

Leaving from Nawiliwili Harbor, **Lahela Sportfishing** (635–4020) uses a 34-foot Radon. They do mostly private charters with 14 people max and allow you to take all of the catch if you like. *Shared* charters are expensive at $219 because they only take 3 anglers.

Kai Bear (652–4556) has a 38-foot and a 42-foot Bertram. Their new motto is, "We do sportfishing for the discriminating big game fisherman." Sounds a little snooty for cheap beer and fish guts. Half day is $159; 6-hours is $239. Half day private is $795. 3-day cancellation policy.

Freshwater Fishing

There are dozens of lakes (actually manmade reservoirs) strewn throughout the island. Largemouth bass are plentiful. You'll also find smallmouth bass and a tough-fighting South American import called tucunare or peacock bass. Avoid fishing when the water is real muddy after a heavy rain; fish won't bite. **Tom Christy** is the local tucunare guru, and you can book time with him from **Sport Fish Kaua'i** at (877) 388–1376.

The **Pu'u Lua Reservoir** in Koke'e (on the west side, see map on page 84), as well as several feeding streams, are stocked yearly with rainbow trout fingerlings. Lake waters are too warm for trout to spawn. Trout season in Koke'e is restricted to the first Saturday in July until the end of September. The rules are complicated. **Division of Aquatic Resources, Department of Land and Natural Resources** (274–3344) can fill in any additional blanks you may have.

Places to obtain licenses are: **Lihu'e Fishing Supply** (245–4930) in Lihu'e and **Waipouli Variety** (822–1014) in Kapa'a. Squid and shrimp can be obtained from most supermarkets.

GOLFING

With its bountiful nightly rainfall and warm, sunny days, Kaua'i is a perfect environment for golf. Its nine golf courses are diverse, ranging from a wealthy sugar magnate's private course donated to the island to a world-class resort course rated #1 in the all the islands by *Golf Digest*. If golf is your game, Kaua'i is sure to please.

The prices described under Fees in the table (next page) reflect the highest category of fees. Check the specific course descriptions below for more information and possible discounts. Many have additional twilight specials.

Princeville Resort Kaua'i: Makai Golf Club (826–3581)

Designed by Robert Trent Jones, Jr. and first opened in 1971, the course had a giant renovation back in 2010. The **Makai Course** offers an impressive 18 holes with commanding and outstanding views. The greens and fairways are in great shape and the layout fairly open. Make sure you bring your sand wedge, because there is a *lot* of sand between you and your destination. For hole 3 consider playing from the blue Ts, even if you're playing white. Not much farther but a heck of a lot better view. Take the crosswind into account on signature hole 7, and don't play sand-trap-roulette at the green. From hole 8 you'll see more sand than grass from the Ts. And 14 has a killer ocean view and a sandy prison to aim for. Makai is a really fun course and is easy to recommend. No food cart, though.

Located off Highway 56 inside Princeville; see map on page 49. Fees for the Makai Course are $210 for standard, $150 if you're staying at the St. Regis Resort. Westin guests pay $155. Kama'aina rate is $70. Carts are included. Walking is allowed, but you pay for a cart anyway. Note: The proper golf attire rule is more rigidly enforced at Princeville courses.

Princeville Resort Kaua'i: The Prince Course (826–5070)

Now you've reached golfing nirvana. This course is often rated #1 in all the islands by *Golf Digest*, and for good reason. With 390 gorgeous acres to work with, Robert Trent Jones, Jr. took full advantage of the cliffs, gorges and natural rolling scenery. When it opened in 1990, the Prince Course was hailed by *Golf Digest* as the best new resort course in the country. And it became known throughout Hawai'i as one of the most challenging and rewarding courses

Course	Par	Yards	Rating	Fees
Kaua'i Lagoons	72	6252	72.2	$175*
Kiahuna	70	6214	70.3	$103*
Kukuiolono (9 hole x 2)	72	6154	70.0	$9 x 2
Po'ipu Bay Resort	72	6127	69.5	$240*
Princeville Resort Kaua'i:				
Makai Course	72	6476	71.4	$210*
Prince Course	72	6521	72.1	$240*
Puakea Course	72	6061	71.0	$99*
Wailua Municipal Course	72	6585	71.6	$48–$60

* Indicates power cart included in fee.

one can play. But for some years up until 2011 it was somewhat encroached upon by vegetation, and the bunkers were hurting. A massive renovation that year returned it to its former glory and really improved the fairways, which used to get pretty soggy. The design stresses unobstructed expansiveness, with the rolling topography and deep gorges serving as the main hazards and obstacles. There are 9 miles of cart paths, and the layout allows for considerable room between holes. Hole 6 offers a delightful march toward the ocean cliffs. At hole 7, you must shoot over a gorge onto a narrow finger of land containing the green and little else. The 13th green is accompanied by a charming waterfall coming out of a hole in the mountain. You won't find a lot of flat areas on this course, but you will find tough, challenging, world-class golfing. In fact, if you're *really* into self-flagellation (*hey,* getting pretty personal, aren't we?), the black tees measure a whopping 7,309 yards with a rating of 75.2. If it's your first time here, the $7 course guide is handy to have.

The clubhouse is spectacular. If you've never played golf before, this probably isn't the course on which to learn. But if you have a little experience and don't mind being humbled a bit, this course can't be beat.

Located just before Princeville off Hwy 56; see map on page 46. Fees are $240 for standard, $160 if you're staying at the St. Regis Resort and $70 for kama'aina.

Wailua Municipal Course (241-6666)

At one time this course was rated the best *municipal* course in Hawai'i and one of the best in the United States. Although it certainly has fallen from its once vaulted position, today Wailua still rates as a pretty good municipal course with a great location.

As it parallels the beach on Kaua'i's Coconut Coast, Wailua constantly reminds you that you are near the ocean. The smell of sea air, the constant crosswind and the roar of the surf are all comforting companions, making this course extremely popular with locals. (The $15–$20 kama'aina rates might also be a factor). Weekends are very busy; Fridays tend to be the slowest. While the course is long, there are relatively few hazards, making it a leisurely course. Wind is always a consideration here. Hole 17 requires restraint, lest you drive it into the sand (the *real* sand and its accompanying surf). The locker room and other facilities are no-frills. Singles are paired up. Rates are $48 on weekdays, $60 on weekends (plus $18 for the optional cart, $10 for a pull cart). Club rentals start at $32. (Oddly, it's cash only for most things, except *you* have to use a credit car for pull carts. Yeah…weird…we know.)

Kaua'i Lagoons Golf Course
(241–6000 or 800–634–6400)

Formerly two separate 18-hole courses called the Mokihana and the Kiele, this Jack Nicklaus design is now three sets of 9, and they will be working on one of the sets during your visit. The renovated Kiele Moana 9 is the star of this course, and even if the other nine were a kid's *put-put course,* it would be worth it. Moana embraces the ocean like no other, and the views and layout are outstanding. Right from the get-go things are impressive. Hole 2 brings you astoundingly close to the airport runway—very cool. Hole 4 is a beautiful march toward the ocean. Number 7 is a long, downhill journey to the green next to the ocean at the bottom of a hill. Hard line drives are death here. For No. 8 ya got the T-box, the green and nothing but water between you.

The Mauka 9 are more about the foliage. Longer, straighter and lesser views. Hole 5 is short but challenging in the crosswind and includes a beautiful cart ride through the jungle, as does 6.

The Waikahe is probably the least interesting but has a few nice views.

Located at Kaua'i Lagoons, take the Rice Street entrance and proceed past the Marriott hotel. Fees are $175, with discounts if you are staying at one of sev-

For those who venture off the fairway here at Po'ipu, we have some advice: Take the stroke.

eral resorts. (For example, Marriott customers pay $120.) Kama'aina rates are $60. Carts are included in the price and are mandatory. Price drops to $95 at noon. Club rentals are $50.

Puakea Golf Course (245–8756)

Fairways were not in the best of shape in our most recent visits, and the course tends to be pretty windy. You don't have many ocean views, but nearby Ha'upu Mountain makes a very pretty backdrop. Hole 3 requires some restraint. Go for the green and you'll simply get wet. Use your 3 wood and come up short of the water, and you'll live to shoot another day. And stay to the left at hole 8, or you'll be presented with a posse of bunkers lined up with their mouths open to arrest you.

In all, Puakea is a fun and moderately difficult course. It's not in the same league as some of the resort courses, and the fees reflect this. Located behind Kukui Grove Shopping Center; see map on page 65. Fees are $99 for the general public, and the kama'aina rate is $50. Carts included in price and mandatory. Collared shirts required. Club rental available for $40, and they have surprisingly nice clubs for rentals.

Po'ipu Bay Resort–Hyatt (742–8711)

With its location on the "sunny south shore," **Po'ipu Bay Resort** is a sprawling 210 acres of wide-open golfing. In fact, if it has a flaw, it's that it is *too* wide open. Even course personnel privately mumble about a dearth of hazards. But this nitpicking aside, **Po'ipu Bay Resort** offers spectacular scenery, impeccable grooming and attention to detail. (They like to brag that they imported their bunker sand from Australia and Idaho.) Greens are real consistent. Designed by (here he is again) Robert Trent Jones, Jr., the links style course is nicely designed with particularly smashing views

from holes 15–17. Look for turtles in the water when you're near the heiau (an ancient Hawaiian structure) on hole 16. During winter months you might even see whales off the coast. The course is not as challenging as Princeville's Prince Course (but it can be windier), and players less comfortable with the game will enjoy it as much as the more advanced. Collared golf shirts are requested. They have GPS distance locators in the golf carts—which is cool—but we're uncertain as to their accuracy. We found we could drive carts to within 15 yards of a hole, yet the locator would indicate 40 or 50 yards to go.

Located off Po'ipu Road (520); see map on page 75. Fees are $240 for the general public, $160 for Hyatt guests and a kama'aina rate of $68. Carts are included in the price and are mandatory. At noon price drops to $145. By the way, so you don't go blind looking for it, there *is* no such place as Po'ipu Bay.

Kiahuna Golf Club (742–9595)

Another Robert Trent Jones, Jr. design, the greens are fast, but the fairways seem like they could use a bit more water. Holes 3 and 7 share a water hazard and a green, so be sure to shoot for the correct pin. The back nine has five left doglegs, the biggest being at 15. At 495 yards from the blues, you have to play short to set up the second shot. Drive too far and you'll have to contend with a Sahara-sized trap to the right of the green. Rock walls and rock gardens dot the course and will devour your balls. They also have silver tees for senior golfers.

Homes are all around the course, detracting from the natural beauty and ocean views are scarce. (The mauka views are better.) But price (less than half of Po'ipu Bay) makes it tempting. Behind the Poipu Shopping Village along Kiahuna Plantation Drive. Standard fees are $103. Carts are included and have GPS that is fairly accurate. Kama'aina rate is $47. Club rentals are $52 for Calloways.

Kukuiolono Golf Course (332–9151)

In 1919, sugar magnate Walter Mc-Bryde donated his personal 9-hole golf course and some surrounding land to the people of Kaua'i. This land, complete with a trust, has been cherished by Kaua'i residents ever since. To get into the park, you pass through a magnificent metal gate with lava stone pillars. Once inside, the personal nature of the course is apparent. The links are not as lavish as others on the island; its location in Kalaheo does not afford it much rainfall, and the maintenance budget is not in the same league as the big boys. And it was not designed by Robert Trent Jones, Jr.; in fact, they don't know *who* designed it. But this course might leave you with a smile. They even sell bird seed to feed the ubiquitous tame chickens. The price can't be touched. $9 *per day* with power carts costing $9 and pull carts $3 per nine holes. Club rental for $9 are available, but check in advance. No credit cards. Course personnel can be snotty and unprofessional, but don't let it get to you. It's the course that's the star here. If you're playing 18 holes, play from the blue tees for the back nine—6,154 yards of pleasant, easy-going golf. Especially good for beginners since there aren't many hazards. If you want to personally thank Mr. McBryde, you'll find him buried near the 8th tee in the middle of his lovely and cherished Japanese garden. This charming garden is worth a look, and local weddings occur here almost every weekend.

Open to everyone, this course is located ⁸⁄₁₀ of a mile from Hwy 50 on Papalina Road (the only stoplight in Kalaheo). From Papalina look for a gate on your right. No advance tee times.

First, I need to get something out of the way. Flying a powered hang glider (known as a trike) is different than any other type of aircraft. When I was growing up, I used to have a recurring dream that I could flap my arms and fly like a bird. My father flew little Cessnas, which, though fun, felt more to me like a car in the air than flying like a bird.

I had forgotten my flying dreams until **Birds in Paradise** (822–5309) began giving lessons in these odd-looking aircraft. I was skeptical at first. Is this for real? Is it safe? Are you *really* allowed to do this? After checking into it a bit, I discovered that these newest generation crafts are *far* safer than they were two decades ago *if operated properly*. As soon as my instructor and I took off, I realized that a person *really could* fly like a bird. *This* was what the flying bug felt like! I was so smitten with the craft that I eventually paid the owner to teach me, and now I fly trikes myself in addition to fixed wing airplanes. So, although I have *no* personal interest in any company teaching trikes in Hawai'i, my perspective isn't as remote as it is for most activities. After all, it's not possible to *anonymously* review Birds in Paradise because I now know the pilots. (We're all members of the small aviation community.)

With that explanation, powered hang gliding is an activity I love and recommend. Don't confuse this with hang gliding. This craft has an engine, it's bigger and more stable, and it even has a powered parachute attached to the craft...just in case (a safety feature rare

Flying along in a powered hang glider is as close as you'll ever get to feeling like a bird.

on traditional airplanes). Trikes take off and land on regular runways, and the ease and grace of the craft is glorious. (Watch the movie *Fly Away Home* if you want to see what they're like.)

Trikes have become quite a love of mine and are, in my opinion, one of the safest form of light sport flight available. (I'm not a daredevil and wouldn't fly them myself if I felt unsafe in them, though any time you're in the air you're potentially at risk—even on the airlines. And two preventable crashes in 2011, by two small pilot-run companies I was already nervous about because of their questionable flying habits, certainly marred the industry.)

I grin like a fool *every* time I fly and have never reviewed an activity that generates more enthusiastic responses from other participants. It seems that whenever I see people coming off a trike (I sometimes use the same airport that Birds in Paradise does), passengers are *frothing* at the mouth with excitement, proclaiming that it's the best thing they've ever

done on vacation. (Unless they're on their honeymoon, of course; then it's the *second* best thing.)

Birds in Paradise has a camera mounted on the wing to take photos of you during the lesson for $35 and up—just in case no one back home believes you. They often have two or more trikes running so couples can fly together in formation. There's a 265-pound weight limit. The cost of a half hour in-air lesson is $165. It's $235 for an hour. Expensive? Perhaps. But it's so unspeakably cool that the memories will stay with you for a lifetime.

HELICOPTERS

If ever there was a place made for helicopter exploration, it's Kaua'i. Much of the island can be seen only by air, and helicopters, with their giant windows and their ability to hover, are by far the preferred method for most. Going to Kaua'i without taking a helicopter flight is like going to see the Sistine Chapel and not looking up. You will see the ruggedly beautiful Na Pali Coast and marvel at the sheerness of some of its cliffs. This is an area where razor-thin, almost two-dimensional mountains rise parallel to each other, leaving impossibly tall and narrow valleys between them. You will see vertical spires and shake your head in disbelief at the sight of a goat perched on top. The awe-inspiring Waimea Canyon unfolds beneath you. A good pilot will come up over a ridge, suddenly exposing the glorious canyon, often timed to coincide with a crescendo in the music you hear in your headphones. You will see the incredible Olokele Valley with its jagged twists and turns and stair-step waterfalls. It is impossible to keep track of all the waterfalls you will see on your flight. You will get a different view of Kaua'i's fabulous north shore beaches and reefs. You might see whales, depending on the time of year. And best of all, you will be treated to the almost spiritual splendor of Wai'ale'ale Crater. You have never seen anything like the crater—a three-sided wall of waterfalls 3,000 feet high, greens of every imaginable shade and a lushness that is beyond comprehension. Many people find themselves weeping when they enter the crater. Others find that they stop breathing—it happened to me the first time. If it has been dry lately, it's simply great; if it's been "pumping," it is spectacular.

When you are finished with the flight, you will either be speechless or babble like a fool—it happens to everyone.

Bear in mind that we're not rabidly pro-helicopter statewide. In our Maui book, *Maui Revealed*, we were lukewarm on flights there (fearing a bang-for-your-buck deficit). O'ahu, too, doesn't lend itself well to air tours. But on Kaua'i it's absolutely worth it.

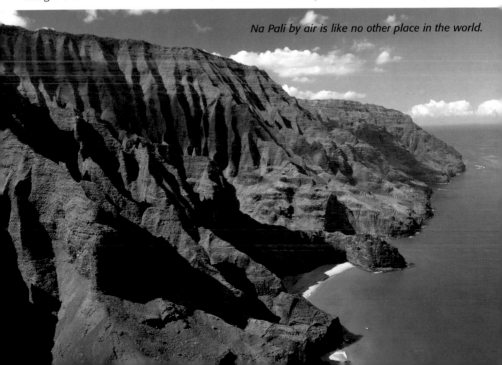

Na Pali by air is like no other place in the world.

One concern you may have is safety, and that's a valid point. As far as the industry safety record is concerned, there have been crashes and "incidents," when a craft has had to make an unscheduled landing. You can ask the companies directly about safety, but you should be aware that over the years when we've tried it, we were often misled or directly lied to. Not every time, but many times.

When we checked with the FAA, we discovered that, like many things, safety evaluation isn't that simple. A company might be cited for maintenance violations—*that* sounds ominous. Then you find out that the maintenance was carried out properly, but a log was dated incorrectly, or the company didn't fill out a particular form. Should we steer you away from them for this reason?

In the end it comes down to a matter of judgment. Below is a list of companies that we feel are qualified. Not all have spotless safety records. Things happen—a warning light comes on, and they have to land immediately. Even if it was a false alarm, it is still considered an "incident." These companies struck us as honest and forthright in their concerns about safety.

One issue that all the companies have to deal with is weather. As a pilot myself, I appreciate a company that will *cancel* due to marginal weather. Setting aside the safety factor, if cloud base is super low and it's dumping rain, how much will you get to see? When we don't like the weather, we call the companies to see which ones are canceling. The companies that seem most willing to fly when we wish they *wouldn't* are **Safari** and **Island**. Safari, especially, has really disappointed us by flying during what we consider very ugly conditions.

As far as seating is concerned, the front seat is the best. To console you, some companies might tell you otherwise when they direct you to a back seat. From the front, the island rushes at you with incredible drama. The problem is that seating arrangements are *supposed* to be made on the basis of weight. Lighter people are generally seated up front. If you are seated in the back, the **right seat** is the best since much of the action will be on the right side. (By common agreement, companies fly clockwise around the island, making Na Pali and other areas best from the right side, though good pilots will rotate often to accommodate left seat passengers.) Although companies won't guarantee you the *front* seat, ask them if they'll at least keep you on the *right side* of the craft and let them know you'll consider them weasels if they don't comply. Most will accommodate. If they don't, consider going elsewhere.

There are different types of helicopters. **A-Stars** seat two passengers up front and four in the back, leaving two people in the middle. Helicopter companies like these crafts since they can fly six passengers at a time. There are usually no windows to open, so glare may be a factor with your pictures. **Eco-Stars** are a

Company	Phone #	Helicopter Type	2-Way *	Departs
Blue Hawaiian	245–5800	Eco-Star	Yes	Lihu'e
Jack Harter	245–3774	A-Star, Hughes	Yes	Lihu'e
Inter-Island	335–5009	Hughes	Yes	Hanapepe
Safari	246–0136	A-Star	Yes	Lihu'e
Sunshine	245–8881	A-Star, Eco-Star	No	Lihu'e, Prince
Island	245–8588	A-Star	Yes	Lihu'e
Ni'ihau	335–3500	Agusta	No	Hanapepe

* Indicates whether craft contains a microphone for you to talk to the pilot.

ACTIVITIES

roomier and more luxurious version of A-Stars. They have lots of window space, are quieter and cost more, so tours are sometimes more expensive. **Blue Hawaiian** and **Sunshine** use Eco-Stars. At press time nobody was using **Bell Jet Rangers**, but it's a popular tour helicopter nationwide and one we try to avoid due to poor seating. **Hughes 500** aircraft seat two passengers in the front and two in the back, a great arrangement. The Hughes has the pilot sit on the left side, out of the way. (*Some* A-Stars like Jack Harter's do, as well.) Hughes have large, removable windows. While the back is a bit cramped and doesn't allow the forward view that other back seats do, their side views are better. Currently, only **Inter-Island** and **Jack Harter** have these because the Hughes cost more per person to operate per passenger than A-Stars. Both companies fly with the doors off. Windy and cold in back but an awesome experience.

All helicopters on Kaua'i are allowed to fly 500 feet over most scenic areas. (Companies that claim *only* they can fly that low...are full of beans.)

This is a hard section to write. You're going to spend a lot of money, and we *really* want to point you in the right direction. Most of the companies do a pretty good job, but they're very different. (Of course, like another activity that comes to mind—*wink, wink*—even when a helicopter ride over Kaua'i is bad...it's still good.) The difference between helicopter companies is the difference between a very pleasant flight and really experiencing the island. It's the difference between coming off the craft with a pleasant smile and coming off with a stupid grin on your face that won't leave you all day—between having a tale to tell and experiencing something so moving that it will stay with you for a lifetime. All this said and done, our favorites are **Blue Hawaiian** and **Jack Harter** (with a caveat on the latter).

Prices

We hesitate to print the prices for helicopters these days because, with wildly fluctuating fuel prices and cutthroat competition, it's too variable. At press time it was *around* $230 per person for hourlong flights *before* fuel surcharges and so-called discounts. They like it when you book direct and avoid the commission-driven "activity booths," Some might give you a 25% discount, maybe even more, if you book on the Internet. Many companies have coupons available in ads or give discounts for booking directly or on-line. (Just ask them.) Charter rates for the whole bird are between $1,000 and $2,200 per hour.

Most Recommended

Blue Hawaiian (245-5800)—This is the company to go to if you want the cushiest flight. Their Eco-Stars are the most comfortable choppers on the island and the roomiest. Giant windows (with gobs of glare, too, if you're into photos) provide a great viewing area. Price *might* be a bit higher than similar A-Star tours. They make DVDs of the trip from their four on-board cameras.

Other Qualified Companies

Jack Harter (245-3774)—This was the guy who started it all on Kaua'i in the early '60s, and his company's tours are still in demand, so book in advance. Their A-Star layout keeps the pilot on the left side, which is good for the front seat passengers. Harter has 60–65 minute flights and an excellent comprehensive 90–95 minute flight for about $120 more. They're the only one with such a flight and the experience is relaxed and unhurried. Their narration had been super accurate for years, but they had gotten a little sloppy with the facts in our last edition. For this edition, we tried *three times* to anonymously book a flight with them, only to have them can-

If you ever saw Jurassic Park, you'll remember this waterfall (real name Manawaiopuna Falls). The only other way to see it is by helicopter (unless your last name happens to be Robinson).

cel at the last minute *all three times,* so I'm afraid we can't tell you if they're shooting straight at the moment. (In fairness, single seat bookings tend to be cancelled more, but this was ridiculous.) If you want a sportier trip (we think it's more fun), they also have a 4-passenger Hughes with the doors off similar to Inter-Island's. *Very* cool and great for photographers. Unlike their cheaper A-Star flights, the Hughes has no background music. For this it's a 250-pound weight limit, 400 *per couple.*

Inter-Island (335–5009)—They depart from Port Allen Airport in Hanapepe, so their route is a bit different than other operators with some impressive locations. As with Jack Harter, it gets pretty cold and sometimes wet in the back, and the wind in your eyes and hair might be an annoyance (so pony-tail those long locks), but the 60+ minutes in the air in an aerial sports car can be a hoot. While not as comfortable or cushy as the other flights, it's a fun, if slightly pricier, adventure. They also have a flight that, for an extra $50, you spend an extra 20 minutes scoping out additional waterfalls.

Safari (246–0136)—We're not a big fan of their tours. One interesting difference, however, is that they record your entire trip from multiple on-board cameras. (It's $40 extra.) The quality may be pretty bad (we get hypnotized by watching the dirt on the camera lens moving back and forth), and frankly, we think you'd be *much* happier with a professionally made DVD, rather than one taken on the fly (so to speak). But at least you'll get to hear your voice if you asked the pilot questions. Readers have told us that they are the most accommodating to larger passengers. They also have a trip that lands at a remote canyon where you get out and listen to a lecture about the Robinson Family history and their plans. Overpriced at $300.

Sunshine Helicopters (245–8881)—They use A-Stars and Eco-Stars (which they call Whisper-Stars). Although helicopter companies always claim that weight distribution decides who sits up front, if you pay an extra $50 (on top of the $279 for the Whisper-Star), they'll distribute your butt up front. (They call them "first class seats.") Otherwise, their flights are a bit shorter and a bit cheaper, though their flights from Princeville are about $45 more.

Island Helicopters (245 8588) has standard 50–60 minute tours in their A-Stars. For $349 (check for discounts) they'll land at Manawaiopuna Falls (they should offer half off if you can pronounce *that* one properly) and let you get out for photos and some area info. No swim-

ming, and people over 250 pounds may have to purchase an additional ticket.

Be wary of some of the information imparted during some of these flights, especially from bigger companies that may have pilots from the mainland with little knowledge of Kaua'i. They mean well, but often their "facts" are way off.

Helicopter Tips

- Never take a flight of less than 50 minutes; you will only get your appetite whetted. It's too rushed.
- With a still camera, zoom lenses work best since the size of the field changes rapidly.
- Use a fast ISO speed of 400 or higher.
- Beware of the glare from the inside of the windows, and don't let your camera touch a vibrating window while shooting. Circular polarizers (which you'll have to adjust constantly) are *vital* for reducing glare. Wearing dark clothing helps, too. Polarized sunglasses help in the glare department.
- Don't get so caught up taking pictures that you lose the moment. It's hard to soak up the magic of your flight through a camera viewfinder.
- If you're in a craft that has two-way communication, don't be afraid to ask the pilot to turn so you can take a shot of something. Most will.
- If you're prone to motion sickness, take something *before* you fly.
- Remove any earrings before putting on the headphones.
- If you can't hear the pilot over the music, ask him to adjust the sound.
- If there are four or more of you, consider chartering a helicopter. It might actually be cheaper and will allow you to call many of the shots during the flight: "Pilot, please hover here for a few minutes, and turn a little more to the right." If only your group is on the flight, you are effectively chartering the flight whether

you realize it or not, so take advantage of it.

- Morning is usually the best time for flights (though Na Pali looks best in the afternoon). Rainy weather brings more waterfalls.
- If you take a helicopter trip, do it early in your stay. It'll help orient you to the island.
- When you see people getting off a helicopter after their tour, try not to be downwind from them. They are often foaming at the mouth from their experience and might drool on you.

For an off-island helicopter experience, **Ni'ihau Helicopters** (335–3500), owned by the powerful Robinson family, flies groups to their privately owned island of Ni'ihau. For $385 you get 1-hour of flying, circumnavigating Ni'ihau, and land at one of its beaches for snorkeling and a picnic. The problem you encounter with them is that they require at least 5 people on a flight and don't usually have enough customers to ensure a flight for you. Even if they do, their twin-engine Agusta is often being chartered for commercial work (such as the military, which uses it for electronic warfare exercises). If you are determined to take the flight, contact them as much in advance as possible to maximize the chance that they can organize a flight, but don't be surprised if it doesn't work out.

Airplane Tours

If you don't like helicopters and still want to see Kaua'i by air, **Wings Over Kaua'i** (635–0679) has a four-passenger Cessna 172 and a 6-passenger Airvan with circle island tours for $125. Visibility is better with the Airvan, but it scoots along pretty fast. Airplanes can't go into the narrow valleys the way helicopters can. It's nowhere *near* as thrilling as a helicopter tour, and if your objective is to see the sights, go with helicopters. But if you just want a plane ride over Kaua'i, here's your chance and they're friendly folks. Weight limits are higher (350 pounds). You can get the whole plane for $500.

Air Ventures Hawai'i (651–0679) also does tours in their 6-seat Airvan for $130 for the hour.

Tropical Biplane (246–9123) also provides tours, but in a biplane (two wings). At $386 per couple for an hour-long flight ($208 for 30 minutes), it's not much cheaper than helicopters, but they only take 2 passengers at a time, so tours are more personalized. Biplanes have fairly rotten views. The wings dominate everything you see. They also have a Cessna 182 for $109 per person per hour.

Of all the Hawaiian Islands, none offers more trails or better hiking than Kaua'i. You could spend an entire month on Kaua'i, hiking every day and not see half the trails that the island has to offer. And those are just the officially *maintained* trails.

We have *lots* of hikes in this book. We've also made some close-up maps to assist on specific hikes. Additionally, there are several *excellent* hikes listed in the ADVENTURES chapter since they're a bit...different.

If you plan to do a lot of hiking, contact the agencies below for information packets on their trails:

Hawai'i DLNR Division of State Parks
3060 Eiwa St., #306
Lihu'e, HI 96766
(808) 274-3444

County of Kaua'i Parks & Recreation
4444 Rice St., #150
Lihu'e, HI 96766
(808) 241-4463

We defy you to find a finer setting for lunch than this one along the Po'omau Canyon Ditch Trail.

If you need to **rent** camping or hiking gear, your best sources will be **Kayak Kaua'i** (826–9844) in Kapa'a and Hanalei or **Pedal 'n Paddle** (826–9069) in Hanalei. For walking in streams or anything slippery, nothing beats **tabis**. Like felt-covered mittens for your feet, they provide impressive traction on mossy rocks. (No ankle support, though.) **Waipouli Variety** (822–1014) and **Kmart** in Lihu'e are your best bets.

Good places to buy other gear include: **Village Variety** (826–6077) in Hanalei, **Waipouli Variety** (822–1014) in Kapa'a and **Discount Variety** (742–9393) in Koloa. Also in Koloa is **Da Life** (742–2925), which has lots of outdoor clothing, shoes and camping gear. Don't forget **Walmart** and **Kmart** in Lihu'e.

A **hiking stick** can be helpful on some trails. We sometimes even use two on long hikes and find that they greatly ease climbing and descending and give better balance, in addition to their usefulness in probing mud puddles. It's also handy during the months when tiny **crab spiders** are active. Their minor bites

aren't dangerous, just annoying, especially if you get one in the face. Just wave a stick in front of you if you notice any on the trail. In a flash of brilliance, they were brought to the islands on purpose to attack a farming pest. Didn't work—smooth move, guys! (Next, they'll probably want to bring in *tarantulas* to get rid of the mosquitoes.)

Lastly, it's nice to be able to visually see *where* you are on a trail and know you're going in the right direction. But many of the trails on the island do not show up on a typical GPS or Google maps. *Well,* it just so happens that we GPSed every trail on the island, and they are in our iPhone app available on iTunes.

KOKE'E/WAIMEA CANYON AREA

In Koke'e State Park you'll find exceptional hiking, with the additional benefit of higher altitude and its accompanying cooler temperatures. The map on page 140 shows the layout of the trails and dirt roads. The dirt roads, even when graded well, become *very* slick when wet. As a result, you may have to walk to some of

Koke'e Trails

The nature of the terrain at Koke'e makes it difficult to convey the type of hiking each trail provides. This accurate, computer-generated, shaded relief map is drawn from an angled perspective to give you a feel for the lay of the land. Since this is a perspective map, the mileage scale should be a little smaller at the top of the map (since it's "farther away" from your eyes) and a little bigger at the bottom of the map.

0   1 MILE

Honopu Valley

Kalalau Lookout
18

Honopu Trail

Awa-'awapuhi Trail

See Nu'alolo Hike map on page 145

Kaluapuhi Trail (2.0)

Koke'e Rd
17

Nu'alolo Trail

Water Tank Trail

4WD From Here

Koke'e Museum & Lodge

Chlorine Water Valves

Pu'u ka Ohelo Trail

Berry Flat

Pole ☎ #320

16

Pumping Station

1.3

1.6

Miloli'i Ridge Rd

Koke'e Rd   0.0
Waineke

Mohihi

0.9

Mohihi-Camp 10

Kumuwela

Unnamed Trail

0.5

Waininiua Trail

Spur Rd (0.75)

15

Camp Sloggett

Waimea Canyon Dr

Halemanu-Koke'e Trail

Kumuwela Trail (0.8)

Makaha Ridge Rd (Paved)

Hale

Manu 4WD

Kumuwela Rd (2.0)

14

End of Ditch Trail

Po'omau Canyon

Pu'u Hinahina Lookout

Canyon Trail (2.4)

Black Pipe Trail

Koke'e Ditch

Grassy Bank
22°06.599
159°38.638

13

Waimea Canyon Dr

Waimea Canyon

550

Waipo'o Falls

Note: Distances given for trails are one way. Distances listed along Mohihi-Camp 10 Road are from the intersection of Waineke Road and Kokee Road near telephone pole 320. Don't be fooled by a sign at that intersection saying Kumuwela.

Kilohana Lookout
22°09.375
159°35.624

Pihea Vista

Kalalau Valley

Pu'u o Kila Lookout

Alaka'i Swamp Trail (2.0 to the end)

Pihea Trail (1.8 to Intersection)

End of Road

Alaka'i Swamp Trail (1.2 to Intersection)

Pihea Trail (1.15 to Intersection)

22°08.799
159°37.070

Bridges with Metal Slats

Tall Rock & Cliff Face

Kawaikoi Stream Trail (1.75)

2.25

22°07.819
159°37.902

3.0

3.7

Sugi Grove Campground

Short Spur Road Above Small Dam

4.2

Ditch Trail (3.6)

Excellent Views

Foot Bridge

Mohihi-Camp 10 Rd

4.5

Po'omau Canyon Vista (0.3)

5.2

6.0

Po'omau Canyon

Kokua Ridge Trail (2.5)

Mohihi-Wai'alae Trail

Koaie Canyon

Legend:
- Indicates Foot Trails
- [17] Roadside Mile Markers
- Unpaved Roads
- Waimea Canyon Drive
- A Campsites
- Restrooms
- Water Tunnel

W   N   E
        S

© 2012 Wizard Publications, Inc.

the trailheads, lest you find yourself
stranded. It's a good idea to check in at
the **Koke'e Museum** (335–9975, open
10 a.m. to 4 p.m.) before you hike to get
up-to-date information.

By the way, some of the trails in
Koke'e require a 4WD vehicle (or a *long*
walk) to get to them. As an alternative to
a 4WD, consider renting a mountain
bike and bringing it up to the canyon in
your car. Then ride it out and hide it in
the forest near the trailhead, and you will
find that your hiking options greatly increase. One such hike is listed in ADVEN-
TURES on page 200.

Po'omau Canyon Ditch Trail

Formerly called the Ditch Trail, this is
an outstanding hike and one of our favorites in the park. This trail was closed
for over a decade after 1982's Hurricane
'Iwa and a series of landslides scuffed it
up, but it was reopened in the 1990s. It
sports incredible views, lush and exotic
surroundings, and a dizzying finger of
land that sticks out into the canyon and
overlooks two glorious waterfalls at one
shot. It also has a smashing grassy overlook with a canyon view custom made
for a picnic lunch. This is a truly beautiful
trail. Originally cut in 1926 to assist
Koke'e Ditch workers, it's unofficially
kept up by volunteers. There are two segments. The first is moderately strenuous,
if that, and the second is more strenuous
and less maintained. Long pants can be
useful if the blackberry bushes (and their
evil thorns) are sticking out into the trail.
The footing is occasionally obnoxious, especially on the second half, and there are
opportunities for the genetically clumsy or
the vertiginous to take a long roll.

To get there, take Waineke Road
(across from the Koke'e Museum) to Mohihi-Camp 10 Road and drive on the
main dirt road. Either park at the intersection of Mohihi and Kumuwela Road
and walk a mile on Mohihi Road to the

trailhead, or drive farther, until you're
1⁹/₁₀ miles from Hwy 550. From here, it's
a ¾ mile walk to the trailhead. (4WDs
won't have a problem with the last ¾
mile, but cars may unless it's *real* dry and
you're *real* confident it will stay that way.)
The unmarked trailhead is *on your right,*
angling back toward the road exactly 2¼
miles from Hwy 550. (If you come to a
bridge with metal slats, you've gone 600
feet too far. The trailhead is *just before* a
road turnout and might be marked with a
near-invisible metal signpost (missing a
sign). Look for it on your right when the
30-foot-high, road-cut wall of rock and
dirt on your left is about to end. See map.
If you have to cross a concrete walkway at
a small dam at the beginning of the trail,
you're on the wrong trail.

Almost as soon as you start the trail,
you will come to a small valley with a running stream. This is your canary in a coal
mine. If the vegetation is too thick to
walk through, it means you are unlucky
enough to be here toward the end of this
trail's volunteer-run maintenance cycle,
and that the rest of the trail is overgrown,
as well. Might want to do a different hike.

The trail winds its way through primor-
dial-looking jungle with ferns, birds and
often the sound of running water to keep
you company. Toward the end of the first
half, there is a narrow ridge of land on
your left; look for it. This is only for the intrepid, as the drop on either side is rather
conclusive. At the end is a vista from a
poet's dream. On the far wall is a thun-
derous cascade pounding its way down.
Next to it is a multi-step waterfall plunging
into a deep pool with the awesome
canyon all around you. You will probably
interrupt other visitors—bleating goats are
almost always perched up here.

After the ridge, continue on the trail
until it encounters a spur road to Kumuwela Road. Either circle around on
the road, or continue on the second half
of the trail. It's hairier in spots but worth

it. The worst part involves traversing a landslide over 200 feet across. It requires a sturdy gait and some focus. Look for the trail on the other side before you choose a path to cross on. If you decide to go over the top of the rubble, you'll have to figure out a way to get back down to the trail.

Half a mile from the end, you cross a stream. If you take the short trail to the left first, you will be rewarded with a perfect place to have your lunch. It's the grassy bank of an old waterfall (before the ditch cut it off), which overlooks the valley in a setting that is right out of a movie. Sit under the sugi tree for a while, and you won't *ever* want to leave.

At the end of the trail, you can walk 2 miles on Kumuwela Road (or take Kumuwela and Waininiua Trails) back to Mohihi-Camp 10 Road and your awaiting car. Now *there's* a hike to savor!

Pihea Trail to Alaka'i Swamp

This trail starts at the end of Waimea Canyon Drive at the Pu'u o Kila Look-

out. It combines awesome views of Kalalau Valley and takes you through the highest swamp in the world. The terrain in the swamp is like nothing you've ever seen, and we've been told many times that it was the highlight of many people's hiking experience on Kaua'i. You're insulated from the mud *most* of the time by a wooden boardwalk.

The Pihea Trail skirts the edge of Kalalau Valley, passing through native 'ohi'a and fern forest. (See map on page 141.) About a mile into it, a very short but *steep* spur trail leads to the Pihea Vista. Nice, but tricky to walk up to—it's optional. (Long legs help.) Just past this junction, the trail is covered in most spots by a boardwalk to keep you from wallowing in the mud. (The part of the trail before the boardwalk is sometimes pretty muddy and slippery, so be forewarned.) When the trail intersects the Alaka'i Swamp Trail, go left (east); it's 2 more miles to the end. (Many readers have said it's *way* more than that—hey, sorry, the GPS don't lie.) The Alaka'i Swamp Trail

The Alaka'i Swamp Trail's boardwalk meanders to a spectacular end at a sheer cliff overlooking the island's north shore 4,000 feet below the lookout.

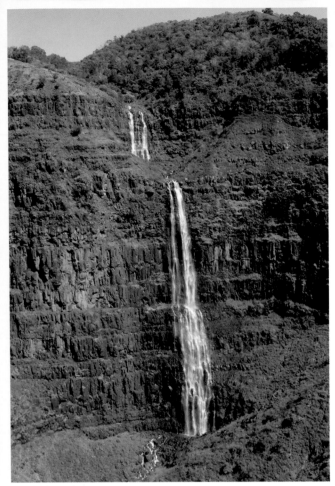

You'll end up at the top of these two falls when you do the Waipo'o Falls hike.

to the valley floor and along the sloping valley to the ocean. All this for westsiders to visit family on the north shore in the winter. (Remember this the next time you think you're too busy to drive across town to see Mom.) Along the trail you'll see old telephone poles. They were erected by the military after the attack on Pearl Harbor and stretched across the swamp, down the cliffs of Kilohana and into Hanalei. They served as a backup communications line in case the Japanese captured Lihu'e.

Even without the view at the end, it's probably the most unusual hike on the island. Full grown trees on the flats rarely exceed 5 feet tall. Submerged grasses, vines and moss-covered trees sheltering endemic birds (found nowhere else) make this a memorable hike. Fog rolls in and out constantly, adding to the mystery of the scenery. You've *never* seen wilderness like this. While you're on this boardwalk, you'll have the same thought as everyone else—"My *God*, this must have been a wretched hike before they installed this." Darned straight! It's about 8 miles round trip from your car, but you can just go as far as your desire takes you. The boardwalk system was created in the late '90s and was quite a task. Even with it, expect to get a little muddy from patches where the boardwalk was left out. If you want to avoid the sometimes sloppy stretch of the Pihea Trail, you can just do

leads to the edge of a cliff where the Kilohana Look-out affords a majestic view of Ha'ena on the north shore, clouds permitting. Imagine hiking to this point before the boardwalk was installed. Then imagine that the hard part was *still to come.* That's because the ancient Hawaiians used this trail to get to the north shore when the surf precluded going by sea. Once at Kilohana, they went over and down the 3,400-foot cliff the Alaka'i Swamp Trail from its beginning off Mohihi-Camp 10 Road. (See map.) You'll probably need a 4WD or mountain bike to get to the Alaka'i Trailhead off Mohihi. Pihea's car access from the end of Waimea Canyon Drive makes it the better route.

Canyon Trail to Waipo'o Falls

Another favorite, this one is also moderately strenuous and will probably take you 2–3 hours, depending on how long you linger. Along the way you will get unparalleled views of the canyon from the other side, visit two waterfalls and find a cold pool to swim in, if you like.

You park your car at the Pu'u Hinahina Lookout between the 13 and 14 mile markers, walk to the back of the parking lot, through a clearing and to the trail to your left. If there's no parking, you can park at the top of Hale Manu Valley Road between the 14 and 15 mile markers on Waimea Canyon Drive and walk 8/10 mile down the road (with a 240-foot loss in elevation) to another trailhead, unless you have a 4WD. (See map on page 141.)

About ½ mile into the trail from Pu'u Hinahina you have the option of going to the lookout off to your right. You might want to save that for the end, since other views will be better.

After you are exposed to the great canyon views, you will come to the top of a ridge. Keep an eye out for goats on the opposite walls. Look south for a provocative-looking rock arch, out where it's impossible for man to have created it. (You will see it closer from the larger waterfall ahead.) The light in this part of the canyon is usually best in the late afternoon (around 3 p.m.).

Just past and below the ridge, you'll come to an intersection, with a small falls to your left and a bigger one to your right. The first one is tiny, but the pool is cool and refreshing. The bigger falls takes a two-step plunge down 800 feet. You're at the top. These falls sometimes flow a bit low, especially in the summer, so don't be disappointed. Just enjoy the delicious scenery, complete with wild ginger everywhere, before making your way back.

Nu'alolo Trail/Nu'alolo Cliffs/ Awa-'awapuhi Grand Loop

This is a great hike! It takes most of a day and is strenuous, but you're treated to views that will stay frozen in your

Nu'alolo/Awa-'awapuhi & Honopu Trails

Kokee Rd

3,660'

4,120'

4,000'

Kalalau Lookout

Awa-'awapuhi Trail (3.1)

Honopu Trail (2.1)

Nu'alolo Trail (3.8)

Seasonal Waterfall

Nu'alolo Cliff Trail (2.1)

Kalalau Valley

2,980'

2,400'

Honopu Valley

3,000'
22°09.325
159°40.347

2,600'
22°09.207
159°40.824

Nu'alolo Valley

Lolo Vista
—2,234'
22°09.020
159°41.803

Awa-'awapuhi

Kalalau Trail

© 2012 Wizard Publications, Inc.

"Fat Man's Misery" rock

Map continued on page 192

Nu'alolo Valley looks radically different from every angle.

mind for a lifetime. If you're up for a long day hike on Kaua'i, this is the one. And you may be surprised at how few people you see along the way.

First, the gory details. It's either 9²⁄₁₀ or 10⁷⁄₁₀ miles (the latter if you have to walk Waimea Canyon Drive back down to your car) and involves about 2,000 feet of altitude change, 1,500 of which is climbing the last leg. But *oh,* the sights you will see. The vertiginous may object to a place or two, but they won't want to miss it.

There are three trails. Nu'alolo Trail starts near the Koke'e Lodge and heads toward the ocean, Awa-'awapuhi brings you back up, and Nu'alolo Cliffs links the two. When you finish at the Awa-'awapuhi trailhead, you're 1½ miles up the road from your car. So either leave a car there, or you'll have to walk back down narrow Waimea Canyon Drive to your car.

This hike is downhill for the first third, mostly flat for the second and a somewhat gentle but constant incline for the last third.

Start at the Nu'alolo Trailhead just south of Koke'e Lodge. (This is better than doing it from Awa-'awapuhi first.)

Coming from the lodge, the 3⁸⁄₁₀ mile-long trail is on your right. After a short climb you'll descend through a landscape that will change from bird-filled koa forest to patches of wild flowers to dryland forest to exposed ridge. All are a tribute to the rain's infatuation with increasingly higher altitudes. The trail will split in a few places but quickly rejoins. By the way, part of this trail is open to hunting during some parts of the year. It's highly unlikely that you'll encounter a hunter, but it's probably best to avoid practicing those new pig calls you just learned.

Less than 3 miles into the hike is the turnoff for a hunter trail. Bypass it and stay to the right. At 3²⁄₁₀ miles is the intersection of Cliff Trail. Don't take Cliff Trail just yet; instead continue another ⅓ mile to Lolo Vista Point. Swallow hard. You're on the upper edge of an Eden-like valley. The view will take your breath away—and then some. Nu'alolo Valley is unimaginably beautiful, and the Na Pali Coast looks endless beneath you. This is the bluff where Harrison Ford had his tree-choking tantrum in *Six Days/Seven Nights*. (Though *he* got here by helicopter.) Surely it can't get better than this.

Think again. As you go back and start the 2 mile-long Nu'alolo Cliffs Trail, you are almost immediately presented with an even more dramatic view—if that's possible. So here *you* are, at the back of the valley looking toward the ocean, half a mile below and a mile in front of you. *This* has got to be the best view on Kaua'i, right? So you'd think. A liability sign tells you to proceed at your own risk. We're assuming you do. It refers to a washed out section ahead that can be unnerving, but it's short.

After a rest at the picnic shelter a little farther, the trail turns into deeper forest. This stretch is one of the loveliest in the park, where birds abound and the scenery is delicious. There are a few false trails that lead to nowhere. Stay on the main trail. After playing in your own personal waterfall (yep, it's got one of those, too, though it's sometimes dry), you hit the Awa-'awapuhi Trail. The highway is to your right, but you head left ⅓ mile.

Nothing can prepare you for what you are about to see. Just when you thought it couldn't get any better, the Awa-'awapuhi Lookout steals your heart with cliffs so sheer and green they can't possibly be real. Can *this* be the same Nu'alolo Valley you saw before? High altitude-flying, white-tailed tropic birds laugh and soar *beneath* you. Knife-edge ridges you didn't even know were there stand against the cliff. This is a side of God's handiwork that you never knew existed. Revel, savor, remember.

The view from past the guard-rail is even better, but you're unprotected. If you fall, the first step is a fairly jarring 2,000 feet. To the right is the almost vertical Awa-'awapuhi Valley. Check out the spires at the valley mouth.

Rested? Good. It's time to pay the piper. You're at 2,600 feet, and the road is 3 miles away at 4,120 feet. Fortunately, it's fairly gentle most of way.

Some warnings: You should start this hike no later than 10 a.m. (earlier if possible). Hiking boots are a good idea. This is not a good trail if it's been raining a lot in Koke'e. Avoid when muddy, or bring your bobsled. Hiking *up* Nu'alolo when it's muddy is awful—another reason we come back up via Awa-'awapuhi. As for water, bring at least twice as much as you think you'll need. After all, the first ⅔ is downhill or fairly flat, so lugging the water that far is relatively painless. Drink up before you start your ascent, and dump any water you don't want to carry. That's infinitely better than walking up Awa-'awapuhi dry (as *we* did the first time). There's a brochure at the museum that identifies marked plants on the

Take a break along the Nu'alolo Cliffs Trail.

Awa-'awapuhi Trail. It's great if you took the trail *down* (which we advise *against* since you're better off taking Nu'alolo down), but you're probably too pooped to care coming up. Besides, many of the markers have been removed.

Kuku'i Trail

While gazing into Waimea Canyon, you may wonder if there's a trail down into it. Yup. And lucky for you, it's down the road at a lower elevation near the 9 mile marker, so you *only* have to descend (and, of course, *ascend*) 2,300 steep, unrelenting feet. Ah, but what views you'll see on your way down as the canyon changes in appearance. It's 2½ miles to the river below. (Not much distance to lose almost half a mile in elevation, so the grade is steep.) At the bottom is Wiliwili Camp (slightly trashed at press time, but there's a rest room). Make *sure* you bring enough water for the trek back up. Too many people underestimate the climb, and they're fanta-

sizing about water on the way up. The climb back up is pretty grueling, and you'll be sore for a few days.

If you don't want to go all the way down, there's a good viewpoint ⅓ mile into the trail and a *spectacular* viewpoint 1 mile into (and 750 feet below) the trailhead. Past this, the trail goes through forest.

Mohihi-Wai-'alae Trail

First things first. If you don't have a 4WD vehicle, you probably won't be doing this trail unless it's *real* dry, you have *lots* of confidence it won't rain, and you're willing to beat your car like a rented mule. That's because it starts at the end of Mohihi-Camp 10 Road, 6 miles from Waimea Canyon Drive (Hwy 550). See map on page 141 and the description of the road in the Po'omau Canyon Ditch Trail hike.

If you are blessed with a 4WD vehicle, you'll be treated to one of our favorite trails on the island. Not for any sweeping

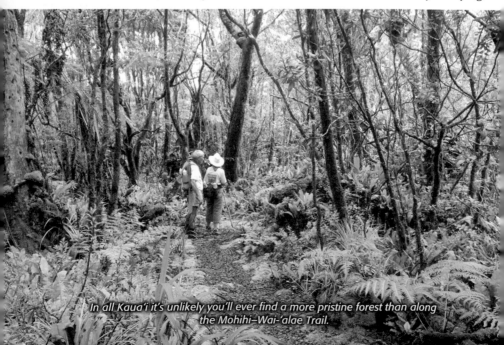

In all Kaua'i it's unlikely you'll ever find a more pristine forest than along the Mohihi–Wai-'alae Trail.

views—you only get one or two of those. This trail shines because it passes through one of the finest forests you'll ever see.

After parking at the end of Mohihi Road near picnic tables, you'll take the trail down a few minutes (the word "Waialae was scratched off the sign), across a footbridge, and walk toward and to the right of more picnic tables. A sign there saying FOREST RESERVE marks the continuing faint trail to the right of the sign.

Down through a forest of sugi trees, you'll have to cross a stream that you can usually boulder hop. A few dozen feet after the stream there's a shack. Don't pass it! The trail angles back to the right.

From here it's not so confusing. The trail gains 250 feet, levels out and climbs a bit more until you come to a broken bench. From here there's a grand view of Koai'e Canyon, part of Waimea Canyon.

For another 1½ miles the trail undulates then brings a plateau with a rain gauge. Until now the trail has been fairly wide. From here it's narrower, with passages through ferns, and there are a few areas that require care since they're on the side of a hill.

If you're game, the next mile is well worth it. It will drop to a luxuriant fern forest, then keeps getting better and better. When you're about 2½ miles from your car, the trail completely levels out. The forest has gotten more and more exotic looking. Gone are the introduced plants of Koke'e. This is an old growth, native forest that looks utterly primeval. It's as if someone had a bucket of life and splashed it all over the ground. Be careful not to walk on the mosses themselves.

The ground is soft and gentle, like walking on a thickly padded carpet, and the area feels ancient and undisturbed. The 87 inches of rain this area gets per year are absorbed by the forest floor. Walk slowly and observe how life bursts from every nook and cranny. Native

birds, though not numerous, show little or no fear of humans. We've been lucky enough to be here on a sunny day, but even rain won't obscure the healthiest, happiest and most prosperous forest you may ever walk through.

Although the trail keeps going for many, many miles, 3–3½ miles is a good turning-around point since it'll get swampy and harder farther on. (There are mile markers.) Though this last portion is *reasonably* marked, keep track of where you've been for your return. Try to start early—by 9 a.m., if possible, so you can take your time on this trail. Camping at Sugi Grove can be handy for this.

NORTH SHORE HIKES
Hanalei 'Okolehao Trail

So you've been especially gluttonous since you've been here, and the guilt is keeping you awake at night. Here's your chance to work off that lu'au you attended. This trail is a puffer. It gains 1,250 feet in less than 2 miles. That means the grade is steep, tiring and unrelenting. It will seem much longer than it is.

Most of the first ⅔ mile is on the dull remains of a steep old dirt road. By the time the road ends and the *real* trail starts (at a huge power pole whose lines swoop into the valley below), you'll probably hate the trail and hate us for mentioning it. Look to the left, and the trail continues through forest. It's prettier, as it quickly starts climbing the ridge, but just as strenuous. Climb, climb, climb, climb. Then climb some more. There are breaks in the vegetation affording grand views, but you couldn't care less because you're puffing so hard. After about 30 miles (really 1⁸⁄₁₀, but you'll swear we're lying) you are richly rewarded. A lovely plateau dotted with ti plants offers impossibly sweeping views. (Just before the trail ends at the plateau, a different spur trail to the right leads to a

Ti plants grace the end of the 'Okolehao Trail. Turn around and you'll see more of the island from up here than perhaps any other trail on the island.

separate ridge. Nasty, scary, hard-core and death-defying make that a *must-miss* alternative.)

From the trail's end at the plateau you can see ⅕ of the entire island, weather cooperating, from Anahola all the way around to the end of the road at Ke'e. Behind you, you'll see Wai'ale'ale and the Hanalei River chiseling its way out of the mysterious center of the island, the Kilauea Lighthouse, Hanalei Bay...nowhere is there a more expansive view.

Was it worth it? Only you can say, but we think so. Is the hard part done? 'Fraid not. Coming down is also hard because the constant downhill is hard on the knees...and 'okole if it's wet and you slip.

To get to the trailhead, drive past Princeville and turn left just after you cross the Hanalei Bridge at the bottom. (See map on page 49.) At ⁷⁄₁₀ mile from Hwy 560 is a parking lot on your left. The trailhead's on the opposite side at a

small foot bridge. After 500 feet you'll encounter a chain gate with an old road rising steeply to your left. Climb till the end or until you run out of sweat.

Incidentally, the word 'okolehao refers to liquor made from ti roots. In the old days, bootleggers planted ti up here to supply them with raw materials.

Pools of Mokolea

For those looking for a beautiful, wild shoreline hike but who don't want something too long and strenuous, this may be the ticket. It only travels ½ mile from you car but has some tasty rewards.

From Kahili (Rock Quarry) Beach, cross Kilauea Stream and head to the right. (The stream is usually shallow—don't cross if it's raging.) You'll see a road, but earlier portions are on private land—hence your need to start the hike the way we're describing it. You'll eventually either go up and down next to a wire fence, or around—either way ending on the lava bench. You'll soon see tide-pools. Fish and crabs scatter at your approach. Lots of ancient metal equipment and parts are scattered along the shore. For 100 years the sugar company dumped worn-out gear here. What was once junk has been transformed by a century of melting rust into an intriguing part of the landscape.

More tide-pools and more lava. It's slow going because you're mostly boulder-hopping on lava rocks, so take your time. Only 800 feet from the end of the road is a large, Jacuzzi-sized hole in the lava where the ocean surges in and out. It's great to watch, but beware of large sets of waves that can surprise you. (This goes for much of the walk along here. Monster surf needs to be evaluated.)

Soon you reach Mokolea Point. What a spectacular place! Waves often pummel the area, creating rivulets of water flowing across the lava bench. During low surf a wonderful lava pool graces the area. Several small pools behind the large rock make nice soaking pools if the surf isn't too high. Moderate waves sometimes wash over the bench, replenishing the pools. Overhead, white-tailed tropic birds and shearwaters often soar on the thermals. Kilauea Lighthouse and Crater Hill are 1⅓ mile across the water with Makapili Rock in front. During winter (October–April) the surf may overwhelm the area. Low tide is best then and only when they ocean isn't raging.

Just past the pools is the end of your hike. The ocean has cut a trench in the lava all the way to the cliff. When there's surf, the ocean comes roaring into the trench, which gets narrower and narrower, eventually undercutting the cliff in a small pocket. The result is a violent ricochet as the water and compressed air explode out of the trap that the lava has set for it. It's like a dragon, breathing water instead of fire. Some waves even hiss as they are expelled. Sometimes rogue waves pound with such ferocity you think the ground will split beneath your feet. Some explosions of water may shower you, so be careful.

To get to the marginally defined trailhead, take Wailapa Road between the 21 & 22 mile markers off Hwy 56 near Kilauea. Then take the smooth dirt road to Kilauea Bay. Park and find the best place to wade across the stream.

The Pools of Mokolea top off a short but sweet shoreline hike.

Kalalau Trail

The ultimate hike is also the most famous hike in all Hawai'i. Eleven miles of switchbacks, hills and beautiful scenery. This hike can be a real adventure. Because of this, we discuss it in detail in ADVENTURES on page 191.

Secret Lava Pools

People often assume that when you live on an island with several editions of a guidebook already out, there must not be anything left to discover. Well, maybe on some islands, but they don't know Kaua'i. This place is constantly revealing new wonders to us, and the potential discoveries are seemingly endless. Take this location. We'd hiked around this area many times and flown over this point at least a hundred times by ultralight. Yet it wasn't until a flight during the last edition that we saw this area for what it is.

Near Kilauea, it's about a 10-minute walk down the path to Secret Beach 200 feet below. (See directions to Secret Beach on page 104.) Once at the bottom, nearly everyone is attracted to the large, beautiful beach section to the right. Too bad. The most unusual part is to the left. Walk along the sand until it ends. Some lava rock may make further progress awkward, depending on the surf and tide. Beware of getting slapped by a rogue wave here. You shouldn't consider this hike if the ocean is angry, which is reasonably often, except in the summer.

After about 500 yards, a large channel/tide-pool filled with small fish much of the time makes a fascinating diversion.

About 600 yards to the left of where you first encountered Secret Beach at the bottom of the path (it'll seem like more because of some awkward footing), you'll come to one of the most perfect bathing pools on the island. Over 6 feet deep in one place, cut off from the ocean's waves during low to moderate surf, the calm, clear and beautiful water beckons. Oh, yeah. Life is good.

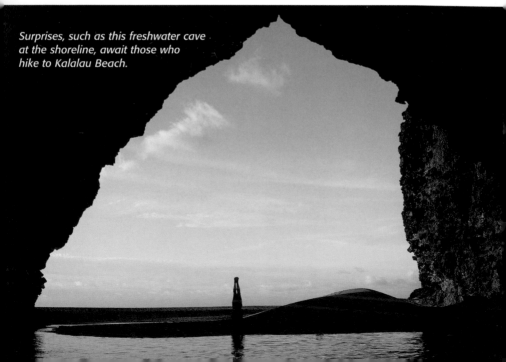

Surprises, such as this freshwater cave at the shoreline, await those who hike to Kalalau Beach.

A family enjoys the Secret Lava Pools—what's not to love?

If the surf is not up and you want more action, another pool closer to the ocean gets jostled at bit by waves. Only consider this other pool when the ocean is calm. Big surf or a rogue wave can turn that second pool into a washing machine and turn you into a limp rag. Enjoy the natural black bottom pool, which is a bit warmer than the ocean.

Yeah, but what about the salt from the ocean? I don't want to drive back all salty. Oh, aren't *we* getting spoiled? OK, if you insist. Past the pools around the rock cliff, look for a place to scramble up the short lava wall, continue a few minutes to the right, and you'll come to your very own waterfall to rinse off. The rocks below the falls (which you access by walking *way* past the top of the falls, then doing a U-turn) are *exceptionally* slippery, so either bring tabis (page 139) or rinse in the shallow pool above the falls.

We want to stress that this whole hike isn't doable when the surf's up. The ocean can clobber this coastline, especially in the winter, and could kick the living daylights out of you if it wanted to. Even calm seas could surprise you. Stay observant and don't push it just because you're itching to visit. This hike, like so much outdoor activity in Hawai'i, depends on nature being in a good mood.

An easier, if less dramatic route, is to take the first Kalihiwai Road for 7/10 miles and park at a pullout on the right near a skinny, yellow fire hydrant. A possibly hard-to-spot trail here leads 10 minutes down to the top of the falls. There may be a metal rung in the cliffside to the right of the falls to help you down. The trail can be slippery, but it's shorter.

EAST SHORE HIKES
Sleeping Giant (Nounou Mountain)

This is a moderately difficult trail. Actually, it's three different trails. The vertical elevation you will gain from the East Trail is 1,000 feet. A thousand feet sounds like a big rise (OK, it *is* a big rise), but this is a hike worth experiencing. Nearly the entire hike is through forests with pretty views. This is a real trail, not an abandoned road like some hiking trails. Of the three trails, the East is the prettiest, longest (at around 2 miles each way) and the least steep, though it involves the most elevation gain. If you take the eastern route, at the third switchback after the ½ mile stake, the trail seems to split into two paths. *Do not take the left fork, which is on the side of the mountain!* This is probably a pig trail and not part of the main trail. You won't like it. In fact, other trails that deviate from the main trail are usually bad. Take the time to savor some of the luscious views of the entire east shore from spots. When you get to the main fork in the trail (diligently guarded by hala trees with their A-frame, cage-like roots), take the fork to the left for 3 or 4 minutes to the picnic table. From here you can see the entire Wailua Valley from Anahola to Lihu'e. The view is not to be missed and well worth the climbing effort expended. Anyone who becomes dizzy from heights should be aware that there are areas along the east side trail where the beautiful sweeping view off to one side is quite steep.

Up at the picnic table, there is a short trail dipping south across the giant's neck up to his forehead and nose. Or is it his chin? Hard to say. The view from up there is, literally, a once-in-a-lifetime experience. The vista is without rival. Think *real hard* before you take this part. It is steep, and the spine is almost vertical on both sides. A wrong step, or a slip anywhere near the nose, would almost certainly cost you your life. Just before the summit there is a short trail to your left leading to the hole in the giant's chin, seen from the bottom of Kuamo'o Road. This part of the Nounou Trail is what they call a real 'okole squeezer. Stop at the picnic table unless you are very brave, very foolish and very well insured.

If you take the West Trail or the Kuamo'o-Nounou Trail, you'll find the climbing steeper. It's a good workout; we like to climb it every other day if we've enjoyed a few too many restaurant reviews lately. Kuamo'o-Nounou Trail and West Trail combine at a magnificent strand of Cook Island pines (a very tall and straight pine tree thought, during the Age of Discovery, to make good ships' masts).

Of the three trails to the top, we recommend either the East Trail or the Kuamo'o-Nounou Trail. (The latter has a stretch where mosquitoes might mug you. Use a repellent.) The map on page 59 makes it easy to find the three trailheads.

Kuilau Ridge Trail

This trail begins 1¾ miles past the Kaua'i Research and Extension Center. The trailhead marker is on the right side as you are driving west on Kuamo'o Road and there are a few parking stalls. Otherwise, park at the nearby Keahua Arboretum.

This is a very nice hike. The first part is a gentle but constant incline that takes you past a myriad of birds. Watch and listen for them. At the end of the incline (about 30 minutes), you will come to a small picnic area overlooking a lovely valley. If it's clear, you will get a stunning view of Mount Wai'ale'ale. This is a nice place to have lunch or just enjoy a long sip of water. *Make sure you go past the picnic tables.* The payoff is 5 minutes later. You will be rewarded with a wonderful razorback, winding, rolling, trek into paradise. *Gorgeous!* There are lush hillsides filled with ferns of every size and shape. Off in the distance you can see the ocean at Kapa'a and all the way to Lihu'e at another point. Very nice. Turn around where the Kuilau Trail ends and the Moalepe Trail begins (see map on page 58) at a quaint wooden bridge. (Or continue onto Moalepe Trail, if you like, though Moalepe isn't in as good condition due to horses stomping the snot out of the trail base.)

The entire hike should take you 2½ to 3 hours if you hike at a semi-steady pace. Bring water. Hiking boots recommended, but tennis shoes OK.

Jungle Hike

If you want a *taste* of the steamy jungle and forest (but without the need for a machete and a gallon of insect repellent), this might be what you're looking for. It leads to a government stream gauging station and passes through some magnificent scenery. Your reward at the end is a small, picturesque stairstep little falls where two streams come together adjacent to a water diversion ditch. (The word ditch has ugly connotations, but often these small dams can make a nice place for a picnic.)

To get there, take Kuamo'o Road (580) all the way until it becomes dirt. (A sign at the Keahua Arboretum says 4WD ONLY, but the road's not *that* bad...usually.) The pavement stops, but you won't. You'll cross *under* a couple streams and stay on the dirt road for over 2½ miles. When you come to a Y take the left fork and reset your odometer. Then at almost 1 mile is another Y, then a gate; take the left fork. (If the gate's locked, you have to walk an extra ³⁄₁₀ mile.) At 1³⁄₁₀ miles is the second gate. The map on page 201 shows all of this. (This road can get a bit junky between scheduled maintenance. Regular cars are *usually* OK, but there's a chance you may have to stop sooner without a 4WD.) Park here and walk down the dirt road. The gate is on state land and was erected to prevent vehicles from going any farther, but it's perfectly legal to go through the gate and continue on foot. Near this gate is where they filmed the ENTRANCE GATE scenes in *Jurassic Park*. It probably won't stop a T-Rex, but it'll keep your car out. The views into Wai'ale'ale Crater from this dirt road can be exceptional, especially in the morning.

After walking 10–15 minutes from the gate (½ mile), you'll come upon an ascent. There will be an old turnout on the left

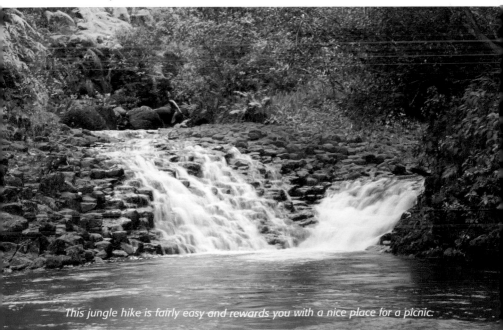

This jungle hike is fairly easy and rewards you with a nice place for a picnic.

side. Listen for gurgling water here. The trail leading off to the left from this turnout immediately parallels for a short time a water ditch and passes through extremely lush territory. The ferns, birds and trees are abundant along this easy-to-follow but sometimes slippery trail. A pleasant 10–20 minute trek up and over a 150-foot high ridge will bring you to a nice, freshwater pool, formed by the small dam. The area around the dam is covered with plant life and can be slippery. A wonderful, secluded spot to eat lunch.

If you don't want to walk *over* the hill to get to the falls, you can walk *through* it. Where the ditch becomes a tunnel (at a circular cement opening), you can access the tunnel that goes under the mountain. Most people will have to duck the entire 800 foot length and, of course, if the water flow rate should change while you're in there, you'd have a big problem to deal with. Hmm, maybe that over-the-hill trail isn't so bad after all. Anyway, it's an adventurous option that we've done (when the flow wasn't too high and we had a flashlight), and it's a hoot. Inner tubes and boogie boards are also fun in the tunnel.

The falls are actually formed by two streams. If you swim across the pool and climb the rocks, then take the right fork for only a few (slippery) minutes, you'll come to a small, hidden falls. At the base is something we call the **Jacuzzi**. During low to moderate stream flow the falling water creates bubbles and jets of air that feels remarkably similar to a spa (albeit a cold one). It's *wonderful* to soak in. Just stay out if the flow is too heavy, and read page 33 for precautions on swimming in streams. Use your own good judgment.

Powerline Trail

The Powerline Trail is an old dirt road cut through mostly untouched wilderness. It was carved by the electric company to facilitate the installation of (surprise!) powerlines in the early 1900s. It was recut in 1996 and goes from northeastern Kapaʻa to southern Princeville over a span of $10^{4}/10$ miles. If you ever wondered why some local trucks have 2-foot lift kits, this road is one reason. It has giant ruts that can swallow stock trucks.

This trail is best taken as a shuttle, starting from Kapaʻa side (the prettier part of the trail) past the end of Kuamoʻo Road, just past the Keahua Arboretum. (See maps on pages 58 and 46 for the two trailheads.) You could leave your car there and take The Kauaʻi Bus back from the north shore, but you'd have to take a cab up Kuamoʻo Road to your car. Otherwise, just take the trail until you get tired, then come back. If it's been raining much, the trail becomes pretty muddy and should be avoided.

There aren't any super long climbs, just lots of small ones on the hilly first half of the hike. The second half is mostly a gentle descent into the north shore. The area is lush and undisturbed for most of the way—except for the road and those pesky poles. (I guess we shouldn't whine too much about the poles. If they weren't there, the trail wouldn't be either.) The area is so lush that the absence of plants on the trail is easily visible from space. Look at the front cover—the Powerline

Ho'opi'i Falls

N / W—E / S

Kapa'a Stream

Kealia Stream

Falls

Old Dirt Road

Falls

Kapahi Rd

Trails approximate

Kawaihau Rd

See map on page 59 to get here.

© 2012 Wizard Publications, Inc.

Trail is unmistakable. Watch for waterfalls along the way, though none are close enough to visit. At about halfway you will be able to see the ocean on the north shore. What a lovely sight! You can see great distances at many places along the trail. This hike, though tiring, is a fine way to see Kaua'i's wild side.

Along the trail there are numerous short spur roads leading to individual poles. Some offer great views. Since the road stays fairly near the poles all the time, and since the main road is easy to stay on, you shouldn't get lost. It ends at Kapa ka Road. (Kapa ka Road is between the 27 and 28 mile markers on Hwy 56.)

Ho'opi'i Falls Hike

Waterfalls have an amazing ability to bring piece of mind. Although Kaua'i is studded with many waterfalls, most of them are inaccessible for one reason or another—but not this one. There are two falls on the Kapa'a Stream—and one of them is named Ho'opi'i. Some locals call the first one Ho'opi'i—government maps give that name to the second falls.

Look at the map on facing page. There are additional trails in this area, but the one shown is on state land. The top of the map on page 59 shows you where Kapahi Road is. An old *public* dirt road (now used as a trail) is on your left as you come down Kapahi Road. Please be re-

Some call this Ho'opi'i Falls. Others use that name for the next falls down the river. These keiki couldn't care less. They're just enjoying the sound.

spectful of the neighborhood here. Residents don't want you driving faster than 15 MPH on Kapahi Road. One resident even posted an irate review of our book on *Amazon.com* because he was upset that we told you how to get to these falls.

Walk down the dirt road, and it leads to a trail. Go downstream and eventually there's a side path leading down to the first falls. Wow, what a place! A flat lava bench offers a magnificent place to sit and breathe in the falls. The only way to get under those falls is either to go downstream and wade back upstream or jump into the pool as some of the daring

From the summit of Wai'ale'ale, the Wailua River is a half-mile below your feet.

locals do. (At your own risk; check out the water first to make sure there's nothing dangerous submerged.)

Back on the trail, the path eventually parallels the stream. Once there, you need to stay within 10 feet of the stream (except in one area) to stay on state land.

This area is lush and the sound of the stream hypnotic. Just before the second falls a side trail crosses the stream, but you shouldn't. Near the top of the second falls the trail hooks around and descends to the bottom.

If you don't bring mosquito repellent, bring an extra pint of blood for the walk through the woods. Tennis shoes are OK. Bring water and your camera.

Hiking to the Top of Wai'ale'ale

A question we're often asked is *How can I hike to the summit of Wai'ale'ale?* The answer is…you can't. In ancient times Hawaiians used to hike up a ridge on the northeast side of the crater (the ridge that's over the Tunnel Hike on page 200). Near the summit they had rope ladders for the final portion. A landslide and lack of use in the 1800s shut off that route. In the 1970s a person tried, with a helicopter overhead to give radio guidance, and he failed. In 2006 another person tried and had to be rescued by helicopter.

The other route used to be through the Alaka'i Swamp, and some government maps still show that trail. It's been gone for years, and even people born and raised here aren't able to make it through the swamp anymore. A few adventurers have made it, but we don't recommend it. The rain gauge at the top is now read by helicopter.

We generally shy away from describing places that the reader won't be able to see. After all, what's the point? Our books are meant to be *used*, and the things *we* see are things that *you* can see.

But over the years we've been asked *so* many times what the summit of Wai'ale'ale is like, we feel obliged to describe it. We were able to fulfill a long-time dream when we arranged a trip up here by helicopter once. It requires jumping through a lot of bureaucratic hoops—and it requires dependably clear weather at the summit—a rare event. (You need a high pressure system parked over the island retarding cloud growth.)

The summit of Wai'ale'ale is an other-worldly place. Other than a few clumps of sickly-looking 6- to 10-foot trees, there is nothing over a foot tall for more than a mile in any direction. Not even the ubiquitous ferns are genetically programmed to deal with so much rain and cloud cover. So the dominant features carpeting the ground are moss, lichen and short grasses. The 3,000-foot cliffs plunging into the crater define the eastern portion, which is so shear, you can literally walk up to it and look nearly straight down to the crater over a half mile beneath your feet.

Walking around is a bit awkward. The sponge-like ground is constantly threatening to steal your shoes. It takes about 2 hours just to go from one end of the summit to the other. Unfortunately, pigs and goats have taken up residence in this hostile terrain, so the state has fenced off a large portion to keep those pests out, but it's been ineffective. No mosquitoes live up here, but huge dragonflies are everywhere. Only a handful of birds can be heard, some of them endemic—found nowhere else in the world except on this watery mountaintop.

SOUTH SHORE HIKES
Po'ipu Shoreline Sandstone Hikes

The lithified cliffs of **Makawehi** next to Shipwreck Beach, as well as the **Maha'ulepu** area, offer excellent shoreline hiking. The Makawehi cliffs are easily accessed by taking the trail from the parking lot between the Hyatt and the Po'ipu Bay Resort golf course (or simply walking to the east end of the beach). It's over half a mile long, formed from cemented sand dunes deposited here during the last ice age. The wind and salt have clawed and thrashed at these cliffs with impressive results. Take your time and wander about. Look for (but don't remove) fossils in the sandstone, and enjoy the views.

Maha'ulepu is described in detail in BEACHES on page 111. Another good hike is to start from the end of Gillin's Beach (see map on page 75). It's beyond the stream and past the last pocket of sand. It's wonderful to walk along here when the surf is raging. At one place there's a hole in the floor of the cliff, allowing you to see the ocean exploding beneath your feet on the lithified bench below. This area looks like an alien landscape. Weekends bring fishermen who tend to leave reminders of their hobby here.

You could walk all the way to the Hyatt, if you wanted. The wind, pounding surf and beautiful cliffs create an amazingly relaxing walk, even if the ground is a bit lumpy. About ⅔ of the way to the Hyatt, the cliff gives way to a sandy pocket affording a luscious view of the cliffs.

Melted Metal & Keyhole Cave at Swiss Cheese Shoreline

Here's an area that's alluring despite numerous reminders of the sometimes untidy nature of man. It starts near the industrial part of Hanapepe (technically 'Ele'ele) and leads to an isolated beach. Along the way the Swiss cheese-type of lava shoreline provides ample opportunity to explore how the ocean carves up the land, while an old dumpsite makes for some surprisingly interesting discoveries.

Start by driving to Glass Beach (see directions on page 116). After the beach the road continues, terminating at an old cemetery. Here you may see trash or junk cars. That's because this area used to be (and to an extent still is) a place locals use to dump equipment. Go to the lava bench below and head to the right. You'll see that the sides of the cliff are embedded with old and new junk, mostly metal and glass. (That's where Glass Beach got its glass.) On the lava is an amazing assortment of ancient engine blocks and car frames. I know it sounds ugly, but you have to see what the ocean has done with them. Many of the hulks have completely melted from the rust, often interwoven with the lava itself. Nature has had almost a hundred years to reclaim the metal, and the results of this long-time environmental abuse are oddly fascinating. Even old porcelain and ceramics have been rounded so much that you'd swear they're stones.

After exploring the junk area, backtrack by heading left along the shoreline. You'll see areas where the ocean has chiseled its way inland. Continue along the shore (east), and you soon come to a **lava arch**. Water floods under the arch, filling and draining the swimming pool-sized opening in seconds, creating a chaotic, washing machine effect. (Look, but don't swim.)

Tides and surf can alter the shoreline here. There are several blowholes that spout when the wave direction is just right. Always be alert to the potential of large waves.

Past the arch is a 20-plus-foot-long cave we call **Keyhole Cave**. It's got a small opening on the bottom where the ocean surges in and out. At the back is a keyhole-shaped opening. It's fascinating to watch the interplay of the cave and the ocean here.

There are other holes, then a tall column of lava looking down toward the frothing ocean. Although you've left the old dump site behind, local fishermen use this coastal area on weekends and don't always clean up their mess. Try not to let it bother you.

You can either continue along the shoreline or occasionally use the old road paralleling the coast. (Most likely you'll use both.) The landowner doesn't want you driving on the road but has traditionally let people walk along here.

Keyhole Cave is just one cool reason to check out the Hanapepe shoreline.

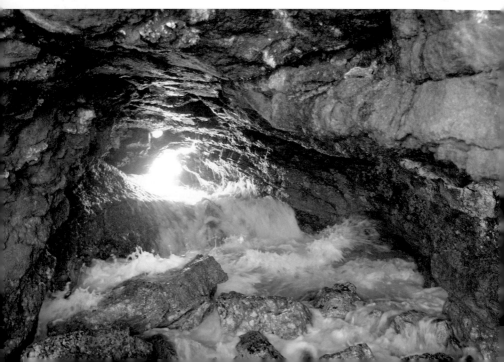

The crops behind the shoreline, however, are off limits.

After 20–40 minutes (depending on how often you stop and explore—hopefully a lot) you come to Wahi-awa Beach. It's a lovely looking bay, though the water visibility is usually poor due to river runoff. During the week, if the tour boats aren't there for lunch, it's often empty.

HORSEBACK RIDING

If you want to let someone else do the walking while you tour the island, try horseback riding.

Silver Falls Ranch (828–6718) inland (mauka) of Kilauea is hands down our favorite. Their 300-acre ranch looks more like a palm arboretum, and the guides seem thrilled to see you and show you around their little piece of paradise. The horses are well-groomed and the trails well-kept. This is how rides should be done if you're looking to be pampered in a stunning location (although it's nose-to-tail). $95 for the 1½-hour ride. For $115 it includes another hour and a trip to their small waterfall and large pool. Swim and lunch there. The only downside is that their location is rainier than some of the others, so you take your chances with the weather. Their weight limit is fairly high at 300 pounds but also based on your height. One caveat: Some of their guides have interesting personalities that readers either seem to love…or not.

CJM Country Stables (742–6096) has three rides available. The afternoon picnic ride is 2 hours of riding, 1 hour for lunch. The ride is mostly along or near the coast to a "secret" beach (it's Ha'ula). $130 per person. Then there's a 9:30 a.m. and 2 p.m. Scenic Valley Beach Ride—2 hours of riding on mountains and along the coast. Beverages included. $103 per person. No riding experience necessary. 250-pound weight limit. Don't expect much narration, just a nose-to-tail ride for up to 24 people (in three groups) along a beautiful coastline in an area that gets less rain than the others. The leader may spend the entire trip on his cell phone (which has happened to us more than once). But fantastic scenery makes up for most of the shortcomings the company may have and creates an easy second choice for us. The experience is pretty relaxed, and the horses are cooperative. They take lots of riders and feel a bit like a rider processing machine, but the rigid structure will make beginners feel pretty comfortable. Experienced riders may be champing at the bit (wow, I *finally* got to use that horse phrase in the proper context!) for some more spark.

Esprit de Corps (822–4688) is mostly for experienced riders. They have numerous rides. (The 6-hour is the best.) This includes up to an hour of training/refreshing. Unlike most companies, they'll let you trot and canter—a lot if you like. They ride a dirt road (Moalepe) with pleasant views of the mountains. They *strongly* stress proper riding habits—drilling you on posting (rising trot)—and it's more of a riding adventure instead of an animal tram ride like CJM. Their depth of knowledge is admirable and freely shared. Ask about the tasty rose myrtles along the way. Prices are $130 for the 3-hour intro, $270 for the 6-hour meditation ride and $390 for the all-day (includes lunch and swimming) trip. 220-pound weight limit.

Princeville Ranch Stables (826–6777) tends to have more spirited horses and is probably not a good choice for beginners as the horses will be in charge of you rather than the other way around. Experienced riders, however, might enjoy the trip on this working cattle ranch without the nose-to-tail aspect. They also have a ride and glide, which interrupts your horseback tour with a few zipline rides for $145.

They also have a 4-hour ride to a "secret" waterfall (Kalihiwai Falls—it's the falls seen from the bridge right after the 25 mile marker on the north shore.) $145 per person; includes 1 hour for swimming and lunch. There's a 230-pound weight limit. Bring your camera and something to swim in. There's also a 3-hour ride for $125. Overall, nice scenery on this ranch. Past the 27 mile marker on Hwy 56.

JET SKIING

Jet ski rentals are outlawed on Kaua'i, so if this is what you came to the island to do, you're out of luck.

A kayak can be a marvelous way to see Kaua'i. The quiet, peaceful nature of kayak travel appeals to many. There are four rivers on Kaua'i you can kayak and, of course, there is the open ocean.

River Kayak Trips

We've kayaked all the rivers in several kinds of craft. We prefer the rigid two-person, self-bailing kayaks for beginners, single person self-bailers for those who have kayaked before. Some use canoes, but we're not as fond of them since they can fill with water if tipped. (Inflatables are terrible since they are easily deflected by wind—called weathercocking, in case you're taking notes.)

Of the four rivers, the **Wailua** is by far the most popular. (See map on page 59.) It's very scenic, and there's a water-fall called **Secret Falls** (sometimes called Sacred Falls) on the north fork you can hike to if you like. (Some brochures call it the most spectacular waterfall on the island. That's bunk, but it's a nice one just the same.) There's a more dubious trail just before the falls that goes to the top and exposes you to the more beautiful upper falls, but the trail is pretty sketchy and not recommended. It's 5 miles round trip and takes most people about 3 hours plus stopping or hiking time. Since large boats take passengers to the Fern Grotto, kayakers should always stay on the north side of the river. If you want to visit the Fern Grotto, consider pulling ashore *before* or *after* the docks. To be honest, the grotto is not the same as it used to be and is barely worth the effort to get there. The best part about kayaking this river is the scenery and hiking to the waterfall. Just enjoy the Wailua for its lushness, and watch out for the large boat tours.

Past the Fern Grotto, you *might* see a rope swing at a well-known swimming hole. (The state has an ongoing war with pesky rope swing builders. State workers, with marching orders from their lawyers, relentlessly cut 'em down almost as fast as people put up new ones.) People line up to jump off the cliff into the water there, despite a state sign warning them not to. If you do, too, make *sure* there's nothing under the water first. The African village scene from *Outbreak* was filmed on a secluded plain here on your right; look for it. The wind will probably be in your face coming back, so hug the north bank tightly to minimize the wind. The earlier you leave, the less wind coming back, and you'll avoid crowds on the river and at the waterfall. (We start at 7 a.m. and strongly suggest you do, even if you gotta rent the kayak the afternoon before.) To kayak this river *on your own,* which we prefer, there are special logistical considerations—see RENTING A KAYAK FOR THE RIVER below. No kayak renting on Sundays.

The **Hanalei River** is the longest and goes mostly through plains. (Beautiful plains, but plains.) There are no power-boats past the mouth where you put in, so it'll be quieter. It takes about 3 hours (6¾ miles) round trip for most people to kayak this peaceful river. After a heavy rain, waterfalls etched in the distant valley walls can enhance the trip. The wind usually helps you a little coming back.

The **Hule'ia River** in Lihu'e is 5 miles round trip (2 hours or more). It starts from Nawiliwili Harbor, and the water flow is not great, so expect ickier water here. There are majestic mountains on your left as you go out, and you will pass the easy-to-miss Mene-hune Fishpond and an area where they filmed the swing-on-a-vine-to-the-waiting-airplane scene from *Raiders of the Lost Ark*. (Keep an eye out for the opening to the fishpond.) Lots of jumping fish in the shallow parts of the pond. The last navigable part is our favorite part of this river. This river goes through a wildlife refuge, but you'll see and hear more birds on the Hanalei River. The wind will probably be in your face coming back. If you're doing this on your own, you'll run into large guided groups at times.

The **Kalihiwai** is short but *very* sweet. You can kayak it in an hour (taking your time) if you decide not to do the additional 10 minute hike (more like a grope up the river, then through the jungle on the right side) to Kalihiwai Falls. Put in at Kalihi-wai Beach. You might not see the waterfall from where you

stop kayaking. The scenery is the best of the four, and you might want to do it if you have any juice left after a Hanalei River trip. Expect to be hassled if you visit the beautifully manicured falls in any way that doesn't bring money to the horseback company that leases the land where the falls are.

Renting a Kayak for the River

You can rent a kayak and paddle any river you like, *except* the Wailua River. The state has rules making it harder to rent a kayak *on your own* to kayak the Wailua (which is the best one). They want

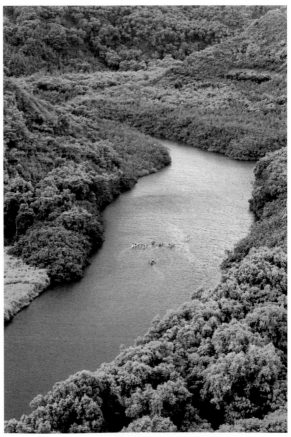

If the ocean surf's up, how about a day on the river instead?

you to go on a *guided* tour. (It's not a safety issue; it's a political one—long story.) So although we recommend doing river trips *on your own*, this may be harder to do on the Wailua. Companies that have permits can only rent so many kayaks, and they might *pull* those from the rental pool if they can make more money putting a guided passenger in it. Of the companies mentioned below, **Kayak Kaua'i**, **Wailua Kayak Adventure** and **Wailua Kayak & Canoe** have them for rent for the Wailua River. (The last one is the most

expensive, but they're right on the river and open at 7 a.m.) Call weeks in advance to maximize your chances of getting one. An alternative is **Kamokila Hawaiian Village** (823–0559), which rents kayaks for $35 from a location so far up the Wailua River, that your paddle to Secret Falls is probably less than 10 minutes. They also *claim* they'll rent them on Sunday. (Nobody else is allowed.)

All the other rivers on the island you can kayak on your own without a guide.

Prices change a lot in this competitive business, and prices for rentals on the Wailua cost more. For single-person kayaks (which are getting harder to find) consider Pedal 'n Paddle in Hanalei or Wailua Kayak Adventures—rent for $25–$30 per day. Two-person kayaks are $40–$75 per day. Sometimes they are cheaper if you are willing to arm wrestle timeshare salesmen. Most cars will hold 2 or 3 kayaks on the roof and staff will help you strap them on.

Guided River Trips

For guided tours of the Wailua River, see list of companies below. Most companies charge around $85 *per double kayak*.

Although the Wailua is our favorite *unguided* kayak trip, the best *guided* river trip we've seen is a one-way trip up the Hule'ia River in Lihu'e. 7-hour Hule'ia River kayak/hike/zip trip from **Outfitters Kaua'i** (742–9667) called the Kipu Zipline Safari. About 2 miles of kayaking then a half mile of hiking to

On the Wailua River, first you kayak, then you hike...then you frolic!

a small falls with a rope swing. Then you're on a tractor-pulled wagon to two ziplines (the second one is 1,800 feet long, and you'll do about 35 MPH) and lunch. Finally, you finish it off at a place they call "blue hole," which has a water zipline. Then back to an outrigger canoe that brings you to your car. We recommend the morning trip. The hiking and paddling are not overly tough, though you'll get wet and muddy, and some of the trail involves boulder-hopping. The guides do a good job, they're great with kids (who *love* the part where they feed some pigs and peacocks), and they don't rush you during the trip. However, they may have some accuracy issues in their narrations, and you need to know about the water you're swimming in. See page 184 for more on that. It's not cheap at $178 per person, 20 people max, and you'll be tired and happy at the end. The only downsides are mediocre food, and the wait for the second zipline can be over half an hour. Bring shoes that can get wet.

A more modest trip is **True Blue** (246–6333). Their "island adventure" tour is not as physical as Outfitters' and there's no ziplining. Groups are small (except on cruise ship days), and their lunch is much better. The hiking is on the prettier wildlife refuge side of the river, and you'll visit two small falls where you can swim. Not as much ooh-aah as Outfitters, but they do a great job and the slow pace will appeal to some. $89.

Ocean Kayak Trips

Ocean kayaking can be an experience of a lifetime. The crown jewel is a summer Na Pali Coast trip. *National Geographic* named it the second best adventure in the United States. (Rafting the Colorado was #1 and dog sledding in Alaska was #3.) Na Pali can be an *incredible* trip for those who can do it, either guided or unguided. We try to do it

every summer and camp along the way. Because paddling Na Pali is so involved, we have a complete description in ADVENTURES on page 188.

In addition to Na Pali, **Kayak Kaua'i** and **Outfitters Kaua'i** have Kukui'ula Harbor to Port Allen trips in the winter for around $145. There's usually a tailwind on this 7-mile, 4–5 hour paddle. Certainly not the most interesting shoreline on the island, but the Lawa'i Bay stop is nice.

If you want to do this by yourself, you can stop at remote Palama Beach on the way down and, once at Port Allen, call a cab to take you back to your car at Kukui'ula.

What if I want to rent a kayak and paddle the ocean on my own? Well, unlike all the other Hawaiian islands, Kaua'i is a very difficult place to rent a kayak *for the ocean*. Whether it's because companies want to make more money guiding you or because Kaua'i's ocean waters are not as calm (probably a little of both), most will turn you down cold if you tell them you're taking a kayak into the ocean. Of course, if it's the sit-on-top variety (which most here are) as opposed to canoe-types, that's what we use on the ocean anyway. If you have some experience and good judgment, there's no one to stop you from taking it to the ocean.

Kayak Companies

The companies described below provide a variety of services.

Kayak Kaua'i (826–9844 in Hanalei and Kapa'a. From May through September they have one-day guided Na Pali tours for $205 per person. Lunch included at either Miloli'i or Nu'alolo Kai. They also have ocean trips to Lawa'i Bay on the south shore for $145. The more involved the trip, the better it is to call them in advance, *especially* for Na Pali. For the Wailua River they have doubles for $55. They have the best location if you're going to kayak the Hanalei River. Guided Wailua trips with lunch for $85 *per double*.

Outfitters Kaua'i (742–9667) in Po'ipu has summer Na Pali trips for $225. Guided Wailua River kayak tours with lunch are available for $98 *per double*, as well as the awesome trip described under GUIDED RIVER TRIPS. Outfitters is a big company with lots of offerings beyond kayaking. They do things well, for the most part. Our biggest complaint is that their guides seem pretty fast and loose with their "facts" lately, and narrations have lots of factual errors.

Pedal 'n Paddle (826–9069) in Hanalei specializes in one-stop shopping. They rent kayaks for the Hanalei, camping supplies, beach cruiser bikes and snorkel gear.

Wailua Kayak & Canoe (821–1188) operates near the Wailua River, and you'll probably be able to walk your kayak down to the boat launch on a kayak dolly. Their gear (seats and such) are not as good as others, and customer service is scant. Doubles rent for $75. Guided Wailua trip is $100 *per double* with *no* lunch.

Wailua Kayak Adventures (822–5795) has river kayaks for rent—$30 for single kayaks, $60 for doubles. Guided Wailua trips are $85 *per double*, snacks only.

Kamokila Hawaiian Village (823–0559) is located far up the river, less than 10 minutes from the Fern Grotto and the trail to Secret Falls. Good for families with kids or anyone who wants a short paddle. They rent kayaks for $35. If you don't want to paddle yourself, you can take a short canoe trip from there for $30 per person.

Kayak Wailua (822–3388) is a no-frills family operation. They don't offer you lunch (they suggest you eat before and after), and you'll pay extra for a seat-

back upgrade. Their price for guided trips, $46, includes a mandatory 15% tip. That's still pretty cheap.

Ali'i Kayaks (241–7700) is a local outfit that does tours of the Wailua for $50 per person. They meet at Wailua Visitor Center at Hwy 580 (Kuamoo Road) and Hwy 56.

In addition to standard bus tours, there are other land tours worth considering.

Aloha Kaua'i Tours (245–8809) provides 4WD tours. Trips include the Kilohana area (which is private and gated) and the mountains behind Wailua town (which are open to the public). Prices are $80. The Rain Forest Tour includes a 3-mile hike.

If you're interested in chocolate, **Steelgrass Chocolate Farm** (821–1857) gives 3-hour tours of their 8½ acre farm for $60 (cash); kids 12 and under free. (There's lots of standing around, so kids under 8 may get too antsy.) The tour is about an hour too long and costs double what it's worth, but it's educational and you'll get to nibble on tons of different gourmet dark chocolates. (Not from here; their plants are too young to be processed.) Once you learn what's involved in making chocolate, you'll wonder why anyone was *ever* able to discover the joys of this plant.

Garden tours are numerous here on the Garden Island. You can either do them on your own (and set your own pace but learn less) or have a guide, many of which stretch things longer than necessary.

The big daddy is the **National Tropical Botanical Garden** (742–2623) in Lawaʻi. Rich and lush with remarkably varied plants and abundant birds, tours here are guided and last about three hours. The fee for the tour is $20 per person (self-guided) for McBryde, $45 for the more exotic and photogenic Allerton. Reservations are required. Kids must be at least 10 years old on the Allerton tour. They won't take you as far as the beach or the old Allerton home. For that you have to take the sunset tour, but that one is $60 and will cost you some of the time in the garden. Personally, we'd skip the sunset in favor of the regular tour. The self-guided McBryde garden ($20) is more of a park atmosphere, and you've got room to roam for around 1½ hours. A pretty nice garden. Don't be late for your tour; they will *not* be accommodating.

In Haʻena on the north shore, **Limahuli Garden** (826–1053) has good guides and is the most educational regarding native plant life, but those looking for a multitude of colorful tropical plants might be disappointed. $30 for the 2½-hour (no bathroom break) guided tour, which is better than the $15 self-guided tour.

Na ʻAina Kai Botanical Gardens (828–0525) near Kilauea is described on page 48. The garden is beautiful and the setting dreamy. Guided tours only, and their pace is exceptionally slow. Lots of sculptures and very manicured. $35 for the formal garden walking tour. If you prefer riding, it's $50. (Don't do the walk/ride combo.)

Ahonui Botanical Gardens (634–5505) near Princeville is small (8 acres) but packed with exotic tropical plants and fruits (which they are generous in letting you eat), including their own chocolate. They spend 3 hours covering the acreage,

and it's a bit overpriced at $40, but you can feel the family pride (and they have the juiciest oranges we've ever seen).

Ocean Tours

When Hollywood needs a beautiful, remote coastline studded with majestic cliffs and glorious valleys to film movies, they often choose Kauaʻi's Na Pali Coast. *Pirates of the Caribbean 4*, *Six Days/Seven Nights*, *King Kong* and others have all used a Na Pali backdrop to convey an idyllic paradise. From the sea, this area of the island takes on a magical quality. Many people dream of seeing the Hawaiian Islands by sea. The Na Pali region is surely the most popular area to cruise, but there are others, as well. This can be a fantasy trip. Rough seas are rarely part of the fantasy, but they can be part of reality, depending on conditions.

Seeing Na Pali by boat is an incredible thrill that we highly recommend. Soaking up this coastline and being on a boat are exquisitely relaxing. You can see it by leaving from the west side or the north shore. They are two very different experiences.

If you leave from the **west side** you'll only see half of Na Pali (and not the best half), and ¾ of the trip isn't even along Na Pali. The boats that leave from Port Allen travel 23 miles along the relatively uninteresting (by sea) Mana Plain, then head up the dry side of Na Pali before turning around at Kalalau. (Boats that leave from Kikiaola Harbor shave 9 miles off the duller part—see map on page 84.) If boats would cruise past Kalalau to Hanakapiʻai, we'd be much happier, because that short stretch has some beautiful sights. But most turn back at Kalalau.

A few companies, however, have permits to leave the **north shore**. Those boats that leave from Hanalei or 'Anini on the north shore have a *far* better and more exciting route, though the return trip is usually into head seas (meaning into the swells) and headwinds, so it can be bumpy.

Some west shore companies switch to south shore tours in October and return to Na Pali in April; others can do Na Pali year-round. Some combine it with a trip to Ni'ihau. If you do Na Pali in winter, expect bigger seas.

There are two main snorkeling spots: *Nu'alolo* (which is pretty good) and a spot near Polihale that the bigger boats often use called *Makole* (which is pretty bad). If you're at *Makole*, the best snorkeling is away from shore, not toward it.

Some of these boating companies give you discounts for booking online.

These passengers know what Hollywood knows...Na Pali is mesmerizing.

What & Who

We've spent a lot of time anonymously reviewing these boats, and here's the deal. If it's May through September and you really want to see Na Pali, you want to do this from the north shore—*period*. That means you want **Na Pali Sea Breeze**, **Na Pali Catamaran** or **Captain Sundown**, or if you want no frills, **North Shore Charters**. As mentioned, *nothing* a west side company can do can compete with the route these four take. They could probably *flog* you on this trip, and they'd still be better than anyone leaving from Port Allen. If you can't book these or it's not these summer months (April and October are borderline), we recommend **HoloHolo** and **Liko Kaua'i**.

Our favorite is **Na Pali Sea Breeze** (828–1285). They have a 34-foot power cat, carrying at most 16 people for $150. Capt. Bob was a resident of the Taylor Camp in 1970 (see page 55) and has over 30 years experience on Kaua'i waters. He's a salty dog with a profound knowledge of the coast that other companies lack. The deli lunch is better than most, with a variety of sandwiches. The boat is comfy even when full. Leaving from 'Anini, it takes 10 more minutes to get to Na Pali than the Hanalei guys, but the better amenities are worth it.

Next on our list is **Na Pali Catamaran** (826–6853). Their 34-foot power cat (no sailing) takes up to 16 people. $150 for the 4-hour tour includes snorkeling at Nu'alolo (they're often the first one there for the morning tour) and a cheap deli lunch. There's no shade and no trampoline to lie on with this narrow cat, but we really like how they'll usually go into the sea caves during the trip. Morning is much better than afternoon here. We like them because of their route and their low profile that lets them enter the caves.

Another north shore catamaran, **Captain Sundown** (826–5585), uses a 40-foot sailing catamaran. They'll usually sail part of the way down the coast far from shore, then motor back a bit closer. Because of the tall mast, they don't go into any of the caves, which is a shame. Their narration is not very good (or accurate), but the boat is comfortable and they'll usually only take 15 or so, making it feel nice and roomy. Food is minimal—nothing at breakfast, deli sandwich at lunch and cookies just before you return to your starting point at the Hanalei River. Consider riding the net (trampoline) on the way out. (The way back is much wetter and bumpier.) Although they do go out sometimes in the winter, it's rougher at that time on the part of the north shore that these boats explore. We believe they are flat out *too expensive*, and if they didn't have a north shore launching point, we'd probably be talking stink about them. Morning 5–6 hour trip is $199, afternoon (less recommended—no snorkeling) is $150. This includes your *mandatory* gratuity.

All the north shore companies are good about letting you venture away from the boat a bit during your snorkel at Nu'alolo.

Na Pali Coast Hanalei (826–6114) is also out of Hanalei, but their 28-foot boat and $150 3½ hour tours aren't as good as the other north shore companies.

HoloHolo Charters (335–0815) has a large, 65-foot power catamaran. Their trips are distinguished in that they go to the "forbidden" island of Ni'ihau. For $179, the 7-hour trip leaves in the morning from Port Allen and makes a beeline to Kalalau Beach on Na Pali. In light seas they're close to shore; heavier swells call for greater distance. Then they tour part of Na Pali before heading to Ni'ihau where they snorkel. (Clean, clear water and lots of fish, but currents can sometimes make snorkeling there more work.) Continental breakfast and a good deli lunch included. After the snorkeling, the open bar serves drinks, but they refuse to serve cookies until they're 5 minutes from port. (Maybe they're afraid you'll toss them otherwise.)

There are two large trampolines at the bow for sunning, but they and the entire bow section are off limits most of the time while motoring. Easy steps into and out of the water from the boat. HoloHolo is a good outfit and is easy to recommend. The boat is good, pretty stable, there's plenty of shade available, and the crew is very professional. They have a freshwater shower hose, adequate snorkel gear but no wetsuits available. Our only complaint is that the boat design makes it feel crowded on nice days. Most of the seating is inside, but when it's reasonably calm and sunny most people want to be outside, which is somewhat spartan and lacking in seating, so people tend to crowd around the railings.

Their sunset tour is $99 for appetizers, beer, wine and champagne.

They also have a smaller cat called the Leila, but we don't recommend it as much.

Liko Kaua'i Cruises (338–0333) offers a relaxing 5-hour tour of Na Pali on a 49-foot power catamaran with 34 people. You'll leave from Kikiaola Small Boat Harbor near Kekaha and cruise north up the coast, often going as far as Ke'e Beach if the weather's good. (That's farther than any other west shore power cat goes, which pleases us greatly.) On the way back you stop and snorkel at Nu'alolo Kai or sometimes lousy Makole. Liko, a native Hawaiian, narrates with legends and stories. $140 for adults, $95 for keiki (kids), it includes snacks and sandwiches. They do a particularly good job with kids. Afternoon/sunset tours also available in the summer.

Catamaran Kahanu (645–6176) is a small boat (20 max, which would be pretty tight) run by a gruff but likable Hawaiian captain. This is a small outfit, and what they lack in cushion (literally) is made up with their family feel. But like a real family (at least one of my uncles) they can be a tad patronizing by listing all the ways you could die on the water that they themselves can handle easily. Might be true, but it can be a bit grating. Overall, a pretty good trip, however, with a tasty lunch. Morning 5-hour trips from Port Allen are $144. Three-hour sunset trips are $111. They sometimes give family discounts.

Other Big Boats

Captain Andy's Sailing Adventures (335–6833) is the biggest operator on the island, leaving from Port Allen, and they tend to run pretty tight ships. They have three types of boats—their luxury catamaran (Southern Star), regular catamarans and their rigid hull rafts. The Southern Star is large (65-foot), plush and comfortable, and their 6-hour snorkel tour has a good BBQ lunch and free beer and wine for $159. If they take their full load of 49 people, it's *a bit* tight. But otherwise, it's an easy trip to recommend. Their 5-hour Na Pali trips in the smaller

catamarans are $139. Snorkeling when conditions permit, but at lousy Makole. Deli lunch with free beer and wine. It would be a better product if they didn't pack up to *49* people on their nice 55-foot catamarans (and it *feels* crowded). You're best off if there's *more* than 49, because then they'll split the group onto two boats. These are sleek sailing cats, but they only sail a short time, and when they *do* raise the sail, it seems to activate the cookie-tossing instinct in some people, especially if they're using the indoor shade. But they are pretty capable sailboats, which will excite sailing enthusiasts. Sunset tours are $139 with a hot buffet and snorkeling. They also have a Zodiac tour for $159. Their excellent dinner cruise is described in ISLAND DINING on page 239. With so many boats, they have *way* too many options to describe here.

Kaua'i Sea Tours (826–7254) leaves from Port Allen for Na Pali trips for $149. They have a 60-foot power/sailing cat called the Lucky Lady, which rides well. Think of this as a power cat, because at best they'll probably only raise the sails *while motoring* downwind. (The sails are more for decoration since this type of vessel sails like a pig.) They also use a 24-foot rigid-hull inflatable that lands at Nu'alolo (in the summer) for $155, but it's not in the same league as Na Pali Explorer's nicer inflatable. They also have a dinner cruise described on page 239.

Blue Dolphin Charters (335–5553) has two catamarans called Blue Dolphin I and II, similar to the Lucky Lady above. Up to 49 people, continental breakfast (good cinnamon rolls) and deli lunch. They have a slide into the water. $149 for Na Pali trips. You can try SCUBA for an extra $35, which is quite reasonable. (But we've seen them very hesitant to give you a wetsuit. Don't believe their ridiculous overestimates of the water temps. You divers *want* a shorty in the summer, and a *full-sized* suit in the winter.) Note that divers and snorkelers usually won't stray far from the boat. Some days they also offer a Ni'ihau trip similar to HoloHolo's for $196. The crew is pretty good and their narrations fair. Plenty of shade, but avoid the inside seats at the front of the cabin. You never sail; at best they'll motor sail downwind. For us, the deal-killer with this company is that they *make* you wear awkward flotation devices, even if you're an Olympic swimmer. If you want to wear one, that's fine, but the mandatory policy is annoying. You won't be able to dive under or get around as easily. Sunset tours are $105.

Rigid-Hull Inflatables (RIBS)

North Shore Charters (828-1379) leaves out of 'Anini Beach *in the summer* with 14 passengers in their 26-foot boat. It has inflatable sides but with a hard hull—amazingly smooth and fast for a Zodiac. No frills, no shade, deli sandwiches, and you'll snorkel at Nu'alolo for $140. The best route of the RIBs.

Na Pali Explorer (338-9999) leaves from the west side and heads north in their 48-foot boat. There is some shade on board. They also have a less impressive 26-foot boat with no shade. $149 for the morning 4½-hour Na Pali/ snorkel trip. These include continental breakfast and a light lunch. $105 for the 3-hour Na Pali dash, no snorkeling.

Na Pali Riders (742-6331) has a 4½-hour trip, but it's a decidedly mixed bag. Think of them as a low-budget trip. On the positive side they leave from Kikiaola Harbor and, during the summer season, they go all the way to Ke'e on the north shore, so you'll see all of Na Pali. (Winter is whale watching heading south.) When they encounter dolphins, they get amazingly close. Also, inflatables can be fun on calm seas. But if seas aren't reasonably smooth, it's a rough ride because you'll feel every bump. On the negative side there's no shade or restroom, and they only serve drinks and snacks. Price is $120. Afternoon trip is cheaper, but snottier seas in a Zodiac ain't fun.

While you're eating lunch on Na Pali...so are they.

Boating Tips

Many companies offer morning and afternoon trips. Morning trips usually have snorkeling and better food on board. Morning is also when you're more likely to encounter smoother seas and better weather, so that's what we recommend.

Be wary of the information given during narrations. Many boat companies, like their helicopter brethren, are particularly prone to repeating inaccurate nonsense in their attempt to "educate" you, and we've seen some who literally made it up as they went along.

Seasickness can strike anyone. If you're concerned that it will be a problem, strongly consider taking Dramamine or something similar at least an hour *before* you leave. (The night before and morning of are best. It's useless to take it once you're on the boat.) Also, avoid any alcohol the night before. (A *big* no-no.) No greasy foods before or during the trip. And some think that citrus juices are a cause of seasickness. Ginger is a very good preventative/treatment. Below deck or in anything enclosed is a bad place to be if you're worried about getting seasick. Without a reference point, you're much more likely to let 'er rip. Scopolamine patches work but have side effects, including (occasionally) blurred vision that can last a week. (Been there, done that, on a 10-day boat trip.) If you're feeling sick, put something cold on the back of your neck. As far as the Ni'ihau trips are concerned, we've had people tell us they were prone to seasickness and ask where they should sit. The answer is...on land. The boats can be mighty rockin' in that channel between the islands, and if you have a history of easy-queasy, that trip might not be for you. Coming back from Ni'ihau is almost always rough.

From the west shore, the best views are off the right (starboard) side going out to Na Pali and off the left (port) side coming back. It's the opposite when you leave from the north shore. Also remember that most boats are a lot smoother in the back than the front, but you may inhale diesel fumes back there. Just slightly ahead of the back seats is our preferred position.

People come off these trips *toasted*, especially in the summer. Make sure you slather on the sunscreen early and often, or you'll be sorry for the rest of your trip.

Since most trips involve driving early in the morning, consider doing the trip early in your vacation—when your body clock is still on mainland time, and it's easier to rise early.

Most companies make you remove your shoes. Also, agendas are not carved in stone. Weather, seas and opportunities along the way can alter the best laid plans. So be flexible.

There are a number of smaller boat companies with smaller boats that are crowded and have no shade, and we don't recommend them for these waters.

PARASAILING

Parasailing is outlawed on Kaua'i. Hey, *that* was easy.

Kaua'i is the only Hawaiian island to offer river trips, and there are two ways to do it. You can take a riverboat ride up the Wailua River (often referred to as the only navigable river in all Hawai'i, but this is a relative term) or paddle your own kayak. **Smith's Motorboat Service** (821–6892) goes 3 miles up the Wailua River and stops at the Fern Grotto, a large natural amphitheater with ferns all about. This is a popular place to get married. It's 30 minutes each way with entertainment and interesting information provided throughout. They spend 30–45 minutes at the site. $20 per person, and they leave many

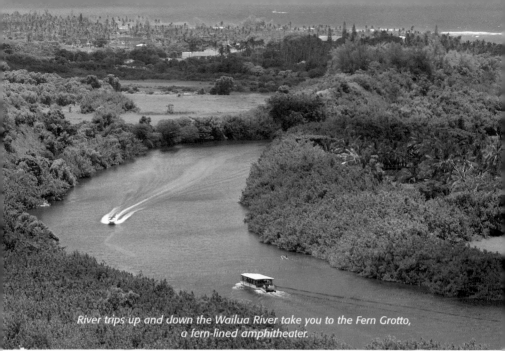

River trips up and down the Wailua River take you to the Fern Grotto, a fern-lined amphitheater.

times each day in their 100+ passenger boats. If you've heard of the Fern Grotto before and seen photos, be forewarned that those photos, even in current ads, might be *very* old. Hurricane 'Iwa in 1982 thinned out the ferns, and the closing of the nearby sugar company—and its leaky reservoir above the cave that accidentally created the grotto in the first place—has resulted in a greatly diminished attraction. They've tried to rejuvenate it somewhat, but it's still a bit of a letdown.

You can also rent a kayak at any of several places and paddle the Wailua, the Hanalei River, the Kalihiwai River or the Hule'ia Stream. The best thing about kayaking the Wailua River isn't the Fern Grotto. (In fact, they discourage landing kayaks there.) Instead, it's the overall scenery and a hike to a waterfall, if you like. See KAYAKING.

Kaua'i is justly famous for many things: its incomparable lushness, gor-

geous beaches and balmy nights. But Kaua'i is not famous for its diving. This is a shame because Kaua'i has some very good dive spots. Turtles are common, and many of them are downright gregarious. Lava tubes, ledges and walls are sprinkled around the island. Fish are abundant and varied. Coral growth is not as good as around the Big Island—at 22° latitude, Kaua'i is on the fringe of the coral belt. Kaua'i's many rivers and streams cut visibility in some areas, but you can still see more than 100 feet on good days.

Granted, you might find better conditions on the Kona coast of the Big Island or around Lana'i. It is dryer there and the lava's porous, so the ocean receives virtually no runoff. But this should not dissuade you from enjoying the wondrous underwater sights the Garden Island has to offer.

Kaua'i's ocean pattern is small summer surf on the north shore, larger summer surf on the south shore, and the opposite during winter months, so you should plan your diving activities accordingly. Summer is very popular and the best companies book up early, so call them as soon as you know when you want to dive. The dive boat operators conduct their tours on the south shore year-round since the local government doesn't allow the boats to moor on the north shore. Some also have dives on the west side at Mana Crack and at Lehua Rock off the coast of Ni'ihau. Those dives are generally considered advanced due to the depths and currents involved, and prices are higher than the spread we show in the table. The Ni'ihau dive in particular involves at least 4 hours travel time (round trip), so those who get seasick (and those who aren't sure) should take Dramamine or Bonine *before* they depart.

Off Ni'ihau, however, you're treated to ridiculously clear water, lots of big life (sharks, rays, dolphins and your best chance at a Hawaiian monk seal) and a close view of the "Forbidden Island." (The Robinsons, who own Ni'ihau, *hate* it when you call it that.) See ADVENTURES chapter for more on this dive. Book in advance to ensure space.

So you'll know **our perspective** when we review companies, we should tell you what we do and don't like when we go on a dive. On a bad dive, the dive master takes the group on a non-stop excursion that keeps you kicking the whole time. No time to stop and explore the nooks and crannies. Good outfits will give you a briefing, tell you about some of the endemic species here, what to look for and will point out various things on the dives, keeping it moving but not too fast. Bad outfits kick a lot. Good outfits explain the unique qualities of Hawai'i's environment. Bad dive masters may tell you what *they* saw (but *you* missed). Good companies work around your needs, wishes and desires. Bad companies keep everyone on a short leash. Good dive masters know their stuff and share it with you. Bad dive masters don't know squat but imply they know it all in order to impress you. As divers, we tend to like companies that wander toward the boat for the latter part of the dive and allow you to go up when you are near the end of your tank, as opposed to everyone going up when the heaviest breather has burned up his/her bottle.

During times when we feel the diving conditions are bad (poor vis or big swells), we like to call around and ask about con-

Dive Operator	Services Available	Price of Dive	Rent Gear For a Day	Boat Size / Passengers	Dive Computer	Ni'ihau 3-Tank Dive	Dive Certification	Rx Masks
Aquatic Adventures 645–0927	Boat Dives & Shore Dives	$159–$295 (2 tank)	No	40' / 12	Yes	$320	$450	Yes
Bubbles Below 332–7333	Boat Dives & Shore Dives	$140–$325 (2 tank)	No	35' / 8 32' / 6	Included	$340–$370	$450	No
Fathom Five 742–6991	Dive Shop & Boat Dives	$125–$195 (2 tank)	$40	25' / 6 35' / 6	Included	$350–$390	$275–$495	Yes
Kaua'i Down Under 742–9534	Shore Dives	$119–$149 (2 tank)	No	N/A	No	None	$375–400	Yes
Ocean Quest 742–6991	Shore Dives	$90–$150 (2 tank)	$40	N/A	No	None	$275–$495	Yes
Seasport Divers 742–9303	Dive Shop & Boat Dives	$125–$150 (2 tank)	$45	32' / 12 48' / 18	Included	$310–$350	$245–$400	Yes

ditions. We appreciate the companies who admit it's bad, and we hold it against those who tell us how wonderful conditions are.

If You've Never Dived Before

If this is your first dive, the recommendation is a no-brainer. **Fathom Five** wins by default since other companies have poor systems. For instance, **Seasport Divers** soaks up too much pre-dive time since they make you do a pre-dive class in a pool (perhaps the day before) prior to taking you on your boat dive. If you don't do well in the pool, they won't take you on the boat. We don't think that such measures are necessary. Most first timers in Hawai'i do fine going straight to the ocean, *if* the instructor does a good job, which, fortunately, **Fathom Five** does. They will take you out for an introductory shore dive for $100 (one-tank) or $140 (two-tank).

Kaua'i Down Under has a one-tank shore intro for $109 and **Aquatic Adventures** has them for $110. Some of the other dive companies encourage you to do your intro off their boat. That's a concept we disagree with since shore dives make beginners *far* more comfortable than jumping from a boat into water over their heads with unfamiliar gear.

If you're interested in getting **certified** or did your book work on the mainland and want an open water referral, **Fathom Five** is your best bet. The open water referral method allows you to do your class work at home, saving your Kaua'i vacation for the *fun stuff*.

Recommended for Certified Divers

As anonymous certified divers (who sometimes pretend to be novices), we are able to experiment with different operators. The outfits we recommend are **Fathom Five** and **Bubbles Below** for boat dives and **Ocean Quest** for shore dives. They are all well-qualified, professional and knowledgeable. **Fathom Five** and their shore dive arm, **Ocean Quest**, is probably the best outfit on the island. We've been impressed at how they run their boat dives, and the personalized service really shows. They use a 25-foot and 35-foot 6-pack, so they're able to keep the groups smaller and respond more to what individual divers want—a nice touch. As for their Ocean Quest arm, we've never seen a better shore dive outfit. Experienced divers will love their shore dives, and beginners will find them perfect for their introduction to the world of SCUBA. In addition to standard 2-tank dives, they have twilight dives, night dives, premium 3-tank dives and Ni'ihau dives, including an extraordinary overnight dive.

Bubbles Below has discovered many of the island's great dive spots, and they are pretty good with customers. During the summer their Mana Crack dives can be exciting. They say they'll take a maximum of 8 on their 35-foot Radon, but you'll want to verify that when you book. They also have a 32-foot power catamaran that takes 6 people. Na Pali and North Shore dives are pricier.

Sometimes it's tempting to go with the cheapest dive operators. Remember that if you're herded in and out with a cheap company that doesn't know the underwater terrain, you may find that your "better deal" was no bargain at all. The spreads in our price table often reflect a short boat ride vs. a long trip to the north shore.

Dive Shops

There are a couple of dive *shops* (as opposed to dive operators) on the island. Although not the biggest, the best is **Fathom Five**. Although their shop is on the small side, they have *two* boats (they tend to use one for more experienced divers, the other for rustier divers), so they don't mix the two unless you *want*

Tunnels Beach sports a fabulous reef, perfect for snorkeling, swimming and SCUBA.

them to. (Certifieds will *love* that.) They feed you better than anyone else, get you on the boat quicker and have a good ascent policy. We also like how they'll keep and rinse your personal gear, if you dive on multiple days. They're on Po'ipu Road in Koloa.

Seasport Divers in Po'ipu (with a smaller satellite office in Kapa'a) is the largest shop on the island with the best selection if you're looking to *buy* gear, but we don't recommend their boat dives as much, except perhaps their Ni'ihau trips in the summer.

For **renting gear**, either of the two shops will do fine.

For the heavy breathers among you, **Bubbles Below**, **Fathom Five,** and **Seasport** have 100s available, so feel free to *suck 'em up.*

Dive computers are available for your own *independent* dives and can only be rented from **Fathom Five**. *Disposable* underwater cameras in a watertight box for snorkeling are available at most gro-

cery stores and sundry shops. **Fathom Five** rents better cameras for SCUBA.

Some of the dive boats on Kaua'i feed you little or nothing between dives. I don't know about you, but I'm tempted to gnaw on the side of the boat after a dive. Bring a package of cookies with you. You'll probably be able to sell them to other hungry divers at prices confiscatory enough to pay for your dive. *I have a bid of $9 for a chocolate chip cookie...Do I hear $9?*

Shorties are usually sufficient for most people *in the summer only.* Surface water temperatures range from a low of 73.4° in February to a high of 80° in October. Any company that will *only* provide you with shorties doesn't seem to care much about your comfort. Or maybe we've just lived here too long and have gotten wussy about the cold.

Between morning and afternoon dives, morning is almost always best.

Nitrox (or enriched air) is available at **Fathom Five, Bubbles Below** and **Seasport Divers**.

Kaua'i has many boat dive spots. Since the more resourceful operators are always finding new spots, and since you basically go where the boat operators go, we'll forgo a detailed description of all boat dive destinations. Suffice it to say that Sheraton Caves, General Store, Brennecke's Ledge, Turtle Bluffs, Amber's Arches and Fishbowl are all popular. Some sites, such as Sheraton Caves, are nice but a bit over-dived.

Remember not to drive up to Waimea Canyon or the Kalalau Lookout after diving. As far as your nitrogen level is concerned, you're flying.

Below is a list of the best shore dives on the island:

- **Ke'e Beach, north shore**—If the seas are flat on a calm summer day, this area offers interesting shallow relief. The area near the reef drop-off is good, again on calm days.
- **Tunnels, north shore**—Easy access, lots of turtles, reef sharks, lava tubes, caves and nice underwater relief. Tunnels' allure is not its visibility, but the dramatic underwater topography. *If* you dive with someone who really knows the reef, this is unquestionably the best shore dive on the island and is often better than a boat dive. Low tide is best.
- **The Hole, north shore**—Located just off the St. Regis Resort. Like the name says, a hole in the reef. Acceptable underwater relief and easy access.
- **Kahala Point, east shore**—Entry and exit is a bugger on the lava rocks with crashing surf. Underwater relief is good, and there are lots of fish. Near Anahola Beach Park.
- **Koloa Landing, south shore**—Easy entry, usually calm conditions year-round and decent coral near the shore. After slightly murky water on entry, the sea is usually quite clear. High tide is best.

Skydiving is available at Port Allen Airport on the west side. You don't need us to tell you whether you should try this or not. It's either, *Yeah, cool. Where do I sign?* or, *Yeah, right. Are you out of your mind?*

The company here, **Skydive Kaua'i** (335–5859), isn't in the same league as those at Dillingham on O'ahu. Skydiving there is a big business, and the reliable onshore breeze on O'ahu's north shore makes it a pretty good place to do tandem jumps. This company is newer and lacks the track record of O'ahu companies. Their plane doesn't exactly inspire confidence, and you're grateful that there are parachutes onboard. And Port Allen isn't an ideal spot to do tandem skydives. It's a peninsula, surrounded by water on three sides, and shifting winds make it more difficult to target your landing area. In fact, during our jump, a solo jumper missed the airport entirely and had to land at a nearby park. You're equipped with an inflatable life vest in case you drop into the water, and the jumpmasters were professional and seemed honest about describing the inadequacies of this jump location. But hey, as long as you understand the risks here, you'll still have the thrill of leaping from a plane at 10,000 feet, the overload of adrenaline that makes things feel like slow motion when you exit the aircraft, and the blissful satisfaction of seeing the parachute inflate above you and your instructor.

It'll run you $229 plus $2 for every pound you weigh over 200 pounds. You can buy a pretty slick DVD of your jump for $79.

If you have ever looked into a saltwater aquarium and marveled at the diversity of the fish life, snorkeling is an experience you might want to try. Anyone who has ever hovered over hundreds of colorful fish can attest to the thrill you feel being in their environment.

Where to snorkel depends on how good you are and what kind of experience you want. The best place for beginners is **Lydgate Beach Park** in Wailua. There you will find an area protected by a ring of boulders that shields you from the strong ocean. Mornings are best. The intermediate snorkeler will find **Ke'e** or **Tunnels** on the north shore to be fabulous during the calm, warmer months. **Hideaways** is also great during calm seas. **Po'ipu Beach Park** on the south shore usually offers good snorkeling and calm seas in cooler months on either side of the tombolo. The BEACHES chapter has a description of all the beaches and the different characteristics they possess.

As far as gear goes, there are numerous places to rent gear on the island. We always snorkel wearing water shoes and divers' fins (which fit over water shoes). This way we can enter and exit the water without worrying about stepping on anything. Cheap water shoes can be found at many places, including Kmart. Bootie socks or women's thin, ankle-length socks will keep you from rubbing the top of your tootsies raw. Divers' fins can be rented at most dive shops. If enough people ask snorkel companies about them, they will start to carry them, too.

If you're looking to buy snorkel gear, you can pick it up pretty cheap at Wal-mart in Lihu'e on the highway or Kmart in Kukui Grove Shopping Center, also in Lihu'e.

Many people prefer to rent gear when they get here and leave it in the trunk, so they may snorkel when the opportunity arises. Your hotel or condo may have gear available. If they don't, try any of the following:

North Shore Rentals

Hanalei Surf Company (826–9000) has pretty good equipment for only $6 per day, $22 per week. *Rx* masks available for nothing extra.

Pedal 'n Paddle (826–9069) in Hanalei rents gear for $5 per day, $20 per week.

East Shore Rentals

Boss Frog (822–4334) on the highway in Kapa'a has decent gear for $2–$8 per day, $10–$30 for the week. *Rx* masks available.

Seasport Divers (823–9222) on the highway in Kapa'a has similar rates, and they also have divers' fins (the kind worn over water shoes) available.

Snorkel Bob's (823–9433 or 742–2206) has two locations: one on the highway in Kapa'a and the other located on Po'ipu Road past Koloa. You're likely to be drawn by the $2.50 per day gear, but be tempted by the $9 or even *$11* gear. Although the equipment is pretty good, it's not *that* good. $6 gear is your best bet. Weekly rental is $9–$35. *Rx* masks available. You can also rent on Kaua'i and return equipment Snorkel Bob's on another island.

South Shore Rentals

Nukumoi Beach & Surf Shop (742–8019) rents beach equipment, including snorkel gear, boogie boards and the like. A good selection. Convenient, since they are right near Po'ipu Beach Park. $6 per day, $20 per week.

Fathom Five (742–6991) in Poʻipu has gear for $6 per day, $30 per week. Divers' fins available.

See also **Snorkel Bob's** listed above.

Snorkel Tours

If you've never snorkeled before and desire lessons and assistance, **SeaFun Kauaʻi** (245–6400) offers guided snorkel tours for $80 per person (children 5–12 cost $63). We once tried to teach a friend to snorkel and were unsuccessful even getting her to put her face in the water (she was terrified). We were very impressed that in only a few minutes they had her snorkeling like an expert. Even *non-swimmers* go out with them. For this price, they'll pick you up at some hotels, take you to a place like Tunnels or Lawaʻi Beach and provide you with gear, wetsuit (which helps you float), lunch and assistance. Prescription masks are available.

Snorkel Tips

- Tropical gloves make snorkeling much more enjoyable. You can grab rocks to maneuver in shallow or surgy areas. (Please don't grab coral, however.)

Even when the ocean looks angry, Lydgate's protected ocean pool offers relatively safe snorkeling on all but the highest surf days. Morning is best.

Hawaiian Reefs—*Why is it that...?*

What is that crackling sound, like bacon frying, I always hear while snorkeling or diving? For years this baffled people. In the early days of submarines, the sound interfered with sonar operations. Finally we know the answer. It's hidden snapping shrimp defining their territory. One variety is even responsible for all the dark cracks and channels you see in smooth lobe coral. A pair creates the channels, then "farms" the algae inside.

Why are there so few shellfish in Hawai'i? It's too warm for some of the more familiar shellfish (which tend to be filter-feeders, and Hawaiian waters don't have as much stuff to filter). But Hawai'i has more shellfish than most people are aware of. They hide well under rocks and in sand. Also, people tend to collect shells (which is illegal), and that depletes the numbers.

Why do coral cuts take so long to heal? Coral contains a live animal. When you scrape coral, it leaves proteinaceous matter in your body, which takes much longer for your body to dispatch.

Why do some of the reefs appear dead? Much of the "coral" you see around Kaua'i isn't the kind of coral you're used to. It's called coralline algae, which secretes calcium carbonate. It's not dead; it's *supposed* to look like that.

What do turtles eat? Dolphins. (Just teasing.) They primarily eat plants growing on rocks, as well as jellyfish when they are lucky enough to encounter them. Unfortunately for turtles and lucky for us, jellyfish aren't numerous here.

Is it harmful when people play with an octopus? Yes, if the octopus gets harmed while trying to get it out of its hole. Best to leave them alone.

Why does the ocean rarely smell fishy here in Hawai'i? Two reasons. We have relatively small tide changes, so the ocean doesn't strand large amounts of smelly seaweed at low tide. Also, the water is fairly sterile compared to mainland water, which owes much of its smell to algae and seaweed that thrives in the bacteria-rich runoff from industrial sources.

Why is the water so clear here? Because relatively little junk is poured into our water compared to the mainland. Also, natural currents tend to flush the water with a continuous supply of fresh, clean ocean water.

Why do my ears hurt when I dive deep, and how are scuba divers able to get over it? Because the increasing weight of the ocean is pressing on your ears the farther down you go. Divers alleviate this by equalizing their ears. Sounds high tech, but that simply means holding your nose while trying to blow out of it. This forces air into the Eustachian tubes, creating equal pressures with the outside ocean. (It doesn't work if your sinuses are clogged.) Anything with air between it gets compressed. So if you know someone who gets a headache whenever they go under water...well, they must be an airhead.

- Use *Sea Drops* or another brand of anti-fog goop. Spread it *thinly* on the inside of a dry mask, then do a quick rinse. The old-fashioned method of spitting in the mask is not very effective. (It's particularly frightening to see tobacco chewers do this. Yuck!)
- Don't use your arms much, or you will spook the fish. Gentle fin motion. Any rapid motion can cause the little critters to scatter.
- Fish are hungriest and most appreciative in the morning (before their coffee).
- If you have a mustache and have trouble with a leaking mask, try a little Vaseline. Don't get any on the glass—it can get *really* ugly.
- In general, it's not a good idea to feed the fish. It upsets the balance by giving some fish an unnatural advantage over others and has the perverse effect of reducing both fish counts and variety. That said, the fish at **Lydgate** are such longtime people-food junkies that you won't do any harm feeding them there. You can find rabbit or fish food at most grocery stores, Kmart or Walmart. Fill a Ziploc bag and, at the proper time, make a small slit in a corner to let the water fill the bag. You can dispense the food by squeezing the bag and using a slight wiggle motion to attract the fish. Be careful that the zip part doesn't unzip—a common occurrence. If you can get a few fish interested and they start darting around, others will come. Dispense the food *sparingly*; too much and they will grab a bite and run. If they have to compete, they will increase in numbers. Too much food also makes the water murky—fish don't like murky water and will depart. If you don't want to use rabbit food, a tightly compressed ball of bread works well. Again, dispense *sparingly*. Don't use frozen peas. Although many think that this food is benign, in fact, it can be harmful due to the fish's inability to digest it properly. We cannot stress enough the importance of not losing your plastic bag in the water. If a turtle encounters it, he will surely think it is a jellyfish and choke to death. If you encounter a bag discarded by a thoughtless jerk, please pick it up and wedge it in your suit until you get out of the water.
- Several manufacturers, including Kodak and Fuji, sell disposable waterproof cameras. They are cheap and can provide wonderful souvenirs.

If you've always wanted to see what it's like to SCUBA dive but are a bit worried or don't want to go through the hassle, try SNUBA. That's where you take an air tank and place it on a raft that floats above you. Anyone 8 or older can SNUBA. From the raft there's a 20-foot hose attached to a regulator. There you are, underwater up to 20 feet deep, no tank on your back, no hassle. You'll have some instruction before you go under, and the dive master stays with you the whole time. It can be an exciting way to see the underwater world for the first time. **SNUBA Tours of Kaua'i** (823–8912). They do their thing off Lawa'i Beach on the south shore. $69. It should take a little over an hour.

If you're looking to be pampered, there are several spas on the island worth mentioning, and the range is huge. You can go from a spoiled, opulent setting to someone's house where clothing throughout your experience is optional.

The grandest tropical experience by far is **Anara Spa** (742–1234) at The Hyatt in Po'ipu, and their fabulous 45,000 sq. ft. full-service spa is guaranteed to turn you to jelly. It's pricey, but their attention to detail and overall surroundings make it worth the splurge. (You'll love their lava rock showers and their optional thatched huts.) You also get full use of all spa facilities.

The most opulent is **Halele'a Spa** (826–9644) at the St. Regis Princeville. Super rich decor (you won't want to leave the showers), and they really sweat the details. Though the surroundings are not particularly Hawaiian or tropical unless you're really paying attention, their services are top of the line. They have adequate gender-specific lounges, but the co-ed lounge is the one with all the trimmings. Also, if you get a massage, you're allowed to come back later in the day and continue to enjoy the spa's amenities.

Spa by the Sea (823–1488) at the Waipouli Beach Resort in central Kapa'a is your next best bet. The facilities are nice (though there are no day spa facilities), and after your treatment, you can access their incredible meandering pool with its waterfalls. Good shower and locker room facilities and professional staff. Our only gripe is that although they have tons of hair-related products to use, most of the other lotions and potions you'd like to have are absent.

(Aunty) Angeline's Lomi Kaua'i (822–3235) is in a category all by itself. Forget the grand spa facilities of the resorts. This experience takes place in Angeline's home/farm and the atmosphere is casual, open and co-ed. This is not for the bashful since nudity is common for your treatments, which includes the co-ed steam room. (They will work with the

more modest as best they can.) Hawaiian chants start things off, and for $150 you get two hours of treatment, including a four-handed lomi lomi massage. Nice people, family-run, and they've been around for decades, but don't be surprised to hear house noises throughout your treatment. BYOT.

Ho, braddah, da shreddin's da kine! (Just trying to get you in the mood.) Surfing is synonymous with Hawai'i. And why not? Hawaiians invented *da bugga*. Learning isn't as hard as you may think. Depending on conditions they may put you on a large, soft board the size of a garage door (well…almost), so it's fairly easy to master, at least at this level.

Hanalei Bay is justly famous islandwide as one of the best and *most challenging* in Hawai'i. The chapter on BEACHES can assist you in picking beaches with surfing possibilities. **Cannons, Hanalei Bay, Kalihiwai, Kealia, Kalapaki, Infinities (Pakala Beach)**, are all well-known surf spots. If you want lessons, the best teacher we've seen on the south shore is **Learn to Surf** (826–7612). For $40 they'll spend 90 minutes with you at whichever beach has the right conditions. Good attitude and good place to rent a board.

Most of the companies on the south side teach at Kiahuna Beach. They might seem distracted and disinterested, but that's only because they're distracted and disinterested. But you'll probably eventually ride a wave here. Companies there include **Margo Oberg Surfing School** (332–6100) and **Garden Island Surf School** (652–4841).

Titus Kinimaka Hawaiian School of Surfing (652–1116) teaches out of Hanalei Bay, and you won't have the same crowd issue as on the south shore. With the sandier bottom at Hanalei (the south shore is reefier) it might be worth the higher price ($55 for 90 minutes).

Hawaiian Surfing Adventures (482–0749) has 2-hour group lessons for $65, $95 for private. We found them patient and eager to get you riding your first wave. They mostly go out of the north shore, too.

If you just want to rent a board, contact your hotel activity desk or any of the following: **Progressive Expressions** (742–6041) and **Nukumoi** (742–8019), both in Po'ipu, **Hanalei Surf Company** (826–9000) in Hanalei, or **Kaua'i Waterski, Surf & Kayak** (822–3574) in Kapa'a.

Contrary to what you see in the movies, beginners should look for crumbling waves, not the picturesque, breaking waves that slap the water.

By the way, a collection of surfboards is known in surfing lingo here as a *quiver*. A little kid surfer who doesn't have a job or car yet is called a *grommet*. Double *overhead* is when the waves are really big, and if you get good enough, you might get a chance to visit the *green room*. If someone says your girlfriend is *filthy*, it's a compliment. And a *landshark* is someone who says he surfs...but doesn't.

Stand Up Paddling, or **SUP**, is the latest craze in the surfing world. The hardest part about learning to surf is standing up on the board while it's moving. This sport has made things easier by giving you a board big enough to dance on. SUP boards are wider, thicker and longer than the biggest longboards people commonly learn to surf on. SUP instruction focuses on keeping your balance while using a tall paddle to move you into the waves. (This provides an excellent central core workout, with your feet—of all things—hurting the most.) The sight of people standing and dipping long paddles in the water has earned SUP surfers the subversive title

Local surfer dudes combing the beach for the perfect morning wave.

"janitors" or "moppers" from traditional surfers. The size of the board, as well as the fact that you are already standing up, gives you an advantage in catching waves early. You don't have to drop in exactly where the wave is breaking. Moppers can catch waves behind the lineup, but all surfing rules apply once you've caught the wave. Traditional surfers will be more inclined to drop in on your wave since they'll feel that you didn't work as hard to get it as they did.

Most of the surfing companies give lessons in SUP. We've had good luck with **Hawaiian Surfing Adventures**. Lessons start in the river. If you're comfortable on the board, you'll want to ask for a Stand Up *Surfing* lesson.

An alternative is **Outfitters Kaua'i** (742–9667). They have a trip that goes 2½ miles up the Hule'ia River (usually downwind), then adds 2½ miles of hiking in beautiful jungle and lunch at a waterfall with a deep pool to jump into. They you motorboat back upwind. Only downfall is that your paddling instructions are practically nil. You won't learn much about the sport. Also their guides are friendly but are often factually-challenged with their narrations. Also, though your group may repeatedly be told that the waterfall and "blue pool" (which is *not* blue) you're playing in is pure and clean, "straight from the top of Mt. Wai'ale'ale," analysis of topographic maps appear to us (we're not certified topographical surveyors) that the feeder stream water you're playing in comes from Haupu and through the Kipu cattle ranch. But it's a fun 5 hours for $120. Bring shoes that can get wet.

If you are into tennis, Kaua'i has no shortage of courts. Many hotels offer free courts for their guests. (Check our resort reviews.) If your hotel doesn't have one, you may contact the courts listed below to arrange court time. Kaua'i County has 10 separate municipal courts scattered around the island, some lighted. They won't be as pristine as the private courts, but they are free to the public. You can call the county at 241–4463 to get the location of the court nearest you.

Other places to rent a court include **Princeville Tennis Club** (826–3620), **Grand Hyatt** (742–1234) and **Kiahuna Tennis Club** (742–9533).

Tubing is where you sit in an inner tube and slowly drift along an old irrigation ditch. It's actually quite relaxing and calls for so little physical expenditure that you'll be tempted to look for your remote control and a can of beer while you're sitting there. Overall, however, we're kind of lukewarm on this. It's semi-lame, and there doesn't seem to be enough bang for your buck.

Kaua'i Backcountry Adventures (245–2506) does their tubing in an old sugar cane field between Lihu'e and Kapa'a. They'll pick you up in Hanama'ulu and drive you out to the area, narrating along the way. Then they'll put a helmet and gloves on you (wetsuits are extra), plunk you and 11 other people in inner tubes and off you go. This is *not* a whitewater adventure. Builders of these ditches didn't want to give up precious elevation quickly. So you'll putt-putt along at about 2 miles an hour. The best parts are the five tunnels, which represent about half your trip. They're dark, and the sounds of you and your fellow tubers bounce around in there.

Overall, the company does a pretty good job with what they have to work with, though you won't see much in the way of views—the ditch banks block most of that. Deli lunch is included, but you'll be forgiven if you think the price—$102 per person—is pretty darned steep considering you're only in the water an hour. People with bad backs might not like the posture they're in for the ride. They also have kid-size tubes, but they'll ride at the adult-sized price.

At **Kaua'i Waterski, Surf & Kayak** (822–3574), you can waterski the Wailua River. They rent a ski boat for $140 per hour, $75 for half hour. This includes the boat, driver, ski equipment and lessons, if you wish. Since you pay for the boat and not for skiing, non-skiers come along for free, up to 5 customers in the boat. If you've never skied before, it's *much* more tiring than it looks, but it's gobs of fun.

Although Maui sees more whales than Kaua'i, they are still very common here. Whales work in Alaska in the summer, building up fat, then vacation here from December or January to March or April, when the females give birth and the males sing the blues. Only the males

sing, and they all sing the same song, usually with their heads pointed down. Humpbacks don't eat while they're here and may lose ⅓ of their body weight during their Hawaiian vacation. (I doubt that many *human* visitors can make that same claim.) These gentle giants are very social and have been known to come right up to boats to check out the sightseers. Regulations prohibit the boat companies from initiating this kind of intimacy, but they get close enough to enjoy the whales. If you want to go on a whale watching boat tour, see OCEAN TOURS for a description of the tour boat operators.

Windsurfing

If you want to try windsurfing, you'll find that your options are limited on Kaua'i. Higher winds and more reefs mostly favor the experienced. A notable exception is 'Anini Beach. Celeste at **Windsurf Kaua'i** (828–6838) specializes in lessons for beginners on the north shore. Rates are $100 per person for 3 hours of lessons and practice. $25 for an hour for rental. Since county laws prohibit renting boards at the beach, you will probably have to pick up a board at another location if you don't want any lessons. Take it to Maha'ulepu or Salt Pond on the south shore, if you like. The west side just south of the Pacific Missile Range Facility can also be very exciting for the experienced. There the winds that wrap around Na Pali can create ideal conditions.

Kiteboarding/Kitesurfing

We're hesitant to give this sport its own section because so many people still don't know what it is, and because it's an offshoot of windsurfing. It's all the rage here in Hawai'i and is called

kitesurfing or **kiteboarding**. Imagine a modified surfboard, shorter and boxier than a normal board, with fins at both ends and straps for your feet. Then let a special, controllable, two-line kite drag you along. Like windsurfing, you don't have to go the direction the wind takes you, you have control (though not as much as on a windsurf board). It's harder to learn than windsurfing, but *oh, what fun it is!* More fun than windsurfing, if you can get over the steeper learning curve.

The problem for Kaua'i visitors is that it takes a big investment of time and money to learn, and we haven't found a reliable source for lessons. Some part time instructors are **Aloha** **Surf and Kiteboarding** (639–9283) and **Kaua'i Kiteboarding** (951–415–0261). If you have your heart set on kitesurfing, you're better off doing it on Maui where there is a larger learning infrastructure.

Ever seen movies where military commandos don a harness, hook a pulley onto a steel cable and zip down into the action? This is similar—without the hostile fire at the end. You'll need to weigh between 80 and 280 pounds.

A kitesurfer soars overhead. Though Kaua'i waters are difficult for beginners, more advanced kiters can snag as much as 50 feet of air.

There are four companies doing zip-lines on Kaua'i.

Outfitters Kaua'i (742–9667) has a 9-zip tour on Kipu Ranch near Lihu'e for $152. The longest is 1,800 feet and has two lines so couples can race each other or snap each other's picture during the zip. The zips are varied and fun and the company does a good job. Afterward, they take you to a swimming hole and waterfall, but see our comments on page 184 before swimming there.

Princeville Ranch Adventures (826–7669) has 9 lines. Most are under 500 feet. The last three are the best. There's not much hiking except on both sides of the last and longest line, King Kong. At 1,200 feet long, I got up to 30 MPH—not bad. Their scenery isn't as nice as the others, but the zipping is more diverse. They also have the best swimming hole (Swimming at a water-fall and lunch in addition to the zipping for $145. Zipping only is $125.) Only complaint is that some (not all) of the guides can be kind of attitudy, snippy or *too cool for school*.

Kaua'i Backcountry Adventures (245–2506) has 7 lines, the longest of

Ziplining can bring a new perspective on how you view the world.

which is 940 feet. But they're all over the same valley, and they seem so pre-occupied with "safety" that it takes some of the fun out of it. It's $130, which includes lunch and swimming in a stream.

Just Live (482–1295). Their concerns about safety seem more justified since they literally keep you in the trees—a big grove of Cook Island Pines—the whole time, so you'll need to stay clipped in. Think of it more like a ropes course with seven zips. You also have to cross two challenging bridges that will spook some of the less adventurous. Too bad their zips are shorter and slower—the longest is about 800 feet—and you're much closer to the ground than others. The waiting is longer between zips since they have more safety procedures to do up in the trees. They are the cheapest at $120. No lunch and no swimming. For $125 you do 3 zips, 3 bridges, rock wall climbing, a little repelling and get to go on their 60-foot swing, which is a scream (literally). In Puhi.

OK, so 16 miles is a long way to paddle, whether over one day or several. But the wind, current and luscious scenery help propel you along.

The activities described below are for the serious adventurer. They can be experiences of a lifetime. We are assuming that if you consider any of them that you are a person of sound judgment, capable of assessing risks. All adventures carry risks of one kind or another. Our descriptions below do not attempt to convey all risks associated with an activity. These activities are not for everyone. Good preparation is essential. In the end, it comes down to your own good judgment.

NA PALI KAYAK TRIP

If you really want adventure, consider a kayak trip down the Na Pali Coast. June through August are normally the only months where ocean conditions permit kayak transit. Kayakers put in at Ke'e Beach on the north shore, exiting at Polihale Beach on the west shore, a total of 16 miles. Along the way you'll encounter incomparable beauty, innumerable waterfalls and sea caves, pristine aquamarine seas, turtles, flying fish and possibly dolphins. If you're doing this as a maverick trip (below), at night you can camp on beautiful beaches, sleeping to the sound of the surf. The experience will stay with you for a lifetime.

There are two ways to do this trip—either on a guided tour or on your own. Guided tours do the entire trip in one day, offering a more structured—though less leisurely—way to see the coast. These trips, usually led by experienced guides, offer the *relative* safety of an expert. The drawbacks to this method are a lack of independent movement, a more brisk paddling pace (it can be *tough* to do in one day) and the lack of an opportunity to camp. **Na Pali Kayak** (826–6900), **Kayak Kaua'i** (826–9844) and **Outfitters Kaua'i** (742–9667). Of the three, we like Kayak Kaua'i for their deeper expertise. Expect to pay around $200–$225. They bring the gear, food and know-how; you bring the muscles.

If you want twice as much cost and hassle but *ten times* the gratification, you can do a **maverick trip**. Na Pali Kayak and Kayak Kaua'i will give you a personal guide who will travel with you to Kalalau and then make a judgment call as to whether you're up to continuing on your own. You'll need a permit with a kayak landing stamp for Kalalau before even applying for this service. See page 192 for info on permits and expect to pay between $275 and $400.

Doing it on your own allows *you* to set the pace and the schedule. You go when you like, how you like, where you like and at the speed you like. You can rent a two-person kayak, if you desire. Consideration of this method necessitates a dispassionate evaluation of your skills, abilities, strengths and weaknesses. Although you don't need to be an expert kayaker, it doesn't hurt to have experience. Though we try to do this trip every year, when we *first* did it on our own, our only kayaking experience had been a 3-hour trip up the Wailua River. On that first trip we experienced ideal conditions, which don't always occur, even during the summer. Please bear in mind that this trip is not for everyone. The Na Pali Coast is wild and unpredictable, and you are exposing yourself to the ocean's caprice. The usually calm June through August seas can become difficult with surprising suddenness. Most of the Na Pali boat companies can tell you stories about kayakers who had to be rescued when they got in over their heads (so to speak).

Sunset from the caves of Kalalau is your rich reward for a morning's paddle.

If you decide to do it on your own, here are a few things to keep in mind:
- Learn as much as you can about kayaking. (*Paddling Hawai'i* by Audrey Sutherland was our main reference when we made the first trip.) Proper paddling and loading techniques are *vital*.
- In addition to other essentials, make sure you bring waterproof sunblock, a hat, sunglasses, Chapstick and possibly Dramamine.
- Apply for camping permits *well in advance* (as much as 6–12 months in advance might be needed for Na Pali campsites), and *make sure* you get a kayak landing stamp on the permit.
- Think through your food requirements. (You *won't* be living off the land.)
- Any water source you utilize along the way will require water treatment pills to avoid possible contraction of leptospirosis. Water filters that don't use chemicals are not considered reliable due to the corkscrew shape of the leptospirosis bacterium. (The only one we've trusted enough to drink from is First Need XL, which purifies down to .1 micron, but you have to decide for yourself if it's good enough.) Fresh water is present at the following beaches along the route: Ke'e, Hanakapi'ai, Kalalau, Honopu, Miloli'i and Polihale, as well as some waterfalls that fall right into the ocean.
- Normal June through August conditions mean that the wind and currents are both pushing you in the direction you want to go, but *normal* doesn't mean *always*. Monitor ocean conditions by calling **Hawaiian Waters Forecast** (245–3564) and the **National Weather Service** (245–6001) for weather.
- Paddling in the early morning usually offers the calmest seas (sometimes like glass, if you're lucky) and easier launchings.
- Unless you spring for pick-up service, you'll have to rent an extra car for a couple days and leave one at Ke'e Beach and one at Polihale.

Here's some of what you can expect...

From Ke'e, Hanakapi'ai Beach is slightly over a mile. With campgrounds and a freshwater stream, Hanakapi'ai is a favorite place for hikers to camp, but it's to soon for kayakers. Past Hanakapi'ai, you will start to see caves and waterfalls straight out of your dreams. Some of the caves are horseshoe-shaped, with separate entrances and exits. Explore 'em all if conditions are safe.

Keep an eye out for dolphins and turtles, which become more plentiful as you get farther down the coast. At Kalalau, you have paddled 6 miles. If you're on your own, this is a good place to camp with half a mile of sand, fresh water and portable toilets. We like to pitch our tents in the caves (hoping rocks won't fall on us) at the far end of the beach and walk a few minutes to a waterfall to shower. Kalalau is as far as hikers can go, so from here on you are in exclusive company.

Less than a mile past Kalalau is Honopu Beach. Landing crafts of all types, including *surfboards,* are prohibited. The only legal way to visit Honopu Beach is to swim there from Kalalau Beach (which can be hazardous if there's surf), or you can anchor your craft offshore and swim in (which can also be hazardous).

In all the Hawaiian Islands, and perhaps in all the world, you'll never find a more glorious, moving and mystical beach. Unspoiled Honopu is only accessible by sea. It is actually two beaches, separated by a gigantic arch carved into Na Pali by Mother Nature's furious waves. During the summertime when the pounding Na Pali surf weakens, Honopu is reclaimed from the sea. As you approach by kayak, you're left speechless by the sheer majesty of what unfolds before you. *Vertical* walls 1,200 feet high are the first characteristics you see from the sea. If you're lucky enough to visit here, the giant arch draws you toward it like a magnet. As you approach it, you can just make out the cascading waterfall around the bend. This is no mere trickle. This immense cataract can knock you down with its force. The stream continues through the arch and out to sea, providing a superb way to rinse off the saltwater. The southern beach of Honopu actually makes a better kayak landing than its northern counterpart, but the northern beach is the most dramatic, and its unfolding vista will surely stay with you forever.

Past Honopu, listen for goats. Although considered pests by island officials, it's charming to hear them from your position on the water. At 9 miles you come to a pair of reefs fringing a beach called Nu'alolo Kai. The waters inside the reef offer good snorkeling during calm seas (and you wouldn't be here if the seas weren't calm, right?). From your kayak, when the two signs onshore are aligned, you're heading toward the deeper channel and to shore.

In times past, the Hawaiians mostly lived in the hanging valley above the beach. Access required scaling the vertical wall (actually, it's worse than vertical; it leans outward!) up a ladder and along a "trail" in the cliff, which was often nothing more than cubbyholes for your feet. Worse yet was a large rock in the "trail" that was very difficult to get around. The Hawaiians even had a name for this dangerously placed immovable rock. They called it "fat man's misery."

Next, Miloli'i is 11 miles into your journey. Camping and fresh water make

Miloli'i an inviting respite. There is a reef all along the beach and the same system to mark the channel as at Nu'alolo. You need a permit to camp at Miloli'i.

After Miloli'i, you will see a radio transmitter on top of a mountain belonging to Pacific Missile Range Facility. From the radar transmitter (helicopter pilots avoid getting too close to it, claiming they can feel their *da kines* cook), it's only 3 miles to Polihale. After your surf landing there, you can look forward to dragging your kayak through 500 feet of sand in searing heat, a task that would make a Himalayan Sherpa weep. (Good thing you were smart enough to spring for pick-up service from your kayak company.)

Congratulations—you have now joined an elite club of adventurers who have braved the Na Pali. A not-so-quick shower at Polihale Beach, and you are ready to dance all night. Or maybe not.

THE KALALAU TRAIL

So you don't like paddling or the surf is raging. You can still see Na Pali. Because the ultimate hike is also the most famous hike in all Hawai'i—11 miles of switchbacks, hills and beautiful scenery. See map below. Much of the trail is narrow and not

An open-ceiling cave along Na Pali is one of the many places to poke your kayak into during your voyage.

without hazards. The trail calls for several stream crossings (some flip-flops are handy for this). Don't cross if the water is too high. Don't go if overnight hikes are a problem. To get the proper permits, contact: Hawai'i DLNR, State Parks, 3060 Eiwa St., Room 306, Lihu'e, HI 96766-1875, (808) 274–3444.

Our map is an accurate, computer-generated, shaded relief map drawn at a 45° angle to give you a perspective of when and how much climbing is involved—altogether about 5,000 feet.

The first 2 miles of the trail leads to Hanakapi'ai Beach (sandy in the summer, bouldery in the winter). There are plenty of slippery and muddy sections, and the second mile is steep downhill (and tough coming back up). It's tricky in spots if you're a beginner hiker, but it's worth it. The views along the coast are exceptional. Hanakapi'ai is a beautiful but treacherous beach to swim, and it takes most people 1½–2 hours to hike each way. From here there is a fairly tough 1⁸/₁₀-mile side trail upstream to Hanakapi'ai Falls, one of the more spectacular falls and pools on the north shore. There are lots of false trails, and it's easy to miss some of the river crossings, but you're in a valley so you shouldn't stray more than a couple hundred feet from the stream. Many people like to reward themselves by swimming in the pool under the falls. Watch out for falling rocks.

This is as far as you can go without a permit. The authorities assume anyone going past Hanakapi'ai will be camping. If this is your plan, and you have your state camping permit, keep going. *Only* 9 miles to go from here. At Hanakoa, you have the choice of either camping, continuing to Kalalau or taking the ½ mile side trip to Hanakoa Falls, which is even lovelier than Hanakapi'ai. You'll cross the Hanakoa Stream and take a left at the trail near a shelter. After 50 yards take the left fork for 15 minutes. Watch for falling rocks at the falls. If you've come as far as Hanakoa, go see the falls. It's worth the walk.

Back on the trail, your toughest stretch is the last. From here to Kalalau Beach you'll find lots of switchbacks and a narrow trail at times. The stretch 7–8 miles into the trail has a couple of dicey spots, but they're not as bad as they used to be. The views are stunning. Persevere and you will be richly rewarded. Wow! This is the glorious valley you see from the top

Kalalau Trail

Indicates Foot Trails
3 Miles into Trail
A Campsite

© 2012 Wizard Publications, Inc.

Hanakapi'ai Falls

Nearly 2 mile side trip to Hanakapi'ai Falls

Hanakapi'ai Valley

22°11.200
159°36.913
Hanakoa Falls

Half mile side trip to Hanakoa Falls

22°13.224
159°34.984
End of the Road

Limahuli Stream

560

Kalalau Trail

Ke'e Beach

Hanakapi'ai Beach

Ho'olulu Sea Cave

Waiahuakua Sea Cave

Kalalau Trail

So you'll know what's involved on this trail, the vantage point of this map is looking at the trail from offshore from the air.

Wild, raw and unforgettable—the Kalalau Trail.

of Waimea Canyon Drive at the Kalalau Lookout. The beach, the valley and the isolation all make Kalalau a magic place. There is a 2-mile trail inland, which takes you to "Big Pool," a large natural pool in the stream.

Have you ever read *Ko'olau the Leper* by Jack London? It's based on the true story of Ko'olau, who fled to Kalalau in the 1880s after authorities refused to let

Map continued on page 145

Kalalau Lookout
550
Kalalau Valley
22°09.903 159°38.079
Big Pool
Honopu Valley
22°10.289 159°39.572
Falls
10
Kalalau Beach
Caves
Honopu Beach & Honopu Arch
Open Ceiling Cave
E S N W

his wife accompany him to the Kalaupapa leper settlement on Moloka'i. On July 2, 1893, a ship carrying 12 police, 14 soldiers, the sheriff, many rifles and a howitzer came ashore to capture Koolau and the other lepers who had joined him. After Ko'olau shot two of the soldiers dead and a third accidentally shot himself in the head (oops), the authorities decided to leave Koolau alone. He died in Kalalau in 1896 from his affliction.

As you stand on the beach at Kalalau, it's amazing to think that the entire valley was once populated. It was only in 1919 that this isolated valley was finally abandoned as people sought the life available to them in Lihu'e and other towns.

This is as far as you can go. A half mile farther down the coast is the most beautiful beach in all the islands, maybe in all the Pacific—Honopu Beach. There is none finer. Period. The only legal way to visit the beach is to swim there. If you do this, beware that the current is against you coming back. Only during calm seas, only with fins and only if you're a strong swimmer. In late summer Kalalau Beach snakes its way closer to Honopu, and people walk on the rocks and sand most of the way. Beware of unexpectedly large waves if you do this. For more information on Honopu, see NA PALI KAYAK TRIP above.

Kalalau has composting toilets. The waterfall provides fresh water, which should be treated before drinking as should your en route sources at Hanakapi'ai and Hanakoa streams. In fact, *all* fresh water in nature should be treated to avoid possible bacteriological contamination from animals or people polluting the stream.

NI'IHAU SCUBA DIVE

For SCUBA divers looking for clean, clear, virgin waters, several dive operators offer three-tank dives near the privately owned island of Ni'ihau, mostly off Lehua Rock north of the island. (For more information on Ni'ihau, see INTRODUCTION chapter.) Since this island is in the rain shadow of Kaua'i, there are no permanent streams on the island (and consequently, no run-off). So visibility is often *well* over a hundred feet. This is possibly the best diving in the state. Between dives we've found ourselves snorkeling with dolphins. *Very* cool.

The waters are rich in critters, arches, caves and pelagics. There's a good chance you will share the water with sharks, so be prepared. The dive requires a 70-mile round trip (if you leave from Port Allen) boat ride and involves drop-offs, currents

and sometimes rough seas. This is not for the inexperienced diver. Dives are usually deeper here. The table in the SCUBA section of the ACTIVITIES chapter tells which companies offer Ni'ihau trips, mostly around the summer months. Coming back into the wind is always a rough trip. We like **Fathom Five** (and are grateful for the shade and extra amenities) and **Bubbles Below** the best. It's a very good idea to book a month in advance to ensure space. **Seasport Divers** trolls for fish the whole time, which takes longer coming back, plus their boat is more crowded.

SEE THE ISLAND FROM A NATIVE PERSPECTIVE

This is a hard adventure to describe because it all depends on what you want. Charlie Mokunui Cobb Adams of **Native Hawaiian Conservation Tours** (652–0478) is a Hawaiian outdoorsman who gives small, personalized tours of lands that are often off the beaten track. It works like this: You call him up, tell him what kind of outdoor experience you're interested in, and he'll tailor the tour to what you want. Maybe you want to go into the wilderness hunting for wild boar. *(Definitely* an adventure.) Maybe you want to snorkel beneath a secluded waterfall or explore private land that he has access to. You might want to learn a native Hawaiian dance in an exotic location or repel off a cliff. Charlie is a wealth of information about native plants as well as native traditions, and it's impossible to walk away without having a greater understanding of how the ancient Hawaiians saw and interacted with the island. And you'll get your own personal adventure in the process.

HIKE TO THE BLUE HOLE

The term Blue Hole is widely used on Kaua'i yet is oddly ambiguous. Some use it to refer to Wai'ale'ale Crater. Some use it for

With clear water that drops so quickly, it's easy to see why Ni'ihau dives can be so compelling.

It takes time, a 4WD and wet feet to get to the so-called Blue Hole.

the dam at the end of the dirt road that marks the trailhead. And others say Blue Hole is the pool at the end of an arduous hike. Let's go with the latter.

Getting to the trailhead can be difficult if you don't have 4WD. Read the directions to the Jungle Hike on page 155. Instead of looking for that trailhead, keep walking on the road until it ends at a concrete diversion dam. If the water is turbid and nasty, it's an indication that heavy rains have occurred, and the river might be getting ready to flood. (Of course, *any* river can flash flood at *any* time.)

Walk across the dam. The trail *up* the river starts out strong and quickly becomes vague. After it dumps you out into the river, another trail begins close by. This is the pattern these trails follow and many people have so much trouble spotting them they spend the whole

time in the river. The trails are only along the right (north) side of the river, and you can make good time by searching them out. (Some left bank trails are for hunters and will get you into trouble.) They'll be narrow, muddy and overgrown, but it's easier than walking on slick river boulders. Flagging tape is an obvious sign that a trail is near. Even if you see an unmarked open swath in the trees, it's worth checking out. You'll be gaining 440 feet of elevation, and the boulder parts can be tiring. Tabis (described on page 139) are *strongly* recommended.

It takes 3 hours round trip for *good* hikers, twice that long or more for sketchier trekkers, or if you can't find the trail segments.

At last you arrive at your goal. Three streams come together with two of them

Hike through bamboo, cross the stream several times, step in mud, walk on wet rocks. All this just to marvel at Makaleha. It works for our hiker friend pictured here.

forming a glorious split waterfall. It's like a scene from heaven. You've been in the river and on the trail for less than 1½ miles, but you'd *swear* it's more than that. (We're positive about that number, we promise.) Soak it all in (easy to do since your already wet to the bone) and return the way you came.

For those who are tempted to continue into the crater, you should pass on that idea. The hiking gets harder, and it can't be done in a single day. If you insist on trying, you're going beyond adventure and working your way toward crazy since it involves scaling waterfalls ahead. Anyway, the correct direction is the stream to the left (not up the waterfall), and stay to the right at the next intersection. Stop when you come to a 3,000-foot wall in front of you at the back of the crater.

MAKALEHA HIKE

This hike is in the ADVENTURES chapter because it is only for the advanced hiker. The trail goes along a beautiful stream, through a bamboo grove and offers lush scenery. There are a number of places along the way to bathe in the stream, which can be deep in spots. Past the end of the trail are waterfalls just for you. The problem is that the trail is a trail-of-use and is not officially maintained. As a result, it is splendid in some parts, wretched in others. Some big steps up and down and mud spots keep it interesting. You will have to walk in the stream in some places, so we usually bring tabis (fuzzy mittens for your feet that work well on slippery rocks). Even without the waterfalls, you will get a real Indiana Jones feel for this part of God's country.

The trail starts at the end of Kahuna Road in northern Kapa'a. (See top of map on page 58 to get there.) From here, you park and walk past the water tank to the trail. At one point, the trail on the right (northern) bank veers away to a water tunnel. Don't go there, but instead

Makaleha Hike
© 2012 Wizard Publications, Inc. Map continued on page 58

cross the main stream at the remains of an old concrete dam. Follow the trail close to the stream as much as possible. From here, enter the bamboo. You'll see three large trees; behind the one on the far right is a trail that ascends into the bamboo grove, skirts the cliff edge and gives some opportunities (take the second one) to return to the river below. Remember that place for your return hike. From here, it can be muddy if it's been raining (and it probably has been). This is the real Kaua'i—lush, wet and beautiful.

When the bamboo ends, you have a choice of walking on the trail (which will be muddy and thorny and fern-filled) or walk in the stream on the rocks. (Many will find rock-hopping in the stream *the whole way* their best solution.) At one point the trail dumps into the stream, and you'll have to cross it onto an island in the river. Walk the length of the island, cross the

Sometimes it's hard to capture the immensity of what you're seeing in a photo. The boat offshore and the helicopter (the light blip above our friend's hat) are testament to the grandness of what awaits you on the Honopu Ridge.

stream to the left, and pick up the trail again. Follow it until you come to some large boulders that form a wall. Go over the wall and cross the stream. The trail gets difficult from here. Look for machete marks in the annoying hau trees that cross the trail, sometimes forming a jungle gym of limbs. You should always be able to hear the stream, but if you get into trouble, there probably won't be anyone coming along to help. Bring mosquito repellent or don't go. Footwear should include hiking sandals or boots and tabis (preferable) for stream walking. Bring water. You'll have to walk in the stream the last 50 yards before you come to a fork (where three streams converge at a stunning vista). A waterfall is up the left-most stream. *If you're feeling lucky*, a better waterfall is 20–30 minutes of rock-hopping to the right. It's an easier walk in a tall, narrow canyon, and the falls are two beautiful tiers with good swimming at the base. But that narrowness opens you up to the possibility of getting hammered by falling rocks, if one lets loose above you. Regardless, allow ample time to get back. In all, it's only 1½ miles each way, but the going is pretty slow in many spots, and it *can* take much of the day.

4WD MILOLI'I RIDGE ROAD

The southern, dryer part of Na Pali is defined by a series of ridges. The map on page 84 shows roads such as Kauhao and Ka'aweiki that wind their way along the ridges to the edge of Na Pali. Unfortunately, these are hunter roads, always closed during the week, and you're supposed to get a hunting permit to drive on them on weekends. But Miloli'i Ridge Road (see same map) is open all week long and, if you have a 4WD and it's not raining, you can probably drive to the end where you'll get a beautiful view of this part of Na Pali. Once at the road's end, look for a trail to the left that goes around and up a hill. Intrepid hikers might want to brave the ridge as long as their nerve takes them. (The ridge ends rather conclusively—right above Miloli'i Beach a dramatic 1,400 feet below you.)

Here's the deal: The road is maintained by State Parks, which means it may be rutted, nasty, impassible or even closed if they feel like it. Or it might be fine. Either way, when you get to some picnic tables (shown on the map), you've come to the last part you should consider driving if it's *been* raining or you *think* it will. Because after that the road gets steeper, and you might have problems returning if it's too slippery. All told it's just over 5 miles of 4WD each way. You access Miloli'i Ridge Road ³⁄₁₀ mile into the paved Makaha Ridge Road between the 13 and 14 mile markers on Hwy 550 (Waimea Canyon Drive).

HONOPU RIDGE TO A DROP-DEAD VIEW

Imagine a trail that cuts through forest, ventures down a ridge and culminates in perhaps the most inspirational view on the island. For two decades that's exactly what you had to do...*imagine* it. Back in 1982 one of Kaua'i's most delicious trails was damaged by a hurricane. The State Park, ever grumbling about budgets, decided not to put in the effort to reopen it. Over the course of more than two decades it became unrecognizable. But volunteers have spent the time to bring it back to life. Today Honopu Trail is available to ambitious hikers. Why ambitious? Because, although it's only just over 2 miles each way, there's opportunity to wander off the trail if you're not careful. Most of the trail is obvious, but there are a few hunter trails that might lead you astray. (See maps on pages 145 and 140.)

Located on the west side, you take Hwy 50 to Waimea Canyon Drive (550). At ⁴⁄₁₀ mile past the 17 mile marker (not far from the end of the road at Kalalau) there's a turnout on the curve about 100 feet past a telephone pole. Park there and the trail heads left toward the coast. After just 120 yards you come to your first confusing intersection. The trail to the left is the correct path. (Don't go straight.) At ²⁄₁₀ mile the trail comes to a T intersection at a tree whose branches all point to the right. Turn right. (The incorrect faint left leads down to a stream bed.) From here you'll *really* be grateful for long pants, because the native Pacific false staghorn ferns tend to claw at

your legs. (Jeans can feel heavy—we've become fond of light pants with zip-off legs.)

It's mostly the first ½ mile that has the confusing intersections. Tips to staying on the correct trail include following the most beaten path, looking for logs or other barriers placed to block side trails and staying on the trail that has the most tags (ribbons) on trees.

Soon most of your 1,000 feet of elevation loss will occur. (You actually climbed a bit until now.) Always stay on the most worn path. About 1 mile into the trail (it will seem like more) you'll be on a wide ridge that will eventually get narrow enough to see Honopu on one side and Awa-'awapuhi on the other. Eventually the trail comes to a glorious lookout on a dirt bluff. The vista into Honopu Valley is so magnificent that it defies description. The entire heavenly valley is before you. Honopu Beach and the Pacific are to your left 3,000 feet below. The scene is so intense that it literally looks unreal. If clouds are in the valley, wait a while. They tend to come and go. The trail continues another 15 minutes, terminating at a point where the ridge takes a drop down to a razorback spine (which you *don't* want to visit). From the end you're treated to a tasty view of Na Pali coast.

While on the trail, if you take a wrong turn, keep track of where you've been and backtrack. Nothing's worse than being lost in the forest. Our first time in (when the trail was more vague than it is now) we made two wrong turns, realized our mistakes, and returned to the intersection to find the right way. Also, make sure you're back at your car *at least* 1½ hours before sunset. It will take most people 1½–2½ hours each way, and the trip back up is fairly strenuous. Bring gobs of water down, suck 'em up at the overlook, and bring only what you need back up. The trail has a few areas where there's opportunity to fall or twist an ankle. One short stretch is on the side of a dirt hill that may make some nervous. This hike is in the ADVENTURES chapter because of the poor trail conditions in a few scattered areas and because of the potential to get off the trail. Coming back, the ¼ mile closest to your car seems to present new opportunities to wander off the same trail you already took on the way down.

MOUNTAIN BIKE/HIKE THE OTHER SIDE OF WAIMEA CANYON

There's a trail in Koke'e called Kohua Ridge Trail that leads 2½ miles to a dazzling view of Waimea Canyon *from the other side.* Problem is, the trailhead is 3⁶⁄₁₀ miles from where most cars can go. But bring along a mountain bike to get you there, and you have an afternoon adventure. See map on page 140 and take Mohihi-Camp 10 Road to where the map indicates 4WD only (1⁶⁄₁₀ miles from Hwy 550). The bike ride to the trailhead is along a dirt road through the forest. The sights are beautiful along the way. The biking is fairly strenuous due to the rolling nature of the road. Get a decent bike with shocks and low gears.

At the trailhead, stash your bike in some bushes and proceed. (Be sure to repeatedly refer to the map so you can anticipate the easy-to-miss trailhead sign.) The trail crosses Mohihi Ditch via a small bridge, then heads down to Mohihi Stream. It's usually a boulder hop across the stream. (Don't cross if it's raging.) Then comes the toughest part—¼ mile of steep trail, a slight leveling and then a shorter steep part before the saddle where it veers southwest. (Remember this point for your return.) At the end of the trail is a stunning view of Po'omau Canyon to your right, Koai'e Canyon to your left, with Waimea Canyon in front of you. You're at the apex of all of them. Across the canyon is the Waimea Canyon Lookout, where mere mortals

view the spectacular canyon. *You,* on the other hand, have earned the right to see it from a more exclusive perspective. It's been pretty strenuous getting to this point, but it's soon forgotten in the glory of your own personal overlook.

Take your time, but be back to your car before dark.

SECRET TUNNEL TO THE NORTH SHORE

Imagine that you're in an east shore valley. You come upon a tunnel that's a *mile* long. From the moment you enter, you can see the light at the other end. When you emerge, you're in the virtually inaccessible back of the north shore's Hanalei Valley, surrounded by nearly vertical mountains, a perfect river and no people. Aside from a few hunters, almost no one on Kaua'i had even *heard* of this tunnel until we revealed it. Those who had heard of it considered it one of those urban legends, a myth. Well, it's no myth.

In the 1920s a sugar company was seriously coveting the abundant water flowing out the Hanalei River. They needed the water for their east shore sugar. So for $300,000 they cut this tunnel and diverted 28 million gallons of water a day under the mountain and into a series of ditches to quench their thirsty crops. But times change. As sugar production dwindled on the east shore, they found that they no longer needed the north shore's water. So, years ago, they stopped diverting the water and abandoned the dam. The flume to divert the water is no longer there. They couldn't divert water into this tunnel even if they wanted to without doing major reconstruction on the dam. But the tunnel, blasted out of solid rock, remains.

Getting there will be a sloppy affair. It involves walking 2½ miles along a trail through muddy conditions. (It rains about 160 inches annually here, spread fairly evenly throughout the year.)

A Few Basics

Driving to the trailhead means taking a dirt road (see map). A regular car can usually go past the sign that says 4WD only, but you *may* have trouble on the last part of the road. You'll have to see. This road is sporadically improved, and it depends on your timing. 4WDs are a sure thing. See directions to the Jungle Hike on page 155 and stop *just before* the first gate. Hiking boots are recommended on this trail. Tabis (described on page 139), water socks or old tennis shoes work best *in* the tunnel. (The latter cushion the bottoms of your feet the best.) Tabis the whole way might be desirable if it's real muddy. Long pants are also recommended. Ferns have a habit of sticking out in the trail, scratching at your legs. Jeans are OK, but they get heavy and stick to your legs, making it harder. Lighter pants are preferred.

Look for delicious red thimbleberries along the way. (The redder, the better.) Bring a flashlight/headlamp (or two) for the tunnel. Also bring water and snacks.

The trail to the tunnel is a hunters' trail, and it's *always* muddy. The first 100 yards are very sloppy with a permanent puddle near the place where you park. Several short stretches are on uneven terrain, and caution needs to be taken. In the first 5 minutes you'll have to cross the Wailua River twice. *Usually* it's done by hopping across a couple of rocks. If it's too deep and you aren't comfortable, don't go. If it's been raining a lot, don't go. During very heavy rains you may find that the river isn't crossable coming back, presenting you with a dilemma. Just after the first crossing, go diagonally upstream about 150 feet and look for a trail in the bamboo thicket. (It's not the trail going straight *ahead* from the river). Bamboo is the best

Tunnel & Jungle Hikes

Map continued on page 58

© 2012 Wizard Publications, Inc.

natural material there is for walking sticks, and it's a good idea to have one on this hike. (It makes a good spider stick in case there are webs across the trail.) Cut it so that a knuckle is near the bottom, acting as a natural stopper, preventing dirt or mud from filling the hollow tube.

The trail is intermittently "paved" with 'ohi'a tree logs looking like railroad ties from long ago. Avoid false trails. Remember, you'll never go more than 15 minutes without seeing the 'ohi'a logs. (Hunters—and their dogs—who use the trail mostly on weekends and Mondays often put their own tags on trees, and following them might take you off the main trail.) You've gone al-most a mile when you see your first old, abandoned wooden power pole. Just after this you come to a flat muddy area and a trail to the left. We've walked through the flat part and sunk three feet into a bog. Take the side trail around unless you want to lose a shoe. You'll cross a couple of smaller streams (a foot wide) and a slightly larger stream.

After 1½ hours or so, when the trail encounters a large stream again, it seems to end. This is where people get lost. It actually veers slightly left, away from the stream and over some rocks. Look for muddy stains on the rocks, and they will lead you to the trail in the tall grass ahead. It crosses the stream where the stream makes a right turn. Once you cross, pick up the trail *directly* on the other side, and it's not far before you walk on a skinny plank bridge over a ditch. There are two trails here, one straight and one to the left. *Take the left trail*. It goes to the gauging station and tunnel. It takes us 1¾–2½ hours *to* the first tunnel, and about 45 minutes *in* the tunnel. Coming back is a bit faster. You'll gain about 600 feet with all the ups and downs.

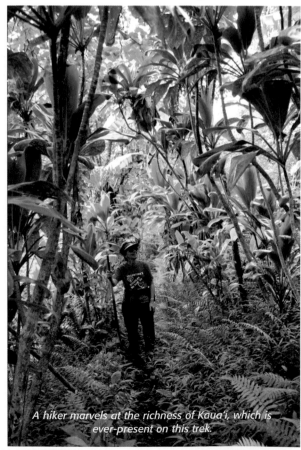

A hiker marvels at the richness of Kaua'i, which is ever-present on this trek.

Once in the tunnel you notice that there's water standing in it. That's from the small amount of water that drips from the ceiling. It's just the right amount to keep about four inches of water fresh. The tunnel is about 6 feet wide and 7–10 feet high with an occasional need for a head duck on the straight portion. The bottom is flat and lined with small rocks, which makes for fairly straightforward walking. The tunnel reverberates with the ever-constant sound of the splashing of your feet in the ankle-high water. About 900 feet above you is the ridge that the ancient Hawaiians used to walk on to reach the summit of Waiʻaleʻale where the remains of their altar, at the wettest spot on Earth, may still be found. As you approach what appears to be the end, you see an odd sight: railroad tracks in the shallow water, probably used to haul the debris out of the tunnel during construction. At the light at the not-quite-end of the tunnel, you can step outside momentarily to visit a small waterfall waiting for you. Then it's back in the tunnel for the remaining ¼ mile. That latter portion is partially lined with cement and shorings, requiring anyone 6 feet tall or more to duck for a bit. At the real end you need to step up on the dike and take the overgrown trail on your right near the tunnel exit. It goes down for about a minute to the Hanalei River. During good weather the scenery is magnificent. The mountains tower all around you. Waiʻaleʻale plateau is above and to your left, its side etched with waterfalls. The river, with some impossibly large boulders, makes a perfect place for lunch.

Most will be more than satisfied with this destination. But if you started early (hiking by 7 or 7:30 a.m.), there is one more challenge for the intrepid. You've been through a mile of tunnel already and are at the river. Directly across from the giant boulder and deep pool (you'll see it), there's a *very* faint trail on the other side of the river that leads 5–10 minutes upstream to *another* ⁷⁄₁₀ mile-long tunnel. It's more dicey. Follow the trail across from the boulder until it meets an old diversion dam (which looks like a waterfall which you'll hear). From the top of the dam look upstream, then turn to your right. You should see a vague trail going directly uphill. It will take you to a cement wall (part of the next ditch). The next tunnel entrance is over the wall to the right.

Once inside the tunnel (known to hunters as Kaʻapoko Tunnel), there's

Hikers entering the tunnel.

lots of head ducking, and it has a more rickety feel. When the tunnel ends, there's an offshoot to the left. Not far from there, you come to a low-ceiling incline with water gurgling down. Scoot up and you'll emerge in a Shangri-La that will make you giddy with joy. A cathedral of 200-foot sheer walls are so steep they actually lean *inward*. Water drips from above, creating an exotic backdrop. To the left is a pounding waterfall. The setting is unbelievable and worth all the effort you went through to get here.

Needless to say, you'll have the opportunity to get big-time muddy, slip on your ʻokole, bump your head, twist your ankle, etc., on this adventure. Use your best judgment. This trail and tunnel are not maintained for this purpose, so please don't complain to *anybody* if you have any problems. This is a strenuous, exciting and memorable adventure with absolutely *no* guarantees. *That's* why it's an adventure.

First a day at the beach, then a romantic evening at the Sheraton Kaua'i.

By their very nature, restaurant reviews are the most subjective part of any guidebook. Nothing strains the credibility of a guidebook more. No matter what we say, if you eat at enough restaurants here, you will eventually have a dining experience directly in conflict with what this book leads you to believe. All it takes is one person to wreck what is usually a good meal. You've probably had an experience where a friend referred you to a restaurant using reverential terms, indicating that you were about to experience dining ecstasy. And, of course, when you go there, the food is awful and the waiter is a jerk. There are many variables involved in getting a good or bad meal. Is the chef new? Was the place sold last month? Was the waitress just released from prison for mauling a customer? We truly hope that our reviews match your experience. If they don't (or

even if they do), please drop us a line. Readers help us *tremendously* in keeping tabs on the restaurants, and we read and digest (so to speak) every e-mail.

We often leave out restaurant hours of operation because they change so frequently that the information would be immediately out of date. These decisions are usually made quite capriciously in Hawai'i. If you're going to drive a long way to eat at an establishment, it's best to call first. Restaurants that stand out from the others in some way are highlighted with this ONO symbol.

In some restaurants around the island you'll see guidebook recommendation plaques, guidebook door stickers and signed guidebooks, but you won't see ours. The reason? We *never* tell them when we're there. We review everything on the island *anonymously*. We're more interested in being treated like everyone else than in copping a free meal. How could you trust our opinion if the restaurant *knew* who we were?

By their reviews, many guidebooks lead you to believe that every meal you eat in Hawai'i will be a feast, the best food in the free world. Frankly, that's not our style. Kaua'i, like anywhere else, has ample opportunity to have lousy food served in a rotten ambiance by uncaring waiters. In the interest of space, we've left out some of the dives. We did, however, leave in some of the turkeys just to demonstrate that we live in the real world.

For each restaurant, we list the price *per person* you can expect to pay. It ranges from the least expensive entrées to the most expensive, plus a beverage and usually an appetizer. You can spend more if you try, but this is a good guideline. *The price excludes alcoholic beverages since this component of a meal can be so variable.* Obviously, everyone's ordering pattern is different, but we thought that it would be easier to compare restaurants using actual prices than if we used symbols like different numbers of dollar signs or drawings of forks or whatever to differentiate prices between restaurants.

When we give **directions** to a restaurant, *mauka side* of highway means "toward the mountain" (or away from the ocean). The shopping centers we mention are on the maps to that area.

Very few restaurants care how you dress. A few discourage tank tops and bathing suits. Some of the fancy resorts like the St. Regis Princeville, Sheraton or Grand Hyatt have dress codes. Their dress codes require **resort wear**, meaning covered shoes and collared shirts for men (nice shorts are *usually* OK), dressy sportswear or dresses for women.

It's legal to bring your own alcohol to restaurants in Hawai'i, and many res-

taurants, especially inexpensive ones, have no objections to letting you BYOB.

Local food can be difficult to classify. Basically, local food combines Hawaiian, American, Japanese, Chinese, Filipino and several other types and is (not surprisingly) eaten mainly by locals.

Pacific Rim is sort of a fusion of American and various countries around the Pacific, including Hawaiian and Asian. We used to categorize them separately, but it's a fine (and subjective) line between American and Pacific Rim, so we just lumped them in with American because even *we* were confused. We don't have a separate **Seafood** section because nearly every restaurant on Kaua'i serves some kind of fish.

Below are descriptions of various island foods. Not all are Hawaiian, but this might help if you encounter dishes unfamiliar to you.

ISLAND FISH & SEAFOOD

Ahi–Tuna; raw in sashimi or poke, also seared, blackened, baked or grilled; good in fish sandwiches. Try painting ahi steaks with mayonnaise, which *completely* burns off when BBQ'd but seals in the moisture. You end up tasting only the moist ocean steak. Generally plentiful Apr.–Sept.

Lobster–Hawaiian spiny lobster is quite good; also called "bugs" by lobster hunters. Maine lobster kept alive on the Big Island are also available.

Mahimahi–Deep ocean fish also known as a dolphinfish; served at lu'au; very common in restaurants. Sometimes tastes fishy (especially if frozen), which can be offset in the preparation.

Marlin–Tasty when smoked; otherwise, can be tough; the Pacific Blue Marlin (kajiki) is available almost year round.

Monchong–Excellent tasting deepwater fish, available year-round. Usually served marinated and grilled.

Onaga–Also known as a ruby snapper; excellent eating in many preparations.
Ono–(Wahoo); *awesome* eating fish and can be prepared many ways; most plentiful May through October. Ono is also the Hawaiian word for delicious.
Opah–(Moonfish); excellent eating in many different preparations; generally available April through August.
'Opakapaka–(Crimson snapper); great tasting fish cooked several ways. Common October through February.
'Opihi–Using a specialized knife, these must be pried off rocks at the shoreline, which can be hazardous. Best eaten raw mixed with salt.
Poke–Fresh raw fish or octopus (tako) mixed with seaweed (limu), sesame seed and other seasonings and oil.
Shutome–Swordfish; dense meat that can be cooked several ways. Most plentiful March through July. The word comes from Japan and literally translates to *mother-in-law*.
Walu–Also goes by other names such as butterfish and escolar. Be careful not to eat more than 6 ounces. The Hawaiian nickname for this oily fish is maku'u, which means—*ahem*, this is awkward—"uncontrollable bowel dis charge." Eat too much, and you may pay more dearly than you intend.

Hanalei Dolphin (826–6113) buys from the fishing boats and has a market that sells fresh, locally caught fish. Other places include **Foodland** (822–7271) and **Safeway** (822–2464) in Kapa'a, **Fish Express** (across from Walmart) in Lihu'e and the **Koloa Fish Market** in Koloa.

LU'AU FOODS

Chicken lu'au–Chicken cooked in coconut milk and taro leaves.
Haupia–Coconut milk custard. Tasty, but too much will give you the… *ahem*.

Hawaiian sweet potatoes–Purple inside; not as sweet as mainland sweet potatoes but very flavorful.
Kalua pig–Pig cooked in an underground oven called an imu, shredded and mixed with Hawaiian sea salt (outstanding!).
Lomi salmon–Chilled salad consisting of raw, salted salmon, tomatoes and two kinds of onions.
Pipi kaula–Hawaiian-style beef jerky.
Poi–Steamed taro root pounded into a paste. It's a starch that will take on the taste of other foods mixed with it. Consider dipping your pipi kaula in it. (Now *that* sounds bad if you don't read it right.) Visitors are encouraged to try it at least once so they can badmouth it with authority.

OTHER ISLAND FOODS

Apple bananas–A smaller, denser, smoother texture than regular (Williams) bananas and a bit tangy.
Barbecue sticks–Teriyaki-marinated pork, chicken or beef pieces barbecued and served on bamboo sticks.
Bento–Japanese box lunch.
Breadfruit–Melon-sized starchy fruit; served baked, deep fried, steamed or boiled. Definitely an *acquired* taste.
Crackseed–Chinese-style spicy preserved fruits and seeds.
Guava–About the size of an apricot or plum. The inside is full of seeds and tart, so it is rarely eaten raw. Used primarily for juice, jelly or jam.
Hawaiian supersweet corn–The finest corn you ever had, even raw. We'll lie, cheat, steal or maim to get it fresh.
Huli huli chicken–Hawaiian BBQ style.
Ka'u oranges–Big Island oranges. Usually, the uglier the orange, the better it tastes.

Kim chee–A Korean relish consisting of pickled cabbage, onions, radishes, garlic and chilies.

Kona coffee–Grown on the Kona coast of the Big Island. Smooth, mild flavor. Better than Kaua'i coffee.

Kulolo–Steamed taro pudding. (Tasty.)

Laulau–Pork, beef or fish wrapped in taro and ti leaves, then steamed. (You don't eat the ti leaf wrapping.)

Liliko'i–Passionfruit.

Loco moco–Rice, meat patty, egg and gravy. A hit with cholesterol lovers.

Lychee–A reddish, woody peel that is discarded for the sweet, white fruit inside. Be careful of the pit. Good, small seed (or chicken-tongue) lychees are so delicious, they should be illegal.

Macadamia nut–A large, round nut.

Malasada–Portuguese donut dipped in sugar. Best when served hot.

Manapua–Steamed or baked bun filled with meat.

Mango–Bright orange fruit with yellow pink skin. Distinct, tasty flavor.

Manju–Cookie filled with a sweet center.

Methley plums–A wild fruit harvested with a permit at Koke'e State Park during the summer months.

Musubi–Cold steamed rice, often with sliced Spam rolled in black seaweed.

Papaya–Melon-like, pear-shaped fruit with yellow skin; best eaten chilled. Good at breakfast. Kaua'i has varieties called sunrise and strawberry papaya.

Plate lunch–An island favorite as an inexpensive, filling lunch. Consists of "two-scoop rice," a scoop of macaroni salad and some type of meat, either beef, chicken or fish. Sometimes called a box lunch. Great for picnics.

Portuguese sausage–Pork sausage, highly seasoned with red pepper. Tastes weird to some people.

Pupu–Appetizer, finger foods or snacks.

Saimin–Noodles cooked in either chicken, pork or fish broth. Word is peculiar to Hawai'i. Local Japanese say the dish comes from China. Local Chinese say it comes from Japan.

Sea salt–Excellent (and strong) salt distilled from seawater. Much of our sea salt comes from Salt Pond Beach Park.

Shave ice–A block of ice is "shaved" (*never* crushed) into a ball with flavored syrup poured over the top. Best served with ice cream on the bottom. Very delicious.

Smoothie–Usually papaya, mango, frozen passion fruit and frozen banana, but almost any fruit can be used to make this milkshake-like drink. Add milk for creaminess.

Taro–Found in everything from enchiladas to breads and rolls to taro chips and fritters. Tends to color foods purple. Has lots of fluoride for your teeth.

NORTH SHORE AMERICAN

Bar Acuda
5-5161 Kuhio Hwy • 826–7081

ONO Hanalei—A pretty unusual concept, it's called tapas food. (Yeah, we didn't know what that meant, either. It's Spanish food served in small, communally shared portions.) In this case, you order lots of small entrées and share them. The menu changes weekly and seasonally, so you'll have to explore it on your own. Expect to see items *such as* (but they may not have) smoked trout, braised short ribs, mesclun salad, garlic green beans or chorizo sausage with chickpea stew *(particularly* good). The food is pricey (and the drinks seriously overpriced), but the flavors are unusual and very effective, and you'll sample a number of them. The molten chocolate cake is incredibly earthy and wonderful—tiny but ONO. And the atmosphere, sort of a contemporary jazzy feel, works for us. **$20–$45** for dinner. In Hanalei Center. Closed Monday.

CJ's Steak & Seafood
5-4280 Kuhio Hwy • 826–6211

ONO Princeville—Hot and cold sandwiches (good and bountiful melts—try the one with crab, shrimp, bacon and cheese), burgers and pricey salads for lunch, with a classic steak, prime rib and seafood house at dinner. The salad bar with locally grown greens is included at dinner, which is uncommon on Kaua'i. Portions are generous and quality is high. CJ's has not always been a recommendable restaurant, but they've really picked things up and currently seem to be operating on all cylinders. No view, though. Lunch is **$12–$15**, dinner is **$30–$40**. In the Princeville Shopping Center.

Foodland Deli
5-4280 Kuhio Hwy • 826–9880

Princeville—Though the Foodland grocery store in Princeville Center will *never* be considered a bargain (their grocery prices are confiscatory), the deli is a good deal. For **$5–$10** you can pick up a fairly decent sandwich (either packaged or custom made) and be on your merry way to the beach. They also have some very inexpensive sushi

Garden at Common Ground
4900 Kuawa Rd • 828–1041

ONO Kilauea—A tiny menu of incredibly compelling and healthy items that knocks our socks off. Maybe just three or four items, such as fish tacos or veggie wraps or a fish sandwich. But ingredients are so fresh and combined so thoughtfully, we love eating here. And their salads taste like they just went out into the garden and picked them for your meal. (Love the dark green leaves salad with non-dressing dressing.) The ginger mint tea has a wonderful burn if you take a big gulp. Ambiance is just as the name says, in an outdoor pavilion next to their calming garden, which is a wonderful place to be during a passing shower. No table service, and flies are sometimes a problem. Just north of the 23 mile marker up Kuawa Rd. **$9–$12** for similarly small but compelling breakfast, **$11–$14** for lunch.

Hanalei Dolphin Restaurant
5-5016 Kuhio Hwy • 826–6113

Hanalei—This is a north shore tradition that over the years, rocks back and forth between really good and really bad. At press time they were in the middle of their sucky phase. They have some outdoor tables on a lawn next to the Hanalei River—very nice at lunch or while waiting for your indoor table at dinner. They are often busy and don't take reservations—so if waiting bothers you, arrive early or you're out of luck. Their seafood selection is excellent. Pick a fish and pick a side item. They have a seafood market, a good place to pick up fish for cooking back at the condo. They do some things well—great char-grilled butterfish and usually good walu. And the western-style sushi is high quality. But food and service have tanked during our most recent visits, and reader e-mail seems to agree—we got a record number of comments for this edition and 90% were horrible. But as they have so many times in the past, they might bounce right back into excellence. **$14–$20** for lunch, **$30–$60** for dinner. On the highway in Hanalei; can't miss it.

Hanalei Gourmet
5-5161 Kuhio Hwy • 826–2524

ONO Hanalei—Quality comes and goes with this place. Currently, they're in the zone most days. Good fish tacos, good fish and chips. Burgers, sandwiches and salads for lunch; steak, seafood, pastas and burgers for dinner. "Gourmet" seems a bit generous, and much of the atmosphere gravitates toward the bar. But it's a pleaser these days. $13–$17 for lunch, $20–$33 for dinner (less if you want a burger). In the Old Hanalei School across from Ching Young Village. Live music some nights.

Java Kai
5-5183 Kuhio Hwy • 826–6717
Hanalei—Also called **Hanalei Coffee Roasters**, a good place to stop for coffee and baked goods on the north shore. The drink selection is vast (love the spicy chai latte), but the hot breakfast items are small and overpriced. Their $8 bagel sandwich is pathetic compared to the $5 equivalent at their Kapa'a location. $5–$12. In the Hanalei Center next to Bubba's Burgers.

Kalypso Island Bar & Grill
5-5156 Kuhio Hwy • 826–9700
Hanalei—Items are hit or miss but rarely rise above acceptable. A lot of readers have told us how much they love the drinks and the food, and we can't help but wonder if the former influenced their opinion of the latter. (I've done more than my fair share of restaurant reviews where the food was great...after a couple of potent drinks, but less stellar with a clearer head.) Decent seafood pasta, unremarkable shrimp and fish, horrible calamari or artichokes. The menu is mostly a single selection of fish, steak, pasta and chicken. And they have an awesome chocolate suicide cake. $10–$17 for lunch, $17–$30 for dinner. On the Hwy; can't miss it.

Kaua'i Grill
5520 Ka Haku Rd. • 826–9644
Princeville—So there you are, at a restaurant with a great view overlooking Hanalei Bay, good food and pretty good service. Why no ONO from us? Because your net worth is now noticeably less, and you did-

n't walk away feeling pampered enough. Forget the $17 drinks and $25 appetizers. This is the place to get your tasty $35 pork chops or your 8-ounce Wagyu steak for $60. And the only thing you get with that steak is...a fork. All sides are extra. And if you order it medium and it comes out less than rare? And if the waitress takes so long to come over that you're halfway finished, you'll get an "I'm so sorry" and maybe even, "The chef is sorry, too." But no offer for a free dessert or a discount. We relay this story to illustrate that you can take great ingredients such as the location and food and still leave the customers wanting. Is it good? Yes. Is it *that* good? Not really. If money's no object, *you'd* give it an ONO. But for the rest of us mere mortals, it's short of the mark. $40–$85 or more for dinner. In the St. Regis, Princeville. Their sister restaurant, **Makana Terrace**, has somewhat inferior food, an even better view and, sorry—no ONO there either.

Lighthouse Bistro
2484 Keneke St. • 828–0480
Kilauea—First of all, you can't see the Kilauea Lighthouse from here. (Sorry to burst your bubble.) But nice ambiance anyway. Although dinner is pricey, lunch is our favorite, and it works fairly well with items such as fish tacos (get two 'cause they're small), fish burritos and burgers. Dinner is mainly fish, shrimp, chicken and pork. Pretty good food at lunch. Consider the creamy carrot soup or, for dessert, the grasshopper pie. $10–$20 for lunch, $20–$33 for dinner. In Kong Lung Center off Kilauea Road.

Mediterranean Gourmet
5-7132 Kuhio Hwy • 826–9875
ONO Ha'ena—Their greatest asset, an awesome oceanside location, is also their biggest curse since most people have made their dining deci-

sions before they drive west of Hanalei, so there have been lots of different restaurants here. The view of the ocean is better standing than sitting (with a low hedge cutting off some of the ocean). The food is pricey and the portions small. But the food is good and the flavors can be pretty strong, like the stuffed grape leaves. The owner's background is Lebanese, and you'll find items like hummus, tabouleh and baba ganush. Most of the items we've had here we'd never heard of, but we liked most of them. Lunch is several tasty wraps and a few other items for **$15–$25**. Dinner is **$25–$40**.

North Shore General Store
5-4280 Kuhio Hwy • 826-7992
Princeville—It's pretty rare that we'd be reasonably happy with food at a *gas* station. (Especially one with *their* prices.) Using quality lean Princeville Ranch beef, these guys make one of the better burgers around. If you're into BBQ sauce, onion rings and bacon, try the Braddah's BBQ burger. Burgers range from $6–$7, a pretty reasonable price *in these here parts*. They also make pizza, which is adequate, Mexican and fish-n-chips. Their breakfast sandwiches are tasty at $6. They come with a hash brown patty that works best when you put it *in* the sandwich. Only a few stools outside, so be prepared to take it to go. In the Chevron gas station at the Princeville Center. Breakfast is **$7–$10**, lunch and dinner are **$8–$15**. Closed Sundays.

Paradise Bar & Grill
5-4280 Kuhio Hwy • 826-1775
Princeville—One of the few places in Princeville that's easy on your wallet. The service is uninterested, the food underwhelming and the experience unremarkable. Breakfast is **$5–$15**. Burgers, sandwiches and fried stuff at lunch for **$9–$14**. Dinner has more expensive options

for **$10–$30**. In back of the Princeville Center.

Postcards
5-5075A Kuhio Hwy • 826-1191
Hanalei—A vegetarian restaurant that also serves fish. The food is distinctive and can be fairly well prepared. They use organic ingredients and have creative selections. Taro fritters make a good pupu, and the fresh fish is recommended. Ambiance is homey. The two areas that need work are the service (often slow), and the wine list is poorly chosen. **$20–$33** for dinner. On mauka side of the highway. Reservations required for parties of 6 or more.

Tahiti Nui
5-5134 Kuhio Hwy • 826-6277
ONO Hanalei—Tahiti Nui is a longtime Hanalei institution that has seen great highs and huge lows. Currently they have an energy that was missing for a decade. Food has gone from hideous to very good, and they have live music some nights. Behind the small dining room is their pizza joint, **Tikiman Pizza**, and next door, the Iti Wine Bar is a tiny (iti) but atmosphere rich cubbyhole hole that might serve Tahiti Nui food, or maybe tapas, or maybe something else. Hard to say here. Iti is so small that *you* may well define the atmosphere. Tahiti Nui is like a living entity, and it's hard to say what you'll find. That's part of the joy. It might be the place with great food and colorful characters, or over-the-top characters bordering on seedy. Either way, this is the center of north shore nightlife, both for visitors and locals, which they win by default. It's because of this we give them an ONO. Dinner stresses seafood and pasta and only a few pupus, and at **$24–$34** is overpriced. Lunch is burgers and sandwiches for **$10–$18**. On the ocean side of the Highway.

The Tavern at Princeville
5-3900 Kuhio Hwy • 826–8700

(ONO) Princeville—Owned by the founder of the local Roy's chain, entrées are creatively conceived and usually well-executed. The food is hard to define, and specials usually outnumber menu items. You may see pork chops with a complicated and tasty result or a lamb shank or blackened ahi. Hard to say. Appetizers aren't as pricey as you'd expect given the preparations, and the wines aren't overpriced. But we're less impressed with mixed drinks from the bar. (Surprisingly bad flavor combinations, hands down the *worst* mai tai on the island and a general elitist attitude from the bar.) Some of the window tables have pleasant views of the rolling Prince Golf Course that the Tavern resides on. If you don't drink or only want wine, you'll be happy. Dinner is $25–$40. Reservations recommended. Just east of Princeville off the highway.

NORTH SHORE CHINESE

Panda's Kitchen
5-5190 Kuhio Hwy • 826–7388

Hanalei—If you want something fast to take to the beach or have a hankering for take-out quality Chinese food, this might do. Fairly good ingredients, prepared well with items like orange chicken, lo mein, sweet & sour pork and the like. Portions are more than acceptable. Add to that really fast service if you order from what you see in front of you. Don't bother asking; if it looks good, it probably is. Grab it and head to the beach. Lunch and dinner are $9–$14. In Ching Young Village.

NORTH SHORE ITALIAN

Hanalei Pizza
5-5190 Kuhio Hwy • 826–1300

Hanalei—A very friendly pizza place in Ching Young Village with an open, breezy atmosphere. Pizza by the slice is a reasonable deal for the size, and beverages are downright cheap. If you have the time to wait, order a whole pie for $20–$35. Quality is average, and they seem to want to add feta to everything, just so you know. Don't be surprised if there's a local musician playing out front (and if you feel the urge, there are extra instruments on the wall inside). Official open mic night is once a month. We like the atmosphere, and if the pizza were a bit better, they'd garner an ONO. $5–$15.

Kilauea Bakery & Pau Hana Pizza
2484 Keneke St. • 828–2020

(ONO) Kilauea—Delicious baked goods and breads. (Try the macaroons or macadamia shortbread cookies.) The pizza is pricey, but the unusual fresh ingredients and the flavor combinations of the whole pizza specials work well. An example: Their island-style pizza is ham, pineapple, roasted garlic and chipotle peppers—much more interesting than traditional Hawaiian-style. More typical pizzas by the slice. As you'd expect from a bakery, the crust is very good. And the Big Kilauea Salad is particularly good. Service is either very friendly or shamefully indifferent—they sometimes seem to pride themselves on their surliness. But the food outshines the attitude. They have a dozen tables split indoors and out. $12–$22 for meals. Bakery is reasonably priced. In Kong Lung Center off Kilauea Road. Open 6:30ish a.m. to 9 p.m.

Tikiman Pizza
5-5134 Kuhio Hwy • 826–6277

Hanalei—The pizza arm of the Tahiti Nui restaurant. It's not bad, but it won't leave you wanting more. $10–$17 for lunch and dinner. By the slice when they feel like it. On the ocean side of the highway.

NORTH SHORE JAPANESE

Bouchons Hanalei
5-5190 Kuhio Hwy • 826–9701

Hanalei—The entrées *can* be good here but haven't been lately, nor has the sushi. Execution seems to be their biggest issue. Besides being slow, it's not as kempt as we'd like, and the kitchen seems eager to close as early as they can. Do yourself in, however, with the deadly chocolate suicide cake. Open air and upstairs in the Ching Young Village. **$22–$55**.

NORTH SHORE LOCAL

Hanalei Wake-up Café
5-5140 Kuhio Hwy • 826–5551

Hanalei—Restaurants around here tend to open late for breakfast, if they open at all. This place opens at 6:30 a.m. Very small menu and less-than-pristine surroundings. They're usually packed. Service is fast, but the food is hastily assembled, and they *hate* substitutions. Omelettes are avoidable but other items will fill the need. Decor is an homage to all things surfing. **$8–$14** for breakfast. On ocean side of the road. Can't miss it. No credit cards.

Kilauea Fish Market
4270 Kilauea Rd. • 828–6244

Kilauea—Besides the usual fresh seafood, they carry some pricey free-range beef. If you don't want to cook at home, we suggest their ahi fajita burrito or the fish tacos. They also have salads, plate lunches and unique specials. The outdoor seating is covered, so if you want some sun, take it to the beach. It's pricier because you're in Kilauea. Behind the Kilauea Plantation Center, kitty-corner from the Kong Lung Center. **$12–$17** for lunch and dinner. Closed Sunday.

Village Snack & Bakery Shop
5-5190 Kuhio Hwy • 826–6841

ono Hanalei—Their baked goods are *excellent* and very reasonably priced. Ambiance is...well, they don't *have* any. But if you want a place that has looked the same since the island rose from the sea, this is the place for you. Hearty, cheap food. Try the apple cobbler—*very* ono and only $2.50. Or consider the chili pepper chicken or a tuna sandwich. **$4–$10** for breakfast and lunch. Not bad food for the price. Simple, homey and cluttered. In Ching Young Village. Open at 6:30 a.m.

NORTH SHORE MEXICAN

Neide's Salsa & Samba
5-5161 Kuhio Hwy • 826–1851

Hanalei—Our ONOs have come and gone with them. Currently the food's reasonably good, but it's too bland to recommend strongly. Though they're Brazilian (with some Brazilian dishes), the Mexican items like the burritos and enchiladas work best, *if* you use some of their salsa. Service is friendly and laid back. For the price, it's a reasonable place to go if you're sandy from the beach and don't want a lot of pretense. In Hanalei Center, at the back of the center. **$12–$24** for lunch and dinner. When they say the plate's hot, what they *really* mean is that you could bake a raw pizza on it.

Red Hot Mama's
5-6607 Kuhio Hwy • 826–7266

ono Ha'ena—Literally a hole-in-the-wall take-out window past the 6 mile marker before the end of the road on Hwy 560 next to the Last Chance Store in Ha'ena. Simple, hearty Mexican food, mostly burritos and tacos with some salads and tuna wraps. Their "small kine" burrito is pretty good-sized for

$8, and the "fat mama" will do most big eaters for $11. The hot sauce is fairly spicy and tasty, but it's an extra $1. Lunch is **$9–$13**, and they close promptly at 5 p.m. or *before*, if they run out of food. Buy your drinks next door and take it all to the beach. Cash only.

Tropical Taco
5-5088 Kuhio Hwy • 827–8226
Hanalei—If you're wondering why there's a likeness of a green truck inside this location, it's because the owner operated Tropical Taco out of one for over 20 years. Located in the green Halele'a Building on the ocean side of the highway in Hanalei, the food is pretty good (though too expensive, and the portions could be bigger), and it's not a bad place to grab a bite when you're on the run on the north shore. Lunch and dinner are **$10–$15**. No credit cards.

NORTH SHORE THAI

Nam Jai Thai
4480 Hookui Rd. • 652–3699
Kilauea—A tiny place with a few covered tables that serves simple Thai food as well as some Thai-inspired items, such as the Thai burger. The selection is reasonably large and prices are fair, but there's no table service and the quality of ingredients seems average at best. Order at the counter and chow down. Heat levels are really tame, even if you order Thai hot. The Thai tea is too sweet to drink, and beverage selection is scant. Mosquitoes can be a problem (as are some unusually aggressive chickens), so consider getting it to go. Summer rolls are good, but overall, we're a bit disappointed. Turn makai on Hookui St. near the 23 mile marker. **$9–$15** for lunch and dinner. Closed Sunday's.

NORTH SHORE TREATS

Kaua'i Nut Roasters
4489 Aku Rd. • 826–7415
(ono) Hanalei—A killer variety of nuts roasted with water (no oil), and the results are excellent. They're generous with the free samples, and there's no chance you'll leave without grabbing a bag or two. Pricey but tasty. **$4–$9**. On the corner of Aku Road and Hwy 560 in Kauhale Center.

Shave Ice Paradise
5-5161 Kuhio Hwy • 826–6659
Hanalei—Good shave ice, but they are inconsistent on the syrup. Sometimes too much, sometimes too little. On expensive side. **$4–$6**. Across from Ching Young Village. Try Wishing Well instead.

Wishing Well Shave Ice
Hanalei—In a truck on the ocean side of the road in Hanalei, their shave ice can be excellent; get it with ice cream on the bottom. But it can also be chunky and bad. Service is strangely moody—sometimes nice as can be, sometimes amazingly snippy or downright caustic. Squirrely, seemingly random hours. Closed Monday. And they don't let you choose your flavor combinations. Take their combos or hit the road. Get 'em on a good day, and you'll be happy, otherwise... **$3–$6**.

EAST SHORE AMERICAN

Bubba's Burgers
4-1421 Kuhio Hwy • 823–0069
Hanalei—826–7839
Po'ipu—742–6900
(ono) Kapa'a—Funky place to get decent (but *small*) burgers, chili rice, etc., with a limited choice of burger toppings. If it wasn't for their sassy attitude, we probably *wouldn't* give them an ONO. Their motto is, "We

cheat tourists, drunks and attorneys." So if you are a drunk attorney visiting the island, you're on your own, counselor. **$5–$10**. On highway in Hanalei and highway in north Kapa'a; can't miss 'em. Also in Po'ipu's The Shops at Kukui'ula near the roundabout. Nothing stands out individually, but overall the place works fairly well at the Kapa'a location. We can't recommend the Hanalei location because it's not run as well. We should point out that our reader e-mail seems to have a pretty consistent 25% negative rating for Bubba's, so maybe we're being too generous with the ONO, even for the Kapa'a location.

Bull Shed
4-796 Kuhio Hwy • 822–3791
Kapa'a—Dinner only, quite popular with both locals and tourists, known for hearty beef and seafood and moderate portions. They really rely on their location to keep you happy. (That's code for bad food.) They seem to strive for mediocrity but rarely climb that high. The window seats are particularly close to the water (we've been there when the waves actually splashed against the glass), but arrive 10–15 minutes before they open (they start serving dinner at 5:30 p.m.) to get one. All entrées come with a choice of salad or...salad. Sorry, no soup. (With a dependably pathetic salad bar, too.) The service can be slow and decidedly unenthusiastic. And if I may rant, you only get rice with entrées. If you pay extra and get a baked potato, they take the rice away. Hey, I'm *paying* for it. Leave it alone! (Whew, I feel better already.) **$15–$30**. Limited desserts such as mud pie and a pretty good and reasonably priced wine list. On the ocean side of highway across from Kaua'i Village. Reservations only for 6 or more.

Caffé Coco
4-369 Kuhio Hwy • 822–7990
(ONO) Kapa'a—Tucked away and hard to find, they serve some very delicious food along with some unusual recipes. Sort of a vegetarian/Pacific Rim/fish menu with other items as well. Specials and regular items change on a whim—you may hear them debate or invent what to fix on the spot. But many items are clever and tasty, such as the fish dipped in panko and cilantro pesto, and the killer potstickers filled with tofu and chutney. Or try the various vegetarian items or the seafood gumbo. Flavor combinations seem well-chosen here. Relaxing ambiance with tables sprinkled around a gravel floor under various umbrellas and awnings with plants all around. (Sometimes mosquitoes are a problem.) Service is so relaxed that it's easy to feel ignored or unwelcome at first. You're not; it's just that they're profoundly laid back. But once you order your food, you are *usually* served well. **$17–$27** for dinner. Across the street from Kintaro Restaurant on Hwy 56 in Wailua (north of 6 mile marker); head toward the back. Closed Monday. Still for sale at press time, so things may change. B.Y.O.B. with a $5 corkage fee.

Chicken in a Barrel
4-1586 Kuhio Hwy • 823–0780
Kapa'a—The name refers to their method of smoking beef, pork, ribs and chicken in a barrel. And if all they served was chicken, we'd give 'em an ONO *in a heartbeat*. It's super moist and flavorful. And they are very nice folks running this tiny stand on the ocean side of the highway with picnic tables in north Kapa'a. But the other meats are bland and don't pick up the flavors, and their breakfasts are pretty tasteless. So by all means, grab the chicken. But that's it. Keep your hands off everything else. **$12–$17** for lunch. Across

from the Kaua'i Products Fair at the north end of Kapa'a. Closed Sunday.

Deli & Bread Connection
2600 Kaumualii Hwy • 245-7115

ONO Lihu'e—An absolutely dandy place to get sandwiches (although you'll often have to wait a while at lunch time). Large selection of traditional meats and veggies, plus some extras. Try the TOPS sandwich. **$8-$12.** In Kukui Grove next to Macy's. Some effective baked goods (though sometimes stale). But overall, a very steady place.

Duane's Ono-Char Burger
4-4350 Kuhio Hwy • 822-9181

ONO Anahola—Duane's Ono-Char Burger is an institution on Kaua'i. Now into their third decade, Duane's still serves some of the better burgers on the island. Though a bit too pricey and with portions that are a bit too small, their specialty burgers, such as the teriyaki burger and the mushroom burger, are delicious. Their milkshakes (especially the marionberry shake) are outstanding. Most customers opt to eat at the cement outdoor tables, which are a bit stark. Marauding wild chickens and cats usually compete for your jettisoned french fries. Or consider taking your food down Anahola Road (south of Duane's) to Anahola Beach Park, where picnic tables at the beach make for a pleasant atmosphere. (Weekends at that beach, however, are a bit crowded.) Service can be gruff—don't take it personally. **$8-$14** for lunch till 6 p.m. On the highway in Anahola; can't miss it. You may want to call in your order because you'll *never* wait less than 20 minutes, often *way* longer, if you order at the counter. We've noticed a slow, steady deterioration at Duane's over time and fear that this may be the last edition we give them an ONO.

Duke's Canoe Club
3610 Rice St. • 246-9599

ONO Lihu'e—Before we talk about the food, we should mention that this is one of the better places on the island to have a tropical cocktail, downstairs outdoors overlooking Kalapaki Bay. We also like the indoor table by the small indoor waterfall. The small menu includes ribs, burgers and sandwiches that can easily serve as a meal and are not as overpriced as most resort foods. Service there is only fair, and prices are **$13-$17.** Now as for the restaurant *upstairs*, the beef and seafood are very good. Consider the fresh catch prepared Duke-style. The prime rib is huge and delicious, and their salad bar is probably the best on the island. Lanai tables at the railing are best, offering a nice view of the bay. **$18-$35,** which is fairly reasonable for the quality of the surroundings. Located at the Marriott. (You can park in their lot or next to Anchor Cove at the beach parking lot.) The also have free valet parking from the road next to Anchor Cove, but it often fills up. Reservations recommended.

The Eastside
4-1380 Kuhio Hwy • 823-9500

ONO Kapa'a—Great food and good service make this a no-brainer to recommend. We've kind of gotten into a rut here, usually ordering the potato crusted mahi mahi entrée. But they also have great ceviche and excellent steak. They *usually* make excellent calamari, but as soon as we fall in love with a particular preparation, they change the recipe. The atmosphere is fairly simple and there's no view other than the highway. *But da grinds work here, brah.* Live music some nights. Try their killer tangerine martini. **$25-$38** for dinner. In the center of Kapa'a town, on the ocean side of the highway.

Happy Shack
4-1586 Kuhio Hwy • 212–8145

Kapaʻa—You probably won't see a sign on this white truck across from the Kauaʻi Products Fair at the north end of Kapaʻa—and you probably won't understand the owner—but they have a bizarre selection of Thai and Mexican items along with some candies, shave ice, sandwiches, hot dogs and some great smoothies. (We classified them under American 'cause we just didn't want to deal with it.) The overwhelming menu is in the form of dizzying lists and photos covering each other, and it's simply hard to make a decision here. But you can get a plate of fish tacos, rice and beans for under $10 or some pad Thai shrimp for $12 and eat it at the nearby picnic tables. How can they have so many items from this tiny truck? Service can be slow. Flavors on some items, like the pork tacos, are great, but some, such as the pad Thai, can be bland if you order it mild. Have 'em crank it up a bit. The frozen bananas are a joke. But for some reason, the experience usually works for us. **$5–$12**.

Hukilau Lanai
520 Aleka Loop • 822–0600

ONO Kapaʻa—Fish is their specialty, and they do it very well. In the past we steered you away from non-fish items, but they seem to operating on all cylinders lately. The complex flavor combinations here are skillfully conceived. The sweet potato raviolis or the lobster and goat cheese wontons make killer appetizers. And don't overlook their bartending skills, which are unusually well crafted. (Try the coconut coast cooler.) The Hukilau Mixed Grill is a tasty selection of seafood items. And their meatloaf is deadly. The atmosphere and views of the courtyard are peaceful and romantic, and if you have kids, you could turn 'em loose on the large lawn adjacent to the dining room. At Kauaʻi Coast Resort, next to Coconut Marketplace. **$25–$35** for dinner. Closed Monday.

Island Palm Steakhouse
4-885 Kuhio Hwy • 823–8828

Kapaʻa—A mixed bag. The atmosphere is islandy and relaxing, though highway noises are never far away. And prices are fairly reasonable. Most items are in the low $20s and include rice and veggies and a trip to the (admittedly small) salad bar. Extras are reasonably priced (such as the $2 baked potatoes). Getting a steak and seafood combo on Kauaʻi for under $25 sounds good. But the "island catch" is likely to be a frozen fish from Southeast Asia, and the steak will probably be a poor cut. Cheap ingredients at cheap prices. That's not a bad thing. You get what you pay for (for Kauaʻi)—nothing more but nothing less. Flies seem to be numerous here. The wine selection is not bad, but they're often out of the basics. **$20–$30** for dinner. On Hwy 56 north of Kauaʻi Village Shopping Center.

Jailhouse Pub & Grill
3-5350 Kuhio Hwy • 246–1110

Kapaʻa—Across the street from our local jail, it's perfectly named. (Nice view of the exercise yard from the parking lot.) They fancy themselves an Irish pub—and they do have some Irish dishes, such as Gaelic steak and shepherd's pie as well as Guinness on tap, of course—but their local regulars respond more to the Korean kimchee and the loco moco. Atmosphere is cafeteria-like with a bar, and it overlooks part of the Wailua Golf Course. Nothing is good, but nothing is expensive. I'd like to say more, but since one of the owners is a criminal defense attorney and the other a bail bondsman (and who knows, I might need either one or the other someday), I won't say any more. **$8–$10** for breakfast, $9–$13 for lunch and dinner. On the Hwy between Kapaʻa and Lihuʻe

Java Kai
4-1384 Kuhio Hwy • 823–6887
Kapaʻa—A small coffee place on the ocean side of Hwy 56 in northern Kapaʻa that serves lots of tasty coffee concoctions and other drinks. (Good chai latte; ask them not to make it too sweet.) You're better off with their baked goods than ordering from their 6-item menu. (Avoid the pre-made breakfast burritos.) Coffee by the pound. $5–$11. On highway in north Kapaʻa. Open at 6 a.m.

JJ's Broiler
3416 Rice St. • 246–4422
Nawiliwili—A longtime steak and seafood landmark. With their location adjacent to Kalapaki Beach they were able to eke out an ONO from us in the last edition, but no more. They have a varied menu at dinner of steak, seafood, pasta, and carryovers from lunch with burgers, sandwiches and salads ($15 and up), which creates lots of choices. But prices are high, and extras such as appetizers and beverages (you can't get a glass of wine for under $10) are pretty overpriced. The atmosphere inside is more sports bar, with the outdoor tables overlooking Kalapaki Bay. (You won't hear the surf, only the sports announcers.) Quality has slipped, and their signature dish—Slavonic steak— seems to be an attempt to bury poor cuts of steak with sauces. $15–$22 for lunch, $15–$40 for dinner. In Anchor Cove.

Kalapaki Beach Hut
3474 Rice St. • 246–6330
Nawiliwili—A small shack that specializes in burgers made from Kauaʻi beef (which they often undercook). They also have a couple grilled sandwiches and fish and chips. Their taro fries are unusual but no more flavorful than any other taro

preparation. They often have lines, and seating is at a long counter with a couple tables and a counter with an ocean view upstairs. Service can be slow—this ain't fast food. We've given them ONOs in the past and maybe should now, but they've been slipping. Consider it a close call. Breakfast is $8–$12 with a scant selection (good breakfast sandwich). $9–$13 for lunch and dinner. Next to Anchor Cove Shopping Center. Open at 7 a.m.

Kalapaki Joe's
3501 Rice St. • 245–6266
ONO Nawiliwili—A broad selection of sandwiches, burgers, steak and a number of seafood items such as fish tacos, salads and pasta. The appetizer list is long and varied—from nachos to ahi poke to steamed clams to their tasty garlic fries. Lots of salads. The atmosphere can be loud with lots of TVs often playing sports, plus you're upstairs across from a busy road with a sliver of a view of Kalapaki Bay. The food is reasonably priced and usually fairly good. Service is hit or miss. Good beer selection. Overall, a reliable place for grinds and a brew. $10–$20 for lunch and dinner.

Kountry Kitchen
4-1485 Kuhio Hwy • 822–3511
ONO Kapaʻa—A dandy place to get breakfast (served till 1:30 p.m.) with pretty good results. Hence the ONO. Lunch also available. You may have to wait during peak times. Large selection of omelette ingredients. (Omelettes are hit or miss—consider the kalua pork; the pancakes, however, are very fluffy.) Be sure to check the board for specials which are usually around $14. Simple American and local food in a small, diner-style atmosphere. $11–$18 for breakfast, $9–$15 for lunch. Our reviews haven't changed much over the years, 'cause they haven't changed either.

Lemongrass
4-885 Kuhio Hwy • 821–2888
Kapaʻa—An interesting and eclectic menu featuring Asian, local and American items, plus pasta, fresh fish and steak. Food can be good here, but usually isn't and is overpriced, plus the quality of ingredients doesn't seem very high. Service has a tendency to be pretty bumbling—always has. $20–$40 for dinner. On Hwy 56 in Kapaʻa north of Kauaʻi Village.

Lihuʻe Barbecue Inn
2982 Kress St. • 245–2921
(ono) Lihuʻe—Steak, seafood and sandwiches with some Asian dishes served in a simple, clean atmosphere. Breakfast can be good. Their French toast creations are pretty unusual but effective. We also liked the breakfast burrito and the benedict. They tend to run out of basic, core items. This place is very popular with locals who appreciate the good food and large portions, though they seem to have shrunk a bit lately. Tasty homemade bread and pies. Teriyaki pork chops, sandwiches, fish, great kalua pig and cabbage—they do most things well. (Avoid the ribs, though. Local style and very fatty.) A good value all around. How nice when you find out your beverages and desserts are included with many meals for $10 or less. It's not the best food on the island. But it *is* an excellent deal. Kress is a side street off Rice St. $7–$10 for breakfast, $10–$16 for lunch, $12–$27 for dinner. Closed Sunday.

Mermaids Café
4-1384 Kuhio Hwy • 821–2026
Kapaʻa—They strive for a healthier meal here and often succeed with their tiny menu. You're best off with the ahi wraps, the fish tacos or the curry plate. Bountiful salads. They have a number of tasty and unusual drinks, such as hibiscus lemonade. Just a few outdoor tables. On Kuhio Hwy near 581. $10–$13 for lunch and dinner.

Olympic Café
4-1354 Kuhio Hwy • 822–5825
Kapaʻa—The menu here is vast and most portions are bulky. Breakfast scrambles are tasty, and the burritos and burgers work well at lunch. Dinner adds some more expensive items like steak, pasta and fajitas. For dessert, the tasty Kauaʻi Pie has nearly a half-gallon of ice cream and can easily satisfy a table of four. Fridays they have a free taco bar during happy hour (3–7 p.m.), which can get really busy. It's a weird night, and you should stay away from the fish. $10–$15 for breakfast and lunch, $11–$30 for dinner. Service can be spotty. Window seats overlook the highway. Across from ABC Store in downtown Kapaʻa.

Ono Family Restaurant
4-1292 Kuhio Hwy • 822–1710
(ono) Kapaʻa—A vast breakfast selection that has something for everyone. Ambiance is old and cluttered (parts of it look like a garage sale), and service is usually quick. Basic eggs, taters and sausage combo is not real compelling, but other items, including French toast with coconut syrup work. $9–$15 for breakfast and lunch. The ono is for value and selection at breakfast, not for the lunch, which is average burgers. On the ocean side of Hwy 56 south of 581. They also have a shave ice stand outside that serves average quality shave ice.

Papaya's Natural Foods
4-831 Kuhio Hwy • 823–0190
Kapaʻa—A good health food store that also serves mostly veggie items, such as veggie lasagna, tofu, falafels and perhaps some sandwiches. Basically you fill a plate once for about $7.50, and results are mixed. We've had some good meals

here...and we've walked away with our inedible plates still full. Hard to say what you'll get. Good fish tacos, though. **$6–$10** all day. If you eat at the tables, be forewarned that you are likely to be dining with individuals who consider bathing an unnecessary and decadent ritual. Located in Kaua'i Village.

Scotty's Beachside BBQ
4-1546 Kuhio Hwy • 823–8480

(ONO) Kapa'a—First things first. Since the initial edition of this book, we've reviewed every company from a dispassionate and unbiased view. We've never had a stake in *any* company. We now have a singular exception, and we want be upfront and tell you why. For years people wrote to us saying, *I want to move to Kaua'i. What does the island really need?* And for years we gave the same response—*You can't get good* BBQ *on Kaua'i.* Much to our surprise, nobody ever took our advice. We missed good BBQ, and with a hugely talented partner we decided to open *Scotty's* at the ocean in Kapa'a. You won't find us working there (our partner, Scotty, is da man), but you will find some of the things we learned after reviewing hundreds and hundreds of eateries in the islands, and we tried to fix the things that always bugged us about restaurants, from the design of the building to the design of the mai tais. (*Lots* of selfless research went into the recipe for *that* one.) For the first year it was open, we *didn't* give it an ONO because it felt unseemly given our ownership. After a year of getting pretty vocal e-mails from readers telling us it deserves an ONO, we relented, but given our interest you are allowed to feel skeptical. *We* believe in it, but we're biased in this case. The menu includes ribs, BBQ pulled pork and beef brisket sandwiches (we always request the sauce be mixed into the meat) and also includes fish tacos, fish and chips, wraps,

etc. Salad bar available for lunch and dinner. It's one of only a half dozen restaurants that's right next to the ocean (on the Kapa'a Bike Path) and built in a series of tiers so every table has an unobstructed, open-air ocean view. On the highway at the north end of Kapa'a, north of Hwy 581, ocean side. It's **$8.50** for the breakfast buffet (includes beverages), **$8–$16** for lunch, **$14–$27** for dinner (more for a full rib rack).

Small Town Coffee
4-1613 Kuhio Hwy • 821–1604

(ONO) Kapa'a—An artsy, hodge-podge café with personality. Their coffee is consistently good and organically grown. Powerful espressos, homemade hot chocolates and lattes. Their breakfast bagels are fantastic with amusing names like the Italian Scallion, the Pig in the Apple Tree and the We Found Nemo (bagel and lox). Diehard regulars usually occupy the outside tables where they solve the world's problems among themselves. It tends to take awhile to get your breakfast. Open 5:30 a.m. (food starts at 7 a.m.). Free Wi-Fi. **$7–$10**. On mauka side of Hwy 56 in north Kapa'a inside the Kaua'i Products Fair next to the Red Dirt Shirt store.

Spicy Island Grill
4-1586 Kuhio Hwy • 652–9543

Kapa'a—A truck across from the Kaua'i Products Fair at the north end of Kapa'a. Here it's garlic or spicy shrimp, jerk chicken and jerk sandwiches. Service can be *achingly* slow. The chicken is fairly tasty and leaves a pleasant burn aftertaste, and the shrimp is loaded with garlic. But because it's unpeeled, you knock all the garlic off in the process of getting to the meat, leaving the shrimp pretty muted. Flies can be a problem. **$8–$14**. Closed Mon. and Tue.

Tiki Room
3501 Rice Street • 246–1100

Nawiliwili—The decor is only mildly tiki (other than the bar), and the music is more apt to be hip hop than Polynesian or reggae. The menu is fairly ordinary with sandwiches, burgers and salads for lunch, some seafood, pasta and steak at dinner. Nothing shines here. Flavors taste bland and canned. With their location within walking distance to Nawiliwili Harbor, they probably do good on cruise ship day, but are otherwise not worth stopping for. In Harbor Mall. **$11–$15** for lunch, **$15–$20** for dinner.

TNT Steakburgers
Kuhio Hwy • 651–4922

ONO Kapaʻa—At the north end of town in Kojima's parking lot on the mauka side of Highway is a trailer that serves up some surprisingly good burgers. They grind their own steak, and the buns are made especially for them. Sizes range from small to their 1-pound slab served on a bun large enough to act as a flotation device. The fries are soaked in vinegar before cooking, giving them a distinct flavor that will either wow ya or turn you off. (Most people love them.) Prices ain't cheap, but not as pricey as a more fixed location. **$7–$15** for lunch and dinner.

Tutu's Soup Hale
4-356 Kuhio Hwy • 639–6312

ONO Kapaʻa—Tutu is Hawaiian for grandma, and although this is *not* just how Nana used to cook (hers was much less healthy), they do an admirable job with lunch comfort food such as soup and hot panini sandwiches, mostly vegetarian. (Love the portobello mushroom BBQ.) Their baked potato soup is consistently good, and the spicy tomato is fatally hot. Breakfast prices are upside down.

The priciest items are the pancakes and the French toast (their signature dish), whereas their breakfast sandwich (the tasty and hearty Bert's Breckie) and potato boat are cheaper. It's a casual atmosphere (order from the chalkboard at the counter) and the service is homey, though rarely fast. They also have kava (made elsewhere) if you want to give this Polynesian woody water a try. Don't sip it; slam it in one gulp. **$8–$15** for breakfast and lunch. Cash only. In the Kinipopo Shopping Center.

22° North
3-2087 Kaumualii Hwy • 245–9593

ONO Lihuʻe—Formerly known as Gaylord's (same owners, same management), the name refers to their global latitude. (Don't worry. Our directions will be a bit more specific.) They stress organic produce and local beef and lamb and strive to be green, even using their beverage boxes as coasters. The lunch menu is small with a dozen fairly well-chosen items such as open-faced roast beef, fish and chips, meatloaf, veggie lasagna, and big burgers made from a randomly-chosen red meat. Their olive poppers make a great appetizer. At dinner you may see lamb pot pie, a steak, seared ahi or spaghetti with prawns. Hard to classify. Quality is usually very good (though avoid the fried green tomatoes), and service tends to be fairly polished. Everything is made fresh, down to the ketchup. The courtyard atmosphere, popular for local power lunches, is relaxing, but the only views are of the old historic building itself. They also have a Sunday brunch for $25 that is awesome and has some unusual selections. **$12–$18** for lunch, dinner is **$25–$35**. Mauka side between the 1 and 2 mile marker on Hwy 50 between Lihuʻe and Puhi in Kilohana.

Wahooo Seafood Grill & Bar
4-733 Kuhio Hwy • 822-7833

Kapaʻa—Ya gotta be willing to ignore the shortcomings here. Great outdoor ambiance courtesy of the large coconut grove and Sleeping Giant, if you can ignore the annoying traffic noise coming from Kuhio Hwy. Some really good and creative seafood entrées, if you can ignore the poor appetizers and very poor bar concoctions. The bananas and cream dessert is fantastic, if you can ignore the fact that the port you ordered with it comes ⅔ of the way through the dish. In short, a seafood restaurant (plus some steak) with pretty solid entrées, but everything else seems to have holes. **$25–$50** for dinner. On Kuhio Hwy, mauka side, just south of Foodland.

EAST SHORE CHINESE

Garden Island Barbecue
4252 Rice St. • 245-8868

ONO Lihuʻe—Despite the name, it's a Chinese restaurant with a local twist, *not* a BBQ. The selection is dizzying—over 150 items! (And no, we haven't tried every one.) Portions are good and the price is reasonable. There will almost certainly be something that interests you. Service is lightning fast. Although the food's not the greatest, you ain't paying for the greatest. You're paying for a large selection, large portions, and you want to get in and out fast. So you're getting what you pay for; hence the ONO. **$8–$12** for lunch and dinner. At Rice and Hardy. Closed Sunday.

Ho's Chinese Kitchen
3-2600 Kaumualii Hwy • 245-5255

Lihuʻe—We don't want to sound mean, but since our very first edition this has been the most consistently hideous food on the island. We've taken "friends" here just to punish them. But Ho's is still here,

so they must be doing something right. We just don't know what it is. **$7–$12** per person. In Kukui Grove Center.

Pacific Island Bistro
4-831 Kuhio Hwy • 822-0092

Kapaʻa—A difficult one to classify. Basically Chinese with a Pacific Rim twist. The menu has lots of compelling choices, including the tasty Peking duck. Other items include flaming satay New York, pot roast chicken and pork tenderloin. Execution is their problem. In the Kauaʻi Village Shopping Center. **$12–$25** for lunch and dinner.

EAST SHORE INDIAN

Shivalik Indian Cuisine
4-771 Kuhio Hwy • 821-2334

ONO Kapaʻa—Here's a good time to remind you that we review restaurants relative to your other dining options here. Shivalik wouldn't stand out in a big mainland city. (And certainly not in India.) But hey, you're in Kauaʻi. And if you're in the mood for an all-you-can-eat lunch buffet, Shivalik fills the need quite nicely. The flavors are good; it's not just quantity over quality. The décor is simple (mirroring their strip mall location). The 11 a.m. to 3 p.m. lunch buffet (**$14**) is a bit on the pricey side, especially since drinks are $3–$5 extra, and there's no salad. But you get about 10 different dishes to choose from, and Indian lovers can't be too choosy here. Nothing is too spicy (loved the tandoori chicken). The curries are more of the spoon type than the dipping type, and they could put a little more love into their naan bread. (Ask for it fresh, but don't expect a smile.) You can order off the menu as well, but it gets pretty expensive. Located in the Waipouli Town Center near Foodland. The ONO is for the lunch buffet only. **$18–30**.

EAST SHORE ITALIAN

Bobby V's
4-788 Kuhio Hwy • 821–8080
Kapa'a—This one's tough. Our readers seem to like it, and the folks here are super nice and friendly, but flavors seem muted and lacking to us, and they skimp a bit on the toppings. The ambiance is somewhat homey and the service prompt. Pizza, calzone and pasta. **$10–$18** for lunch and dinner, sometimes open later than most. Across from Waipouli Town Center. Parking extremely limited.

Café Portofino
3481 Hoolaulea Way • 245–2121
Lihu'e—Their view alone creates a very tasty atmosphere for those fortunate enough to get a railing table. Kalapaki Bay waves create a background hum that can enhance any food. The owner is Italian, and some of the flavors smack of the real Italy, for good and bad. (After spending a month in Italy, we came to expect good wine and bad bread—just like this restaurant.) But the quality has slipped lately, and we've had to pull their ONO. At the Kaua'i Marriott. **$25–$50** for dinner.

JJ's Pizza Pie
4-1345 Kuhio Hwy • 822–5743
Kapa'a—A little pizza place behind the ABC Store in Roxy Square. You order from a window and take it to go, or use their small outdoor gazebo area. They don't offer pizza by the slice, but their whole pies are generous with the toppings. The crust is crisp and thin, and the overall results are hearty and filling. Flavors aren't bland but they aren't... quite right either. Because everything is made fresh, consider going for a stroll or calling ahead 'cause it can take over 30 minutes. Closed Sundays. Cash only. **$10–$15**.

Kaua'i Pasta
4-939B Kuhio Hwy • 822–7447
ONO Kapa'a—A pretty easy place to like for the most part. Expect a few pastas and four sauces, plus paninis and Parmesans for lunch, add pizzettas and some specials at dinner. The quality is good for the price and portions ample except for the tasty bread that they are so stingy with. Their lunch salads are very large and they are happy to split them, so consider ordering only one per couple. You can add chicken breast to any pasta for $5, or add meatballs for a crazy *$10*. Well chosen wine and beer list, but they'll ding you for $15 if you BYOB. Lunch is **$10–$25**, dinner is **$15–$30**. On Kuhio Hwy behind Taco Bell. If you walk through the restaurant, they have another dining room and nice lounge in the back, and the atmosphere seems to be most casual in the front. They also have a location in Lihu'e at 3-3142 Kuhio Hwy that is *not* as good—no ONO there.

EAST SHORE JAPANESE

Hanama'ulu Café, Tea House & Sushi Bar
3-4291 Kuhio Hwy • 245–2511
Lihu'e—Japanese and Chinese served in a *delightful* atmosphere. There are gardens out back, a koi pond and individual tea rooms (if you reserve one with a group). The food here isn't the highest quality, but portions are good considering the price. $8 will get you a heaping plate of their famous crispy fried ginger chicken. On the main highway (56) just outside of Lihu'e in Hanama'ulu. Hours can be squirrely; call to verify. **$9–$15** for lunch, **$12–$25** (more if you go nuts on the sushi) for dinner. Mosquitoes can be a problem at times. Closed Monday.

Kintaro Restaurant
4-370 Kuhio Hwy • 822-3341

ONO Kapaʻa—You will be happy with this selection. *Excellent* sushi bar (try the Hanalei rolls), large teppan yaki section (that's where the food is prepared in front of you by a talented, knife-wielding chef), full bar and a very pleasant atmosphere. The food is expertly prepared using only the freshest ingredients. The service is outstanding. Fun but not stuffy. Filet mignon for those who don't want Japanese food. In fact, they have the best steak and lobster on the island. It's cubed and cooked in front of you, and it melts in your mouth. A bit pricier than others, but worth it. (Occasionally they get over-enthusiastic with the salt.) Just north of Kinipopo Shopping Center not too far from the Wailua River on Hwy 56. Dinner only, **$20–$50**. Reservations recommended for the teppan yaki. (They don't take them for the sushi *bar*, only the tables.)

EAST SHORE KOREAN

Korean Bar-B-Q
4-356 Kuhio Hwy • 823-6744

ONO Kapaʻa—A good place to try some Korean food with a local twist. The combo plates are the best deal. One or more meats—teriyaki beef, kalbi (short ribs), etc.—plus plenty of side dishes—rice, mac salad, kimchee and Korean miso soup, which is excellent, but make *sure* you finish it before the meats arrive. Miso tastes terrible if you eat it with the meats. Overall, consistently good, except for the disappointing chicken katsu. **$9–$16** for lunch and dinner. In the Kinipopo Shopping Village in the south part of Wailua on Hwy 56.

EAST SHORE LOCAL

Dani's Restaurant
4201 Rice St. • 245-4991

Lihuʻe—Clean, cheap and reasonably good. Breakfast is very popular and your best bet here. Lunch is kalua pig, tripe stew, lau lau, pork chops, etc. Service is totally dependent on who your waitress is. It's *very* loud inside and crowded, cafeteria style, but this isn't a bad choice if price is important, though portions are a bit smallish by local standards. **$8–$12** for breakfast (coffee is included with meal) and lunch. Open at 5 a.m. Closed Sunday.

Fish Express
3343 Kuhio Hwy • 245-9918

ONO Lihuʻe—A long-time local favorite, this is the place to get your seafood fix to go. Along with luʻau foods and salads (both very good), they make some wicked fish specials. Seven different preparations are paired with a fresh fish that changes daily. You can't go wrong with macadamia nut crusted fish with lilikoʻi, or have it sautéed with garlic and herbs. Get brave and try some of the unusual but tasty seafood creations at the deli counter. The ahi poke is a good place to start. Portions can be small—sandwiches are their most generous items. **$8–$12**. Across from Walmart on Hwy 56. Open 10 a.m. to 6 p.m. (Grill closes at 2 p.m.) Closed Sundays, and no grilled items on Saturdays.

Hamura Saimin Stand
2956 Kress St. • 245-3271

ONO Lihuʻe—Universally loved by locals and forewarned visitors alike, they have *some of the best saimin on Kauaʻi.* (See page 208 for definition of saimin.) It is wildly popular, and people come from other parts of the island to eat here. Their selection is scant, but the food is good and cheap. Consider the "special" saimin, which has more ingredients and is tastier. Their only dessert—liliko'i pie—is light and fairly good but sells out early. Food is served lunch-counter style—so seat yourself. Though dumpy, it'll be here forever unless the sodium police raid the place. Makes for good takeout, but it's so hot that transporting it almost necessitates a hazardous materials permit. (Spill any on you, and you may burst into flames.) They have good shave ice. (That part of the business is called **Halo Halo Shave Ice**, and they ignore it when they're busy (and sometimes when they're not). Sometimes only on Tuesday. Try ringing the bell. Make sure to get the shave ice with ice cream on the bottom. **$5–$10** for lunch and dinner. Kress is off Rice Street. See map on page 65. Cash only.

House of Noodles
4-1330 Kuhio Hwy • 822-2708
Kapa'a—Diverse menu of saimin, sandwiches, battered lobster and burgers. Items are hit or miss. In general, stick with noodle items like the saimin and won ton soup or a smoothie from the cart. The sandwiches are small and unimpressive, the ambiance is a bit third world, and outdoor tables are besieged with traffic noise. It's fairly overpriced for what you get. Kuhio Hwy south of Hwy 581. **$12–$20** for lunch and dinner with a few cheaper items.

Kalena Fish Market
2985 Kalena St. • 246-6629
Lihu'e—Sort of out of the way and hard to find, which in this case is OK. 'Cause the food is not worth going in search of it. Plate lunches, chicken katsu and some Korean BBQ items served with avoidable results. Oh, and by the way, despite the name, it's not a fish market. **$6–$11**. On Kalena (south of Kress St.) near Rice Street.

Mark's Place
1610 Haleukana St. • 245-2722
Puhi—One of those places that you'd never know was here if someone didn't tell you about it. They probably serve the best local food on the island. The prices are reasonable and the portions ample. Consider the mixed plate with chicken katsu, teriyaki beef and beef stew for around $8.50. That's the most expensive meal. Or try the loco moco, Korean chicken, or one of the specials, such as the occasional kalua pig and cabbage. This is local-style food, so don't expect low calorie or low cholesterol. And don't expect to eat in; everything's to go. But if you want to eat what many locals eat and don't want to spend much, this is the place for you. **$8–$11** for lunch. From Hwy 50, take Puhi Road, right on Hanalima. Closed weekends.

Pono Market
4-1300 Kuhio Hwy • 822-4581
Kapa'a—The friendly folks here serve a great plate lunch with lots of aloha. If you don't know what an item is, they take the time to explain. It's the perfect place to try some local dishes like lau lau or kalua pork. Their ahi poke is arguably the best on island. It can get busy around lunch, but they run it like a well-oiled machine. **$6–$12** with some cheaper sandwiches, cash only. On the ocean side of Hwy 56 in downtown Kapa'a.

Tiano's
4479 Rice St. • 245-6909
Lihu'e—A super varied menu that encompasses lots of local dishes, burgers, pasta, steak and sandwiches. The kalua pig nacho is a fairly good way to start things off (with some papaya relish). Consider their combo, which includes prime rib and their garlic shrimp for a hearty meal. Noise from the busy street might spill over

onto your plate, but the service is usually friendly (though often slow) and the atmosphere casual. Tiano's ain't the healthiest food on the island, but flavors are reasonable good. On the down side, the food may not be hot when it's served, and some portions (such as the tasty garlic shrimp) are too small. (Other items can be more generous.) **$10–$15** for breakfast, **$10–$20** for lunch, add **$2–$5** more at dinner for the same items. Near Kuhio Highway.

Tip Top Café
3173 Akahi St. • 245–2333
Lihu'e—This place is recognized by locals as an outstanding bargain for breakfast and lunch. The menu includes some non-traditional breakfast items, such as beef stew and oxtail soup served first thing in the morning. Banana and macadamia nut pancakes come large, fluffy and light, but hearty and filling. Or try the pineapple pancakes—very tasty. Good coffee. Great cream puffs and pastries in the morning (pass on the cookies, though.) Eggs are their weak spot. Clean, unpretentious heartiness, less-than-bubbly service. Readers are split—half *love* the place, the other half are unhappy. But we still think it's a good breakfast spot. **$7–$13** for breakfast, **$9–$12** for lunch. Closed Mondays.

Waipouli Restaurant
4-771 Kuhio Hwy • 822–9311
Kapa'a—A good place to have some reasonably priced and flavorful (if not particularly healthy) local food. Lunch features items like teriyaki steak, shrimp tempura (which is good), beef sukiyaki, saimin, liver & onions, chopped steak, tofu or burgers. Portions are large, and the place is simple but utilitarian. **$6–$10** for breakfast, **$8–$12** for lunch, **$10–$17** for dinner. In Waipouli Town Center, Kapa'a, near Foodland on Hwy 56. If they don't bring your check, take your money to the counter. They're *real* informal here. Cash only. Closed Monday. They've been slipping a bit lately, so the ONO is marginal.

EAST SHORE MEXICAN

La Bamba
3-2600 Kaumualii Hwy • 245–5972
Lihu'e—In the large Kukui Grove Shopping Center. The food *can* be flavorful, but it's on the wet side. The chile relleno is probably their best bet. Comfortable, not stellar food. Service sometimes slow. **$10–$20** for lunch and dinner.

Mariachi's
3501 Rice St. • 246–1570
Lihu'e—The menu here is a broad selection of standard Mexican items plus some Mexican seafood dishes. Quality is slightly above average, but prices are too high for what you get. The portions are disappointing on some items. Service isn't as quick as you'd expect from Mexican cuisine, but they've put a disclaimer on the menu stating that it takes time, so we can't rightly scold them for it. We like to get the burritos *enchilada* style. The combination plates are a good deal if you get them "as is." Otherwise they'll nickel and dime you with extras. For dessert, try their homemade sopaipillas. **$13–$24** for lunch and dinner. Upstairs in the Harbor Mall.

Monico's Taqueria
4-356 Kuhio Hwy • 822–4300
Kapa'a—A good Mexican menu that goes a bit beyond ordinary selections, such as garlic shrimp quesadillas, chicken mole enchiladas and fish tacos, as well as more typical choices. Seafood is embraced in many items. They seem to use good quality ingredients (the fish taquitos, for example), but flavors are on the bland side, so

you may want to ask them to break out the hot sauce, which isn't on the table. Portions on some, such as the burritos, are generous. It's usually noisy inside, but outdoor tables bring traffic noise as well, and alcoholic beverages aren't allowed out there. Chip refills are extra. Closed Monday. $13–$19 for lunch and dinner. In the Kinipopo Shopping Center.

Verdé
4-1101 Kuhio Hwy • 821-1400

ONO Kapa'a—A small Mexican joint that features less typical items. They call it "new Mexican" (not to be confused with New Mexico), and the results are probably the best Mexican food on the island. Familiar Mexican flavors with refreshing ways to deliver them. Love the stuffed sopaipillas, and the stacked enchiladas *really* work, especially with chunks of pork. Flavors are bold, and they're proud of their chilies. But that boldness seems to turn some people off. (Not us.) Add fish burritos and tacos and limited bar items (a half dozen tequilas, beer and cheap-tasting margaritas), and you have the kind of place that is easy to return to. To go items don't travel well, however. $12–$18 for lunch and dinner, order at the counter. Closed Tuesday (following their $3 margarita Mondays). In Kapa'a Shopping Center near Big Save on mauka side of highway.

EAST SHORE THAI

Mema Thai Chinese
4-369 Kuhio Hwy • 823-0899

ONO Kapa'a—A great selection of Thai and some Chinese dishes, and though not great, it's the best Thai on the east shore. Consider the pad Thai, house curry or one of the vegetable items. On mauka side of Hwy 56 just north of Haleilio Road in Wailua. $13–$30 for lunch and dinner. (Lunch during the week only.) It's BYOB, which you can buy from the *flower* store next door. Service has slipped to the point that we almost withheld the ONO.

EAST SHORE TREATS

Halo Halo Shave Ice
2956 Kress St. • 245-5094

ONO Lihu'e—Good shave ice, poor service. Located in Hamura's Saimin on Kress Street; see map on page 65. They'll ignore you if the restaurant's busy. If that's the case, don't take it personally.

Hanalima Baking Co.
4495 Puhi Rd. • 246-8816

Puhi—On the corner of Puhi Road and Hwy 50 in Puhi, they serve pretty tasty malasadas (a Portuguese donut) three for $1. They have decent blueberry scones and cocoa puffs. Other sweets are not quite bakery-level. $2–$3. Open at 6 a.m. Closed Sunday.

Hee Fat General Store
4-1354 Kuhio Hwy • 823-6169

ONO Kapa'a—This is currently our favorite shave ice on the island. More gourmet than others. Their lava flow is an interesting combination with a snow cap of melted vanilla ice cream on top. Only wish they'd chill the syrups as their ultra-fluffy ice melts fast. We admire that they sweat the ice before shaving. $4–$6. North Kapa'a on Hwy across from the ABC Store.

Icing on the Cake
4-356 Kuhio Hwy • 823-1210

ONO Kapa'a—A bakery with some pretty amazing baked goods, cookies and cakes. (Grab an apple tart if they have any.) Results are consistently great (though we'll keep diligently reviewing them just to be certain), and they also have a smattering of food items, such as a tasty pesto panini, quiche and a couple others for reasonable prices. (They can take awhile, however.) In Kinipopo Shopping Center. **$3–$9**. Closed Monday, free Wi-Fi.

Kaua'i Bakery & Cinnamons
3-2600 Kaumualii Hwy • 246–4765

ONO Lihu'e—Located in Kukui Grove Shopping Center, they have a sparse selection but outstanding quality on some items. Their apple turnovers are the best on the planet when warm. *(Pretty strong words, Andy!)* Other items not as stellar. They open at 6 a.m. and may run out of many things by 11. You won't find bubbly service, *but da grinds broke da mouf, brah.*

Kaua'i Fruit & Flower
3-4684 Kuhio Hwy • 245–1814

Lihu'e—On Hwy 56 near the airport. *$9 for a pineapple!* Need we say more?

Orange Grove
3-2600 Kaumualii Hwy • 632–0055

ONO Lihu'e—A pretty cool, if slightly pricey concept. It's self-serve frozen yogurt where you put your own toppings on and are charged by the pound. (Just over half a buck per ounce, so it's easy to let things get out of hand.) The yogurts may be fat-free, but few of the 75 toppings are. Everything from Captain Crunch cereal to local tastes such as taro, azuki beans, and mochi, so you can make it as healthy—or not—as your little heart desires. In the food court at Kukui Grove Shopping Center. **$4–$10**, and you'll probably take it to go. We have no idea where the name comes from.

Sweet Marie's
4-788 Kuhio Hwy • 823–0227

ONO Kapa'a—This is the place to be a glutton without

gluten, 'cause everything's gluten-free. And they do a good job getting by without it. Brownies, macaroons, cakes, muffins, etc. Compared to other bakeries, it's not as good. But to be this tasty *without gluten* wins 'em an ONO.

SOUTH SHORE AMERICAN

Beach House Restaurant
5022 Lawai Rd. • 742–1424

ONO Lawa'i—A longtime south shore landmark. Steak and seafood with exceptional ocean views—they are right next to the water. Nice sunsets from here. Tables are reasonably spaced. The food quality is usually very good. (Steak is probably their weakest offering—stick with the seafood.) Vast wine list. Dinner, with entrées like lamb, fresh fish, steak and the like, will run you **$28–$45**. On Lawai Road in Po'ipu on way to Spouting Horn. Almost always a memorable meal, this is one of the best restaurants on the south shore. Reservations *strongly* recommended days in advance. Our review doesn't seem to change because they are pretty darned consistent here.

Brennecke's Beach Broiler
2100 Hoone Rd. • 742–7588

Po'ipu—Their motto is "right on the beach" (actually they're across the street from Po'ipu Beach Park) and "right on the price" (which is, unfortunately, dead wrong). Brennecke's is one of those places that has made a great living off their view. Opened in 1983 after Hurricane Iwa opened their view of the ocean across the street, they sailed along and continued to have a great vista after Hurricane 'Iniki pruned the trees across the street in 1992. But it's been two decades since the gardener visited, and the park vegetation has seriously encroached on their view of the ocean. Still good, but pretty limited. As for the food (mostly seafood with steak and a cheaper pasta), flavors are muted and not worth the high prices. Even the charbroiled ono with wasabi shrimp has so little wasabi we literally couldn't taste any. The staff is perky and happy, but it's hard to justify the prices, especially at dinner. $15–$23 for lunch, $30–$40 at dinner, but appetizers are expensive and *really* raise the price. Brennecke's is not a *bad* choice, but it *is* an overpriced one.

Downstairs and next door, **Brennecke's Deli** has breakfast items before 10 a.m., sandwiches, hot dogs and bad shave ice. Though the food's certainly not gourmet, it's amazing how much better it'll taste if you take it across the street to one of the beach park tables and gaze at the delicious scenery. $5–$10.

Ilima Terrace
1571 Poipu Rd. • 742-1234

(ONO) Po'ipu—Located at the Grand Hyatt, they offer good food in a beautiful, open-air setting near a Hyatt waterfall. Breakfast is overpriced (how else can you describe $15 pancakes or $18 loco moco?). And at lunch you have burgers or a cobb salad for $18 or pricier dinner-style entrées for more. They also have a fairly good daily breakfast buffet for $28. A bargain? No. But the location helps take the sting out of it and garners them the ONO. The setting is fantastic—ask for the table next to the waterfall. Reservations recommended.

Joe's on the Green
2545 Kiahuna Pl. • 742-9696

Po'ipu—On the Kiahuna Golf Course next to the driving range, the open-air feel and views of mountains give it a pretty and relaxing atmosphere. Breakfast is your best bet. Lunch is sandwiches (love the Bruddah Reuben and the Marta's Melt), salads, and fish and chips. Service is

friendly. $9–$15 for breakfast and lunch. From Po'ipu Road take the road into Po'ipu Shopping Village. Then drive past it into Kiahuna Golf Course.

Kalaheo Café & Coffee Co.
2-2560 Kaumualii Hwy • 332-5858

(ONO) Kalaheo—Comfortable coffee house ambiance with lots of room, quality breakfast choices and a large list of coffee drinks make this a good spot to stop on your way to a boat tour on the west side. Order at the counter and grab a seat. Great omelettes. We like the bonzo burrito and the bagel benny. Their cinnamon knuckles are deadly and best eaten hot. Sandwiches and salads at lunch. Dinner offers an eclectic menu. We like the open-face enchilada, but the coconut shrimp appetizer will keep us coming back. $7–$14 for breakfast, $15–$30 for dinner (Wed.– Sat.) On highway in Kalaheo. Open at 6:30 a.m. Across from Brick Oven Pizza.

Keoki's Paradise
2360 Kiahuna Plantation • 742-7534

(ONO) Po'ipu—This is a special sort of place that people either love or hate (we love it). The ambiance is the story here with plants everywhere, a large fish lagoon, waterfalls and thatched roof booths (try to say *that* three times fast). It's the South Pacific that never really existed except in movies. The exotic bar area serves burgers, sandwiches and ribs at lunch and dinner for $12– $17. Some people wait there for a table while others make a meal of it to save money. The tables in the main area are arranged on several levels. Purists will sniff that the ambiance is not real—so what?! It's still exotic inside. If you are in the right mood, this is the sort of place you will remember for a long time. As for the food, it's a steak and seafood restaurant with above average food and service. Five styles of fish and steak plus their signature prime rib (including a 32-ouncer for those who swam here from O'ahu). The hula pie is equally large. The place can get pretty busy, which can have an effect on the service. Reservations recommended. **$25–$40** (more for steak and lobster) for dinner. In the Po'ipu Shopping Village.

Merriman's Fish House
2829 Ala Kalanikaumaka Rd. • 742-2856
Po'ipu—Merriman's is a local chain named after the founder, and we've always been impressed with them. This location is the first where we didn't give them an ONO. This really is two separate restaurants. The cheaper downstairs café is more casual and has items ranging from pizzas (tasty) to fish tacos (a bit disappointing) burgers, sandwiches and pastas. Most dishes work well and are reasonably priced for the quality. **$12–$17**. Upstairs is their fish house and, though the food and service are good, it's overpriced given the ambiance, which is tropical plantation. Only a few lanai tables (requestable) have views of the distant ocean. Otherwise, the windows are mounted too high, giving you a penned-in feeling. Items such as their lobster mac and cheese appetizer (super pricey, super tasty) and the crazy good chocolate purse dessert go well with their entrées, most of which are good, but some are underwhelming. (Stick with the fish.) **$30–$50**. If all they had was the downstairs, we'd give 'em an ONO, but they need to do something with the upstairs to make it worth the money. We get the feeling this restaurant hasn't received enough attention from the founder, and we're hoping that changes. In The Shops at Kukui'ula.

Plantation Garden
2253 Poipu Rd. • 742-2121
Po'ipu—A very relaxing tropical orchid, cactus and bromeliad garden setting with mostly outdoor tables (which are preferred). The menu is a small but carefully selected array of fresh fish and a few red meat entrées with a bent toward local preparations. Price is pretty reasonable given the setting, good service and beautiful presentation. But we had to yank the ONO because flavors *across the board* have been so muted on our recent visits. The food *sounds* and *looks* fantastic, but it's too bland and it would take so little effort to correct. You *want* to love the place, but bring your own seasonings. **$20–$30** for dinner. At the Kiahuna Plantation resort.

Po'ipu Tropical Burgers
2360 Kiahuna Plantation • 742-1808
Po'ipu—An unexpectedly large menu for a burger joint. In addition to the *many* half-pound burgers combinations (which start at $9 and include fries), there's spaghetti, fish and chips, sandwiches, lots of salads, veggie items, and lots of cold drinks like smoothies, freezes and floats. They are very reluctant to cook burgers less than what *they* call med/well (which seems well done to us), citing "Board of Health regulations." Plus the burgers aren't very good. **$10–$16** for lunch, add some steak and seafood up to **$25** for dinner. Back of Po'ipu Shopping Village.

Puka Dogs
2360 Kiahuna Plantation • 742-6044
(ONO) Po'ipu—Hard to believe we'd give an ONO for a $6.50 hot dog. Granted, it's overpriced. But these are very good hot dogs served in an unusual way. The dogs are roasted (giving them the slightly crunchy skin), then embedded in a wraparound bun served with a choice of sauces inside. Get some of their mango relish to smear on the tip each time you bite. Only two

dogs—a Polish sausage and a veggie dog. But with their sauces and fixin's you'll be pleased. For a beverage get their lemonade…or bring your drink. In the Po'ipu Shopping Village. It's about $10 for a dog and lemonade. Cash only.

Red Salt
2251 Poipu Rd. • 828–8888

(ono) Po'ipu—The name derives from the strong red Hawaiian sea salt that accompanies most items (and the bread with the unsalted butter). Ambiance is modern with splashes of Asian and tropical. The food is very good and very expensive. Entrées range from red salt-spiced seared ahi, pan-seared opah with king crab fries, wagu New York steak and lamb to their Big Island vanilla bean mahi mahi. They lean toward seared, so if you want it cooked through, let 'em know. They have uncommonly good mixed drinks. Though the Red Coral is their signature martini, consider the Po'ipu Surf, which is more refreshing. Our biggest ding is that their ads show a cleverly photographed oceanfront location, when, in fact, ocean views are poor and fairly distant. Also, appetizers are expensive and tasty, but *incredibly* small. The kalua pork lu'au is absolutely tiny. Take it home and starve your hamster. $30–$55 for dinner. In the Ko'a Kea Hotel. Reservations recommended.

Roy's Po'ipu Bar & Grill
2360 Kiahuna Plantation • 742–5000

(ono) Po'ipu—What started out in Hawai'i is now a chain found in many parts of the mainland. Roy Yamaguchi has a knack for combining flavors. You won't get huge portions here, but the food is extremely well prepared and well presented with prices commensurate with the quality. Atmosphere is somewhat elegant but busy, with a large, glass, sound-proof wall showcasing the kitchen. (Ask for a table in the patio room for a less busy atmosphere.) The service is efficient, attentive and friendly. We've had problems in the past with being rushed, but they seem to have toned that down. Fresh fish, pasta, chicken, beef and a host of nightly specials, all skillfully created. The fish is usually incredible. The signature dessert, baked chocolate soufflé, is obscenely delicious—order it à la mode to actually *counter* the richness. You can BYOB *only* if they don't sell that particular wine, and they charge a hefty $18 corkage fee. Located in Po'ipu Shopping Village. Dinner is $30–$45. Reservations strongly recommended.

Tidepools
1571 Poipu Rd. • 742–1234

(ono) Po'ipu—Located at the Grand Hyatt Po'ipu, their best feature is a very romantic atmosphere. A thatched roof, a stocked freshwater lagoon next to your table and flickering tiki torches outside provide a calm, quiet dinner environment. The limited menu concentrates on fresh fish (their specialty), with some beef and vegetarian items. (Good ahi sashimi, but avoid the prime rib.) $30–$45. Service is adequate. Reservations recommended. Dinner only.

Tomkats Grille
5402 Koloa Rd. • 742–8887

Koloa—A fairly large menu of burgers, plate lunches and grilled sandwiches for lunch, ribs, seafood and shrimp scampi for dinner. All served in a decidedly feline atmosphere. The ambiance is relaxing with an open-air feel next to a small fishpond and garden. But the food isn't good enough, and the service is hiss or miss. (Sorry, couldn't resist.) Lunch is your best bet. Some of their specialties are rather inventive. Not a bad place to bring the kittens, though they also feature a full bar and a huge selection of catnips (beer and tropical drinks) for the adult cats. It can get a bit warm under the hot tin roof. **$10–$17** for lunch, **$18–$30** for dinner. In Koloa town. Look for the sign near Pizzetta.

SOUTH SHORE ITALIAN

Brick Oven Pizza
2-2555 Kaumualii Hwy • 332–8561
4-4361 Kuhio Hwy • 823–8561

(ONO) Kalaheo—We have a lot of affection for this place and we eat here often, but we have to admit that it's overpriced. The pizza is the best on Kaua'i, bar none. Though not baked in a real brick oven, they pride themselves on making their own sauce, sausage and other ingredients. (Inexplicably, though, the mushrooms are canned.) The crust is thin with scalloped edges and brushed with garlic butter with tasty results. The sauce is simply perfect. Simple Italian atmosphere, attentive, friendly service and excellent pizza. But the prices—they've gone from pretty pricy to almost insane. It's just shy of *$40* for a large 4-topping pizza. It's still a great place for pizza and sandwiches, but they only reason we keep the ONO is because the pizza can't be beat. Prices are **$9–$25**. No reservations. Kids are given a wad of pizza dough to play with—nice touch. (And fitting, since adults will *spend* a wad of dough.) Located on mauka side of highway as you enter Kalaheo or the mauka side as you enter Kapa'a from Lihu'e. Buffets some nights for $15, which is recommended.

Casa Di Amici
2301 Nalo Rd. • 742–1555

(ONO) Po'ipu—Good food in a hard-to-find location. Items include standard pastas plus things like Tuscan pork loin and some island-inspired dishes and black prawns in a saffron-orange lobster sauce. The variety is pretty broad. Service can be great, but also sometimes brusque. Light piano music on some nights. **$25–$40** for dinner. In Po'ipu, take Hoowili to Hoone, drive past Brennecke Beach, and when the road goes mauka and changes its name to Nalo, look for it on a corner.

Casablanca
2290 Po'ipu Rd. • 742–2929

Po'ipu—With all due respect to Humphrey Bogart, this is *not* the beginning of a beautiful friendship. We got a number of glowing e-mails from readers recommending this restaurant (and reader e-mail is usually spot on), but we leave scratching our heads in puzzlement. Everything is weak. Food flavors are weak, salads are weak, ambiance—a glorified open pavilion with no view next to a tennis court—is super weak, and drinks are weak. (Maybe if they'd fixed that last one, we wouldn't have noticed the rest.) And you pay *a lot* for all this. Italian items along with some Mediterranean entrées and tapas plus pricey steaks. **$20–$40** for dinner. At the Kiahuna Tennis Club off Po'ipu Road. Closed Monday.

Dondero's
1571 Poipu Rd. • 742–1234

(ONO) Po'ipu—Regional Italian food. Entrées change too often to recommend a specific one here. Pastas, veal, fresh fish and lamb, usually expertly prepared. Outstanding wine list. Elegant dining; their dress code requires resort wear, meaning covered shoes, collared shirts for men, etc. Dondero's never seems to disappoint, but you *pay* for that consistency. Dinner is **$30–$50**. In the Grand Hyatt. Reservations recommended.

Pizzetta
5408 Koloa Rd. • 742–8881

ono Koloa—Although the name stresses pizza, their broad menu includes lots of pastas, parmigianas, ribs, some fish and other items. Prices for non-pizza items are pretty high; the pizzas are more fairly priced. The stuffed mushrooms make a good appetizer. Overall, entrées are pretty dependable, and the variety ensures that one person can get the BBQ chicken pizza, the other the seafood fettuccini, and both will be happy. They also make a pretty decent mai tai (but avoid the mojito). $14–$25 for lunch and dinner (cheaper for a slice and a side salad). On the main road in Koloa Town.

Pomodoro Ristorante Italiano
2-2514 Kaumualii Hwy • 332–5945

ono Kalaheo—Upscale Italian food in small, pleasing surroundings. The owners of the former Casa Italia opened this place when their restaurant in Lihu'e literally blew away. Excellent food quality, attention to detail and great service. The lasagna is *highly* recommended. So are the raviolis. The baked penne is a bit too cheesy and their pestos are disappointing, but overall, this is the best Italian food on the island and has been reliable for years. Dinner is $20–$30. In the Rainbow Plaza. (Ocean side of highway.) Closed on Sundays.

SOUTH SHORE LOCAL

Koloa Fish Market
5482 Koloa Rd. • 742–6199

Koloa—Ordering can be intimidating. You're standing at the counter with locals who *know* what they want. You, however, are trying to figure out what the items are. They serve plate lunches like lau lau, kalua pig, etc. Small selection but decent quality. $10–$13. In Koloa. Closed Sunday. Cash only.

Sueoka's Snack Shop
5392 Koloa Rd. • 742–1112

ono Koloa—Quite possibly the cheapest food on the south shore. Prices top out at around $6. Burgers, beef curry, fish burgers, chili rice and plate lunches. It's been popular forever with locals. Remember, since it's local style, items may be different than you think. For instance, the teriyaki burger isn't ground beef—it's strips of teri beef on a bun. On Koloa Road near Po'ipu Road beside Sueoka's Market. No credit cards.

SOUTH SHORE TREATS

Koloa Mill Ice Cream & Coffee
5424 Koloa Rd. • 742–6544

Koloa—Rather ordinary ice cream, but they make a mean blueberry cheesecake as well as some other baked goods. Smoothies aren't bad. In Koloa Town—can't miss it.

Lappert's Ice Cream
2829 Ala Kalanikaumaka Rd. • 742–1272

ono Po'ipu—A beautiful ice cream shop in The Shops at Kukui'ula. Lappert's has gone from great locally made ice cream, to mediocre, to good quality once again. Compelling flavors and some stupid-rich gelatos, including a nearly-radioactive chocolate.

Papalani Gelato
2360 Kiahuna Plantation • 742–2663

ono Po'ipu—Outrageous gelato made on the premises as well as dairy- and sugar-free frozen concoctions. It ain't cheap, but it's utterly delicious. $3–$7. Next to Puka Dogs in Po'ipu Shopping Village. They also serve it at Pizzetta in Koloa town, but it doesn't seem *quite* as good, and we can only attribute it to perhaps the way it's stored.

Uncle's Shave Ice
2829 Ala Kalanikaumaka Rd. • 742-2364
Po'ipu—Pricy shave ice and smoothies. The ice is ultra light and fluffy, but the syrups are so incredibly sweet, you can't finish one. **$5–$8**. In The Shops at Kukui'ula.

WEST SHORE AMERICAN

Grinds Café
4469 Waialo Rd. • 335-6027
'Ele'ele—Standard breakfast fare, hot and cold sandwiches plus pizza for lunch. Pretty ordinary stuff except for the mean cinnamon rolls. Service can be pretty indifferent. **$7–$10** for breakfast, **$8–$14** for lunch, **$9–$17** for dinner. In 'Ele'ele Shopping Center on Hwy 50 near Hanapepe. Open at 6 a.m.; good if you're doing a boat trip nearby, otherwise a miss.

Island Taco
9643 Kaumualii Hwy • 338-9895
ONO Waimea—Very tasty fish tacos in homemade tortillas. The atmosphere is bare bones (indoor counter and outdoor tables). If you like your burrito with sauce, go for the wet option (and if it's raining, the leaky awning will leave everything else wet, too). Very nice staff with a homey, family feel. Choose from flavorful options such as the Cajun or seared wasabi ahi (say that one out loud) in your tacos or burritos. We prefer the two-taco combo for $10, but we aren't wild about the refried beans and are neutral on the seasoned rice. On the mauka side of the highway. (They close at 5 p.m., so keep that in mind if you're hiking). **$7–$13** for lunch.

Koke'e Lodge
3600 Kokee Rd. • 335-6061
Koke'e—Hearty. That's the word that comes to mind. They classify themselves as local soul food. Consider the cornbread and chili. Their coconut pie is excellent. Lunch only for the most part. **$7–$12**. Located *waaaay* up the road in Koke'e on Waimea Canyon Road past the 15 mile marker. This is the road you take to get to Waimea Canyon and the Kalalau Lookout. Open 9 a.m. to 3 p.m.

Shrimp Station
9652 Kaumualii Hwy • 338-1242
ONO Waimea—A good place for a plate of shrimp with rice or fries. Some items, like the sweet chili garlic shrimp (very tasty), you'll have to peel. Others, like the coconut shrimp, are peeled. Most items are **$12**, though some are less. On the ocean side of Hwy 50 in Waimea just before Waimea Canyon Road. Just some outdoor picnic tables.

Wrangler's Steakhouse
9852 Kaumualii Hwy • 338-1218
ONO Waimea—Well, with a name like Wrangler's, you ain't a' lookin' for no Mongolian food, and you ain't a'gonna find it here. (Cowboy accents are hard to do in print.) The dinner menu is steak, which they do *very* well (the pulehu steak rocks!), and seafood. All entrées come with soup and a trip to the tiny salad bar. Lunch is burgers, steak and some specials. (Try the Kau Kau Tin.) Some outdoor tables in sunny Waimea can make for a pleasant meal. Good food with reasonable service. **$11–$17** for lunch, **$20–$40** for dinner. On the ocean side of the highway in Waimea; can't miss it. Avoid the horrible mai tais. Saturday is dinner only, closed Sunday.

WEST SHORE ITALIAN

Hanapepe Café
3830 Hanapepe Rd. • 335-5011
ONO Hanapepe—A vegetarian and seafood restaurant with

an interesting selection of unusual sandwiches. (Love the grilled vegetable or the portobello sandwiches.) They also have a number of bountiful salads, and ingredients tend to be fresh and tasty. Several garden burgers, and the hibiscus tea is pretty good. Their baked goods are deadly. The carrot cake is insanely moist and over the top good for two...or three. Cookies are just so-so. The atmosphere is simple, plantation style, and the floor shakes as people walk by. **$11–$17**. Lunch might only be Monday thru Thursday. Might have dinner Friday. From the Hwy, drill into the main part of Hanapepe to find them.

Pacific Pizza & Deli
9852 Kaumualii Hwy • 338–1020

Waimea—A reasonably good pizza place on the ocean side of Hwy 50 next to Wrangler's. In addition to the typical ingredients, they have innovations such as teriyaki chicken, shrimp, spicy Thai sauce, salmon, etc. The crust is crunchy on the bottom—very tasty—and their sauce complements things well. They could use a bit more toppings on some, but the pizza is very flavorful. Consider having them go easy on the cheese—sometimes they're too generous, and it's their weakest ingredient. They have other items such as calzone (cheesy, greasy and tasty). Your options are limited on the west side. It gets a bit warm inside, but you can always take it to the beach. **$10–$20** for lunch. Closed weekends.

WEST SHORE JAPANESE

Ichiban Sushi
4169 Waialo Rd. • 335–9989

'Ele'ele—With a name like Ichiban (Japanese for #1) and a location next to a boat harbor, you'd expect great sushi. But the sushi smells as fishy as the harbor, and portions are inexcusably small for the price. Avoid the 2-piece nigiri items starting at $5, because they...well, only come with *two bites*. The makimono rolls ($5–$9) are bigger, but still overpriced. Stick with the small selection of entrées, like chicken katsu, if you are looking for an actual meal. Otherwise, consider this a decent air-conditioned place to have a $3 beer, *maybe* sample some sushi, and perhaps even sing karaoke. Popular with local fishermen. **$11–$30** or more. In the 'Ele'ele Shopping Center.

WEST SHORE THAI

Toi's Thai Kitchen
4469 Waialo Rd. • 335–3111

Hanapepe—It's not very inspiring when you walk in. The place looks like it could use some TLC. And it may take awhile to place your order. The menu has lots of selections at lunch but with some basic items, such as green or red curry, missing. Dinner brings more items for considerably more money. Given the setting, the quality needs to be higher than it is. Overall, the food is flavorful but unusually fatty for Thai food. **$14–$18** for lunch, **$18–$25** (which is overpriced) at dinner. In the 'Ele'ele Shopping Center. Closed Sun and Mon.

WEST SHORE TREATS

Jo-Jo's Clubhouse
9734 Kaumualii Hwy

(ONO) Waimea—*Sometimes* the best shave ice on the island. Expertly prepared, large portions (piled twice as high as the cup), very reasonable prices and an outrageous selection of over 60 flavors. What else is there? Across from the 23 mile marker. Great place to stop on your way to or from Waimea Canyon (we usually do). Some problems can kill the experience, however. They sometimes let the blade get too dull (resulting in more of a snow cone-type product), and it's usually too crowded and under-staffed, so there may be a long wait. Also, we wish they had a way to keep the syrup chilled before pouring onto the ice. When this is done, it keeps hard ice from forming on the bottom of the shave ice. The surroundings aren't so good and service often poor. If you catch 'em on a bad day, we don't vouch for them. But we gave them an ONO because we wanted to call your attention to them, and it's a cheap gamble. **$3–$6**. Not to be confused with **Jo-Jo's Anuenue** around the corner toward the ocean. Their ice is good, too, and it's cleaner and has better service.

Kaua'i Chocolate Company
4341 Waialo Rd. • 335–0448
'Ele'ele—Homemade chocolates, fudge and ice cream. None are great; none are bad. It's solidly mid-level quality. In Hanapepe in the Port Allen Marina Center. **$3–$6**.

ISLAND NIGHTLIFE

I know what you're thinking. "Gee, this section sure is small." True. Let's face it— Kaua'i won't be confused with Las Vegas when it comes to nightlife. That's part of our charm. But hey, it's not like we spend *all* of our nights rearranging our sock drawers. (Usually just Fridays, and *oh, what a crazy time that* is!) Besides, if you did most of the things in the previous two sections, you're too pooped to party.

That said, there is probably enough nightlife on Kaua'i to satisfy *most* people's needs. Many of the restaurants feature entertainment at night, but the schedules are always changing. You can select a restaurant from the listings above and inquire as to their entertainment.

People have different desires when it comes to nightlife. Here we simply try to describe what's available and let you pick what you want.

Po'ipu
On the south shore, nightlife is mostly a resort affair. (So to speak.) **Stevenson's Library** at the Grand Hyatt is designed to appeal to anyone who ever wanted to visit the private library of one of the Rockefellers. Richly decorated, bookcases filled with the classics, pool tables (not billiards), large aquarium, chess tables and a terrace with great ocean views. The bar is the center attraction and is beautifully crafted out of strips of koa and monkeypod. Pupus are available, as is sushi some nights. Good but pricey cocktails. Live music nightly usually starts at 8 p.m. Things can get surprisingly lively. The Grand Hyatt's **Seaview Terrace** commands a fabulous view of the resort and can be a relaxing place to have a drink after a long day. Early nightly music.

Outside the resort, your best bet is **Keoki's Paradise** at 742–7534 in the Po'ipu Shopping Village. They have Hawaiian entertainment in their nice-looking lounge most nights. Hula demonstrations in the shopping center's courtyard some nights.

In Koloa, **Tomkats** often has live music starting around 10 p.m. They cater mostly to local hotel workers coming off their evening shifts. Music, such as reggae, is what they want to hear.

Lihu'e
Duke's Barefoot Bar at the Marriott is a great place for a drink; sporadic music offered. **Rob's Good Times Grill** (246–0311) on Rice Street offers entertainment every night. Mostly a local spot; sometimes a bit rough. **Nawiliwili Tavern** (245–1781) is very visible near the harbor and has pool tables and bar food. Kalapaki Joe's often has lots of sports on TV.

Moviegoers can call **Kukui Grove Cinemas** at 245–5055 for a listing of their features.

Kapa'a

Trees (823–0600) behind Coconut Marketplace in Kapa'a is currently *the* place to go on the east shore for live music, pupus and cocktails. Most of the local musicians featured are pretty good, and the food is better than you'd expect at a lounge. Monday is their best night, usually featuring an *awesome* electric guitar player named Jeff Caldwell. When Trees closes, some of the crowd goes to **Big Wave Dave's** (822–3362) a sports bar on the Hwy north of the ABC Store where the atmosphere can be younger and more local. **Oasis on the Beach** at the Waipouli Beach Resort in across from Safeway in Kapa'a has a good *near*-beach bar and a good selection of rums. (Try the Ron Zacapa on ice when they have it. If you mix it with Coke, we don't want to know about it.) **Cook's Landing** at the Courtyard Kaua'i at Coconut Beach (822–3455) is a decent place for a beverage while you listen to music near the pool. Some like to grab a drink here and stroll along the beach. We also like to grab a drink at the Beachboy poolside bar at **Kaua'i Coast Resort** (next door to Islander on the Beach) and sip it on the beach watching the waves. **Caffé Coco** has offbeat music most nights 7–9 p.m. **The Eastside** often has live music and a small but sometimes lively bar.

North Shore

Hanalei Gourmet (826–2524) across from Ching Young Village sometimes has live music but is only recommended for those on the prowl. **Tahiti Nui** (826–6277) in Hanalei is the center of north shore nightlife. You never know what you're gonna get there but some of the live music is pretty good.

West Shore

Find a bright light bulb and watch the geckos eat the mosquitoes—you crazy party animal, you. In Hanapepe, Friday night is art night, where you can walk the streets and peruse the galleries.

LU'AU & DINNER SHOWS

If you've ever seen a movie that takes place in Hawai'i, odds are there was a lu'au scene. This is where everyone stands around with a mai tai in one hand and a plate of kalua pig in the other. There's always a show where someone is twirling a torch lit at both ends, and, of course, the obligatory hula dancers. And the truth is, that's not far from reality. The pig is baked in the ground (called an imu) all day and is absolutely delicious. Shows are usually exciting and fast moving. Although the lu'au on O'ahu can make you feel like cattle being led to slaughter, Kaua'i's lu'au are somewhat smaller and much more pleasant.

All in all, a lu'au can be a real blast. If your time allows for one, it is highly recommended. On Kaua'i, the lu'au are all different, so your choice might be easier than on the other islands. Kilohana is high-production, story-line oriented, Grand Hyatt is more traditional, St. Regis is super pricey with great views and food but a lousy show, and Smith's is a blend of the three.

Lu'au Kalamaku at Kilohana (245–5247) is one of the largest lu'au in the state. Their 20,000-square-foot pavilion can hold nearly 1,000 people. You may not see it at maximum capacity, as some nights are cruise ship-only performances. Instead of waiting in line at the entrance, you're encouraged to roam their manicured grounds, visit the vendor booths, and grab a drink while the line diminishes. They also offer a 30-minute train ride for $18 (leaves the station at 5:15 p.m.).

Seating is assigned, and there's hardly a bad table in the house. Considering the cost of this lu'au, we expected the food to be better. The main dishes are simple, and there's little variety in the side items. Dessert is very weak, and waiting in line for 20 minutes to get it (as has happened to us) makes it worse. At least the bar is accommodating, but it closes at 7:30 p.m., just as the show begins. There are only eight women's restroom stalls, meaning on a full night it comes to 62½ women per stall. So get it done quickly, gals. Someone is waiting and giving you stink eye.

The show is energetic, captivating and highly entertaining. Instead of the traditional Polynesian revue, they offer a theatrical production of the Polynesian migration to Hawai'i. There is a plot to the show, and each element is presented with quality sound, inventive lighting and a level of intensity that remains constant throughout the show. The fire knife dance is especially exciting but is marred somewhat by a protective net. Shows are Tuesdays and Fridays (which is usually less crowded). **$99**.

We also like **Smith's Tropical Paradise** (821–6895). Lu'au are Mon., Wed., Thur. and Fri. The food is not the star; it's the marvelous setting. (And they need more desserts.) Smith's is surrounded by a huge garden area. Though the garden could use a little polishing, the site works perfectly for a lu'au. After dinner, you move to a separate show area where a small pond separates the audience from the stage. While not authentic by any means, it's dazzling and well-choreographed and is quite entertaining, complete with an erupting volcano. **$78**. Free open bar, but it closes at 7:30. Allow 30 minutes for a garden tour before the imu ceremony. You can also attend the show alone, without the food, for $15.

Next on our list is the **Grand Hyatt Kaua'i Lu'au** (240–6456). The line to get in can be long, and they serve only fruit punch until you're inside. The food is well-prepared. When they have the lu'au in their Ilima Garden, it's a nice setting. But when it's in the courtyard or ballroom, it suffers. And there's no way to know which one they'll use in advance, so it's lu'au roulette. It has a more comfortable dining experience than Smith's and a more traditional MC-dominated show. Seating can be confusing, grab a table in the front center. Free, open bar all night, plus table service for drinks. Sundays and Thursdays for **$94**.

Mailani at the Makana Terrace at the St. Regis Princeville is a wallet-choking **$135** for tables on the outdoor terrace, **$100** for much inferior indoor seating. This includes one (very good) mai tai, one wine or beer and one champagne. Otherwise, it's a cash bar. The positive traits are the great food with killer desserts and stellar views from the outdoor tables. On the negative side the show is pretty bad and takes place on a microscopic stage. Think of the *indoor* tables as simply an expensive restaurant buffet experience, not a lu'au. And it's the only lu'au where you pay *at the end*, with a clear expectation of a tip, adding salt to the wallet wound. Thursdays.

Although this isn't a lu'au, we didn't know where to put it. Every Wednesday night the Hilton Kaua'i Beach Resort (245–1955) hosts a performance of Rodgers & Hammerstein's 1949 Broadway musical, **South Pacific**. Wednesday also happens to be a big cruise ship day. Coincidence? Don't expect the excited atmosphere of a lu'au here. There is no audience participation, and you're not encouraged to drink and cut loose. (The bar makes bad $8 mai tais.) This is true dinner theater, and the audience tends to be older and much more subdued than lu'au audiences. The show is very well rehearsed, and the actors are as talented as the program describes. If you're familiar with *South Pacific*, or just enjoy theater, you'll like their presentation. If not, you might find yourself sleeping through the second act. The buffet is not spectacular, but the desserts are good. $85 and premier seating is $105.

DINNER CRUISES

Maui and O'ahu have multiple choices when it comes to dinner cruises. On Kaua'i the pickin's are more slim. Fortunately, there's a winner here. One of **Captain Andy's** boats is a beautiful 65-foot catamaran called **Southern Star** (335–6833) adorned with nice touches such as wooden decking and lots of high-end furnishings. Food is excellent (though you should eat that prime rib fast because the breeze will chill it). First drink is free, then it's a cash bar. Though the boat cuts through the water well, this is still Kaua'i, so some will get seasick. You'll probably power upwind toward Po'ipu then sail downwind. Don't get too comfortable in the back; suck up some of the breezes on the bow. Some of the narration is classic Captain Andy bad, but the staff is warm and helpful and the experience easy to recommend. $119 for 3 hours. They also have a 4-hour tour with a buffet on a smaller boat that goes to Na Pali (though most of the trip is along the bland Mana Plain). Better scenery on *part* of this one, but poorer boat and food.

Kaua'i Sea Tours (826–7254) has a 4-hour trip with more modest food and beverages for $115. The boat's not as cushy, and the bar serves only beer, wine and mai tais, but it's all included.

DINNER ON A BEACH

How about a romantic dinner by the ocean? For around $350–$500 per couple, the **Sheraton Kaua'i Resort** (742–1661), the **Grand Hyatt Kaua'i Resort** (742–1234) or the **Kaua'i Marriott Resort & Beach Club** (245–5050) will serve you near their beach. What a perfect way to make up for forgetting your anniversary. **St. Regis Princeville** (being the St. Regis) will do it for you for a mere $850.

Heavenly Creations (651–8933) will set a private table, usually at 'Anini Beach, and serve some *very* tasty food for around $350. They'll even light a beachside fire for extra. But don't assume the tip is included in the fee, and expect them to call you days later and shame you into tipping them if you forget. (Which seems kind of rude to us.)

ISLAND DINING BEST BETS

Best Pizza—Brick Oven Pizza
Best Cheap Mexican Food—Red Hot Mamas or Verde
Best View—Beach House Restaurant
Best Phony but Exotic Ambiance—Keoki's Paradise
Best Shave Ice—Jo-Jo's Clubhouse or Hee Fat General Store
Best Saimin—Hamura's Saimin
Best Vegetarian Food—Hanapepe Café
Best Hamburger—TNT Steakburgers
Best Yogurt—Orange Grove
Best Lu'au—Smith's Tropical Paradise
Best Pancakes—Tip Top Café
Best Sushi—Kintaro
Best Sandwich—Deli & Bread Connection
Best Inexpensive Baked Goods—Village Snack Shop
Best Place to Lower Your Net Worth—Kaua'i Grill
Best Lasagna—Pomodoro's
Best Place for a Romantic Dinner—Tidepools or Dinner on a Beach
Best BBQ—Scotty's Beachside BBQ
Best Local Food—Mark's Place
Best Gelato—Papalani Gelato

Hotels shown in this color. Condominiums shown in this color.

Rental Agents

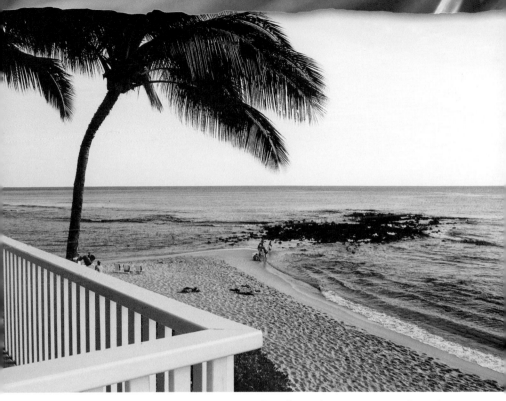

Wanted: Visitor seeking room with a view. Must be willing to burn your return airline ticket.

Your selection of where to stay is one of the more important decisions you'll make in planning your Kaua'i vacation. To some, it's just a place to sleep and rather meaningless. To others, it's the difference between a good vacation and a bad one.

There are four main types of lodging on the island: hotels, condominiums, bed and breakfasts, and single family homes. The vast majority will stay in one of the first two types. But B&Bs and single family homes are often overlooked and can be very good values. If your group or family is large, you should strongly consider renting a house for privacy, roominess and plain ol' value. There is a list of rental agents in the WHERE TO STAY INDEX,

each willing and happy to send you a list of homes they represent. We also have a referral service there.

We have *brilliantly* labeled the four main sections of Kaua'i as North Shore, South Shore, East Shore and West Shore and listed the resorts geographically within in each section. Hotels are in green and condominiums are in blue. Hotels usually offer more services, but smaller spaces with no kitchens. Condos usually have full kitchens, but you won't get the kind of attention you would from a hotel, including daily maid service. There are exceptions, of course, and we will point them out when they come up. You can find their locations on the various maps.

See all Web reviews at: www.wizardpub.com

All prices given are RACK rates, meaning *without any discounts*. Tour packages and direct Internet booking will often bring better rates. Most resorts offer discounts for stays of a week or more, and some will negotiate price with you. Some won't budge at all, while others told us *no one* pays RACK rates. Also, these prices are subject to taxes of around 13.5%.

The gold bar indicates that the property is exceptionally well priced for what you get.

SOLID GOLD VALUE

A REAL GEM

The gem means that this hotel or condominium offers something *particularly* special, not *necessarily* related to the price.

These are subjective reviews. If we say that rooms are small, we mean that we've been in them, and they feel small or cramped to us. If we say that maintenance is poor, we mean that the paint might be peeling, or the carpets are dingy or it otherwise felt worn to us.

HOTELS

All hotel rooms described **(shown in this color)** have air conditioning, an activity or travel desk, telephones, small refrigerators, lanais (verandas), cable TV and have cribs available upon request. None has room service unless otherwise noted. If you are a smoker, call about smoking policies because most hotel rooms in Hawai'i are designated non-smoking.

CONDOS

One of the confusing aspects about renting a condo **(shown in this color)**, cottage or house on Kaua'i is the fact that there's no central rental source for many individual properties. Most condo complexes, whether large or small, consist of individually owned condominiums. Individual owners have the prerogative of renting their units through any rental agent they choose. Consequently, a 50-unit condo resort might be represented by many rental agents. Usually (but not always), prices for comparable units within a given resort are equivalent through different agents. When we describe a particular resort, we will often give the names or phone numbers of one or two companies that dominate the rental pool. But realize that this does not always do justice to the *entire* property. When we describe rates, it is for the larger rental agents. Different agents have different policies for the same complex.

Once you have decided where you want to stay, you can contact the resort. You may also want to contact some of the rental agents on page 236 to determine if they represent any units from the property you have chosen.

Also realize that condominium owners usually have complete autonomy in how they furnish their individual units. Consequently, a resort that we describe as a good deal might have individual units that are not as hot. (Notice how we neatly cover our 'okoles, so that if you get a less-than-charming condo in a resort we recommend, we can always say you got one of the few duds there.)

Many condos have minimum stays—usually three nights. We don't always list this because it changes with different rental companies. More and more rental agents are also requiring you to pay *all* of your condo rental costs before you arrive. It may make you nervous, but you might not have a choice if you're intent on staying at a particular place.

Three bedroom/two bath units are described as 3/2, two bedroom/one bath units are described as 2/1, etc. Differentiation between half baths and full baths is

See all Web reviews at: www.wizardpub.com

not made. The price spread for rooms of a given size is due to different views, different locations within the resort and seasonal fluctuations. So when you see that a 2/2 unit rents for $140–$180, you should figure that $180 units have a better view or are closer to the water. The terms Oceanfront, Ocean View and Garden View are used rather capriciously in Hawai'i, so you should be skeptical of them.

Unless otherwise noted, all rooms come with telephones, complete kitchens, washer/dryers in unit, coffee makers, lanais (verandas), cable TV, ceiling fans and have cribs available upon request. Maid service is usually not available, and none have air conditioning unless otherwise noted. (On Kaua'i, trade winds often make a/c unnecessary, and few opt for it.) Most condos also have an additional cleaning fee and charge more at Christmas. If you are a smoker, you will want to check policies before you book. Most condos don't allow smoking in the units, and some even restrict you from smoking on the lanai and property grounds, too.

BED & BREAKFASTS

Rather than describe the countless B&Bs scattered about the island, you're better off calling **Hawai'i's Best Bed & Breakfast** (800) 262–9912 or (808) 263–3100. We have lots of links to B&Bs on our website, but it's not practical to personally review them the way we do other accommodations.

RENTAL AGENTS

Nearly all the rental agents on the list on page 240 also represent private home vacation rentals, as well as condominiums in various resorts. Contact them in advance to obtain lists of rentals available or hit their websites. (We have

links to all of them from our site.) Many great bargains can be found this way.

WHERE SHOULD I STAY?

What part of the island you want to stay on will dictate, to a degree, what kind of vacation you have. Although Kaua'i is small enough to do a driving tour in one day, where you stay will dominate certain activities.

The **north shore** is probably the prettiest part of the island and is dominated by one large hotel and lots of condos and vacation rentals. The weather is usually great in the summer and can be quite a bit wetter in the winter. Though the scenery is incomparable, the down side is the remoteness you'll feel when you want to venture to other parts of the island.

The **east shore** is the most geographically convenient. Trips to the north or south shore don't feel as daunting. There are plenty of hotels and condos and the most dining and shopping options. The down side is traffic in Kapa'a (especially heading south on Hwy 56) and the scenery and beaches aren't as good as the north shore.

The **south shore** has better weather year round and some great beaches. Several big hotels and lots of condos dominate. But the backdrop isn't as nice as the north or even east shores, and there aren't as many dining or shopping choices as the east shore. Also, construction of new condos will be ever present.

Finally there's the **west shore**. It's nearly always sunny, it's the hottest and driest part of the island and has only one resort plus a few vacation rentals to choose from. If you plan to spend all your time hiking in Koke'e and Waimea Canyon, it's convenient. Otherwise, it's isolated and remote.

See all Web reviews at: www.wizardpub.com

WHERE ARE THE REST?

You'll notice that some of the resorts listed here don't have full reviews. When we review a place to stay, we don't just want to list bare bones information on them. After all, you can get that kind of info on the Internet. We wanted to tell you what we really *think* about a place, and that takes space. Also, we wanted to include aerial photos of the resorts. After all, a picture speaks a thousand words (and a thousand words takes too long to read, anyway). But in the end we only have so much space we can devote to accommodations.

We had a choice—give you *less* info on *all* of them or do *detailed* reviews on only a *portion* of them. Neither choice seemed palatable.

So we came up with a *third* way: List minimal info on all (including if they are GEMS or SOLID GOLD VALUES), print detailed reviews on *most,* and post full reviews of all on our website, **www. wizardpub.com**. After all, most people use this section before they come to the islands. And with the Web (which has infinite space), we can do more, like post larger aerial photos of the resorts with specific buildings labeled when appropriate, provide constant updates when necessary, and put links to the various rental agents or hotels right in the review, allowing you to go to their sites and get more photos of the rooms. You should remember, however, that resorts post photos to lure you in, and some aren't above posting modified or overly flattering shots when they were new and sparkling. Our aerials don't lie and are designed to give you a feel for their ocean proximity (does oceanfront *really* mean oceanfront?), so you'll know what kind of view to expect from a given location within the resort. Resorts whose full

review is posted *only* on our website are identified with WEB REVIEW

Please remember that all these reviews are *relative to each other*. This is important. Even staying at a dump right on the ocean is still a *golly gee!* experience. In other words, *Hey, you're on the ocean on Kaua'i!* So if we sound whiny or picky when critiquing a resort, it's only because their next door neighbor might be such a better experience. It doesn't mean you'll be miserable, it just means that *compared to another resort*, you can do better.

NORTH SHORE

Hanalei Colony Resort
(800) 628–3004 or (808) 826–6235
7130 Kuhio Hwy

52 units, pool and spa, BBQs, coin-op laundry room, small day spa, restaurant, free Wi-Fi resort-wide and at restaurant with computers available, maid service every 3 days, wedding coordinator. No telephones, no TV. Kitchens lack dishwashers. This is the only beachfront resort on the north shore. Some of their units are as close to the water as you will get on Kaua'i *(25 feet).* We especially like units in A, F, G, I and the front J units. The resort is secluded and somewhat isolated, near the end of the road on the north shore. All units are two bedroom

A REAL GEM

See all Web reviews at: www.wizardpub.com

(although the bedrooms aren't completely walled off and second rooms have twin beds). Rooms are nicely kept and were remodeled in 2011. Their location on Kepuhi Beach is outstanding, and the attention to detail is admirable, but expect some rust on metal items in units. (Being this close to the ocean, it's *unavoidable*.) While the lack of room telephones might make arranging your day slightly awkward, others will welcome it. Cell phone coverage may be spotty, depending on your carrier. (You can use the phones by the small pool, which is also where the laundry facilities are, so you won't be bored between loads.) 2/2 units (850 sq. ft.) are $255–$440. Garden views are quite nice. 3-night minimum in high season.

Hanalei Inn
(808) 826–9333
5-5468 Kuhio Hwy
WEB REVIEW

St. Regis Princeville
(877) 787–3447 or (808) 826–9644
5520 Ka Haku Rd.
WEB REVIEW ◆

Hanalei Bay Resort & Suites
(800) 826–7782 or (808) 826–9775
(800) 222–5541 or (808) 826–6585
5380 Honoiki Rd.
WEB REVIEW

Pu'u Poa
(800) 222–5541 or (808) 826–6585
(866) 922–5642
5454 Ka Haku Rd.
56 rooms, tennis court, pool, free hi-speed Internet access, BBQ area. Units are large (1,800–2,079 sq. ft.), comfortable and most are very nice. Most units (especially higher floors) have commanding ocean views. Units vary depending on the care of the particular owner, but

most we saw were nice. The great ocean bluff causes lots of seaspray-induced maintenance headaches. Many bathrooms have deep, round Japanese-style tubs or Jacuzzis next to the shower. Note that some of the unit owners have converted their lanai into a separate room (which they call an atrium). It's nice, but your upstairs neighbors will be able to see you through the glass...so behave yourself. 2/2 units from the first phone number are $175–$225. The second numbers has units mostly of similar quality but are a bit pricer and have a 3-night minimum. Regency Pacific Realty and Kaua'i Vacation Rentals also have units here.

Hanalei Bay Villas
(800) 222–5541 or (808) 826–6585
(800) 367–5025 or (808) 245–8841
5451 Ka Haku Rd.
WEB REVIEW

Hale Moi
(800) 367–5004 or (808) 826–9066
5301 Ka Haku Rd.

40 units, BBQs. Cheap. No, not the price, but the quality. Duplex units share a lanai.

See all Web reviews at: www.wizardpub.com

Inside, the construction feels…cheap. The sound of passing traffic is a given if you leave the jalousie windows open (which you'll want to do). And the mountain views are mixed but generally poor. Top this off with Castle Resort's ridiculous rates of $230–$260 for 471–943 sq. ft., depending on if you want both sides (one of which has a kitchen). Either way, the bed is in the main (only) room. In short, you can do better almost anywhere.

Pali Ke Kua
(800) 826–7782 or (808) 826–9775
(800) 367–5004 or (808) 826–9066
5300 Ka Haku Rd.

98 units, pool, keiki pool and spa, BBQ area, free hi-speed Internet access in some, restaurant. Some nicely furnished units from the second set of numbers, private path to eastern part of Hideaways Beach below the cliffs (which is otherwise only reachable by swimming from the western part of the beach). Nicely tucked away, offering quiet privacy. Many units have very fine ocean bluff views, but it's a bit pricey at rates listed below. Some of the layouts are a bit strange, and the bedrooms feel small to us. Try to get an upstairs unit for a better ocean view. Units 3–16 have poor mountain views. 1/1 units (683 sq. ft.) are $170, 2/2 units (1,067 sq. ft.) are $215–$278. The second set of numbers is for Castle Resorts

whose units are even more expensive. You should check with other rental agents such as Kaua'i Vacation Rentals, RE/MAX, Oceanfront Realty or Ahh! Aloha. (See list page 240.)

Emmalani Court
(800) 222–5541 or (808) 826–6585
(866) 922–5642
5200 Ka Haku Rd.

WEB REVIEW

Villas of Kamali'i
(800) 367–5025 or (808) 245–8841
4141 Lei O Papa Rd.

WEB REVIEW

Alii Kai I
(866) 922–5642
(800) 222–5541 or (808) 826–6585
3780 Edward Rd.

63 units, BBQ area, pool, free hi-speed Internet access (second agent-listed units don't all have Internet access). Most of the buildings are perched on the sea **SOLID GOLD VALUE** cliffs (except #s 1 & 2). Bldgs. 3, 4 and 5 have the best views and can be quite dreamy, though the mountain views from 1 & 2 are really pleasing. Layouts of these 2/2 units are good with even the second bedrooms often having ocean views. Sounds do carry in these buildings. Don't confuse this resort with Alii Kai II next door. Units (1,086 sq. ft.) are $95–$195. 3-night minimum from first phone number. Decor varies *a lot* here from unit

See all Web reviews at: www.wizardpub.com

to unit—some feeling more dated than others. It's worth it to splurge for the ocean view here. Second agent listed has cheaper prices on the top end. Regency Pacific Realty also has units here. See list on page 240.

The Cliffs
(800) 356–8024 or (808) 826–6219
(800) 222–5541 or (808) 826–6585
3811 Edward Rd.

WEB REVIEW

Nihilani at Princeville Resort
(877) 838–8149 or (808) 826–9675
4919 Pepelani Loop

102 units, pool, spa, a/c, BBQ area, free Wi-Fi, 2-car garages (some not available to renters). These 34 triplex buildings were completed in 2008. The close proximity of the buildings, lack of any decent views and roads on three sides of the grounds give the property a claustrophobic feel. If you can get past all that, the interiors are pretty nice. Big bathtubs and separate showers in many of the bathrooms. Very pleasing layouts on the single-story 2/3 units, which at 1,972 sq. ft., make them very livable. We like the large dens and separate living rooms. The 2-story 2/3 (1,406 sq. ft.) units are our least favorite layout here. They show Bali Hai views on their property map, but the views of it are not great, and only a few units can see Bali Hai, mostly buildings 16–19. (Even in

some of those we had to walk out onto the second floor lanai to see it.) 2/3s are $145–$200, 3/3s (1,874 sq. ft.) are $175–$235. 3-night minimum.

Plantation at Princeville
(877) 838–8149 or (808) 826–9675
(800) 367–5025 or (808) 245–8841
4771 Pepelani Loop

WEB REVIEW

SeaLodge
(800) 585–6101
(866) 922–5642
3700 Kamehameha Rd.

86 units, pool, BBQ area, free hi-speed Internet access in most (all units from second agent listed), coin-op laundry plus some units **SOLID GOLD VALUE** have washer/dryers. Most units have incredible ocean bluff views at *extremely* reasonable prices. You'll never get tired of gazing at the extensive offshore reef. Building A will require the most walking to your car. Bldgs. B and F have the poorest views but also the cheapest rates on the property. 1/1 units are 550 sq. ft. and are a good deal at $95–$190, 2/2 units (second bedroom is a loft making it 720 sq. ft.) are $125–$160. 3-night minimum from first phone number. At this price it's an easy place to like due to the location. Units vary *considerably* in terms of quality from both agents listed. Also note that both of these rental agents are based on the mainland, not Kaua'i.

See all Web reviews at: www.wizardpub.com

Kamahana
(800) 222–5541 or (808) 826–6585
(866) 922–5642
3800 Kamehameha Rd.

WEB REVIEW

The Westin Princeville Ocean Resort Villas
(800) 937–8461 or (808) 827–8700
3838 Wyllie Rd.

WEB REVIEW

Puamana
(800) 222–5541 or (808) 826–6585
3880 Wyllie Rd.

WEB REVIEW

Mauna Kai
(800) 826–7782 or (808) 826–9775
3920 Wyllie Rd.

WEB REVIEW

Villas on the Prince
(866) 922–5642
(800) 367–5025 or (808) 245–8841
4141 Queen Emma's Dr.

WEB REVIEW

EAST SHORE

Hotel Coral Reef Resort on the Beach
(800) 843–4659 or (808) 822–4481
4-1516 Kuhio Hwy

21 rooms, pool, beauty shop, juice/sand-wich bar, sauna, free Wi-Fi in lobby and rooms, free room safes, BBQ area, a/c, refrigerators in king bed oceanfront units and 1/1 suites only, coin-op laundry, lanais on all, coffee makers with free coffee daily (in all but garden rooms). The rooms have a fresh tropical feel. The oceanfront unit's bathrooms have deep Jacuzzi tubs. Good oceanfront location, free coffee, fruit and pastries in the lobby in the mornings where you can "talk story" with other guests and staff. Rooms and suites (approx. 200–600 sq. ft.) are $110–$245. Discounts available on their website make some rooms a good deal at certain times of the year and even a SOLID GOLD VALUE.

Kaua'i International Hostel
(808) 823–6142
4532 Lehua St.

WEB REVIEW

Pono Kai Resort
(800) 456–0009 or (808) 822–9831
4-1250 Kuhio Hwy

241 units, 2 lighted tennis courts, pool and spa, 2 saunas, BBQ area, elevators, washer/dryer and a/c in most units, coin-op available, SOLID GOLD VALUE free fitness room, hi-speed Internet access in units. Although it's a fairly old resort, the grounds are well cared for. Part timeshare, part vacation rental. Rates are quite reasonable for renovated rooms done in 2008. The results are clean, but the furnishings feel cheap and don't seem to be holding up well. Spring for the oceanfront (bldgs. A–D), if

See all Web reviews at: www.wizardpub.com

you can. 2-bedroom units have exceptionally large master bedrooms. If you get an oceanfront unit, note that first floor units will allow people walking by on the ocean path to look right into your room. If that's an issue, get one off the ground. Sounds between units seem to carry well. Studios (300 sq. ft.—building K only) are $125, partial kitchens (two rooms with a kitchenette—building K only) at 600 sq. ft. are $125, 1/1 units (740 sq. ft.) are $160 $205, 2/2 units (1,132 sq. ft.) are $179–$240.

Waipouli Beach Resort & Spa
(800) 688–7444 or (808) 823–1401
(877) 838–8149 or (808) 826–9675
4-820 Kuhio Hwy

196 units, pool with keiki pool, 3 spas, free fitness room, restaurant, business

A REAL GEM

center, a/c, day spa, coffee maker with free coffee daily, free room safes, free Wi-Fi, BBQ area. Finished in 2006, this resort has the most upscale condos on the east shore. The area is very congested, and traffic into and out of the property may be an issue at times. Once you are within the grounds, you won't notice that much, as most of the resort is oriented toward the pool and beach. The rooms are richly appointed and furnished. They include dark, imported hardwood trim, granite counters, oversized Wolf ovens, etc. On the plus side,

the bedrooms and baths are large. The baths have deep tubs or Jacuzzis and separate showers. On the negative side, the living area is relatively small. They didn't plan for a dining area, which is usually just a small table often shoved against a wall (an issue especially if you have more than 4 people staying in a room). We were told that the developers planned to have all the dining on the lanais, but with possible passing showers that is not always practical. The oceanfront units have the best layouts with roomy lanais and dreamy views. Second story and above are better, because first story oceanfront units have plantings in front of them that may block some of your view of the beach.

The pool is the star here. It is a saline, 2-acre, river-like pool that meanders through the entire courtyard of the property. One end is sand-lined for the kids (since the beach is not very swimmable), and it has two waterslides. There are three spas, each with a sandy bottom, and one is suitable for kids. The pool is especially pretty at night.

Hotel-type rooms (325 sq. ft. with coffee maker, fridge and are closest to the road) are $275, 1/2s (824 sq. ft.) are $355–$570. 2/3s (1,155–1,414 sq. ft.) are $480–$780. The second set of phone numbers has 1- and 2-bedroom units for much less, but these units don't include daily maid service or free coffee, have a 2-night minimum and charge a cleaning fee.

Courtyard Kaua'i at Coconut Beach
(800) 321–2211 or (808) 822–3455
650 Aleka Loop
WEB REVIEW

Plantation Hale (Best Western)
(800) 775–4253 or (808) 822–4941
4-484 Kuhio Hwy
WEB REVIEW

See all Web reviews at: www.wizardpub.com

Islander on the Beach
(877) 997–6667 or (808) 822–7417
440 Aleka Place

200 rooms, pool and spa, BBQ area, coin-op laundry, poolside bar, empty refrigerator, microwave, coffee makers with free daily coffee, free room safe, free hi-speed Internet access in units, free Wi-Fi in lobby. Wonderful open, plantation-style setting adjacent to Wailua Beach with very relaxing grounds. The Kaua'i and Ni'ihau buildings are fairly close to the ocean, allowing you to fall asleep to the sound of the surf. Grab a beverage from the poolside bar and sip it at the adjacent beach. The resort was converted to a condotel (meaning the rooms are all individually owned), but decor is consistent and pleasing. Rooms are smallish at 311 sq. ft. and go for $134–$290. Jr. Suites at 622 sq. ft. (with full kitchen) are $290–$363. They have lots of specials, and few ever pay the price we listed (and we're assuming you won't either).

Kaua'i Sands Hotel
(800) 560–5553 or (808) 822–4951
420 Papaloa Rd.
WEB REVIEW

Lae Nani
(800) 688–7444 or (808) 822–4938
410 Papaloa Rd.
84 units, lighted tennis court, pool, daily maid service, coin-op laundry, free room safe, BBQ area. Though this gated resort is

still a gem, it's a bit overpriced, so we're hoping that you're getting a discount. Pleasant grounds and a very nice oceanfront location. They have a Hawaiian heiau on the premises, as well as a wonderful boulder–enclosed ocean pond for the keiki (kids). Building 5 has oceanfront units. 1/2 units (around 900 sq. ft.) are $329–$399, 2/2 units (around 1,100 sq. ft.) are $355–$465.

A REAL GEM

Lanikai
(808) 822–7700
390 Papaloa Rd.
WEB REVIEW

Kapa'a Sands Resort
(800) 222–4901 or (808) 822–4901
380 Papaloa Rd.

24 units, pool, BBQ area, coin-op laundry, free Wi-Fi in units and by pool. This is a very good bargain. They have small oceanfront studios (some have a pull down Murphy bed—these are recom-

SOLID GOLD VALUE

See all Web reviews at: www.wizardpub.com

mended for more living space). Small, but they make good use of space for $150. For this price you are as close as 30 feet from the water on a pretty beach. Resident offshore turtles will keep you entertained at dusk. What a deal! The property feels very intimate and tropical. The aerial photo makes it look like some of the oceanfront units (#1–14) are blocked by trees, but the crowns of the trees are above the ocean plane. Nice staff here. Studios (approx. 380 sq. ft.) are $120–$150 (definitely spring for the oceanfront), 2/2 units have a two-story layout (728 sq. ft.) and are $170–$205. 3- or 7-night minimum.

Wailua Bayview
(800) 367–5242
320 Papaloa Rd.
WEB REVIEW

Coco Palms Resort
4-241 Kuhio Hwy
The historic Coco Palms, where Elvis filmed "Blue Hawaii," was whacked by a hurricane in 1992 and spent the better part of a decade trying to get an insurance check, during which time Elvis had left the building. The fate of the old Coco Palms remains unknown at press time.

Aloha Beach Hotel
(866) 774–2924 or (808) 823–6000
3-5920 Kuhio Hwy
WEB REVIEW

Kaha Lani
(800) 367–5004 or (808) 822–9331
4460 Nehe Rd.
74 units, lighted tennis court, BBQ area, pool, computer in office, free hi-speed Internet access in units, coin-op laundry, free room safe, maid service every third day. The grounds are well-tended, and the area is less built up than some places on the east shore. The buildings themselves feel cheaply built (and sound carries pretty efficiently), but they are well-maintained. Most of the units are reasonably decorated, though you still have lots of variation in terms of updating. However, all the units are very clean. We prefer units that are on higher floors for a better ocean view, though views still feel a bit distant. Adjacent to Lydgate State Park and the beach path. RACK rates are on the high side, so hope you got a better deal. The staff is helpful here. 1/1 units (627–739 sq. ft.) are $235–$320, 2/2 units (961–996 sq. ft.) are $295–$415, 3/2 units (1,183 sq. ft.) are $385–$485.

Kaua'i Beach Villas
(800) 367–5025 or (808) 245–8841
4330 Kauai Beach Dr.
WEB REVIEW

Kaua'i Beach Resort
(866) 406–2782 or (808) 245–1955
4331 Kauai Beach Dr.
350 rooms, 4 pools, 2 spas, 7 conference rooms, poolside snack bar, valet parking, room service, day spa, 24-hour fitness room, a couple of shops, hi-speed Internet access in rooms, free Wi-Fi in lobby area, 3 restaurants, lounge, room service, coin-op laundry, empty refrigerator, coffee maker with free coffee daily, free laptop safe, Wi-Fi in lobby area, 3 restau-

A REAL GEM

See all Web reviews at: www.wizardpub.com

320 sq. ft. and so are the lanais. If you opt for ocean view, ask for one of the ocean-facing end units in Bldg. 4.

They charge $13 per day to park your car, $16 for valet. Internet in your room is $13, and local calls are a buck. RACK Rates are high at $338–$498, but few pay them. Suites (650–1,250 sq. ft.) are $600–$1,300. Many good discounts and packages are available with rooms starting at $169.

Tip Top Motel
(808) 245–2333
3173 Akahi St.
WEB REVIEW

Motel Lani
(808) 245–2965
4240 Rice St.

rants, lounge, room service, coin-op laundry, empty refrigerator, coffee maker with free coffee daily, free laptop safe, 24-hour business center, free airport shuttle. We just like the feel of this place. It's relaxing, laid back and not too big. This resort has been through many management changes, but its latest is one of the better ones. In 2007, owners spent $13 million to upgrade the property, pools and rooms. The resort is currently a condotel (individual owners for each room). The rooms all have the same pleasant plantation style decor that was part of the upgrade and are holding up well.

This resort, located between Lihu'e and Wailua, is near a pretty but relatively unswimmable beach. (A short walk farther north leads to better parts of Nukoli'i Beach.) They've augmented their other 3 pools with a wonderful half-sand lined freshwater pool with a water slide complete with man-made waterfalls. We wish they had more umbrellas available for the pool chairs. Service has improved markedly, to the point that it competes with higher-end resorts, and they keep things *very* clean. The staff is warm here. Rooms are fairly small at

8 rooms, BBQ area. They claim this "was probably the first hotel on the island." It's pretty disheveled with old furnishings. Rooms are **SOLID GOLD VALUE** small (most under 200 sq. ft.), have bathrooms and fridges but no phones or TVs. Most with a/c. Best view is of the Dumpster. $55–$70. Cash only. If you stay more than two nights, the rates drop. They have a TV and piano in the lobby, but we doubt you'll find Billy Joel staying here. The reason for the SOLID GOLD VALUE is there are not many places with a private room and bath for this kind of money on the island, but don't expect much more than that.

See all Web reviews at: www.wizardpub.com

Kaua'i Palms Hotel
(808) 246-0908
2931 Kalena St.

28 rooms, coin-op laundry, free Wi-Fi throughout. No phones. This is probably your best bet in Lihu'e (but it is a bit pricier). It has small, clean rooms and few amenities, but the present owner has made an effort with the decor and property. They provide free coffee and muffins in the mornings. Rooms (108–250 sq. ft.) are $75–$85, kitchenettes (250 sq. ft.) are $89. Larger rooms (275 sq. ft.) with full kitchens are $100. The $75 rooms do not have a/c and are on the second floor, but they do have ceiling fans.

Marriott's Kalanipu'u at Kaua'i Lagoons
(888) 236-2427 or (808) 632-8200
3325 Holokawelu Way

78 units, pool, spa, BBQ area, a/c, free Wi-Fi and hi-speed Internet access in the rooms, 42-inch HD flat screen TV, daily maid, coffee maker with free coffee daily, full size washer/dryer in unit, free room safe, 24-hour business center, elevators, free fitness room, golf

A REAL GEM

course. At press time two of these three buildings were finished. Though open as timeshares, they always have vacation rentals available. These buildings sit overlooking very pretty mountains, golf course and more distant ocean views (along with some planned construction of another property). Overall, the views are best from higher floors. The units are modern and spacious with high-end appliances, granite counters and large lanais. The 2- or 3-bedroom units (all have king beds) can accommodate two or three couples nicely as each room also has a TV, and the kids can use the pull-out sofa in the living room. Bathrooms have large showers and separate tubs. The two-level pool by building C has a nice layout, but may become crowded when all the units are up and running. There is a free shuttle to run you back and forth to the Kaua'i Marriott Resort to enjoy the beach (not the pool), and you do have signing privileges at their restaurants. There is a 10 a.m. check-out, but they will store your luggage, and you may use the pool and showers before your flight.

Local calls are a buck. 2/2 units (1,300 sq. ft.) are $407–$567. 3/3 units (1,600 sq. ft.) are $487–$647.

Kaua'i Marriott Resort & Beach Club
(800) 220-2925 or (808) 245-5050
3610 Rice St.
WEB REVIEW 💎

Garden Island Inn
(800) 648-0154 or (808) 245-7227
3445 Wilcox Rd.
WEB REVIEW

Banyan Harbor
(800) 422-6926 or (808) 245-7333
(800) 767-4707 or (808) 245-4711
3411 Wilcox Rd.
WEB REVIEW

See all Web reviews at: www.wizardpub.com

Kaua'i Inn
(800) 808–2330 or (808) 245–9000
2430 Hulemalu Rd.

WEB REVIEW

SOUTH SHORE

Grand Hyatt Kaua'i Resort & Spa
(800) 554–9288 or (808) 742–1234
1571 Poipu Rd.

602 rooms, multiple pools and spas, 3 tennis courts with pro shop, golf course, 24-hour room service, 6 restaurants, 37-inch HD flat screen TVs, Wi-Fi throughout, cocktail lounges, iHome, 9 shops, Camp Hyatt child care program, 23 conference rooms, valet parking, 24-hour fitness center, empty refrigerator, coffee makers with free coffee daily, coin-op and valet laundry, lu'au, complete business services and a 45,000 sq. ft. day spa. It was hard for us to review this resort without sounding like drooling sycophants. But the reality of the Hyatt is that they did almost everything right. Put simply, it's our favorite big resort on the island.

A REAL GEM

As you walk into the lobby and see the ocean framed by the entrance, you realize that here they really sweated the details. The grounds are as exotic as any you will find in all the islands, complete with parrots and other birds. Their pools are incredible. Gallon for gallon, they're more fun than any we've seen on the island. The upper swimming pool seems to meander forever. It even has a slight current and hides such goodies as caves tucked behind small waterfalls (they're easy to miss). Take your time exploring as it winds through lush vegetation. At the end of the upper pool, you can take the "elevator" (a free and respectably fast waterslide) to the bottom. There you will find what they call the action pool complete with a volleyball net, waterfalls, spas and an area for children. An island there hides a hot tub. Above is the adult pool. Across from the lower pool are several *acres* of saltwater lagoon. If you want saltwater without the waves, here it is. The "sand" is actually gravel imported from San Juan Capistrano. (And it's hard on tender tootsies.) Inside the lagoon are several landscaped islands.

The grounds are lush and very well maintained and feature a smashing waterfall below the Seaview Terrace Lounge. The resort is located on a so-so beach called Shipwreck Beach. They have covered cabanas on the beach for $100. (They're coveted, and the Hyatt could use more.) If you're lucky enough to be under one in the evening during a passing shower, it's something you will long remember. Cabanas by the pool and lagoon are free, but you have to get up early to snag one. Large hammocks and loveseat swings are scattered throughout the grounds. Their shops run the gamut from fine art to footwear. They have wedding coordinators on site, and guest services are good.

The Hyatt's an easy GEM, and their awesome grounds keep them in a class by themselves. Rooms are pleasant and were updated in 2010. Rooms with a king bed have a walk-in shower with a hand-held showerhead and bench. Rooms with two queen beds have a tub/shower combination. They even have hypoallergenic rooms available.

They have a *mandatory* $25 per day resort fee covering local calls, self-park-

See all Web reviews at: www.wizardpub.com

ing, Internet, fitness center, laptop room safe and some other things. Valet parking is $10.

If your intention is to come to Kaua'i and never leave the resort (which we hope you *won't* do), the Hyatt is the place to come. You'll never get bored here. This is a *great* place to bring the kids, but adults will enjoy it, too. Camp Hyatt provides an extensive children's program for kids age 3 (if potty trained) to 12 for $80 per day. Anara Spa is massive and complete with couples "treatment hales," lava showers, steam and baths. So what's the catch? Well, amenities like this don't come cheap. Rooms (500 sq. ft.) are $440–$880. Suites (866–2,463 sq. ft.) are $1,570–$5,240. Be aware they have an early departure fee if you opt to trim some days off your stay.

Makahuena
(800) 367–5004 or (808) 742–2482
1661 Pe'e Rd.

78 units, small pool, spa, BBQ area, free hi-speed Internet access in rooms, room safes, lighted tennis court. Every fourth day maid service with the first set of numbers. The developer seems to have spared...well, lots of expenses, actually. Like the endless concrete stairs at every turn, cheap-looking fixtures, etc. Some of the units are fairly nice inside, many are not. We've never been real warm toward Makahuena. The location out on the point

will expose you to *lots* of sea spray-laden wind, so don't expect the windows to stay clean. Those winds, however, tend to keep the units cool. There are 8 different floor plans, so it's hard to say if you'll get a good one. Second floor units are better for views, whereas many first floor units are partly below ground. 1/1 units (732 sq. ft.) are $270–$300, 2/2 units (1,157–1,217 sq. ft.) are $300–$430, 3/3 units (1,380 sq. ft.) are $455–$485. The Parrish Collection Kaua'i and Po'ipu Connection Realty both have a few units here for less money.

Po'ipu Makai
(800) 325–5701 or (808) 742–2000
(800) 367–5025 or (808) 245–8841
1677 Pe'e Rd.
WEB REVIEW

Po'ipu Crater Resort
(800) 367–8020 or (808) 742–7400
2330 Hoohu Rd.

30 units, pool, sauna, BBQ area, tennis court and paddle court (mini tennis). Located in the bottom of a small crater, the grounds are pleasant and well maintained, but there is no view. (Technically speaking, you're in a hole.) When the trade winds aren't blowing, it can get pretty hot in there, and sounds bounce around in an odd way. Lots of rental agents have units here, not just the number listed (which charges for local calls). 2/2 townhouse units (1,240 sq. ft.) are a pretty

See all Web reviews at: www.wizardpub.com

good deal at $160–$214. Prices decrease if you stay longer than 7 nights. No Internet access here.

Po'ipu Palms
(800) 325–5701 or (808) 742–2000
(800) 742–2260 or (808) 742–2233
1697 Pe'e Rd.

WEB REVIEW

Sunset Kahili
(800) 367–8022 or (808) 742–7434
1763 Pe'e Rd.

35 units, pool, free hi-speed Internet access in a few, free Wi-Fi in rec room, BBQ area, elevator. Built in 1968 (you'd swear it was the '50s), it's old but fairly well-kept in the common areas. The units all vary, but mostly they are in need of updating. They all have nice ocean views, with the third floor and above being particularly good. Units ending in 01 and 08 are 2 bedrooms. Master bedrooms are only shut off by shoji doors, which creates less privacy. It's very popular with seniors and long-time repeat guests. An average value. 1/1 units (780 sq. ft.) are $125–$175, 2/2 units (1,037 sq. ft.) are $250. 4-night minimum. Add 3.5% for credit card payments.

Po'ipu Shores
(800) 367–5004 or (808) 742–7700
1775 Pe'e Rd.

39 units, swimming pool, BBQ area, free Wi-Fi by pool, free hi-speed and Wi-Fi Internet access in rooms, room safes, elevator in Building A, daily maid service. Most of the owners (not all) have been spending a lot of money on their units, and they were looking *very* nice on this visit. The grounds aren't much, but the property is well-maintained, but expect sea spray on your windows even though they clean them daily. That's what you're paying for—the extraordinary proximity to, and sound of, the ocean—not the size of the rooms. (Some people actually *complain* that the ocean is "too loud.") The townhouse units in building C are the quietest. The one-bedroom condos are the only units without the master bedroom on the ocean side, but all units have great ocean views. 1/1 units (698 sq. ft.) are $295–$360, 2/2 units (912–1,036 sq. ft.) are $375–$480, 3/2s (1,041 sq. ft.) are $485–$600. They often discount. The staff here is very friendly. They charge $1 per local call (unusual for a condo). The 1,204 sq. ft. penthouse is $550–$650. It was originally built for the developer, is glass-walled and has one of the grandest views on the south shore.

A REAL GEM

Po'ipu Plantation
(800) 634–0263 or (808) 742–6757
1792 Pe'e Rd.

WEB REVIEW

See all Web reviews at: www.wizardpub.com

Nihi Kai Villas
(800) 325–5701 or (808) 742–1412
1870 Hoone Rd.

70 units, pool, keiki pool, free hi-speed Internet access in rooms, some have Wi-Fi, free room safe, 2 tennis courts and a paddle ball court (sort of mini tennis), BBQ area. Well-maintained grounds. The rooms seem to vary *a lot*. The two-story townhouse units have an annoying layout, but single level 2/2 units are an acceptable value. Many of the units had been remodeled on this visit and were looking much nicer. Buildings 1, 2, 4, and some units in 5 and 8 are your best bet for a glimpse of the ocean. The rest are strictly garden views. The agent above rates their units into premier, deluxe and island casual. We didn't find much difference between premier and deluxe. Island casual units have not been updated but are still clean. 1/2 units (1,400 sq. ft.) are $150–$244, 2/2 units (2,100 sq. ft.) are $177–$380, 3/2 units (2,300 sq. ft.) are $300–$625. 5-night minimum.

Hideaway Cove Villas
(866) 849–2426 or (808) 635–8785
2307 Nalu Rd.

WEB REVIEW ◆

Regency II
(877) 595–2824
(800) 325–5701 or (808) 742–2000
1831 Poipu Rd.

WEB REVIEW ◆

Po'ipu Kai Resort
(800) 367–8020 or (808) 742–7400
(877) 997–6667 or (808) 742–7424
1941 Poipu Rd.

WEB REVIEW

The Cottages at Po'ipu Kai
(800) 325–5701 or (808) 742–2000
2391 Hoohu Rd.

WEB REVIEW ▭

The Villas at Po'ipu Kai & Regency Villas
(866) 362–4755 or (808) 742–8410
(877) 595–2824
2373 Hoohu Rd. & 2387 Hoohu Rd.

WEB REVIEW ◆

Marriott's Waiohai Beach Club
(800) 845–5279 or (808) 742–4400
2249 Poipu Rd.

WEB REVIEW

Ko'a Kea Hotel & Resort
(888) 898–8958 or (808) 828–8888
2251 Poipu Rd.

121 rooms, saline pool, spa, free fitness room, restaurant, empty refrigerator, "Nespresso" makers, resort-wide Wi-Fi,

See all Web reviews at: www.wizardpub.com

hi-speed in rooms, laptop room safes, valet only parking, day spa, 24-hour room service, docking stations for your iPod, 42-inch flat screen TVs, conference and hospitality room, free local calls, coin-op or valet laundry. This was originally the Po'ipu Beach Hotel built in the 1960s and whacked by hurricane 'Iniki in 1992. It was left abandoned until the current owners rebuilt this upscale boutique-type hotel on the original footprint of the old buildings in 2009. The resort is airy and modern with themes of ocean life in bright colors scattered about. Most of the rooms are dark chocolate and white with a splash of hot pink, orange or teal, feel larger than the listed size, and are comfortable. They've thought of many nice touches you don't often find at hotels of this size, such as Nespresso machines (6 free pods supplied), ceiling fans in every room so you can leave the doors open and enjoy the ocean sounds, reading lights, Egyptian cotton sheets, down feather beds and pillows (which they can remove if you don't like them), keyboard height pull-out desks on wheels, and showers with rain shower heads mounted in the ceiling and wide benches to sit on. The oceanfront deluxe rooms and suites, which are larger, have separate deep soaking tubs and even a flat screen TV. The oceanfront views are excellent and very close to the water. Their beach is small and varies in width, so you won't have many people parked in front of your room. Since they are on a fairly protected cove, the snorkeling can make up for the minimal sand. Their small day spa offers many treatments (for individuals or couples) to melt your bones. If you stay here, opting for an oceanfront or a courtyard view is worth the money (if you can swing it). The garden views tend to be quieter, but on the side facing the Marriott's Waiohai, they are less private.

A REAL GEM

They have a *mandatory* $15 resort fee that covers valet parking and Wi-Fi. Overall, we really liked this place. We found it relaxing and peaceful and appreciated its intimacy with the ocean. Rooms (335–445 sq. ft.) are $445–$800. Suites (585–680 sq. ft.) are $1,625–$2,575. Discounts are often available.

Kiahuna Plantation Resort
(800) 688–7444 or (808) 742–6411
(800) 367–5004 or (808) 742–2200
2253 Poipu Rd.

WEB REVIEW

Sheraton Kaua'i Resort
(800) 782–9488 or (808) 742–1661
2440 Hoonani Rd.

WEB REVIEW

Po'ipu Kapili
(800) 443–7714 or (808) 742–6449
2221 Kapili Rd.

60 units, 2 lighted tennis courts, elevators, free hi-speed Internet access in rooms and Wi-Fi by the pool, pool, coin-op laundry (washer/dryers in all 2/3s and some 1/1s), maid service once a week, BBQ area, some units have a/c in bedrooms. Well-maintained and sculptured grounds, very spacious rooms for the money, and a second-home atmosphere make this an easy recommendation. Buildings 1, 2, 6 and 7 (all 2/3s) have very nice ocean views and are two-story townhouses. You can pick herbs from their gar-

A REAL GEM

See all Web reviews at: www.wizardpub.com

den if you choose to cook. The staff is top-notch here. 1/2 units (1,120 sq. ft.) are $220–$320, 2/3 units (1,820) are $300–$450. They also have elegant 2,600 sq. ft. penthouses for $450–$600. There is a construction project behind them, but it doesn't appear to be active at press time, and we didn't see or hear anything objectionable. 3-night minimum. Special discounts available throughout the year.

AlIhI Lani
(800) 742–2260 or (808) 742–2233
2564 Hoonani Rd.

WEB REVIEW ◆

Koloa Landing at Po'ipu Beach
(888) 317–0205 or (808) 240–6600
2641 Poipu Rd.

WEB REVIEW ⌐¬

Waikomo Stream Villas
(800) 325–5701 or (808) 742–7220
2721 Poipu Rd.

60 units, pool, free hi-speed Internet access, tennis court, BBQ area. Pretty, well-kept grounds and large rooms (all garden views). **SOLID GOLD VALUE** Some of the garden views are quite lovely with small streams. Lots

of privacy. The rooms are rated by the above agent as premier, deluxe and island casual. We felt the premier or deluxe units were really not that different—both were very nice. Opt for island casual if you want clean but not updated. 1/1 units (1,050 sq. ft.) are $115–$211, the 1,500 sq. ft. 2/2 units (second bedrooms are a loft with limited privacy) are $145–$249. Very nice staff here. 5-night minimum.

Whalers Cove
(800) 225–2683 or (808) 742–7571
2640 Puuholo Rd.

39 units, heated pool and spa, daily maid, elevator, BBQ area, free daily coffee, free room safe, free hi-speed Internet access or Wi-Fi in most in rooms and lobby. This is a lovely property and very **A REAL GEM** serene. The grounds are well-manicured, and the setting for the pool is outstanding. Though individually owned and decorated, they are well-furnished with koa wood doors and even koa floor trim in the closets. In the past the units were some of the most expensively furnished we had seen. On this visit, though still lovely, the newer condos in the area are starting to make some of the units feel a bit dated. The resort is very quiet, and they provide more personalized service than you will find elsewhere. (They will even do your grocery shopping before you arrive and stock your refrigerator.) Some units have Jacuzzi bathtubs, many

See all Web reviews at: www.wizardpub.com

overlooking the ocean. They are not on a beach, but there is a snorkeling cove nearby. 1/2 units are $349–$541. (These actually have two bedrooms, but you are limited to 2 people and charged as if it were 1/2.) 2/2 units are $479–$709. Most units have 1,390 sq. ft. (plus lanai) except the deluxe, which has 2,200 sq. ft. In all, it's expensive, but worth the money if you get a deal. By the way, even at this price they have an obnoxious *mandatory* $15 resort fee. With all the services they provide, do they really have to charge an extra $15 so you can have "free" Internet, coffee and beach towels? (OK, end of rant.)

Kuhio Shores
(800) 543–9180 or (206) 938–5802
(800) 367–8022 or (808) 742–7555
5050 Lawai Rd.

WEB REVIEW

Prince Kuhio
(888) 747–2988
(800) 742–2260 or (808) 742–2233
5061 Lawai Rd.

72 units, pool, coin-op laundry (washer/dryers in *some* units), free hi-speed Internet access, a/c in studios. Grounds are very well-tended, and the pool and BBQ

SOLID GOLD VALUE

area are very pretty. Built in 1962, the resort's clean for its age. Some units are more updated than others. Located across the road from the ocean, this used to be a hotel but was converted to condos, so expect some bizarre room layouts. The ocean views here are not that great, but if you want a glimpse, get a unit above the first floor and closer to the road. Some long-term rentals here. If you are looking at unit numbers ending in 30–37, then you may want to opt for a park-facing, odd-numbered unit for a more pleasant view than the interior courtyard. Studios (338–450 sq. ft.) are $50–$110, 1/1 units (600–720 sq. ft.) are $105–$145. There is also a 2/1 penthouse (875 sq. ft.) with a large roof deck for $200–$275. 4-night minimum from first phone number, which is for a large group of owners. Prices decrease for longer stays, and because you are dealing directly with the owners, they may be more flexible with the price. The second set of numbers has slightly higher rates. Units also available from R & R Realty and Rentals.

Kalaheo Inn
(888) 332–6023 or (808) 332–6023
4444 Papalina Rd.

WEB REVIEW

WEST SHORE

Waimea Plantation Cottages
(877) 997–6667 or (808) 338–1625
9400 Kaumualii Hwy

See all Web reviews at: www.wizardpub.com

54 units, pool and keiki pool, restaurant, conference room, hi-speed Internet access in rooms, Wi-Fi in lobby area, day spa, room safe, stereos, coin-op laundry, BBQ (upon request), volleyball, and maid service every third day. Many of these cottages were once plantation workers' homes, and each is as different as their former owner's tastes. We had a hard time coming up with adjectives to describe the rooms. They have old-style floors and furniture, just like from the plantation days. Units have been refurbished with modern amenities, but they retain the old-style feel inside, without feeling *too* old and worn. They are very clean. At this 27-acre former plantation, peace and privacy are yours—the trade-off is relative isolation given the location on the extreme west side. There is much feeling of 'ohana (family) here, and you will definitely experience the aloha spirit. With their location so close to the mouth of the very reddish Waimea River, swimming in the murky ocean water is pretty poor at this marginal beach. The coconut grove, banyan trees and hammocks scattered about add to the quiet charm of this property, and this is a good place to watch the sunset over the private island of Ni'ihau. There's a *mandatory* $10 per day resort fee, which covers Internet, room safes and DVD rentals. Units vary tremendously in decor, price and proximity to the ocean. 1/1s (approx. 594 sq. ft.) are $238–$447, 2/1s (approx. 726 sq. ft.) are $289–$544, 3/2s (approx. 1,088 sq. ft.) are $406–$620, 4/3s (approx. 1,250 sq. ft.) are $543–$691, 5/4s (1,020–1,240 sq. ft.) are $722–$1,230. Discounts available.

Koke'e Lodge
(808) 335–6061
3600 Koke'e State Park
WEB REVIEW

YWCA Camp Sloggett
(808) 245–5959
Koke'e State Park

60 beds in the bunkhouse, cottage and lodge, huge fire pit (wood available), BBQ area, pay phone (bring change because your cell phone probably won't work), covered lanai with ping-pong table and other games. Built in 1925, this is a clean, no-nonsense camp with a no-nonsense attitude: "leave it as you found it." The grounds are isolated, but the scenery is quite beautiful with a small stream. It's $10 per person for tent camping with access to toilets and hot showers, $25 for the hostel bunkhouse (bring your own bedding and towels). Community restrooms and showers for campers and bunkhouse. The two end units of the bunkhouse have a kitchen and sleep up to four people for $75–$100 per night (you still share a bath with the hostel). They have a cottage available for $85–$120 for up to four people. The lodge has a large kitchen and bath and can sleep up to 15 people for $25 per person (5 person minimum weekdays/8 weekends). Children under 5 are free. They often rent to large groups, so be sure and call two weeks in advance for availability. The cabin and lodge often are reserved up to a year or more in advance with summer being the busiest season. We prefer this over Koke'e Lodge. 2-night minimum for the cottage.

SOLID GOLD VALUE

INDEX

Island Dining Index on page 204, Where to Stay Index on page 240.

INDEX

263

Island Dining Index on page 204, Where to Stay Index on page 240.

Island Dining Index on page 204, Where to Stay Index on page 240.

INDEX

Island Dining Index on page 204, Where to Stay Index on page 240.

Island Dining Index on page 204, Where to Stay Index on page 240.

Island Dining Index on page 204, Where to Stay Index on page 240.